Japanese Demon Lore

Oni from Ancient Times to the Present

Japanese Demon Lore
Oni from Ancient Times to the Present

Noriko T. Reider

Utah State University Press
Logan, Utah
2010

Copyright © 2010 Utah State University Press
All rights reserved

Utah State University Press
Logan, Utah
84322

Cover: Artist Unknown, Japanese; *Minister Kibi's Adventures in China, Scroll 2* (detail); Japanese, Heian period, 12th century; Handscroll; ink, color, and gold on paper; 32.04 x 458.7 cm (12 5/8 x 180 9/16 in.); Museum of Fine Arts, Boston; William Sturgis Bigelow Collection, by exchange, 32.131.2.

ISBN: 978-0-87421-793-3 (cloth)
ISBN: 978-0-87421-948-7 (paper)
ISBN: 978-0-87421-794-0 (e-book)

Library of Congress Cataloging-in-Publication Data

Reider, Noriko T.
 Japanese demon lore : oni from ancient times to the present / Noriko T. Reider.
   p. cm.
 Includes bibliographical references and index.
   ISBN 978-0-87421-793-3 (cloth) — ISBN 978-0-87421-794-0 (e-book) 1. Demonology—Japan. 2. Folklore—Japan. 3. Legends—Japan. 4. Supernatural. 5. Spirits. I. Title.
  GR340.R35 2010
  398.20952—dc22
                    2010029181

To Brent Reider

my husband and best friend

Contents

List of Illustrations	x
Foreword, by Peter Knecht	xi
Acknowledgements	xvi
Introduction	xviii

1	An Overview: What are Oni?	1
	Origins, Etymology and Formation of Oni	2
	The Japanese Line	2
	The Chinese Line	4
	The Buddhist Line	10
	The *Onmyōdō* Line	13
	Characteristics of Oni	14
	Cannibalism	14
	Transformation Power	16
	The Other: The Oppressed, Alienated, and Isolated	18
	Lightning	23
	Prosperity	24
2	Shuten Dōji (Drunken Demon): A Medieval Story of the Carnivalesque and the Rise of Warriors and Fall of Oni	30
	Legends of Shuten Dōji	30
	From Simple to Complex: Troubling the Demon	30
	Texts of Shuten Dōji	32
	The Shuten Dōji Story	34
	Carnivalesque Festivities	37
	Shuten Dōji as Other	42
	Origins of Shuten Dōji	48
	The Rise of the Warrior Class and Fall of Oni	51
3	Women Spurned, Revenge of Oni Women: Gender and Space	53
	Uji no hashihime (Woman at Uji Bridge)	53

	The Stories of Uji no hashihime	53
	Uji no hashihime vs. Shuten Dōji	55
	Sociopolitical Space for Gendered Oni	57
	Noh *Kanawa*: Lingering Affection of a Spurned Woman	58
4	Yamauba, the Mountain Ogress: Old Hag to Voluptuous Mother	61
	Cannibalism	62
	Yamauba as Great Mother and Nurturer	64
	Image of Yamauba in the Medieval Period	68
	Yamauba in the Early Modern Period: Mother of Sakata no Kintoki	69
	Chikamatsu's *Komochi Yamauba* (Mountain Ogress with a Child)	76
	The Alluring Yamauba	84
5	Oni in Urban Culture: De-demonization of the Oni	90
	The Edoites' Belief System	90
	De-demonized Oni	92
	Commercialization and Urban Culture: Oni as an Example of *Yōkai*	95
	Demonic People in Popular Culture of the Early Modern Period	98
	Kotō no Oni (Oni of a Solitary Island): Demonic People in the Erotic-Grotesque-Nonsense Culture	100
6	Oni and Japanese Identity: Enemies of the Japanese Empire in and out of the Imperial Army	104
	Reconfiguration of the Supernatural in Modern Japan	105
	Oni as Foreign Enemy in the Second World War	107
	Teito Monogatari (Tale of the Imperial Capital)	113
7	Sex, Violence, and Victimization: Modern Oni and Lonely Japanese	120

	Nakagami Kenji's "Oni no hanashi" ("A Tale of a Demon")	121
	Yumemakura Baku's *Onmyōji* (The Yin-Yang Master)	131
8	Oni in Manga, Anime, and Film	144
	Apocalyptic and Elegiac Oni	145
	Nagai Gō's Oni	145
	Debiruman (Devilman)	146
	Shuten Dōji (A Child Handed from Heaven)	151
	Akira Kurosawa's "The Weeping Demon"	154
	Modern Female Oni: Powerful, yet Compromised	155
	Urusei Yatsura: The Cute Sexy Oni	155
	Bigheaded Yamauba in *Spirited Away*	158
	Yōkai and Oni Variants	162
	Yasha and Dog in *InuYasha*	163
	Tsuchigumo (Earth Spider) in *InuYasha*	165
	Tsuchigumo in *Spirited Away*	167
9	Oni without Negatives: Selfless and Surrealistic Oni	170
	Kind and Thoughtful Oni: *Naita Akaoni* (Red Oni Who Cried)	170
	Oni Go to Heaven: Inoue Yasushi's Surrealistic "Oni no hanashi" (A Story of Oni)	173
	Conclusion	177
	Appendix A: Translation of Shibukawa's Version of Shuten Dōji	185
	Appendix B: Japanese and Chinese Names and Terms	204
	Bibliography	210
	Index	231

List of Illustrations

Figure 1: An oni in *Minister Kibi's Adventures in China*	8
Figure 2: Sugawara no Michizane in the *Illustrated Legends of Kitano Tenjin Shrine*	22
Figure 3: Shuten Dōji entertains Raikō and his vassals with human flesh	36
Figure 4: Shuten Dōji's head	44
Figure 5: *Yamauba to Kintarō ennenmai* (Yamauba and Kintarō, dance)	86
Figure 6: *Yamauba to Kintarō genpuku* (Yamauba and Kintarō, coming-of-age)	87
Figure 7: *Yamauba to Kintarō kamisori* (Yamauba and Kintarō, shaving hair)	89
Figure 8: Oni on Kamaishi Line	183
Figure 9: Shuten Dōji entertains Raikō and his vassals with human flesh	196
Figure 10: Shuten Dōji's severed head lunges at Raikō	198

Foreword

On the last day of winter, *SETSUBUN*, the parting of the seasons, people perform a ceremony at temples and in many private houses where they throw beans at imagined or impersonated frightening figures called *oni*. When they throw the beans they shout: "*Oni wa soto, fuku wa uchi*" (Oni get out, luck come in). On this year's *setsubun* a foreign colleague participated in this ceremony at a temple only to find himself to be the target of people throwing beans and shouting "*oni wa soto*!" He found himself looked at as if he were an oni. For what reason would he have been considered to be an oni?

It is difficult to translate the term *oni* because an oni is a being with many facets. It may be imagined as some ambiguous demon, or it may be impersonated as an ugly and frightening humanlike figure, an ogre. However, it is not an intrinsically evil creature of the kind, like the devil, who, in monotheistic religions, is the personification of everything that is evil. The difficulty in describing oni, is in itself, it seems to me, part of the oni's character as a basically elusive and ambiguous creature. At *setsubun*, when people throw beans to dispel the oni, they do it with so much fun so that the onlooker may get the impression that an oni is nothing more than a character from children's stories. Yet, as Noriko Reider eloquently shows in this volume, there is much more to an oni. In fact, it can be said that this figure and its actions let us have a glimpse at how the Japanese imagine their own world in its relation with the outside. This relation is continually reinterpreted according to the change of times. For that reason, oni are not simply a product of naïve beliefs of a remote past, they are alive to an astonishing degree still today. The experience of my colleague mentioned above may well be taken as a sign of the oni's continued actuality. The changes as well as the continuity in the image of the oni, are the topic of this volume. Here I do not plan to summarize Reider's argument, because to do so would only take away a good deal of its fascination. However, a recent experience of mine might help to prepare the reader for how complex the concept "oni" in fact is.

On a day in late February a dream I had fostered for many years finally became reality. It was a sunny and, for the season, an unusually warm day, when I visited the "Namahage Museum" on the Oga Peninsula, a wind-stricken peninsula reaching out into the Sea of Japan north of the city of Akita. Although Namahage appear in many villages all along the sea line of Akita and neighboring Niigata Prefectures, those of the Oga Peninsula are particularly well known. Impersonated by vigorous young men they are truly terrifying figures, by their looks as well as by their raucous and impetuous behavior. They appear in pairs or in groups of four or more. Their faces are hidden behind red, blue or black masks with large gaping mouths that expose huge canine teeth. From the top of their head protrude two large horns. Their garments, a shoulder cover, a skirt and shoes are all made of rice straw preserved from the last harvest. These looks and the strange sounds they utter when they visit the houses combine to make them truly frightening. The time of the day when they appear also adds to this fearsome impression: late in the evening of the last day of the year they emerge out of the dark mountain forest. They burst into the houses where they look for lazy or disobedient children or adults, threatening to take them away. They cause great havoc, especially among the children who hide behind their parents' backs or cling desperately to a pillar trying to avoid being taken away. But the head of the family invites them to a formal meal and soothes them with sake until they leave rather quietly, leaving behind pieces of straw that had fallen from their covering. After they are gone, the people of the house gather these pieces and bind them around the head of the children because they are believed to insure good health for the coming year.

Who are these threatening figures? They are one kind of oni. The Namahage Museum offers two kinds of narratives about them: one to explain their presumed origin, the other to explain their and the villagers' behavior.

The first narrative about their origin is related to the striking fact that Namahage appear in numerous villages more or less close to the sea shore, but not in the mountains of the hinterland. In this narrative the wild figures are presented as being foreigners from the continent, probably Russians, who had suffered shipwreck and then were trying to go inland in search of a way to survive. Dressed in their long coats, with large beards and long disheveled hair, it is said that these foreigners must have appeared to the surprised villagers they encountered as wild and threatening giants. In other words, these disquieting figures must have burst upon the villagers as nothing else than real oni, the strange creatures about whom they had heard in their old stories.

The second kind of narrative is an example of such a story. At one time, a group of huge oni appeared in a village and demanded that the farmers hand over to them a village girl. The distressed farmers discussed the matter among themselves and finally decided to offer the oni a deal. For some time they had had in mind to build a stair of one hundred stone steps up the mountain. Now they saw a chance to have the oni do the work in their stead. So they proposed to let the oni have the girl under the condition that the oni build the stair of heavy stones in one single night before the first cry of the cock at dawn. The oni accepted the deal and eagerly set to work. By the time dawn was approaching the farmers noticed that they were about to loose the deal, but when the oni carried the last stone, one of the farmers shouted "cock-a-doodle-doo" imitating the cock's cry. The oni, believing that it had been a cock's cry and that, therefore, they had lost their bet, flew into a terrible rage. One of them pulled up a huge tree with its roots and tossed it back into the earth top down. After that the oni disappeared. Although the villagers had won their bet and were happy about the impressive stone stair, they had some afterthoughts about their own behavior. They were not quite happy that they had deceived the oni. In order to make up for their misbehavior, they built five small shrines on top of the flight of steps where from then on they honored the oni as divine beings.

Today, the young men of Oga Peninsula who impersonate the Namahage—the oni—dress up in the afternoon of the last day of the year at the village shrine. When they are ready, by falling darkness they gather in the shrine's hall of worship. There, in front of the village deity, the shrine priest purifies them ritually before he lets them go out into the dark village in pursuit of their mission. If these oni were conceived of as intrinsically evil beings, as devils set on harming humans, one would be hard pressed to explain why they are sent into the village by the priest who attends to its tutelary deity. In fact, despite the turmoil and confusion they cause on entering a house in the village, they are wined and dined by the head of that house just as honored guests are. And what they leave behind, the straw fallen from their garments, is accepted as a token of the blessings they are believed to have bestowed on the family: that in the coming year its members would be free of sickness and have a good harvest.

The Namahage *are* frightening creatures and their exaggerated strange appearance underlines what they are: beings from outside, from another world. For that reason they appear not just on any night, but on the very night that marks a border, the end of one year and the beginning of another. For the villagers and their ordered world they represent the (seemingly) threatening outside, the unknown other. However, at the same time they are also the harbingers of all the good the villagers hope for. In this function they are mediators between their world, the outside, and the world of the villagers, the inside. In Japanese folk tradition such outsiders are prone to cause fear, yet they are also accepted because they are considered to be beings with special powers that work for the benefit of those living inside the daily ordinary world. These visitors, despite inspiring intense feelings of fear, are also looked at as a kind of divine being. Their distinguishing mark is often that they are clad in shabby garments made of rice straw. The foreigners appearing in the first narrative may not have been dressed in straw garments, but both their unusual foreign dress and their sheer physical size, which the villagers had never seen before, may well have called up associations that linked the foreign figures with the conceptions the people held about visiting deities or beings of the other world.

Oni are denizens of an other world, a world invisible by definition. Yet they are imagined as having a shape that somehow resembles the shape of visible beings of this world. The weird exaggerations in the manner of how they are imagined only underline their very otherworldliness. Yet, the oni that are the target of bean throwing at *setsubun,* as well as the Namahage, are oni made visible. As such they can be grasped and handled so that they may even turn into beings favorably disposed towards humans.

In the examples mentioned above, oni appear to be fantastic expressions of folk imagination, a result of people's efforts to come to terms in some way with the reality of the other, be it either otherworldly or just outside the borders of one's ordinary world. When we go back in history, we find that in medieval Japan the term oni is used to express 'the other' in fields different from folk tradition, namely in medicine and court literature. Under the influence of Chinese medical treatises, early medieval Japanese practitioners of medicine argued that the causes for human diseases are certain entities active inside the human body. These causes were conceived as oni, but at that time oni were not yet the terrifying figures they became later. However, in later interpretations it was thought that types of *mushi* (an imaginary 'insect') were active in the different parts of the body. Challenged by some outside being, these *mushi* were believed to cause a disease together with the intruder. The outside challengers were concretely conceptualized as oni. In this interpretation oni are not only entities of a world outside of the human body, they were also of a negative and noxious nature. In a quite different world, that of Heian court literature, we find still another idea of oni, for example in the expression *kokoro no oni* (oni in one's heart). In this case the oni serves to give concrete form to an otherwise hard to express and invisible disposition in one's mind, namely the dark and evil side of one's heart, such as evil or mischievous thoughts and feelings toward fellow humans. This kind of oni is said to hide in a dark corner of the heart and to be difficult to control. However, in consequence of an impetus from outside it may be thrown into consciousness and its noxious nature may show itself (see Knecht et al. 2004).

There can be no doubt that oni are much more than just the gruesome figures of fairy tales. In Japanese society, ancient and recent, they can appear in various forms and serve a variety of purposes. If we look closely at them we may notice two main aspects. In folk tradition oni are ambiguous beings, at times feared but helpful at other times. In the sophisticated traditions of medieval medicine and literature they are the concrete figure by which otherwise difficult to grasp concepts or states of the mind and heart are made intelligible and, as a result, also controllable. Yet, under both of these aspects, the oni are conceptions of entities generally foreign to normally functioning society. Therefore, as Reider says in this volume's introduction, examining them "reveals a problematic and unstable aspect of the human psyche and of society in general."

Oni are not readily visible yet they help to make hidden problems visible and understandable, in individuals as well as in society. They help people to come to terms with the other. Reider leads the reader skillfully through this mysterious yet ever actual world of Japanese culture. Yet, it is hoped that her work not only makes the oni of Japan visible to foreign readers, but challenges researchers outside of Japan to study in their cultures expressions of the encounter with otherness and the psychic and social problems it causes.

Peter Knecht

Acknowledgments

So, again we wade into Japanese folklore. Modern and ancient, powerful in their ability to express the human condition, oni can always be reimagined. Therein, it is easy to imagine how this work has benefited from the kindness of many people. First of all, I express my sincere appreciation to Peter Knecht, former editor of *Asian Folklore Studies* (now *Asian Ethnology*) who has guided me through a number of journal articles and generously shared information about oni. I am grateful to Shelley Fenno Quinn of the Ohio State University, a scholar and a performer of Noh, for her support throughout my academic career; and to Mark Bender of The Ohio State University, a folklore scholar in East Asian studies, for his encouragement all the way across the Project Oni.

Special acknowledgements are due Richard Torrance, Shinji Nobuhiro, Thomas Rogers, Clark Chilson, Benjamin Dorman, Scott Schnell, Rio Otomo, Judith Snodgrass, Elizabeth Oyler, Gaynor Sekimori, Lloyd Michaels, Hank Glassman, R. Keller Kimbrough, Paul Swanson, Rebecca Copeland, Michael Bathgate, Thomas Kasulis, Michael Mitchell, and Paul Watt for their valuable comments and suggestions on various stages of this project. The contributions from Susan Napier of Tufts University and an anonymous reader of the manuscript were invaluable, and I appreciate their time and comments for this book. The guidance of John Alley, executive editor of Utah State University Press, has been very helpful. Anne Morris Hooke, my neighbor and friend, and Mary Jackson-Smith, editor for Utah State University Press, were skillful and patient in editing my English. Librarians Maureen Donovan of The Ohio State University and Stacy Brinkman of Miami University were always helpful in obtaining the many books I required for research. I thank the staff at museums and historical sites in Japan, the United States, and abroad, and especially the staff at Miami University's Interlibrary Loan office for their help in my research. Chantal Kozyreff and Dominique Hoornaert of the Royal Museums of Art and History—Brussels have been gracious in their assistance and encouragement. My colleagues at the Department of German, Russian and the

East Asian Languages and East Asian Studies Program at Miami University have been supportive and are exemplars of collegiality. Likewise, friendship and encouragement from the members of Midwest Japan Seminar are much appreciated.

With a research leave in the academic year of 2007–2008, financial support from my institution's Hampton Fund for Faculty International Initiatives in 2004, and the constant support of my friends and colleagues at Miami University, I was able to complete the manuscript.

Chapter one of this book is a revised and much expanded version of my article that appeared as "Transformation of *Oni*: From the Frightening and Diabolic to the Sexy and Cute" in *Asian Folklore Studies* 62. 1 (2003), and a core part of chapter two appeared as "*Ōeyama Shuten Dōji*: A Voice of Other and Carnivalesque" in *Japanese Studies* 28. 3 (2008). The main part of chapter four has been published as "Yamauba: Representation of the Japanese Mountain Witch in the Muromachi and Edo Periods" in *International Journal of Asian Studies* 2. 2 (2005). A section of chapter seven appeared as "*Onmyōji*: Sex, Pathos, and Grotesquery in Yumemakura Baku's *Oni*" in *Asian Folklore Studies* 66. 1 (2007), and a section about *Spirited Away* in chapter eight was taken from my article titled "*Spirited Away*: Film of the Fantastic and Evolving Japanese Folk Symbols," which appeared in *Film Criticism* 29. 3 (Spring 2005). A translation of the Shuten Dōji story in the Appendix is a reprint of "Shuten dōji: Drunken Demon" in *Asian Folklore Studies* 64. 2 (2005). I am grateful to the journals for permission to use the articles in revised form.

Finally, the love and encouragement of my family—my husband Brent Reider, daughter MaryEllen, and son Warwick—kept me busy with much needed diversions.

Noriko T. Reider

May 2010

Introduction

WHY THE SUPERNATURAL? "Serious scholars remain very wary about studying supernatural folklore. ... The supernatural has been officially demoted to the nursery, commercial, or fantasy worlds," Gillian Bennett writes, yet at an "informal level, there continues to be a very widespread belief in the supernatural" (1–2). Here, Gillian Bennett refers to contemporary English society, but this is true for Japanese society as well. In varying degrees Japanese people believe in life after death, deities, ghosts, and demons, just to name a few. Indeed, the supernatural is an integral part of their everyday life. To study supernatural lore of the past and present—how the Japanese have perceived, treated, believed or disbelieved the supernatural from ancient times to the present—is to explore fundamental issues of how the Japanese worldview has been shaped and changed or remained unchanged. It is to examine how Japanese people have thought and lived, to study the Japanese psyche and behaviors. Examining the supernatural as a collective whole is far beyond the scope of this book or my capacity, however. In this book I focus on just one of its important elements—the *oni*.

Referenced throughout generations of Japanese literature, religion, art, and in more modern times, through mass media representations in such pop culture icons as anime and film, oni's longevity can arguably be ascribed to their symbiotic evolution alongside Japanese society. Oni are mostly known for their fierce and evil nature manifested in their propensity for murder and cannibalism. Notwithstanding their evil reputation, oni possess intriguingly complex aspects that cannot be brushed away simply as evil. While oni are sometimes likened to their demonic or Western ogre counterparts, the lack of a streamlined western mythos makes the comparisons roundabout and difficult.

In popular Japanese thought, the word "oni" conjures up images of hideous creatures emerging from hell's abyss to terrify wicked mortals. Some scholars assert that the concept of the Japanese oni is a purely Buddhist creation, while others argue that it is not exclusive to the Buddhist cosmos.

Komatsu Kazuhiko, for example, notes that the term oni was used in *onmyōdō* (the way of *yin* and *yang*) to describe any evil spirit(s) harmful to humans ("Supernatural Apparitions and Domestic Life in Japan"). Some scholars find the root of oni in Chinese thought while others claim the creatures are indigenous to Japan. Each theory of origin and formation seems plausible, even though some theories contradict each other. Oni, as a subject of study, thus represent rather eclectic supernatural creatures. These representations came into being adopting, embodying, and assimilating multifaceted elements, concepts and characteristics of entities that draw from Chinese origins, Buddhist religious traditions, and *onmyōdō*. Oni can thus be said to be genuinely pan-Asian in their roots.

While the shape shifting powers of the oni make it possible for them to assume human, as well as other forms, their typically gruesome appearances are often reflective of their allegedly evil dispositions, as one might surmise from the oni's well-known appetite for human flesh. Yet, close examination of oni in diverse contexts reveals more than just monster imagery. For instance, in some traditions, oni can be harbingers of prosperity to humans. This gentler aspect of the oni seems to be closely related to oni as a variation of *marebito* (foreign travelers, or *kami* [Japanese deities] from the other world [*tokoyo*] who visit villagers) as Orikuchi Shinobu describes them ("Oni no hanashi" 17–18). Or it could originate from the dichotomous nature of Indian deities from which many Buddhist gods and demons are adopted. This positive aspect gives a wonderful source for kyōgen plays and other auspicious folklore. On the metaphorical level, the oni can symbolize the anti-establishment, as "other" or outsider, vis-à-vis some form of hegemonic authority. Traditionally, anti-establishment elements are often assigned the appellation of oni as a pejorative against difference. Rosemary Jackson, author of *Fantasy*, suggests: "the fantastic traces the unsaid and the unseen of culture: that which has been silenced, made invisible, covered over and made 'absent'" (4). In this context oni can represent disenfranchised persons, groups and organizations silenced, and/or destined for elimination by those in authority and/or mainstream Japanese society.

Shuten Dōji, a notorious oni known for kidnapping and consuming the maidens of the Capital of Heian, is a good example of all the above. He is a formidable, cannibalistic villain; yet, he may also represent someone opposed to public policy, such as a local deity chased away by a religious authority, or a marginalized being considered by the ruling dynasty to be injurious to the general public or the safety of the court itself. Interestingly, in this vein, Shuten Dōji's narrative reveals the voice of someone or something outside the powerhouse of hegemonic authority.

While the visual image of oni is predominantly masculine—with muscular body and loin cloth—there are numerous examples of female oni in Japanese lore such as Yomotsu-shikome (literally ugly woman of the other world) who appears in *Kojiki* (Ancient Matters, 712),[1] Uji no hashihime (woman at a bridge), and *yamauba* (mountain ogresses). Notably, one hypothesized origin of the Japanese oni is a female named Yomotsu-shikome, born from a female deity who felt shamed by her husband. A great number of female oni seem to be born from the angst and/or shame of being seen as unsightly by male lovers; Uji no hashihime, a protagonist of Noh's *Kanawa*, or contemporary versions of "Kanawa" by Yumemakura Baku[2] all become oni while they are alive because of jealousy, angst and/or shameful feelings related to being watched by someone. There are, of course, exceptions, such as a yamauba who is introduced in a Noh play as "an oni-woman." A yamauba is a woman marginalized by villagers or family members at home and who lives in the mountains either voluntarily or because she is forced to by others. Depending upon the time and social expectations, the yamauba's role changes from an enlightened seeker to a doting mother.

Examining oni—what and how they were and are represented, their vicissitudes and transformation—reveals a problematic and unstable aspect of the human psyche and of society in general, not exclusively endemic to Japanese society. To that end, in this monograph, I will treat the oni as marginalized other, and examine the evolution of their multifaceted roles and significance in Japanese culture and society. "Other," in this sense, broadly signifies a person or members of a group marginalized and/or silenced by hegemonic authority and/or mainstream society, willingly or involuntarily, temporarily or permanently. Those marginalized persons or groups are partially or entirely excluded from participation in politico-historical affairs of their particular society, and they suffer from cultural, intellectual, legal, geographical and/or physical disadvantages attached to their status.[3]

In more limited terms, I follow Komatsu Kazuhiko's notion of other or "strangers." Most pertinent to my work is his explanation about strangers

---

1   For the Japanese text of *Kojiki*, see Yamaguchi and Kōnoshi. For an English translation, see Philippi.
2   Yumemakura's "Kanawa" is included in his *Onmyōji: Namanari-hime*.
3   For the discussion of "other," see Goodich; Dallery and Scott; Huffer.

as those who live spatially far away from a community, and are thus known to members of the community only through their imaginations such as foreigners who live overseas and supernatural creatures who live in the other world ("Ijin ron –'ijin' kara 'tasha' e" 178).

Several years ago when I visited the oni museum in Ōe-mach in Kyoto, I purchased a booklet. A small explanation of the front page picture—monstrous Shuten Dōji's head biting Minamoto no Raikō's helmet—reads, "There is nothing false in the words of demons." A friend of mine who was traveling with me saw it, and repeated the phrase, deep in thought. She was apparently sympathizing with Shuten Dōji as someone who was naively deceived. A great number of people in contemporary society seem to find the idea of oni as marginalized and/or deceived creatures attractive and empathize with them as one of their kind. Thus, as elements of our human psyche, oni are alive with us and within us. One need only examine the work of certain contemporary Japanese authors who take the oni as tantamount to humans and attempt to understand their behavior, to see how this plays out in contemporary Japanese popular culture.

These fantastic creatures—threatening dark forces of society in ancient and early medieval periods—took up residence in remote mountains and rivers, and strode through the realms of art and literature in the Early Modern period. In present-day Japan they have emerged at the forefront of pop culture. Modern lighting technology appears to have deprived oni of their traditional living space—complete darkness of night. But they seem to have relocated via modern technology to a cyber-world comprised of film, anime, and games. Commercialization and commodification of oni come with this reclamation, reflecting contemporary consumerism if not drawing it into the mix. It has to be understood, however, that commercialization of oni did not start in the postmodern age. An *oni no nenbutsu* (oni intoning the name of the Buddha) of Ōtsu-e (Ōtsu pictures) back in the Early Modern age is a good example. Ōtsu-e are folk paintings produced in and around Ōtsu town, one of the fifty-three stations of Tōkaidō (Eastern Sea Route) connecting Edo and Kyoto. Undoubtedly, the Praying oni were popular souvenirs for the travelers who journeyed on to Tōkaidō. Oni's commodification has only accelerated in the postmodern age.

Despite the oni's importance in Japanese cultural history as well as their recent resurgent popularity, scholarly analytical works on the subject in English are limited. While many articles refer to or mention oni, the oni are rarely the major focus of the articles. Ikeda Yuriko's article, "Oni or Ogres in

Japanese Literature" straightforwardly treats the oni; however, it deals with ancient Japanese oni only and does not analyze their representative construction or social function. There are a number of insightful and informative books available in Japanese, and I am indebted to many of these for an appreciation and understanding of the metaphorical and literary treatment of oni, especially Ishibashi Gaha's *Oni* (1909), Kondō Yoshihiro's *Nihon no oni: nihon bunka tankyū no shikaku* (Japanese Oni: Perspectives on the Search for Japanese Culture, 1975), Chigiri Kōsai's *Oni no kenkyū* (Study of Oni, 1978), *Oni no kenkyū* (Study of Oni, 1988) by Baba Akiko, Komatsu and Naitō's *Oni ga tsukutta kuni Nihon* (Japan, a Country Created by Oni, 1991), and *Oni* in Volume Four of *Kaii no minzokugaku* (Folklore Studies of the Strange and Mysterious, 2000) edited by Komatsu Kazuhiko. While these works are all informative and illuminating, they rarely discuss the oni's modern rendition.

Japanese Demon Lore: Oni from Ancient Times to the Present is different from existing studies in both English and Japanese in that it studies the oni's vicissitudes or progression/retrogression in Japanese history from ancient times to the present day, examining and evaluating the cultural implications these astonishing creatures have had for the Japanese psyche and society and culture as exemplified in literature, religion, art, folklore and film. It is my hope that this book will provide an analytical overview of oni, while suggesting connections with broader disciplines. This study thus addresses not only scholars and students of Japanese literature but also general readers interested in history, religion, anthropology, cultural studies, gender studies, and the visual and performing arts.

The monograph is organized into nine chapters. Chapters one through three deal with the ancient and medieval periods. Chapter four is transitional, and examines the medieval and Early Modern periods. Chapters five through nine discuss the oni from the Early Modern through the contemporary periods, and these chapters are further organized according to topics.

Chapter one ("An Overview") examines what has become the dominant representation of oni. The oni's genesis, etymology, and formation are described from the viewpoints of indigenous Japanese, Chinese, Buddhist, and *onmyōdō*. Further, the general features of the oni are discussed with literary examples. Considered a real entity by the ancient and medieval Japanese, the oni frequented both urban and rural areas, and were even seen in the capital, disrupting everyday life. The oni's principal characteristics—cannibalism, the power to change shape, enmity to central authority, social isolation, and the power to discharge lightning and to bring prosperity—are analyzed as established features of the medieval oni.

The second chapter ("Shuten Dōji [Drunken Demon]") explores one of Japan's most renowned oni legends, the story of Shuten Dōji. Shuten Dōji is a dynamic medieval oni with all the typical oni characteristics. He and his cohorts kidnap daughters of the nobility and then eat their flesh. Shuten Dōji is finally eliminated by the warrior-hero Minamoto no Raikō (or Yorimitsu, 948–1021) and his four loyal lieutenants. The legend is intriguing in that, while it clearly praises "the forces of good" (the protectors of Japan with the imperial authority as its center), a sympathetic view of "evil forces" (voices of those outside the central authority) resonates equally. The tale is also insightful in that it anticipates the emerging power of the warrior class in contrast to the declining dominance of oni. Using Mikhail M. Bakhtin's theory of the "carnivalesque" (see *Rabelais and His World*) this chapter examines the Shuten Dōji texts as treatments of the marginalized other.

The third chapter ("Women Spurned, Revenge of Oni Women") examines two medieval stories of spurned women whose angst turns them into ferocious female oni while they are still living. They are Uji no hashihime (Woman at Uji Bridge) as described in the *Heike monogatari* (Tale of the Heike) and a famous Noh play entitled *Kanawa* (Iron Tripod), which is based upon the Uji no hashihime episode. While describing the stories of the spurned women, the chapter primarily focuses on the space and gender that male and female oni, represented by Shuten Dōji, and Uji no hashihime and the woman of *Kanawa*, respectively, occupy. Uji no hashihime's fury causes random disappearance of people similar to those in Shuten Dōji. The chapter concludes with the conjecture that an Uji no hashihime episode may have actually been a source for the male Shuten Dōji.

In the fourth chapter ("Yamauba, the Mountain Ogress"), I examine the female oni known as yamauba or mountain ogress and trace her transformative image from medieval time to the Early Modern period. According to the medieval Noh text entitled *Yamamba*, a "yamamba (or yamauba) is a female oni living in the mountains" (Yokomichi and Omote 279). To many contemporary Japanese, a yamauba is an ugly old woman who lives in the mountains and eats human beings. By the end of the seventeenth century, the legend of Shuten Dōji and the tales of the yamauba were linked in the story of one of Raikō's four lieutenants, Sakata Kintoki. Kintoki, a legendary super-child raised in the mountains, was considered the son of a yamauba. The theme of motherhood in the yamauba tale was gradually brought to the forefront, as exemplified in the Kabuki/Puppet play entitled *Komochi yamauba* (Mountain Ogress with a Child, 1712). Later, the yamauba came to be portrayed as an alluring, seductive woman by *ukiyo-e* (pictures of the floating world) artists. In urban areas, yamauba have been commodified as objects of sexual desire.

During the Early Modern period, Edoites believed in the supernatural to varying degrees. Belief in the oni as a real entity had significantly declined; yet, the oni continued to thrive in the minds of common folks and remain visible in their literary and visual arts. The fifth chapter ("Oni in Urban Culture") examines a general trend of de-demonization of oni in the Early Modern period and looks into an increasing tendency among urban cultures to commercialize and commodify oni. This is seen in Tsuruya Nanboku's *Tōkaidō Yotsuya kaidan* (Yotsuya Ghost Stories, 1824), and Edogawa Ranpo's *Kotō no oni* (Oni of a Solitary Island, 1929–30), a work of the Modern period.

The sixth chapter ("Oni and Japanese Identity") examines the problematic labeling of oni. The imperial Japanese military complex used the oni to define its enemies, particularly effectively as a tool to define foreigners. The idea of outsider or "other," simultaneously promoted a sense of unity among the Japanese. This became especially true during the Second World War. Conversely, Japan's foes could use the oni to define the Japanese. This identification of oni becomes essentially a matter of whose viewpoint one takes, and this is a focal point in some postwar fiction such as Aramata Hiroshi's *Teito monogatari* (Tale of the Imperial Capital, 1983–89).

Authors of any age, with or without intention, tend to impart values and issues contemporary to the age in which they are writing, albeit some aspects—sex and violence, for example—tend to attract larger audiences. The late twentieth and early twenty-first century's portrayal of the oni as a victim rather than the perpetrator of evil seems to be representative of all popular media of the time. In taking this approach, some modern authors essentially seem to tap the Japanese psyche. The seventh chapter ("Sex, Violence, and Victimization") examines oni representations that evince these trends through Nakagami Kenji's "Oni no hanashi" ("A Tale of a Demon") and Yumemakura Baku's extremely popular series titled *Onmyōji* (The Yin-Yang Master).

The eighth chapter ("Oni in Manga, Anime, and Film") examines some noted anime (Japanese animation), manga (graphic novels), and films that utilize oni and oni variants, and studies the signification behind the oni.

A contemporary oni in these media is often portrayed as a creature from a different time and space whose existence has become entwined with cutting-edge technology such as electronics, mechanics, or robotics. Geopolitics may change; but the oni is still an alienated "other." Some oni are used in apocalyptic epic stories like Nagai's *Devilman*, or as representation of a negative emotional state of mind such as in *Shuten Dōji* by the same author; some are cute and sexual such as Lum in *Urusei Yatsura*, and others are employed as allegories or social commentaries as in Akira Kurosawa's "The Weeping Demon," one episode of *Dreams*. Oni-like characters appear in the award-winning animated film *Spirited Away* as well. Just as the subject matter of the contemporary representative pop cultural media varies greatly, the oni's use has a wide range.

The ninth chapter ("Oni without Negatives") studies the oni characters that do not have any negative associations. The modern era has witnessed the birth of an utterly kind, selfless oni as described in Hamada Hirosuke's *Naita Akaoni* (Red Oni Who Cried). Hamada's oni may at first appear to be an anomaly, but in the process of studying various aspects of oni throughout Japan's history, a selfless oni may become understandable. "Oni no hanashi" (A Story of Oni) written by a famous twentieth-century author, Inoue Yasushi, is a keenly personal account. His oni are good people who are deceased. These oni stories do carry cultural baggage and the oni's stigma, and yet, give fresh breeze to the stereotypical oni world, revealing the oni's lasting flexibility and elasticity.

Regarding the way Japanese names appear in this text, according to the Japanese custom, they are written with the family name appearing first. For example, the family name of Orikuchi Shinobu, the name of a scholar of Japanese literature, folklorist, and poet, is Orikuchi. The exception to this rule occurs when the names are well known outside Japan in English circles. For example, the film director, Akira Kurosawa, remains Akira Kurosawa even though Kurosawa is his family name.

In my research I have encountered various images and interpretations of oni. One memorable image is a cute, baby-like chubby, angry-looking oni painted on a train car in the Kamaishi line, Iwate Prefecture in the summer of 2007. It was part of East Japan Railway Company's campaign titled "Another Japan North East North: Aomori, Iwate, and Akita" to attract more passengers and tourists to northern Japan. This particular train had only two cars, and on one car a lovable looking oni and *kappa*—once grotesque or bizarre supernatural beings—are portrayed. They are inviting people to come and increase the train company's revenue as well as to revitalize the areas the train visits with tourism. Rich in folklore and sites of the supernatural, northern Japan and the Railway Company appear to be effectively capitalizing on this unique cultural resource. For the people of Kitakami city in Iwate prefecture, "Oni are ancestors who protect the townspeople and good deities who bring happiness" (Kitakami shiritsu oni no yakata 3). Perhaps boosting tourism is one way today's oni can bring material prospecity. This made me think how times have changed in regard to the oni—from the ancient time when people were helpless before their invisible, awesome force to the present when human beings create and use them to their advantage. As we shall see, oni provide a rich pallet of representations, from a formidable evil force, to forlorn and marginalized individuals, to connoisseurs of art, and harbingers of fortune. They are indeed multifaceted fantastic creatures.

1

An Overview
What Are Oni?

IN AN ENGLISH LANGUAGE TREATMENT OF ONI it is tempting to seek comparisons in Western demonology. Indeed, the concept of oni and the history and development of their representation have some striking affinity to the demonic entities that populate Judeo-Christian myths and the various figures from older Greco-Roman, Celtic, Anglo-Saxon, Germanic, and Norse traditions that became "demonized" as Christianity spread through the European continent, the British Isles, and finally Iceland. Such a comparison, a worthy task in itself, is, however, beyond the scope of this book. It suffices to say that the Western adjective *demonic*, while the closest Western term to describe oni, falls short of capturing the full idea of these creatures.

The popularity and longevity of the oni myth is no doubt partially based on the beings' conventional demonic accoutrements, which have remained relatively constant through the ages: they are dreadful supernatural beings emerging from the abyss of Buddhist hell to terrify wicked mortals; their grotesque and savage demeanor and form instill instant fear; and the oni's omnipresence in the socio-historical and cultural archive of Japan is directly attributable to the moral, social, and religious edification that stories about oni engender. But there is a lesser known side to the oni that will also be examined here—the oni as harbingers of wealth and fortune. This widely disparate dichotomy begs a fundamental question, "What are oni?" This chapter examines the genesis and etymology of oni, as well as their features and attributes as depicted throughout various literary texts.

Origins, Etymology, and Formation of Oni

Considering the diverse roles of oni in the Japanese cultural milieu, one expects varieties of theories about oni's origins, etymology, and formation, and one is not disappointed—they are indeed multiple and varied. According to Anesaki Masaharu, Japanese oni "belong to a purely Buddhist mythology" (238) but the oni cannot be said to be exclusive to the Buddhist cosmic universe. Komatsu Kazuhiko explains that oni was the term used in *onmyōdō* (the way of yin and yang) to describe any evil spirits that harm humans. In early *onmyōdō* doctrine, the word "oni" referred specifically to invisible evil spirits that caused human infirmity ("Supernatural Apparitions and Domestic Life in Japan" 3). Takahashi Masaaki identifies oni as an epidemic deity (4), while Kumasegawa Kyōko interprets an oni as an individual and/or societal shadow (204). It is little wonder then that overwhelmingly negative forces have often been attributable to oni. This section examines the origins, etymology and formation of oni and explores the four major lines from which oni stories have evolved: the Japanese, Chinese, Buddhist, and *onmyōdo*. There are many overlapping elements across the four lines; some descriptions are contradictory and yet believed simultaneously. Others are interwoven as if to reinforce themselves. There are many ambiguous and even ambivalent descriptions. While some conflicting and/or ambiguous explanations reveal the process of integration and adoption of various origins in the early stages of history, they also disclose Japanese attitudes toward something foreign: a selective adaptation while trying to keep their indigenous beliefs. The oni remind anyone researching their origins how strong and influential the dominant culture, be it Chinese or Buddhist, stood in relation to indigenous beliefs in *kami* or Japanese deities. Without a solid philosophical and intellectual background, evil or negative *kami*, like their European pagan counterparts, are *demonized* and incorporated into the large corpus of oni.

The Japanese Line

Kondō Yoshihiro describes the genesis of oni as a historical product of people's fear of the destructive power of phenomenological occurrences such as thunder and lightning, storms, and earthquakes (14–15). Among the natural forces, thunder and lightning are most strongly associated with the oni. That thunder and lightning instilled fright in people is evinced by the sheer number of shrines dedicated to the thunder gods (Kondō 16). According to Wakamori Tarō, the inhabitants of ancient Japan believed in the existence of evil spirits that resided deep in the mountains. He also asserts that the Japanese referenced the presence of oni well before the advent of Chinese thought and Buddhism in Japan (119–122). For the appellation of the "oni" itself, Orikuchi Shinobu asserts a Japanese origin, meaning giant people 大人 (pronounced oni) who lived in caves ("Oni to sanjin to" 121). Furthermore, Orikuchi suggests that there may have been no clear demarcation between an oni and a *kami* in Japan's ancient past. Both were "awesome" beings, although the oni may not have been worshipped. Orikuchi asserts as well that the negative and fearful aspects of *kami* came to be considered oni ("Shinodazuma no hanashi" 283–284). He writes that the oni concept before the introduction of Buddhism was a variation of *tokoyo-kami* (*kami* who live in the other land or the land of the dead) or *marebito* (foreign travelers, *kami* who visit villages) who give blessings on the lunar New Year's Eve and/or New Year's Day for the coming year. *Marebito* wear *minokasa* (straw raincoats and hats) and come from a distant land beyond the sea. Villagers treat *marebito* well because they are foreigners with awesome power and the villagers want them to return soon. Orikuchi equates *marebito* to oni. He writes, "fearful oni rouse sometimes close (*shitashii*) and dear (*natsukashii*) feelings—not at all like Buddhist oni." After Buddhism was introduced in Japan, he continues, oni became mixed up with such Buddhist creatures as *rasetsu* (rākṣasa), *gozu* (ox-headed demons), and *mezu* (horse-headed demons).[1] If one accepts Orikuchi's connection between *marebito* and oni one can see how oni came to be considered harbingers of wealth.

In the same vein as Orikuchi's suggestion that *kami* are worshiped while oni are not, Komatsu Kazuhiko explains that supernatural deities worshipped by Japanese are known as *kami* while those that are not worshipped are called *yōkai* (hobgoblins/monsters), and the *yōkai* with the most negative association are oni ("Yōkai" 334, 342). As we shall see in detail in chapter eight, people performed religious rituals in order to transform *yōkai* to *kami*. If there is not worship enough for a particular supernatural being to be considered *kami*, then that *kami* becomes *yōkai* (*Yōkaigaku shinkō* 193).

Citing eighteenth-century Japanese Nativist scholar Motoori Norinaga (1730–1801), Ishibashi Gaha considers an origin of the Japanese oni in Yomotsu-shikome (literally ugly woman or women in the nether land), who

---

[1] Orikuchi, "Oni no hanashi" 16–18; "Kokubungaku no hassei" 13, 21; Also see the discussion of *tokoyo* and *marebito* in chapter one of Yamamoto's *Namahage*.

appears in Japan's creation myth in *Kojiki* (Ancient Matters), the oldest extant chronicle or record in Japan, complied in 712 (4). After the death of Izanami, the female creator of Japan, Izanagi, her husband and male counterpart, misses her so much that he goes to the nether land to retrieve her. But Izanami says that she has already eaten the food from that realm, implying that it would be difficult for her to return easily to this one. The food produced in the other world has the power to make one stay in that world, so she tells him to wait and not to look. The taboo against "looking" is a familiar folk literature motif—unable to resist temptation, a protagonist often breaks a promise not to look. Izanagi breaks his promise not to look at Izanami—just as Orpheus does on his journey to bring Eurydice back to the world of the living in the Greek myth. When Orpheus looks back, beautiful Eurydice slips back into the world of the dead. When Izanagi looks at Izanami, however, she is ugly, with maggots squirming and eight thunder deities growing around her entire body. Izanami is furious, probably because he broke the promise/taboo and looked at her changed appearance. Instead of bemoaning her fate and going back to the nether land quietly, she attacks him saying that he has caused her undying shame. Terrified, Izanagi quickly makes his way back to this world, whereupon Izanami dispatches Yomotsu-shikome from the underworld to avenge her shame.[2] It is interesting that a precursor of Japanese oni is a female born from a goddess who feels "shame" and is spurned by a male lover, for this pattern continues to appear throughout the ages in Japan, as we shall see in the following chapters. While the Japanese can identify with a primordial form of oni in Yomotsu-shikome, Ishibashi attributes the appellation, oni, to Chinese thought (104).

The Chinese Line

Ancient Japanese literature assigns a number of different written characters such as 鬼, 魑魅, and 鬼魅 to express oni (Tsuchihashi 95). Among them, the character used now is 鬼,[3] which in Chinese means invisible soul/ spirit of the dead, both ancestral and evil. The letter 鬼 is a hieroglyph that presents the shape of a dead body at a burial during the Yin Dynasty (1500–770 BCE);

---

2   For the Japanese text, see Yamaguchi and Kōnoshi 45–47. For an English translation, see Philippi 61–64.

3   According to Kosugi Kazuo, the oldest example of the character, 鬼, in Japan appears in an inscription written on the halo of the statue of Shaka and two attendants housed in the Golden Hall of the Hōryū-ji (*Chūgoku bijutsushi* 203).

the fundamental meaning of 鬼 is, therefore, a dead body itself.[4] According to *Wamyō ruijushō* (ca. 930s), the first Japanese language dictionary, oni is explained as a corruption of the reading of the character *on* 隠 (hiding), "hiding behind things, not wishing to appear… a soul/spirit of the dead." Apparently the concept of oni in *Wamyō ruijushō* is based upon the Chinese concept (Takahashi Masaaki 41). Tsuchihashi Yutaka writes that the term oni came from the pronunciation of *on* 隠 plus "i." Similar to Orikuchi, he writes that many types of *kami* possessing powerful spiritual forces existed in ancient Japan. Among *kami*, those harmful to humans are quite similar to the *mono* or evil spirits. Both beings are invisible; the *kami* are, however, the object of awe and respect, while the *mono* are universally feared, but not respected. Oni are spiritual beings very much like the *mono*. Tsuchihashi surmises that the character, 鬼, was employed probably because the meaning of 鬼 is close to the concept of *mono* (95).[5] But as Takahashi suggests, it is unclear whether the negative meaning of *mono* had existed before applying the character 鬼, or the Chinese meaning unwittingly seeped into *mono* when the character 鬼 was applied. In the end, Takahashi asserts that oni, *mono*, and *goryō* (vengeful spirits of the dead that will be discussed later), are all heavily influenced by Chinese concepts (41).

The early examples of 鬼 appear in *Nihongi* or *Nihonshoki* (Chronicles of Japan, 720 CE) and in *Izumo fudoki* (Topography of Izumo Province, 733 CE),[6] describing evil and/or antagonistic beings. In *Nihongi*, for example, when Takamimusuhi, one of the central deities of the Plain of High Heaven and an imperial ancestor, desires his grandson to rule the Central Land of Reed-Plains (i.e., Japan), he pronounces, "I desire to have the evil Gods of the Central Land of Reed-Plains expelled and subdued."[7] He calls

---

4   See for example, Li, "'Kiki' seiritsu ni okeru 'oni' to iu 'hyōgen'" 425. Izushi Yoshihiko explains the original character of 鬼 (without ム, which was added later) is made up of two parts: 甴 and 儿. 甴 presents a dead person, and 儿 is a hieroglyph for a person. So he surmises that the various changing appearance of dead people or a difference between a living person and a dead person was displayed by 甴 (416–418).

5   Orikuchi explains that the oni were something to be feared and that *mono* was the abstract being, possessing no particular shape or form ("Oni no hanashi" 9).

6   *Izumo fudoki* is included in Akimoto 1958 and Uegaki 1997.

7   For the Japanese text, see Sakamoto et al. I: 134. For an English translation, see Aston 1: 64. In *Kojiki*, Amaterasu, rather than Takamimusuhi makes this announcement. The corresponding section is written as "kono kuni ni chihayaburu araburu kunitsu kami domo" (unruly earthly deities in this land). See Yamaguchi and Kōnoshi 99; Philippi 121. The 鬼 character is not used in *Kojiki*.

the inhabitants of the Central Land who are not subjugated "ashiki 鬼," or evil gods. In *Izumo fudoki*, a one-eyed 鬼 appears in a reclaimed land in the community of Ayo of Izumo Province (present-day Shimane prefecture) and devours a man (Akimoto 238–39). Komatsu Kazuhiko writes, "People who had different customs or lived beyond the reach of the emperor's control" were considered some form of oni ("Supernatural Apparitions and Domestic Life in Japan" 3). This concept is actually not unique to Japan. Targets of subjugation and different ethnic groups that do not assimilate the precepts of hegemonic authority are described as 鬼 by the Han race even before the period of Six Dynasties (220–589) in China (Li 427).[8] It is not certain, however, whether the character, 鬼, was pronounced as oni or *mono*. Indeed, the character is rendered as *mono* in *Man'yōshū* (Ten Thousand Leaves, ca. eighth century).[9] There exists no definitive example of the term "*oni*" in the ancient literature (Tsuchihashi 94–95).[10] As Shelley Fenno Quinn notes:

> [T]he oldest myths and legends of Japan, material that is assumed to have been orally transmitted from ancient times, has been handed down to us in scripts that are written either in classical Chinese or in characters taken from Chinese and used for their phonetic values in writing Japanese. It was not until the ninth century that simplified phonetic scripts for writing vernacular Japanese came into general use, and thus much of what we know of these preliterate, oral discourses, reaches us through the filter of a continental writing technology or adaptations thereof. ("Oral and Vocal Traditions of Japan" 258)

Thus, when something called oni comes to be identified as 鬼, that entity seems to emerge from this kind of process.[11]

During the Heian period (794–1185), *mononoke* (evil spirits)—sharing the same *mono*—exerted great influence on the lives of Japanese people. Though *mononoke* is often written as 物の怪 (*mono*'s mystery), the original meaning is 鬼の気 (oni's vital energy), or that which employs 鬼 (Tsuchihashi 96). *Mono*, 物 as in 鬼, was a spiritual perception that negatively affected the

---

8   Li, hence, finds Chinese influence in the use of 鬼 in *Nihongi* and *Fudoki*.

9   For the text of *Man'yōshū*, see Kojima, Kinoshita, and Tōno.

10 While Baba Akiko surmises that the rendition of 鬼 as *oni* probably started around 600 CE, other scholars such as Ōno Susumu consider the appellation of "*oni*" starts to appear in literature in the Heian Period, and until then, 鬼 is rendered as "*mono*." See Baba 31 and Ōno, Satake and Maeda 228.

11 For the detailed influence of the Chinese character, see Li.

human, 怪 as in 気 was shapeless energy, integral to the essence of the human body. A story in Keikai's *Nihon ryōiki* (Miraculous Stories from the Japanese Buddhist Tradition, ca. 823) recounts the tale of a mysterious messenger from the netherworld, documented as 鬼. When 鬼's 気 was attached to the human character, that human either fell violently ill or died (Takahashi 3–4). In any case, the rendering of the character 鬼 as oni was mostly established in and after the tenth century.

As the use of the character 鬼 became popular, the invisible oni gradually became omnipresent in popular Japanese consciousness and began to be represented in more tangible form. Reflecting this trend, artisans and entertainers of the day often represented oni in literature, paintings, and in the performing arts. Oni are customarily portrayed with one or more horns protruding from their scalps. They sometimes have a third eye in the centre of the forehead, and varying skin color, most commonly black, red, blue, or yellow. They often have large mouths with conspicuous canine teeth.[12] More often than not, oni are scantly clad, wearing a loincloth of fresh tiger skin. The combination of the horn and the tiger skin may trace its origins back to an ancient folk belief. The image of oni with an ox horn(s) and tiger skin loincloth is said to have come about from a play on the word *ushitora*. *Ushi* (ox) represents the direction thirty degrees east from due north (north-north-east); *tora* (tiger) is the direction thirty degrees northward from due east. Ushitora was considered an ominous direction called *kimon* 鬼門—oni's gate 門. Hence, ox horns and tiger skins are used to depict oni (Baba 46–47; Toriyama 80). Oni are often depicted carrying an iron rod used to torture their human victims.

Although descriptions of oni vary, there are certain common physical traits that tend to be relatively constant from one representation to another, such as their three-fingered hands. As they are described in *Konjaku monogatarishū* (Tales of Times Now Past, ca. 1120),[13] in the medieval period, the oni usually have only two or three fingers and toes with long and sharp nails. Indeed, some oni depicted in *Jigoku sōshi* (picture scrolls of Buddhist Hell, ca. 12th century), *Gaki sōshi* (picture scrolls of hungry ghosts, ca. 12th century),[14] and *Kibi daijin nittō emaki* (Minister Kibi's Adventures in China, late 12th century) are depicted with three toes (see Figure 1).

---

12   Some *gokusotsu*, prison guards of Buddhist hell, are ox-headed (*gozu*) or horse-headed (*mezu*).

13   For the Japanese text of *Konjaku monogatarishū*, see Mabuchi, Kunisaki, and Inagaki. For English translations, see Ury; Tyler, *Japanese Tales*.

14   For the texts of *Jigoku sōshi* and *Gaki sōshi*, see Komatsu Shigemi and Akiyama.

Figure 1. An oni. Artist Unknown, Japanese. *Minister Kibi's Adventures in China*, Scroll 2 (detail), Japanese, Heian period, 12th century. Handscroll; ink, color, and gold on paper; 30.04 x 458.7 cm (12 5/8 x 180 9/16 in.). Museum of Fine Arts, Boston, William Sturgis Bigelow Collection, by exchange, 32.131.2. Photograph © 2010 Museum of Fine Arts, Boston.

Oni are frequently considered to have imposing physical stature. This may have some relationship to Orikuchi's explanation of oni's etymology, which is that the term was used to describe gigantic people. According to *Fusō ryakki*, a 12th century history book, on the twenty-fifth of the Fourth month of 929, a man saw an oni who was taller than the beam of a house (see Kōen 688). According to a story included in *Konjaku monogatarishū*, an oni that a man encountered at Agi Bridge in Ōmi province was nine feet tall.[15]

Sometimes oni are described as hairy. According to (*Yashiro-bon*) *Heike monogatari* (Yashiro version of the *Tale of the Heike*, ca. early 13th century), the oni who attempts to kidnap Watanabe no Tsuna (953–1025) to Mt. Atago has a black arm full of white hair,[16] and an oni described in *Ōkagami* (The Great Mirror, ca. 1085–1125) has "a shaggy hand with long, knifelike nails."[17] As mentioned earlier, a primordial form of oni is female, and there are a number of notably fierce female oni in Japanese literature and performing arts. But the popular image of oni remains predominantly male.

Furthering the theory that the concept of oni bears the mark of Chinese influence, Kosugi Kazuo asserts that the root of the visual image of Japanese oni is found in Chinese *gui-shen* 鬼神 (ghosts and spirits), and the oni's shape has remained surprisingly unchanged from that of its Chinese predecessor. The *gui-shen* was originally an indigenous Chinese being and had no foundation in Buddhism. Buddhism, however, seems to have assimilated *gui-shen* into its pantheon. According to Kosugi, Chinese *gui-shen* came to Japan with Buddhism, and gave a shape to what was heretofore a shapeless oni. Kosugi finds evidence that indigenous Japanese concepts of the oni bore no clear visual image by merit of fact that when the Chinese *gui-shen* were introduced to Japan around the seventh century the Japanese applied the form to oni with little apparent change (*Chūgoku bijutsushi* 188–206).[18]

As the image and character of oni spread in popular use and recognition, the *aratama* (malign spiritual entities) of humans, animals, and various

---

15　The story of an *oni* at Agi Bridge is found in Mabuchi et al. 38: 46–52. For an English translation, see Tyler, *Japanese Tales* 19–22.

16　The story of an *oni* and Watanabe no Tsuna is found in Asahara, Haruta, and Matsuo 518–22.

17　Translated by Helen Craig McCullough. An episode is found in McCullough, *Ōkagami: the Great Mirror* 106. For the Japanese text, see Tachibana and Katō *Ōkagami*, 95.

18　The earliest *oni* figure in visual art is *rasetsu* on the Tamamushi no zushi (miniature shrine decorated with wings of jewel beetles, Asuka period [538–645]) at Hōryūji temple (Mizuo 190).

phenomena, which previously had not been represented visually, came to be recognized as oni and were likewise depicted with oni features. Similarly, the label 鬼 was applied to the specters of ordinary household objects such as tools and containers after they reached a hundred years of age.[19]

The Buddhist Line

As mentioned earlier, Anesaki Masaharu writes that Japanese oni belong to a purely Buddhist myth. Although the oni cannot be said to be exclusive to the Buddhist cosmos, Buddhist influence is profoundly significant in all of the oni's elements. As we have seen, the image of oni came to Japan with Buddhism. The dreadful supernatural creatures that reside in the abyss of Buddhist hell to terrify mortal sinners are, one can rightly claim, Buddhist oni. Conversely, the creatures stepped on by *shitennō* or Four Heavenly Guardians,[20] often seen at a temple gate representing evil beings that go against Buddhist Law, are also oni. Just like humans, there are a variety of oni, from the minions in Buddhist hell punishing wicked humans to the beings punished by divine Buddhist protectors.

In broad terms, Buddhist oni include cannibalistic beings of Indian origin as *yasha* (*yakṣa* in Sanskrit) and *rasetsu* (*rākṣasa* in Sanskrit). *Yakṣa* in Sanskrit and Pali literature is generally synonymous with *deva* or deity, "sometimes in the highest sense, and sometimes in the lower sense of goblin or spook" (Coomaraswamy 9).[21] *Yasha* share a truly violent aspect with oni in that they are said to suck in a human's vital energy and devour her or his flesh (Mochizuki and Tsukamoto 5: 4895). This image seems to be underscored in Japan. *Rasetsu* is an evil creature that devours human flesh and drinks human blood. In Buddhist mythology, *rasetsu* punishes the sinners in hell (Mochizuki and Tsukamoto 5: 4953–54). Both *yasha* and *rasetsu* are the followers of Bishamonten (Vaisravana), also known as Tamonten.

A little deeper explanation of *yakṣa* helps to better understand the

---

19 These animate objects are called *tsukumogami* (tool specters). For a discussion of *tsukumogami*, see Rambelli 211–258; Reider "Animating Objects"; Lillehoj 7–34; Tanaka *Hyakki yakō no mieru toshi*; Komatsu Kazuhiko *Hyōrei shinkō ron*, 326–342.

20 Four Heavenly Guardians are pre-Buddhist deities that were incorporated into the Buddhist pantheon to protect Buddhist teachings. They are Tamonten (North), Jikokuten (Dhrtarasta, East), Zōchōten (Virudhaka, South), Kōmokuten (Virupaksa, West). Each of them rules one of the cardinal points and a race of earthly devas.

21 Also *yakṣa* and *yakshis* are known as three spirits, the chief divinities of a popular non-Vedic cult (Robinson and Johnson 21).

Buddhist influences on the representational development of the oni. *Yakṣa* are not only a representational predecessor of oni, they are quite popular in present-day Japanese culture as *yasha*. With the rise of Buddhism, *yakṣa* that appear in the *Vedas* (sacred canonical texts for Brahmanism, 1500 to 500 BCE) are integrated into the Buddhist pantheon. Among the earliest figures in the images of Buddhist art, *yakṣa* and *yakshis*, their female counterparts, represent fertility and abundance and often adorn the decorations around stupas and entrances to cave temples (Fisher 22).[22] Powerful deities among *yakṣa* acquire important positions in the Buddhist cosmos. The best example is the aforementioned Vaisravana or Bishamonten, one of the *shitennō*. While high-class *yakṣa* such as Vaisravana are promoted to the Heavenly realm, low-class *yakṣa* remain as they are and become oni to serve the *shitennō*. Those oni called *jaki* (evil oni) who are stepped on by *shitennō* at temples are of the lower class of *yakṣa* (Mizuo 93–97). *Shitennō* and *Jūniten* or Twelve Devas[23] that become quite prominent by the Heian period are said to exercise power over minor gods and demons. The Indian Buddhist devas that belong to the heavenly realm are by and large fearful deities with dichotomous natures; they are said to cause misfortune but may bring good fortune as well (Ōshima, "Shichifukujin no denshō" 310). As will be discussed in more detail in the section on "Prosperity," this is another branch in the oni's genealogy and one source of the idea of oni as harbingers of good fortune. Historian Ōsumi Kazuo writes:

> Buddhist priests gave a form to this invisible being and explained oni with *jaki* that rebel against Buddha. The priests also carried out rituals that drive away oni. As Buddhist hell was being explicated, the hell's prison guards were explained as oni. In the minds of Japanese people, various types of oni such as *mononoke* and vengeful living spirits were

---

22   The earliest example of *yakṣa* as a Buddhist deity appears on the reliefs from Bharhut (2nd century BCE) (Mizuo 93).

23   The Twelve Devas or tutelary deities who control varied directions became quite prominent as protectors of Buddhism, and by extension, as harbingers of peace and prosperity to Japan. They were originally Hindu devas and were incorporated into Esoteric Buddhism. The highest in status among the Twelve Devas are *Bonten* (Brahman, rules upper direction) and *Taishakuten* (Indra or Sakra, rules east). *Bonten* and *Taishakuten* are followed in the descending order as follows: Suiten (Varuna west), Bishamonten or Tamonten (Vaisravana, north—he is one of the Four Heavenly Guardians), Enmaten (Yama, south), Katen (Agni, southeast), Rasetsuten (Raksasa, southwest), Ishanaten (Isana, northeast), Fūten (Vayu, northwest), Nitten (Surya), Gatten (Candra), and Jiten (Prthivi, downward direction).

believed to exist, and their activities were threatening the lives of people. Buddhism took the role of exorcising these feared beings with incantations and prayers. Buddhism was the civilization that had a power to make the invisible visible, and it possessed methods of negotiating with and fighting the unseen. (238)

This is true not only in the psychological and spiritual sense that Ōsumi describes in this passage, but, as we have seen, in the representational sense as well—from the standpoint of the oni's representation, Buddhism can literally be said to "make the invisible visible." The fearful beings mentioned in this passage include *goryō*.

According to Hori Ichirō, the *goryō* belief "possibly originated in the ancient belief in *hito-gami* of the shamanic and charismatic folk religion, and under the influence of Buddhism and Yin-yang or religious Taoism was transformed into belief in individual evil spirits of the dead" (*Folk Religion in Japan: Continuity and Change* 112).[24] The pinnacle of *goryō* belief is presented in the case of Sugawara Michizane (849–903), a statesman and scholar. Indeed, if those who go against the will of the emperor are given the label oni, Sugawara Michizane might well have been regarded by the imperial family as a chief among oni (Komatsu Kazuhiko and Naitō 117). Not only is Michizane's case a prime example of *goryō*, it reveals an interesting relationship between Buddhist deities, Shinto *kami,* and oni. Michizane fell victim to Fujiwara no Tokihira's slanderous tongue and was relegated from the position of Minister of the Right to the chief administrator in Kyushu. After Michizane died at his place of exile in Kyushu, a rumor arose that his angry spirit might retaliate against his enemies. His dead spirit became Daijō-itokuten (Heavenly Great Merits) whose dependents, one hundred sixty thousand evil spirits (*akushin*), were said to cause various natural disasters. His attendants look like *kongō rikishi* (guardian gods), thunder gods, oni kings, *yaksa*, and *rasetsu*. Legend has it that Michizane as Daijō-itokuten had received permission from Bonten (Brahman) and Taishakuten (Indra or Sakra) to cause thunder and lightning to strike the emperor's residence in 903.[25] Further, the emperor whose ancestors include the Sun Goddess and who bestows *kami* status is

---

24   Further, Hori writes, "The magical Buddhist priests and upāsaka-magicians, as well as the shamans and Yin-yang priests, actively promoted this trend in collusion with each other and also possessed the confidence of the troubled persons by means of their magic" (*Folk Religion in Japan* 116).

25   For a text of the *Illustrated Legends of Kitano Shrine*, see Sakurai, Hagiwara, and Miyata 141–68.

sent to Buddhist hell because of sins against Sugawara Michizane. Buddhism's influence on the Japanese system of belief becomes clear in this story as we see both the emperor and indigenous Shinto gods subordinated to Buddhist deities.[26] As ensuing emperors bestow high court rank, and *kami* status on Michizane and build shrines in his honor, his anger is said to subside—it thus appears that there is the give and take of a symbiotic relationship between high Shinto priests and Buddhist deities. Michizane's story reveals this as well as the relationship between *kami* and oni proposed by Komatsu Kazuhiko, which we touched on earlier. That is, angry spirits turn into *kami* by way of people's worship. Indeed, these fearful aspects of *kami*—or rough and rowdy *kami* anyway—seem to earn them the moniker oni simply for want of a better word. We will return to this transformation from oni to *kami* later when we look at lightning, one of the oni's attributes.

The *Onmyōdō* Line

Onmyōdō is an eclectic practice whose roots are found in the theory of the cosmic duality of yin and yang and the five elements (metal, wood, water, fire, and earth). To these ancient Chinese roots, *onmyōdō* added elements from Buddhist astrology (*Sukuyōkyō* or *Xiuyaojing*) and indigenous Japanese *kami* worship. As mentioned earlier, Komatsu Kazuhiko explains that in early *onmyōdō* doctrine, the word "oni" referred specifically to invisible evil spirits that caused human infirmity. It is noteworthy that in each of the four lines of origin explored here, be it Japanese, Chinese, Buddhist, or *onmyōdō*, invisibility is a predominant feature of oni in their very early stage. Something one cannot see yet causes her/him to fall is dreadful, because there is absolutely no way to prepare against it. One need only watch someone stumble over her or his own feet and look back to see what caused her or him to trip to get a sense of just how innate this fear is. The Heian period was the apex of the oni's hold on popular imagination as a real entity. Within the Heian period, the era of Engi-Tenryaku (901–947) is considered a time when *onmyōdō* prospered and produced excellent practitioners of its tradition. The official practitioners of *onmyōdō*, which included Abe no Seimei (921?–1005), were the employees of a government ministry that observed and examined astronomy, astrology and divination, and the

---

26 The primary source for the *Illustrated Legends of Kitano Shrine* was produced by priest(s) of *Shingon* esoteric Buddhism who were in search of measures against and prevention of disasters based upon the *Golden Splendor Sutra* (Imahori 26–40).

current almanac.[27] But the Engi-Tenryaku era is the transitional period when the official *onmyōdō* tended to become the aristocrats' private cat's-paws (Murayama, "Kyūtei onmyōdō no seiritsu" 378, 385). More precisely, as descendants of the northern branch of the Fujiwara clan were establishing their authority through the Regency, the court practitioners of *onmyōdō* were consolidating their own power by serving the Fujiwara (Murayama, *Nihon onmyōdō sōsetsu* 112, 172). It was believed, in this period, that the practitioners of *onmyōdō* could use magic, and that some could see, and even create oni. Komatsu Kazuhiko writes that the foundation of the practitioners' magical force is *shikigami* or invisible spirit (*Hyōrei shinkōron* 222). Using *shikigami*, the practitioners were actively involved in the lives of aristocrats. The *onmyōji* or yin-yang diviners used their magic at the request of their royal and aristocratic patrons and not infrequently against their patrons' political enemies. Importantly, Tanaka Takako surmises that the *shikigami* that were left underneath the bridge—not just any bridge but Modoribashi Bridge in the capital—by practitioners of *onmyōdō* such as Abe no Seimei, became various oni who stroll on certain nights in the capital (Tanaka, *Hyakki yagyō no mieru toshi* 141).

Expansive and dynamic, the oni of legend were said to thrive in all corners of ancient and medieval Japanese society. They could appear anywhere and often did. The oni frequented both urban and rural areas, and were even seen in the capital and within the imperial palace compound, disturbing everyday life, spreading fear and causing trouble. Indeed, the oni were the objects of awe and fear, and considered real entities among ancient and medieval Japanese. The modern oni, despite their continued evolution and changes, still exhibit many of the characteristics of medieval oni.

Characteristics of Oni

Cannibalism

One of the oni's major and most gruesome attributes is their huge appetite for human flesh. Oni are often portrayed feasting on human flesh. It is said that oni can eat a person in a single gulp. Indeed, the phrase "oni hitokuchi" (oni in one gulp) more than suggests the oni's cannibalistic inclinations. The sixth episode of *Ise monogatari* (Tales of Ise, 945 CE) tells of a man who falls

---

27   The agency is called *onmyōryō* (the Bureau of Divination). See Bowring, *The Religious Traditions of Japan, 500–1600* 171–92.

hopelessly in love with a woman well above his social status. The man decides to kidnap her. On their runaway trip, near the Akuta River, a severe thunderstorm forces the woman to shelter in a ruined storehouse. Even though the man stands gallantly on guard at the entrance of the shelter, the lady is eaten by an oni in one gulp. Although she screams, the pounding thunder muffles her cry and the man does not realize what is happening until she is gone.[28] In the story, nobody sees the oni eating the woman, or even the oni itself for that matter. But the gruesome act is attributed to oni. "Oni in one gulp" suggests an instantaneous action, exemplifying an oni's atrocity and enormous appetite. But these creatures do not always consume the victims so quickly. As will be discussed in chapter two, in the story of Shuten Dōji, the oni deliberately savor the delicacies of human flesh during special banquets.

Another example of an oni's ravenous appetite appears in *Nihon ryōiki* (Miraculous Stories from the Japanese Buddhist Tradition, ca. 823). The story is entitled "Nyonin akuki ni kegasarete kurawareshi en" (On a Woman Devoured by an Oni). During the reign of Shōmu (724–749) in the province of Yamato, there lived a wealthy family with a beautiful daughter. Many suitors came seeking the girl's hand in marriage but the daughter never consented to wed. One day, a suitor sent her a number of luxurious gifts including three carriages full of splendid silks. Pleased with this suitor's overtures, she accepted his proposal. On their wedding night, from the bedchamber of her house, painful cries were heard. Her parents dismissively concluded, "perhaps she feels pain because she is not used to it." So they took no action. On the following morning, her mother went to her daughter's bedchamber to wake up the newly wedded couple, but there was no reply to the mother's call. Thinking this strange, she opened the door only to find her daughter's severed head and one remaining finger—the rest of her body had been completely devoured. People claimed it was the work of an oni.[29] In the story, no one sees the enemy or its act of cannibalism, but as the title denotes, this abhorrent act is attributed to oni.

Stories of cannibalism are frequently recorded in Japan's official history, too. According to *Nihon sandai jitsuroku* (True Records of Three Generations in Japan, 901), on the seventeenth of the eighth month of 887 three beautiful women walking near Butokuden, one of the buildings in the

---

28 She is supposedly devoured by an oni. For the Japanese text, see Sakakura et al. 114. For an English translation, see McCullough, *Tales of Ise* 72–73.

29 For the Japanese text, see Endō and Kasuga 274–277. For an English translation, see Nakamura Kyoko 205–206.

imperial palace compound, see a good-looking man under a pine tree. The man approaches one of the women and begins talking with her. When the remaining two women look back in the direction of the pine tree, they are horrified to see the dismembered woman, limbs strewn on the ground, her head missing. At the time, people believed that an oni transformed into the handsome man and then ate the woman.[30]

While showing the oni's cannibalistic side, this tale also illustrates the oni's exceptional metamorphic abilities. Changing from its grotesque form to a handsome man allows the cunning oni to gain the trust and interest of his victim so that he can devour her with little or no resistance. Oni are capable of transforming into both male and female forms at will.

Transformation Power

One exemplary tale that attests to the oni's gender-crossing powers of transformation appears in *Konjaku monogatarishū*. In the story, a man who brags about his prowess goes to Agi Bridge in Ōmi province in an attempt to exterminate an oni haunting the area. The oni, disguised as a beautiful young woman, is presented waiting at the bridge. As soon as the oni attracts the man's attention, it reveals its true form: greenish skin color and nine-foot-tall frame, three fingers on each hand and dishevelled hair. The man narrowly escapes. Later, the same oni, disguised as the man's younger brother, visits his house and finally murders him.[31] It is intriguing to note that this oni changes its shape freely to female or male in its confrontation with the man.

A similar but better known story, one that became a source for a famous Noh play entitled *Rashōmon* in fact, appears in "Tsurugi no maki" (Swords Chapter) of *Heike monogatari*.[32] According to the "Swords Chapter," during

---

30 For a text of the episode, see Fujiwara et al. 464.

31 The story of an *oni* at Agi Bridge is found in Mabuchi et al. 38: 46–52. For an English translation, see Tyler, *Japanese Tales* 19–22.

32 For the texts of "Swords Chapter," see Asahara, Haruta, and Matsuo 3: 514–47; Mizuhara 1: 59–88. For an English translation, see A. L. Sadler, 1921: 325–354. There are numerous texts of *Heike monogatari* such as *Yashiro bon*, *Kakuichi bon*, *Shibu gassenjō bon*, *Nanto bon*, *Enkyō bon*, etc. These various texts have been classified in many ways. The classification used here, one of the recognized standardized classifications, is to divide the texts into two lineages: (1) *kataribon kei* (recitation lineage) which includes *Yashiro bon*, *Kamakura bon*, *Kakuichi bon*, *Rufu bon*; and (2) *yomihon kei* (reading lineage) which includes *Shibu gassenjō bon*, *Genpei jōsuiki* (Vicissitude of the Genji and Heike Clans), *Enkyō bon*, *Nanto bon*.

A number of texts were in existence by the end of the thirteenth century, and the most prevalent text of *Heike monogatari* today is *Kakuichi bon*, which was compiled

the time of Minamoto no Raikō (or Yorimitsu, 948–1021), people begin disappearing in the capital. Around that time, Raikō sends Watanabe no Tsuna, one of Raikō's *shitennō* (four heavenly guardians), on an errand. Thinking that the capital is dangerous, Raikō lends his famous sword to Tsuna to guard himself. At Modoribashi Bridge in the capital, Tsuna encounters a beautiful woman of about twenty years of age who asks him to take her back to her house. Tsuna agrees and lifts the lady on his horse, just as the lady reveals her true identity—she was a monstrous oni. Grabbing Tsuna's topknot and flying in the air, the oni declares that s/he is going to take Tsuna to Mt. Atago. Tsuna manages to cut off one of the oni's arms. The oni flies off, leaving the severed arm (with Tsuna) behind. Later, the same oni, disguised as Tsuna's foster mother,[33] attempts to gain entry to his house. The foster mother/oni asks Tsuna to show her the famous oni's arm. Believing that the woman is actually his foster mother, Tsuna takes the disguised creature to the chest where he has placed the oni's arm. Seeing the severed arm, the creature reveals its true identity to Tsuna, grabs the limb and flies away with it.[34]

An oni often uses the power of transformation to prevent warriors from

---

in 1371. *Yashiro bon* is considered an older version among the texts of the *Kataribon* lineage, which includes the *Kakuichi bon*. The *Kakuichi bon* contains the "Swords Chapter" in Volume Eleven, but this is different from more elaborate *Yashiro bon*'s "Swords Chapter" or that of *Genpei jōsuiki*. In the "Swords Chapter" of *Kakuichi bon*, the episodes Minamoto no Raikō (*tsuchigumo*), Watanabe no Tsuna, and Uji no hashihime (will be discussed in chapter three) do not appear.

There are four English translations of the *Tale of Heike* as follows:

1. Sadler, "The Heike monogatari." This translation, the oldest one, is based on the *Rufu bon*. The *Rufu bon*'s "Swords Chapter" is similar to *Yashiro bon*'s "Swords Chapter," and it appears from 325–354 of vol. 49, part 1.
2. McCullough, *The Tale of the Heike*. This translation is based on the Kakuichi text published in Takagi Ichinosuke et al. *Heike monogatari*. Takagi's *Heike monogatari* is based upon the Ryūtani daigaku version of the *Kakuichi bon*.
3. Kitagawa Hiroshi and Tsuchida, *The Tale of the Heike*. This translation is based on the same *Kakuichi bon* published in Takagi Ichinosuke et al.
4. Burton Watson, *The Tales of the Heike*. This is a selected translation of the *Heike monogatari*, and is based upon Ichiko, *Heike monogatari*. This book is based upon the Kōya version of the *Kakuichi bon*.

For the explanation of the *Heike* texts, see Takagi Ichinosuke et al. 33: 12–46; Asahara, Haruta, and Matsuo 1: 387–97 and 3: 548–51; Yamashita 390–98; Matsuo 406–07; Oyler 9–16.

33 She is also Tsuna's aunt.
34 For the episode of an *oni* and Watanabe no Tsuna, see Asahara, Haruta, and Matsuo 518–522.

accomplishing their heroic tasks. An example of this can be found in the Noh play entitled *Momijigari* (Maple Leaf Viewing), authored by Kanze Kojirō Nobumitsu (1435–1516).[35] The warrior Taira no Koreshige (the end of the 10th century) receives an imperial order to subjugate the oni residing on Mt. Togakushi. On the mountain, Koreshige meets an enchanting lady (an oni in disguise) and the two have a banquet under the maple trees. Seduced by the lady, he sleeps alongside her, completely intoxicated. In his dream, a messenger of the deity of Hachiman bestows a sword upon him and tells Koreshige to use it to kill the oni. Waking, Koreshige is shocked to find the sword from his dream at his side. He is even more shocked when he realizes what he is now lying next to; in place of the beautiful lady of his amorous tryst is a gruesome female oni with horns on its head. The oni in *Maple Leaf Viewing* is female and the performer who plays the role of the oni wears a *hannya* (she-demon) mask. Koreshige kills the oni with the sword given to him by the deity. The oni of Mt. Togakushi had transformed itself into a voluptuous woman to make Koreshige lessen his guard. It is not at all uncommon for an oni to use female sexuality as a ploy to achieve its goal.

The Other: The Oppressed, Alienated, and Isolated

As mentioned in the section on Chinese origins, people who had different customs or lived beyond the reach of the emperor's control were considered to be some form of oni. Indeed, one could argue that any person or people who are forced to and/or voluntarily live on the periphery of mainstream society are marginalized and thus, considered oni (Komatsu Kazuhiko and Naitō 11).

In the aforementioned *Maple Leaf Viewing*, it is worthy to note that the oni were to be eliminated by imperial command because they were deemed to be troublemakers, even seen as a threat to imperial authority. The oni in these tales are often "beyond the reach of the emperor's control," so suppressing them means dispatching special warriors to remote regions. When the being is "beyond the reach of the emperor's control" or is considered an enemy of the establishment, that being is often labeled oni, thus becoming a target of subjugation. Using the oni label to connote difference, apartness or oppression is a theme previously seen in *Nihongi*. For example, when Emperor Keikō tells Yamato Takeru to conquer the rebels in the east, he

---

35 For the Japanese text, see Sanari 5: 3079–3092. For an English translation see Weatherby 33.

says, "So by cunning words thou mayst moderate the violent Deities, and by a display of armed force sweep away malignant demons (kadamashiki 鬼)."³⁶ The corresponding phrase in *Kojiki* is "the un-submissive people" (matsurowanu hito-domo).³⁷ As many scholars point out, the character, 鬼, does not appear in *Kojiki*. Ōwa Iwao writes that the editors of *Nihongi* employed the character, 鬼, for those who were against the emperors (48).

An interesting example of an oni defying the emperor and actually triumphing over him in the end can be found in a story in *Konjaku monogatarishū*. A holy man of Mt. Katsuragi, who gains miraculous power through asceticism in the mountains, is summoned by imperial order to heal the illness of the emperor's beautiful consort. The holy man successfully cures the consort's illness, but while staying in the palace, he becomes increasingly infatuated with her. Acting upon his carnal desire, he is caught in the act and consequently imprisoned by the emperor. Thus imprisoned, the once ascetic, devout man swears an oath that he is prepared to die and reincarnate into an oni to possess the royal consort, the object of his carnal obsession. Hearing this ominous promise and obviously afraid of the holy man's curses, the emperor and Fujiwara no Yoshifusa (804–872), the prime minister and the consort's father, release the holy man from prison. Back in the mountain, the holy man proceeds to starve himself to death, determined to make good on his threat and return to earth as an oni. No sooner has he effected his death, than he appears before the consort as an oni apparition—a huge, statuesque, black-skinned, big-eyed, wide-mouthed being with sharp teeth. He seduces the consort and realizes his carnal desire—in public and in front of the emperor no less—who is helpless to stop it.³⁸ This oni reveals his extraordinary determination to realize his sexual desire. It is his determined will that makes him oni. His determination is such that he spurns the wishes of the emperor and powerful Fujiwara and brings about their ultimate humiliation. This example shows how the oni was indeed to be feared but not necessarily respected.³⁹

---

36   For the Japanese text, see Sakamoto et al. I: 302. For an English translation, see Aston 1: 204. Ōwa Iwao surmises that Yamato Takeru's story was originally probably a story of Amaterasu conquering violent deities. But the emperor's power is augmented in *Nihongi* to enhance the emperor's authority (51).

37   See Yamaguchi and Kōnoshi 223. For an English translation, see Philippi 81.

38   The Japanese text is found in Mabuchi et al. 37: 46–51. For an English translation of the story, see Tyler *Japanese Tales*, 178–180.

39   Iizawa Tadasu writes that the holy man of Mt. Katsuragi was actually Bishop Shinzei

Baba Akiko states that the oni were a representation of those suppressed people and/or those who were not a part of the Fujiwara Regency (from the 10th century through the 11th century). The Fujiwara Regency reached its peak with Fujiwara Michinaga (966–1027), and Baba observes that oni are said to be more rampant during Emperor Ichijō's reign, the zenith of the Fujiwara Regency, than at any other time in Japan's history (141,150). One of the best examples of those who "lived beyond the reach of the emperor's control" is the story of Shuten Dōji. Shuten Dōji, the chief of an oni band, lives on Mt. Ōe. During the reign of Emperor Ichijō, Shuten Dōji and his oni band abduct people, particularly maidens, enslaving them and eventually feasting on their flesh and drinking their blood. The concerned emperor orders the warrior hero Minamoto no Raikō and his men to stop the abductions by vanquishing Shuten Dōji and his band of oni followers. Raikō and his men disguise themselves as *yamabushi* (mountaineering ascetics) and by means of guile, deception and some divine help, they eliminate Shuten Dōji and his oni band. There are many theories regarding the origins of the Shuten Dōji legend, including the notion that Shuten Dōji and his fellow oni were nothing more than a gang of bandits who lived on Mt. Ōe, or that Shuten Dōji was a Caucasian man who drifted to the shore of Tanba Province (present-day Kyoto) and drank red wine. But, as will be examined in greater detail in the next chapter, what is most striking among these theories is that all the characters are disenfranchised either by geography, customs and/or different lifestyles.

En no gyōja (ca. 7th–8th century), revered as the founder of *Shugendō* (Mountain ascetics) has two oni attendants: Zenki (anterior demon) and Goki (posterior demon). According to *En no gyōja denki* (History of *En no gyōja*), Zenki and Goki are humans born in a village at the foot of the mountain. They are orphaned when young and go to the mountains to

---

(799–860). Shinzei was greatly admired by Emperor Montoku, who had conferred the position of archbishop on the former. When Montoku became gravely ill, people had great hope for Shinzei's magic power to cure the emperor. But Shinzei failed and the emperor died at the age of 32. People were terribly disappointed, and Shinzei was greatly criticized from all directions. Shinzei retired in disappointment. With this background, not to mention the monks who had been jealous of his superior talent and intelligence, Shinzei was turned into the character of oni. Regarding the imperial consort, Izawa assumes that having lost her husband at a young age, over time, she would become hysterical from sexual frustration. In her later years, she resorted to extreme behaviors as written in the texts (142–53). Here, too, the person who was made into oni is someone who ultimately could not help the emperor's life, and was heavily criticized by society. Also, see the similar story in *Fusō ryakki* (Kōen 602).

survive. Their appearance is ugly, and the villagers who encounter them in the mountains call them oni. They in turn avoid humans, and make the mountain their territory before they become En no gyōja's disciples and protect the practitioners of *shugendō* (Chigiri 312). Ishikawa Tomohiko writes that those who lived in the mountains beyond the reach of imperial authority probably came to be known as Zenki and Goki (Ishikawa and Ozawa 12). Also in "Yama no jinsei" (Life in the Mountain) Yanagita Kunio writes of babies born with teeth—different from ordinary babies. These babies were widely believed to be *onigo* (oni's child) and were badly abused, particularly prior to the Edo period. Yanagita cites various documents including *Tsurezure nagusamigusa*, which records "... a deplorable custom in Japan where a baby born with teeth is called oni's child and is killed." In *Higashiyama ōrai* (Letters from Higashiyama) Jōjin (1108 –?), a Buddhist monk, chronicled how "a maid gave birth to a baby with teeth. The woman's neighbours advised her to bury the baby in the mountain, rationalising that the baby had to be an oni. The maid came to me for consultation and I [Jōjin] suggested that the baby be sent to a temple to become a monk" ("Yama no jinsei" 234). This appears to be the bleak destiny of any child thought to be of oni lineage—death, abandonment or more mercifully, the priesthood. People seriously believed that babies born with teeth would become oni (Satake, *Shuten Dōji ibun* 44). As many social scientists cross-culturally have come to observe however, it is human nature to apply social stigma to those displaying any difference or anomaly.

Indeed, the act of labeling people with different customs as 鬼 appeared as early as in *Nihongi*. The *Nihongi* states that during twelfth month of the sixth year of Emperor Kinmei's reign (544 AD), "At Cape Minabe, on the northern side of the Island of Sado, there arrived men of Su-shēn in a boat, and stayed there. During the spring and summer they caught fish, which they used for food. The men of that island said that they were not human beings. They also called them devils 鬼魅, and did not dare to go near them" (Sakamoto et al. II: 92).[40] The "men of Su-shēn" (Mishi-hase) was an old name for Tungusic ancestors of the people living in the coastal area of northeastern China. They must have drifted ashore from that region. The native people were thus observing Su-shēn from a distance while labeling them as 鬼. A similar case is found in *Izumo fudoki* regarding a one-eyed 鬼 who devoured a man. Referring to the one-eyed 鬼, Akimoto Kichirō

---

40   For an English translation, see Aston 2: 58.

Figure 2. Sugawara no Michizane as shown in *Nichizō's Journey to Hell*, from *Illustrated Legends of the Kitano Tenjin Shrine*. Japan, Kamakura period (1185–1333). Late thirteenth century. Set of five handscrolls; ink and color on paper. (b): 11 5/16 in. x 28 ft. 3 3/4 in. (28.8 x 763 cm). Fletcher Fund, 1925 (25.224. b). The Metropolitan Museum of Art, New York, NY, U.S.A. Image copyright © The Metropolitan Museum of Art/ Art Resource, NY.

notes that those with physical characteristics of a different race were probably described as such (238). Again, "difference" seems key to receiving the label of 鬼. Akimoto further notes "it may have some relation to metal workers whose deity of profession is *Ame-no-hitotsu-kami* (one-eyed deity)" (238). In other words, this 鬼 may have something to do with metal workers or their lifestyle. The first metal culture was brought to Japan either by Chinese or Koreans from Southern China (Tanigawa, "Seidō no kami no sokuseki" 31). The non-Japanese races or their descendents may have been looked upon as "different" by native Japanese and, therefore, described as 鬼. This may also explain why the oni are often depicted carrying an *iron* mace. Could it be that these early smiths, geographically and socially distinct from the rest of the populace, were what helped spawn the medieval revival of an even older myth? In creating metal equipment or weapons, sparks are emitted by hammering, sparks which visually resemble lightning. Perhaps these same blacksmiths' propensity for metals is what caused the masses to attribute the impressive power of lightning to the oni.

Lightning

Oni are often associated with one of nature's most powerful forces—lightning. Indeed, as mentioned earlier, Kondō Yoshihiro finds the genesis of oni to be in people's fear toward the destructive power of phenomenological occurrences, especially thunder and lightning (16). This results, no doubt, from the combined visual and auditory intensity of the experience, coupled with the threat of potential, instantaneous destruction. Recall that in *Ise monogatari*, the woman is eaten by the oni during an intense thunderstorm.

Also recall that Sugawara no Michizane (849–903), the dauntless adversary against imperial power, uses lightning as a weapon against the imperial family. In 955 a young child of a Shinto priest announced the divine message and "proclaimed that the spirit of Sugawara had become the deity of disasters and a chief deity of the thunder demons. The imperial court would dedicate a shrine to Michizane" (Hori, *Folk Religion in Japan* 115). Indeed, Sugawara is posthumously endowed with the highest rank, and is enshrined by the imperial household with various rituals, and now more than a thousand years later, he and his shrines are thriving as the *kami* of school entrance examinations for numerous boys and girls. In *Kitano tenjin engi emaki* (Illustrated Legends of the Kitano Tenjin Shrine, ca. 13th century) Michizane's vengeful spirit turns into a thunder god and reincarnates Michizane as Daijō-itokuten. Remarkably, Michizane's/Daijō-itokuten's appearance as a thunder god is portrayed as similar to the oni who torments wicked mortals in hell in the picture scroll.[41]

As the noted painter Tawaraya Sōtatsu's (early 17th century) portrayal of a thunder god reveals,[42] a thunder god is often depicted with features similar to oni. A thunder god usually appears standing on the clouds and carrying an array of drums. This similarity is understandable when one considers the extent to which oni stories originated from people's fear of thunder and lightning. Another interpretation of their resemblance is through the *kami-oni* (or *yōkai*) paradigm proposed by Komatsu Kazuhiko (*Yōkaigaku shinkō* 193). As mentioned earlier, people performed religious rituals in order to transform *yōkai* (oni being the most negative of *yōkai*) to *kami*. When a particular supernatural being is not worshipped abundantly and devoutly enough to be considered *kami*, then that entity is said to become *yōkai*. Thus as a vengeful spirit, Michizane was a terrifying oni; but with ample rituals and sincere apologies from imperial court authorities, he gradually changes (or is promoted) from oni to *kami*. Yet, by fostering vengeance and with a smothering destructive force, he retains the form of oni at the moment he inflicts his disastrous wrath on his enemy. It makes sense then, that Michizane as Daijō-itokuten and a thunder god takes the similar form as the oni who afflicts humans. In the popular military literature entitled *Taiheiki* (Chronicle of Grand Pacification, ca. 14th century) Sugawara Michizane himself is said to have actually transformed into the lightning that struck the imperial palace (Gotō and Kamada 406–407). By superimposing the oni onto natural disasters or inexplicable destructive phenomena like thunder or lightning, people had a clear target for their fear and anger; in this vein, the oni represent a self-designed coping strategy, helping people come to terms with nature's unpredictable fury by personifying it and giving substance to the inexplicable.

Prosperity

A literary survey throughout the ages would no doubt reveal that more often than not, the oni's evil side is what is emphasized. Yet, the oni are not

---

41 In the earliest extant hand-scroll of *Kitano tenjin engi* owned by Kitano ten'mangū in Kyoto, Michizane's/Daijō-itokuten's appearance as a thunder god is portrayed almost identically to the red-skinned oni who torments wicked mortals in hell. See Komatsu Shigemi, Nakano, and Matsubara 25, 29, 31–35.

42 As "Fūjin raijin zu" (the god of wind and the god of thunder), the painting is housed in Kyoto National Museum in Kyoto.

exclusively represented as evil beings. Oni can also be supernatural entities that bring good fortune and wealth. An example of how the oni can be seen as harbingers of wealth and fortune appears in the *kyōgen* play entitled *Setsubun* (on the lunar New Year's Eve). Traditionally, on the night of *setsubun*, people scatter beans, one for each of their years alive, saying "oni wa soto, fuku wa uchi" (Demons out, Fortune in). In some rites, a male from the community goes to a house pretending to be an oni (wearing a paper oni mask) and is chased out while people scatter their beans. In this *kyōgen* play (see Koyama 125–131), however, an oni from *hōrai*, the land of eternal youth, goes to Japan, wishing to eat beans. The oni visits a house where the husband has gone on a religious retreat leaving his wife at home, alone. The oni immediately falls in love with the wife. She is scared of him at first, but quickly realizes how to make the most of her situation by going after the oni's fortune and treasures, saying: "If you really love me, give me your treasure." The oni zealously agrees, replying, "My treasures are a straw raincoat of invisibility, a hat of invisibility, and a wish-granting mallet (*uchide no kozuchi*),"[43] and he hastily gives her the cloak and the hat he wore to Japan. As soon as she receives the treasures, the wife chases the oni away with beans. Portrayed in the spirit of *kyōgen*, which makes fun of serious and frightening figures, this oni is humorous and quite credulous.

This *kyōgen*'s oni that comes from the land of eternal youth, and visits on New Year's Eve bearing treasures, probably descends from the Japanese line of oni which is, as we have seen, a variation of *marebito* coming from a distant land at a certain time, notably on the lunar New Year's Eve and/or New Year's Day, to give blessings to villagers. The *marebito* wear a straw hat and cloak.[44] The treasured cloak and hat with the power to make their wearer invisible might have been a main source of the oni's powers of invisibility. Such equipment was considered highly prized treasure; by being

---

43 These three treasures are also listed as oni's treasures in the story, "Momotarō," or Peach Boy, that is discussed in chapter six. See Antoni 167.

44 An oni's association with a hat is mentioned in *Nihongi*, although it does not describe the hat as invisible. It says, on the evening Empress Saimei died, "on the top of Mt. Asakura, there was a demon (鬼) wearing a great hat, who looked down on the funeral proceedings." Translated by Aston (2: 270). For the Japanese text, see Sakamoto et al. II: 350. By the early tenth century, an oni is widely associated with an invisible hat and cloak. Ōshikōchi no Mitsune, a late tenth century poet, writes in his private anthology of poems titled *Mitsuneshū* that "Oni sura mo/ miya no uchi tote/ mino kasa o/ nugite ya koyoi/ hito ni miyuran" (Even an oni/ takes off his cloak and hat/ in the imperial court/ this evening/ and lets people see its appearance, I wonder). The preface to the poem gives the date as 918 (Fujioka and Tokuhara 137).

invisible, one could acquire tangible and intangible wealth, from precious metals to valuable information. The theme of invisibility may also hark back to the *kami* being invisible (or oni being originally invisible).

A number of stories present a wish-granting mallet as an oni's valued possession. One such story is a famous folk tale entitled *Issun-bōshi* (Little One-Inch).[45] In the story, a boy is born to an elderly couple far past the years of conception and childbirth. For years, the couple prays for a child and eventually, the woman conceives. The boy she gives birth to however, never grows any larger than an inch (hence his name, Little One-Inch). One day, Little One-Inch decides to go to the capital in search of fortune and success. He gets a job as a servant to an aristocratic family and falls madly in love with the couple's beautiful daughter. He tricks her parents into believing she has stolen his rice and they disown her; she comes under his care, and they both soon leave the family's compound. On their journey with no destination, Little One-Inch and the daughter meet up with a band of oni. One of the oni swallows Little One-Inch in one gulp but he fights against the oni, plunging his little sword into the being from inside its body. Severely injured, the oni coughs up Little One-Inch and the demon band scampers away, leaving behind a magical wish-granting mallet. Little One-Inch picks up the mallet and with the help of its supernatural power, he is transformed into a normally sized human. He uses the mallet to produce food and treasures. Little One-Inch becomes rich, marries the princess, and they live happily ever after, primarily because of the oni's wish-granting mallet. Although the mallet was not given to Little One-Inch as a present but was left behind by the band of oni, the fact that the implement of good fortune was brought by the oni to the mortal world remains unchanged. Through their wish-granting mallet, the oni in the story become the bringers of fortune.

A mallet that produces food and wealth is indeed an invaluable treasure, and it seems a wish-granting mallet was widely considered to be a standard possession of an oni by the thirteenth century. A chapter entitled "Gion nyogo" from the Kakuichi version of *Heike monogatari* describes a mysterious being as an oni, adding "That thing in its hand is probably the famous wish-granting mallet."[46] To many contemporary Japanese a wish-granting mallet is most associated with Daikokuten (the Great Black Deity), one of the Seven

---

45 For the Japanese text, see Ichiko, *Otogi zōshi* 319–26. For an English translation, see McCullough, *Classical Japanese Prose* 495–98.

46 Translation by McCullough (*The Tale of the Heike* 215). For the Japanese text, see Ichiko, *Heike monogatari* 461.

Fortune Deities (*shichifukujin*). Daikokuten carries a wish-granting mallet in his left hand. I conjecture that Daikokuten came to possess a wish-granting mallet partly through its association with an oni. Daikokuten is:

> a direct translation of Mahākalā [Great Black Deity], a Hindu deity already adopted by Buddhism in India. In the *Commentary to the Mahāvairocana Sutra* he is described as a manifestation of Mahāvairocana who can subdue demons. The *Sutra of the Wisdom of the Benevolent Kings* speaks of Daikokuten as a god of war, and in Buddhist iconography he is often portrayed with a fierce and angry countenance. (Reader and Tanabe, Jr. 158)

Indeed, the facial expression of the earliest Daikokuten sculpture housed in Kanzeonji temple in Fukuoka prefecture is stern (see Miyamoto Kesao 61). So is one of the most famous Daikokuten sculptures enshrined in Mt. Hiei: he is a fierce-looking three-faced, six-armed Daikokuten. Notably, neither sculpture has a mallet. It is plausible that the image of Daikokuten as the Great Black Deity, a fierce-looking war god, became conflated with oni images because of its original angry countenance and its black skin color. There is a belief that one day Dakini's consumption of living human flesh disgusted Mahāvairocana. Mahāvairocana changed his appearance to Daikokuten, caught Dakini, and ate it to remonstrate the latter's behavior (later Dakini was allowed to eat only the bodies of deceased humans). From this story, another belief that Dakini was subjugated by Daikokuten and became Daikokuten's attendant was born (Naganuma, *Fukujin kenkyū Ebisu to Daikoku* 266). Eating live humans, or supernatural creatures like *yasha*, is part of the oni's repertoire. The conflation of representations in these gruesome stories may have led to oni's possessions becoming associated with Daikokuten.

Although Daikokuten was a god of war in India, his image was also placed in monastery kitchens in India and China as a deity of food and its abundance. In Japan, from the Kamakura period (1185–1333) to the Muromachi period (1336–1573), Daikokuten is claimed as a protector of Buddhist teaching. This time period corresponds with the Japanization of Daikokuten according to Naganuma Kenkai (*Fukujin kenkyū Ebisu to Daikoku* 309),[47] and during this time Daikokuten comes to be worshipped

---

[47] Two statues of Daikokuten, one housed in Kōfukuji in Kyoto and the other in Daikokuji in Osaka have a mallet held by the right hand. Naganuma assumes the production period to be the very late Kamakura period through early Muromachi period (*Fukujin kenkyū Ebisu to Daikoku*, 297).

mostly as a deity of food and good fortune. This attribute is strengthened as Daikokuten is also identified as Ōkuninushi no mikoto, an agriculture deity, through a homonym when their names are written in kanji. During the Muromachi period, Daikokuten came to be worshipped as a fortune deity with a big amiable smile and was quite popular among people of all walks of life (Kanai 331). Perhaps Daikokuten is widely considered to carry a mallet by this time, because an entry from Prince Fushiminomiya Sadafusa's (1372–1456) diary dated 1 Third Month of 1416 of *Kanmon nikki*, records that there were "Daikokuten's large straw raincoat and mallet of fortune"[48] at the tea gathering at Fushimi Mansion in Kyoto. The mallet is often explained in relation to agrarian moral values because of the homonyms "for the mallet (*tsuchi*) that hammers out wealth (*takara*). '*Tsuchi*' also means dirt or earth, and 'takara' can also be read with two words: '*ta kara*' (from the rice field)" (Reader and Tanabe 158). It makes sense that Daikokuten, who is worshipped as a deity of food and the kitchen, has an agrarian tool. But perhaps Daikokuten carries a mallet because of its strong association with oni.

It is interesting that Daikokuten, originally an Indian deity of war already adopted by Buddhism, was incorporated into one of the Seven Fortune Deities as *kami*, which are Shinto gods. More important perhaps is what this re-creation and realignment of representations demonstrate about the evolution of people's expectations since, as Miyata Noboru suggests, it was humans who selected the seven supernatural beings (six of them from either India or China) and put them together to create a set of fortune *kami* ("Kankō ni attatte," 2). By the time Seven Fortune Deities became popular in the early modern period, it really did not matter whether a deity was of Buddhist or Shinto origin. What mattered was that they brought fortune in this world.

As a bringer of fortune, the oni of *Haseo sōshi* (Story of Ki no Haseo, the 14th century)[49] who brought the most beautiful lady to Ki no Haseo (851–912), a noted scholar, should be mentioned here as well. This oni, unlike many other oni, does not harm humans; rather he is an oni of word. One day the oni, apparently an eager player of *sugoroku* (a Japanese kind of parcheesi), approaches Ki no Haseo because of the latter's excellent ability

---

48 In a small letter, Sadafusa explains that "a *sake* barrel is named "Daikokuten's large straw raincoat" and that inside a wish-granting mallet are tea cakes and extra sake (Gosukō-in 1: 18).

49 For the Japanese text, see Komatsu Shigemi and Murakami 1–39.

at *sugoroku*. Similar to the oni of Rashomon Gate who plays the lute, this oni appreciates art. Haseo and the oni play *sugoroku* with a bet that if Haseo loses, the oni receives all of Haseo's treasures, and conversely if the oni loses, Haseo receives a strikingly beautiful woman from the oni. Needless to say, the oni loses. As he has promised, the oni brings the ethereal beauty to Haseo. He warns Haseo, however, that he cannot touch the woman for a hundred days. Haseo cannot resist however, and after eighty days he attempts to make love to the woman. No sooner does he touch her than the woman melts into water. The lady, the oni explains, was made of the best parts collected from various dead bodies, and her soul was to enter the body after a hundred days. Had Haseo been patient, he could have kept the most beautiful woman created by the oni. Interestingly, in *Haseo sōshi*, it is the oni who strictly keeps his promise and a human who breaks it.

The idea that demons are honest and not manipulative is not novel. For example, in the tale entitled "Miyoshi no Kiyotsura no saishō no ie-watari no koto" (The Eviction) from *Konjaku monogatarishū*, Minister Miyoshi no Kiyotsura (847–918) says "real demons know right from wrong and are perfectly straight about it. That's what makes them frightening" (Tyler, *Japanese Tales* 123).[50] Also an *onmyōji* in "Harima no kuni no oni hito no ie ni kite iraruru koto" of *Konjaku monogatarishū* says that "(the oni) will come from the gate in the shape of a human. Such an oni is not wicked or unjust. He follows a righteous way" (Mabuchi et al. 38: 79). Though generally considered evil, when one thinks of its role as an attendant of Buddhist protectors and/or a variation of *marebito*, it is understandable that he is more honest than normal human beings. An utterance of this kind is also heard from Shuten Dōji as we shall see in the following chapter.

Through the medieval period, oni with these attributes had a forceful presence in the consciousness of nearly all elements of Japanese society. Much of whatever was inexplicable and/or mysterious to human intellect and perceived as negative eventually took shape as oni. An abundance of records on oni in the ancient and medieval periods reveal how oni were perceived as real by the Japanese masses. In the following chapters, representative oni or labeling of oni from the medieval through contemporary times will be examined in more detail to see how oni were treated and/or what roles they played with the changing contemporary psyche and society of Japanese culture.

---

50   The Japanese text is found in Mabuchi et al. 38: 97–101.

2

Shuten Dōji (Drunken Demon)
A Medieval Story of the Carnivalesque and the Rise of Warriors and Fall of Oni

Legends of Shuten Dōji

From Simple to Complex: Troubling the Demon

MORE THAN ANY OTHER TIME IN JAPANESE HISTORY, the medieval period was the oni's time. "Shuten Dōji and Ibaraki Dōji, so infamous that they are considered oni's pronoun, were born in this era," Komatsu Kazuhiko writes, "...many oni in performing arts and literature were also born during this time [the medieval period]" (*Shinpen Oni no tamatebako* 306). The story of Shuten Dōji is one of Japan's most renowned legends,[1] with its title character possessing all the oni's characteristics delineated in chapter one. The tale belongs to the genre *otogi zōshi* (companion stories), short stories written from the fourteenth to the seventeenth century for the purposes of both entertainment and moral or religious edification.[2]

According to legend, during the reign of Emperor Ichijō (r. 980–1011), people begin to disappear mysteriously from the royal court. Abe no Seimei (921?–1005), an official diviner of the Heian court, discovers that it is the

---

1 The many versions of "Shuten Dōji" are the most famous monster-conquering stories in the genre of *otogi zōshi* and have exerted more influence on later literature of monster-conquerors than any other work of *otogi zōshi* (Ichiko and Noma 78). See also Sakakibara, "*Ōeyama ekotoba* shōsai" 144; Nomura 72.

2 The definition of *otogi zōshi* as a genre is still controversial among literary scholars. For the study of *otogi zōshi* in English, see Kimbrough, *Preachers, Poets, Women, and the Way*; Steven 303–31; Mulhern, "Otogi-zōshi" 180–198 and "Analysis of Cinderella Motifs" 1–37; Keene, *Seeds in the Heart* 1092–1128; Skord; Childs 253–88; Araki 1–20; Ruch, "Medieval Jongleurs and the Making of a National Literature" 279–309; Putzar 286–297.

work of the archfiend, Shuten Dōji, the chieftain of the oni. Shuten Dōji and his cohorts abduct and devour young Kyoto maidens. The warriors Minamoto no Raikō (or Yorimitsu, 948–1021) and Fujiwara no Hōshō (or Yasumasa, 957–1036), as well as Raikō's *shitennō* (the four heavenly guardians) are charged by the imperial court to destroy Shuten Dōji and his evil minions. The warriors, with the help of their attending deities, carry out their mission, ultimately slaughtering the oni, rescuing the surviving captives and restoring peace and the security of the country. While on the surface Shuten Dōji provides a potent literary example of "good" triumphing over "evil," internal tensions in the text blur these distinctions. Although praise for some central authority[3] is clear, especially when the virtues of the emperor and his warriors are extolled, the voice of the marginalized "other" also resonates throughout the text in the form of the arch demon himself. Thus, the representation of the Japanese imperial court and the noble warriors fighting on its behalf as the force of all that is "good" becomes a troubled one. To explicate this alternate viewing of the drunken demon and to prize out these tensions within the text, Shuten Dōji will be examined through the lens of Mikhail Bakhtin's concept of the *carnivalesque*.

Taking its name from the raucous medieval celebration of Carnival, carnivalesque literature inverts power structures, demystifying and lampooning that which a particular culture holds serious or sacred. The carnivalesque upsets the structures of everyday life by its flagrant violations of class, gender, and religious boundaries. Examining the carnivalesque elements of *Shuten Dōji* sheds new light on certain aspects of Japanese culture, and a subversive and marginalized group identified as threatening "evil" by Japan's central authority becomes more familiar and sympathetic. Who is Shuten Dōji and what is his identity within Japanese society? In spite of socio-cultural

---

3   In the texts of *Shuten Dōji*, the "central authority" signifies the Heian imperial court with the emperor and the Fujiwara regency as its center. In the extra-literary context, during the fourteenth century when *Ōeyama ekotoba*, a picture scroll, was produced, tension existed between the imperial court and military government in terms of political power, with the latter increasingly exerting influence on the former. In the ensuing periods, while the imperial court clung to its cultural heritage as the main source of tradition, its political power declined precipitously. The political power rested completely in the military government at the time of the Shibukawa version of *Shuten Dōji*. Thus the central authority of the Shibukawa version in the extra-literary sense indicates the Tokugawa government. Whether the central authority signifies the imperial court, military governments, or both, depending upon the periods, the *oni* remain in varying degrees outsiders or strangers.

differences[4] between medieval European and Japanese traditions, the confluence of discursive practices in this medieval Japanese text and Bakhtin's theoretical ideas regarding the carnivalesque offers striking parallels. The application of Bakhtin's insights to Shuten Dōji yields a deeper understanding of the Shuten Dōji story and of the way society, in the world of the text, functions.[5] Thus viewed, the texts of *Shuten Dōji* offer possibilities of multilayered readings, on multiple levels of significance, into the complexities of what might otherwise be dismissed as a simple moral story from a distant time. The texts of *Shuten Dōji* offer people of this current age a chance to rethink and repossess these tales, breathing new life into heroes, demons, spirits, and texts that would otherwise be lost in too simplistic a reading.

Texts of Shuten Dōji

Although we know of the tale of Shuten Dōji through the written texts, evidence suggests that the story derives from a much older oral folk tradition.[6] As is the case with popular stories with an oral origin, the story of Shuten Dōji has an array of textual versions, interpreted and presented differently. Essentially, though, there are two versions of Shuten Dōji: the Ōeyama (Mt. Ōe) version and that of Ibukiyama (Mt. Ibuki). The major differences between them are twofold: one is the location of the oni's fortress. In the

---

4   There may have been no equivalent carnival festivities in Japan where the carnival laughter lampooning the serious (religious) rituals and customs in society were openly practiced. And yet, in Japan similar epistemological concepts of heaven and hell were strongly forwarded by Buddhism. Importantly, I believe, binary concepts of sacred and secular as well as distinctions of high and low strongly existed, although this binary concept is similar to yin and yang rather than water and oil. As Barbara Ruch comments, the world of commoners (*shomin*) portrayed in *otogi zōshi* is cheerful and hopeful as a whole. Authorship of *otogi zōshi* is not known, but contributors to the creations of the texts must have included not only educated people but also itinerant performers of low social status (see Ruch, *Mō hitotsu no chūseizō* 34, 143–84.) Bakhtin's utopian "folk" is unspecified, but I would interpret that it would include religious and secular itinerant performers who help the creation of *otogi zōshi*.

5   Bakhtin's *carnivalesque* is applicable across barriers of culture, time, and language. A twentieth-century Russian, he wrote about medieval French works; *carnivalesque* is certainly a useful tool in examining medieval Japanese literature.

6   *Otogi zōshi*'s anonymous authorship, brevity, and context indicate an oral-derived literature (Steven 303–331). Many works in this genre originated in history or legend and evolved in the oral tradition before being recounted in written form. This is characteristic of a folklore process (Honko, *Textualising the Siri Epic*). Standardized expressions and the mnemonic repetition of keywords and phrases often typify this oral-derived literature. Another indicator of *otogi zōshi*'s origin in oral tradition is the "emphasis on events and comparative lack of concern for details typical of auditory literature" (Steven 305).

Ōeyama version, the fortress is located on Mt. Ōe whereas the Ibukiyama version situates the oni's den at Mt. Ibuki. The second difference is that the Ibukiyama version includes a section of explanation on Shuten Dōji's *honji*, that is, an explanation of their "true nature" or "original form." Thus, in the Ibukiyama version we are told that Shuten Dōji is *dairokuten no maō* (the evil king of the Sixth Heaven in darkness) and the archenemy of Buddha. Likewise, the text tells us that Raikō's *honji* is Bishamonten (Vaiśravaṇa); Emperor Ichijō's, Miroku (Maitreya); and Seimei's is Kannon-satta (Kannon Bodhisattva).[7] The Ōeyama version does not contain this section, with the exception of the oldest text of this type entitled *Ōeyama ekotoba* (Picture Scroll of Mt. Ōe, early 14th century).[8] It is now generally accepted that the Ōeyama version came first. Satake Akihiro asserts that the Ibukiyama version was formed by incorporating a historical incident, the murder of a bandit named Kashiwabara Yasaburō at Mt. Ibuki in 1201, into the Ōeyama version (*Shuten Dōji ibun* 119). The earliest extant text of the legend is the above-mentioned picture scroll *Ōeyama ekotoba* made during the fourteenth century, which is kept in Itsuō Museum of Art in Osaka, Japan,[9] and depicts the Ōeyama version of the legend. Another picture scroll treating this story, *Shuten Dōji emaki* (Picture Scrolls of Shuten Dōji), owned by Suntory Museum of Art, in Tokyo, dates to the early sixteenth century, and represents the latter, the Ibukiyama version.[10] There are a number of copies and versions of the story, but it was the eighteenth-century printed version of the Shuten Dōji story that reached the broadest audience, thanks to a bookseller by the name of Shibukawa Seiemon.[11] For all intents and

---

7   See for example, "Ibukiyama Shuten Dōji" in Yokoyama and Matsumoto, 2: 426.

8   Separate sheets, presumably written in the middle of the Muromachi period, are believed to be copies of the *Ōeyama ekotoba,* and have a *honji* section. Satake Akihiko assumes that the *honji* section of the Ōeyama versions may have been eliminated as exposure to the audience became more frequent. *Shuten Dōji ibun* 152.

9   The scroll is also referred to as Katori-bon because the work was formerly in the possession of high priest of Katori Shrine in Shimofusa Province. It is reprinted in Yokoyama and Matsumoto 3: 122–140; Komatsu Shigemi, Ueno, Sakakibara, and Shimatani 75–103, 144–160, 171–178.

10 For various Ibuki versions of texts, see Yokoyama and Matsumoto, 2: 357–426; Matsumoto *Muromachi jidai monogatari taisei hoi* 1: 245–68, 335–59.

11 The Shibukawa edition is almost identical to a *tanroku-bon* (a picture booklet illustrated in green and orange), which was published during the Kan'ei era (1624–1643) (Matsumoto, "Otogi zōshi no honbun ni tsuite" 172). Regarding the text of Shibukawa version, see Ichiko, *Otogi zōshi* 361–84. For an English translation of the Shibukawa version, see Appendix A.

purposes, the popularity of the Shibukawa edition put an end to creations of further variations (Amano, "Shuten Dōji kō" 16). The location of the fortress in the Shibukawa edition is on Mt. Ōe, and Shibukawa published the "Shuten Dōji" story in an anthology of twenty-three short stories under the title of *Goshūgen otogi bunko* (Auspicious Companion Library).

The Shuten Dōji Story

According to the oldest extant text titled *Ōeyama ekotoba*, the story is set in the late tenth or early eleventh century in the Japanese capital of Heian. As mentioned earlier, Abe no Seimei's divination that the oni living on Mt. Ōe are abducting people sets the plot in motion. When the emperor commands the famous warriors to assemble their men and conquer the demons, Raikō and Hōshō are at first alarmed by the formidability of their mission, for oni possess supernatural powers and are able to transform into anything, making them difficult to hunt down, much less destroy. Despite their uncertainty, the warriors set out on their quest taking with them several loyal retainers. The troupe stops to pray for success at four separate shrines. Their faith is rewarded, for while on their way to the oni's lair on Mt. Ōe, the group encounters four deities disguised as priests. The old priests advise Raikō's party to disguise themselves as *yamabushi* (mountain priests), providing the men with the necessary clothing. Thus attired in what one might view as an inversion of their royal livery, the warriors, now joined by the deity-priests, continue on their quest, disguised as *yamabushi*. At a river on Mt. Ōe, the group meets an old woman who had been kidnapped by oni. She warns the heroes about the activities of Shuten Dōji and his band of oni. She tells the ersatz monks that Shuten Dōji forces kidnapped maidens into domestic servitude, and at the whim of the oni, they are dismembered, their flesh devoured, and their blood imbibed. Thus warned, the heroes are prepared to confront the arch demon in his lair. Arriving at the demon's mountaintop palace, the royal troupe lies to the oni guard, telling him that they are a band of lost *yamabushi* in need of lodging for the night. Shuten Dōji promptly allows them into his palace and jovially regales the men with stories from his past; he entertains his guests, offering them unknown flesh to eat and a detestable liquid to drink. In turn, one of the deity-priests offers Shuten Dōji his own *sake*, which causes Shuten Dōji to fall into an inebriated stupor.

After Shuten Dōji retires, a number of oni, disguised as beautiful women, visit Raikō and Hōshō in the palace guest quarters. The oni-women fail, however, to entice the warriors. Raikō gives the oni-women an intense glare, and the demons scurry off. Soon after, another group of oni disguised as a *dengaku* (field music) troupe emerge to entertain Raikō and his band. Again, Raikō's fierce stare wards them off. Raikō and Hōshō then decide to scout out the palace compound, an impressive structure described as a place where the splendor of heaven and the torment of hell simultaneously exist. In their search, the men discover a cage holding a kidnapped page of the Tendai sect's head priest. Although protected from death by Buddhist deities, the page remains trapped alongside the other captives. Raikō's and Hōshō's troupe moves quickly to Shuten Dōji's grand bedchamber. There, they find the entrance to his quarters blocked by a seemingly impenetrable iron door; but as the deity-priests pray and chant mystical incantations, the once impervious door magically melts away. Inside, Shuten Dōji lies in drunken repose, fully reverted to his true monstrous form. He is a giant, over fifty feet tall and with his red body and five-horned head, the epitome of demonic appearance. He has one black leg and one white, a yellow right arm and a blue left. The fifteen-eyed oni sleeps peacefully, oblivious to the fate that awaits him. While the four deity-priests hold each of Shuten Dōji's colorful limbs, the warriors behead him. Shuten Dōji cries as he is decapitated, *"Korera ni hakararete, ima wa kou to miyuru. Teki uteya!"* (Deceived by these men, I am now to be done with. Kill these enemies!). As Shuten Dōji's head hurls through the air, his mouth tries to bite Raikō. Thinking quickly, Raikō dons his helmet, and is thus saved from Shuten Dōji's final blow. With Shuten Dōji dead, Raikō's band kills the rest of the oni and frees the surviving captives. Before parting with the warriors at Mt. Ōe, the four deities reveal their true identities: they are the same deities to whom Raikō and Hōshō prayed at the shrine. The deities also show the heroes their own *honji* (true nature or original form): Raikō is a reincarnation of *Daiitoku* (Yamantaka, Great Awe-Inspiring Power) and Abe no Seimei, that of Ryōju bosatsu (Nāgārjuna).

On the troupe's return to the capital, Shuten Dōji's head is placed, by imperial command, in Uji no hōzō (Treasure house of Uji). Both Raikō and Hōshō are generously rewarded for their heroic deeds. Fulfilling the *otogi zōshi* genre's function of providing moral edification as it entertains, the Shuten Dōji story reveals how, with the help of holy deities, warriors faithful to the emperor can defeat even the most monstrous of villains and reap rich rewards.

Figure 3. Shuten Dōji entertains Raikō and his vassals with human flesh. Freer Gallery of Art, Smithsonian Institution, Washington D.C.: Purchase – Friends of Asian Art, F1998.26.2 (detail).

Carnivalesque Festivities

Shuten Dōji is a story rife with festival scenes and therein lies one of the most essential of its many connections to Bakhtin's concept of the carnivalesque. In *Rabelais and His World,* Bakhtin describes the medieval carnival as a form of pressure release from the political, class, and religious restrictions of everyday medieval folk life. The physical and rhetorical practices of defamation and inversion underlying the carnivalesque embody grotesque laughter at the official "real" world. This "carnivalesque laughter" differs sharply "from the serious official, ecclesiastical, feudal, and political cult forms and ceremonials" of the day. The carnival experience produces "ever-changing, playful, undefined forms. ... It is to a certain extent a parody of the extra-carnival life, a world inside out" (5–11). The carnivalesque is, however, dependent upon the very forms it mocks for its critical efficacy. Carnivalesque laughter, according to Bakhtin, is "ambivalent laughter" because it both "asserts and denies" the object of its laughter and because, unlike modern satire that assumes some place "above the object of [its] mockery, ... [t]he people's ambivalent laughter. ... expresses the point of view of the whole world; he [sic] who is laughing also belongs to it" (12). Which is to say, that the critical efficacy of the carnivalesque rests in this very ambivalence, in the idea that the official form implies its own mockery and vice versa. The low implies the high. The yin implies the yang. Such distinctions are inextricably caught up in one another in the interplay of life and text. Thus (and this is paramount to this analysis) the self, or in this case the ideal, is caught up in the other in the grotesque mockeries and inversions that characterize the carnivalesque. It is pertinent at this juncture to state that all that follows in this analysis probably lies outside the realm of the original author's intention.

In one of the festival scenes from Shuten Dōji, he eats a human servant without an inkling of hesitation—remember, cannibalism is a fundamental attribute of oni. The old woman at Mt. Ōe recounts that Shuten Dōji dismembers abducted humans with a kitchen knife, in much the same fashion that one prepares a meal. Shuten Dōji and his followers seem to fête regularly and human flesh is an important part of their banquets. The feast that the arch demon serves to Raikō and Hōshō, in *Ōeyama ekotoba,* the "unknown flesh and detestable liquid," we can assume is of human origin. Indeed, many Shuten Dōji picture scrolls contain vivid depictions of severed human legs (thigh meat) on a cutting-board in the banquet scene.[12]

---

12 See for example, *Shuten Dōji emaki* (illustration by Kanō Motonobu, 1476–1559)

The portrayal of preparing and eating human flesh is certainly grotesque in a carnivalesque sense. And, if we follow Bakhtin's logic, it is precisely this grotesqueness that lends this scene its carnivalesque ambivalence. Thus, while fearing and sympathising with the plight of the kidnapped maidens, in the portrayal of the banquet's beverage and entrée, the author(s) (and possibly the readers as well) of "Shuten Dōji" may be simultaneously amused by the grotesquery, goriness, and inebriated merriment of the oni's feast. This banquet scene displays the very characteristic that Bakhtin calls grotesque realism. Bakhtin writes:

> The essential principle of grotesque realism is degradation, that is, the lowering of all that is high, spiritual, ideal, abstract; it is a transfer to the material level, to the sphere of earth and body in their indissoluble unity.... Degradation here means coming down to earth, the contact with earth as an element that swallows up and gives birth at the same time.... it has not only a destructive, negative aspect, but also a regenerating one. (19–21)

Bakhtin further stresses that "Folk humor denies, but it revives and renews at the same time.

Bare negation is completely alien to folk culture" (11). Shuten Dōji boasts of his supernatural power and material wealth. Indeed, it is implied that feasting on a varied diet, including blood and human flesh, helps him maintain his supernatural longevity. His longevity, in turn, is demonstrated by the fact that the story takes place during Emperor Ichijō's reign (r. 980–1011) and by Shuten Dōji's own confession, he was active before the time of Priest Dengyō, who died in 822. The old woman that Raikō meets on Mt. Ōe says that she has served Shuten Dōji for more than two hundred years. Much in the same vein as Bakhtin sees culture consumed and renewed in the carnivalesque, human flesh is consumed and renewed in the regeneration of Shuten Dōji's power and his realm.

This scene functions inter-textually on another level of significance as well. The proto-image of the aforementioned human legs on a cutting-board in *Shuten Dōji* is found earlier in a scene from *geshin jigoku* (hell of pulverized flesh) in *Jigoku sōshi* (scrolls of Buddhist Hell) in the twelfth century

---

in Suntory Art Museum, *Shuten Dōji e* (ca.17th century) in Tōyō University Library, *Shuten Dōji* (1700) of Freer Gallery of Art, Smithsonian Institution [illustration in the main text], and *Ōeyama emaki* (ca. 17th century) in the Chester Beatty Library. Also, the widely distributed Shibukawa woodblock version (ca. 18th century) contains the similar picture of a severed leg.

(Amano, "Shuten Dōji" 105).[13] *Jigoku sōshi* was produced with the purpose of serious religious edification in mind, ostensibly so that the observers of the imagery would be awakened to the presence of abhorrent hell. In the *geshin jigoku* scene three oni are slicing men's bodies into pieces on oversized cutting boards. Conspicuous are the big legs placed on the boards. Other oni sit nearby, placing the neatly cut flesh onto plates. Although it appears that the demons intend to make a meal of the human flesh, they are punishing mortal sinners through the pain of dismemberment. *Geshin jigoku*'s sinners are priests who break the Buddhist precept against killing and therein resides its moral precept. While in the story Shuten Dōji and his minions consume human flesh for pleasure as well as sustenance, and while Shuten Dōji's victims are innocent, one can readily perceive Shuten Dōji as a carnivalesque inversion of *geshin jigoku*. Bakhtin asserts that in "the folklore of primitive peoples, coupled with the cults that were serious … were other, comic cults which laughed at the deity" (6).

Shuten Dōji considers the great Buddhist priests, Kōbō Daishi (774–835)[14] and Dengyō Daishi (d. 822)[15] as villains. In the Ibukiyama texts, he is the evil king of the Sixth Heaven in darkness, an avowed enemy of Buddha. In this sense the character, Shuten Dōji, can indeed be said to mock the deity. Also, if we accept the depiction of Shuten Dōji's banquet scene as a folk repossession and comic inversion or parody of the serious text of the *geshin jigoku* scene, and by its extension, the Buddhist concept of hell, and if we recall that Shuten Dōji, as *otogi zōshi* has as its purpose religious and moral edification as well, we see again how that which is moral and that which seeks to mock it are caught up in the ambivalent flux of carnivalesque laughter.

Bakhtin writes that a leading role in the banquet image is played by the gaping mouth, which is related to the theme of swallowing (*Rabelais and His World* 279, 325), symbolizing not only death and destruction, but also regeneration. Likewise, Shuten Dōji, with his huge mouth, swallows human flesh and blood, leading not only to the destruction of human lives but of the Heian capital as well. One of Shuten Dōji's victims, the daughter of Lord Munenari, laments that she "was appreciating the moon in a past autumn,

---

13 For the picture of *geshin jigoku*, see Komatsu Shigemi and Akiyama, 72–73.

14 Kūkai. The founder of the Shingon sect of Buddhism; he founded Kongōbu-ji on Mt. Kōya in present-day Wakayama prefecture.

15 Saichō. The founder of the Tendai sect of Buddhism; he founded Enryaku-ji on Mt. Hiei in present-day Kyoto.

when she was suddenly kidnapped." She cries of the "uncertainty in her life, for at any time she could be the oni's next victim." But the perpetuation of the oni's power is the ultimate result—destruction and regeneration ever in flux—Shuten Dōji's consumption of humans helps maintain the oni's realm and his supernatural power.

We see similar examples of the carnivalesque in the scenes where Shuten Dōji's oni minions attempt to ensnare Raikō, Hōshō, and their men through their awesome powers of transformation, one of the signature characteristics of the oni. We are told in the story that five or six oni transform themselves into beautiful maidens in layered costumes and appear in front of the *yamabushi*. Without saying anything, the oni eagerly cast amorous glances at them (see Yokoyama and Matsumoto 3: 132). But Raikō's penetrating eyes reveal their true identity and the oni flee. Indeed, one might argue that this scene and the very characteristic of transformation and gender switching mark the oni as the ultimate embodiment of the carnivalesque as the transformed demons represent the comic inversion of what ought to be the warriors' objects of sexual desire and at the same time are the objects of the oni's own appetites. The scene, depicting the oni in various costumes running away from Raikō, is quite amusing. A more intriguing and complex scene follows this humorous scene when the oni transform into a *dengaku* troupe.

Dengaku in its broad meaning refers to all rituals related to agriculture and thus to fertility and regeneration (Plutschow 169).[16] In more limited terms, it is a dance form whereby people play musical instruments such as drums, flute, and *binzasara* (wooden clapper-type instruments) while dancing in various combinations. *Dengaku* is considered a most typical performing art of medieval Japan (Moriya 39). As we shall see, the art itself has many elements of the carnivalesque and as we shall also see, the juxtaposition of distinct *dengaku* scenes within the text is yet another example of the carnivalesque in *Shuten Dōji*.

Earlier in the *Ōeyama ekotoba* picture scroll, at Hie Shrine, when Raikō and Hōshō visit the shrine to pray, they are entertained by *dengaku*. A child

---

16 *Dengaku* is broadly divided into two categories. First, as the rites of actual planting in paddy fields are performed in spring, dance and music are presented to pray for a good harvest. The other, as a ritual performed at shrines, is designed to pray for a good year's harvest by artistic imitation of routine agricultural tasks such as sowing, planting, and harvesting. *Dengaku* became fashionable for urban dwellers at that time to parade around the city in various costumes, imitating the *dengaku*'s actual movements used in the planting of rice in the paddy field (Honda 359; Plutschow 169–80).

performer is pictured dancing *dengaku* at the shrine, while other performers play music and dance in the yard in front of the Hall of Worship. Similarly, in the scene at Shuten Dōji's palace, the oni also perform *dengaku*. In both cases, the location of the performance shares the same depiction—outside, in a courtyard in front of the building. The angle of the buildings, the Hall of Worship and Raikō's and Hōshō's quarters in the Shuten Dōji's palace is also the same. Significantly, three of the oni's postures and costumes are portrayed identically to the *dengaku* performers depicted in front of the Hall of Worship; only the face is changed from human to oni.[17] The oni's *dengaku* is clearly a parody of the earlier more wholesome dance at Hie Shrine. The performance at Hie Shrine is to pray for the success of Raikō's quest to kill the oni, whereas that of the oni-*dengaku*'s is to trick Raikō's group and to kill and to eat them.[18] One need not push the scene any further to see its carnivalesque aspects.

The more complex functions of the *dengaku* scenes and of the very art of *dengaku*, however, require a closer look. The dance scenes in *Ōeyama ekotoba* are actually a reflection of a contemporary folk belief portrayed in art form. Much like the festivities of carnival, *dengaku* were popular festivities for all classes, and, amusingly, an account in *Azuma kagami* (ca. 13th century) indicates that it was popular among non-humans as well.[19] In medieval Japan, the sudden surge of *geinō* (performing arts) such as *dengaku* had an ambivalent reception. Indeed, this fertility ritual was considered a bad omen by some segments of medieval Japanese culture (Moriya 7–37, 79).[20] An interesting example of this is the demise of Hōjō Takatoki (1303–1333), the ninth regent to Minamoto Shogun, who was much taken with *dengaku*. As

---

17 For the pictures, see Komatsu Shigemi, Ueno, Sakakibara, and Shimatani 80, 88.

18 The oni's intention to kill Raikō's group is clear in the Shibukawa version of *Shuten Dōji*. In the Shibukawa version, after the exchange of *sake* between Shuten Dōji and Raikō, Shuten Dōji commands his minions to entertain Raikō's party. One demon named Ishikuma Dōji rises to sing out, "From the capital what kind of people lost their way to become condiments of *sake*? How interesting." Ishikuma Dōji's song suggests that the demons should make condiments and *sake* out of the *yamabushi*.

19 An entry dated 16 Ninth month of 1247 of *Azuma kagami* records that the villagers of Nakayama in Sagami province reported strange creatures (*bakemono*), and that the creatures danced and sang in the costumes of *dengaku* every night (Kuroita 395).

20 Historically *dengaku*'s enormous popularity among the high and low plunged the capital of Kyoto into chaos in 1096. This affair or disturbance is called "Eichō ōdengaku." The extraordinary *dengaku* fever which engulfed the whole capital was put to an end by the sudden death of Princess Ikuhōmon'in (1076–96). People considered in retrospect that the impulsive vogue of *dengaku* foreshadowed the Princess' death (Moriya 15).

some graffiti at Nijō Riverside (Nijō gawara) in 1335 tell it, "Dogs and *dengaku* have caused the Hōjō downfall, but *dengaku* is still thriving" (Hanawa 504). It is commonly considered (and even satirized) that *dengaku* caused the collapse of the Kamakura shogunate,[21] and the demise of Hōjō Takatoki. Conversely, in *Taiheiki* (Chronicle of Grand Pacification, ca. 14th century), the *dengaku* is described as being feverishly welcomed by all classes for its ecclesiastic fund-raising ability. An itinerant monk organized a *dengaku* competition to raise funds for the building of a bridge. On the day of the performance, in the sixth month of 1349, everyone from members of the imperial court, the regent, and the shogun on down to commoners were equally rapt and enthralled by the *dengaku* performance at the Shijō Riverbed (Shijō gawara). That is, of course, until the reviewing-stand galleries collapsed, claiming the lives of men, women, and children of all backgrounds. The contrast between this celebratory atmosphere of a fertility ritual, marked by excitement and merriment, with the grotesque deaths of innocent people, is indeed pertinent, for it is the carnivalesque festivity itself that inherently and concurrently embodies elements of both destruction and renewal.

Thus, just as the surge of performing arts was for some segments of Japanese society considered a bad omen, the sudden appearance of oni as a *dengaku* troupe in the story can be interpreted as the harbinger of Shuten Dōji's doom. One might argue that the carnivalesque ritual contributes to the demise of Shuten Dōji at the peak of his prosperity just as the Shijō Riverbed *dengaku*, at the height of its performance, foreshadowed the destruction of Hōjō Takatoki and the Kamakura shogunate. In the Shuten Dōji story, the oni's defeat ushers in an era of peace in Japan, marked by a renewal of imperial authority, and eventually contributes to greater power and recognition for the nation's warrior class, creating the shogunate. Thus in its carnivalesque way, the dance is at once the dance of death and rebirth.

Shuten Dōji as Other

Inasmuch as the carnivalesque characterizes the narrative, rhetorical, and/ or discursive structures of *Shuten Dōji*, it also defines the way images of

---

21 See the head note of Hasegawa 1: 254. According to *Taiheiki* (Chronicle of Grand Pacification, ca. 14th century), around the time of the Genkō era (1331–1333) in the capital, "men made much of the dance called field music [*dengaku*], and high or low there was none that did not seek after it eagerly." (Translated by McCullough. *The Taiheiki* 131; the original text is found in Hasegawa, 1: 254.) It is recorded in the *Taiheiki* that Hōjō Takatoki was dancing inebriated at a banquet with various specters.

marginalization and otherness are transacted. Kidnapping innocent people and eating them is enough, perhaps, to suggest that Shuten Dōji is evil. As we witness in the various versions of the Shuten Dōji legend, the archfiend brings disaster to the land of Japan sometimes as storms, sometimes as famine (see, for example, Yokoyama and Matsumoto, 3: 130). Abe no Seimei, who sets the plot in motion and who protects Japan from the capital with his divination and prayers, calls Shuten Dōji a *tenma* (demon). Lest we wonder what the tale proposes as its ideal, and where our sympathies are supposed to rest, an imperial counsellor asks, "Living in the imperial land of Japan, how could even a supernatural creature not obey the imperial wishes?" (Komatsu Shigemi, Ueno, Sakakibara, and Shimatani 159).

It is refreshing and entertaining, perhaps, to see a monstrous creature dangerous to one's country completely smashed by good, heroic warriors. A close examination of the texts, however, reveals a different picture of Shuten Dōji, the monster. During the festivities, Shuten Dōji is presented as overly naïve and trusting. Although he is presumably a mighty and shrewd creature, the arch demon fails to see through either the disguises of his enemies or the ruse they use to gain admittance to his palace. He cheerfully talks about his personal history without doubting Raikō's true intentions, and even shares his favorite food with him, human flesh.[22] At his dying moment, Shuten Dōji cries out, "Deceived by these men, I am now to be done with. Kill these enemies!" In other versions, including the Noh text entitled "Ōeyama," his righteous claim is even stronger, for he laments, "How sad, you priests! You said you don't lie. There is nothing false in the words of demons."[23] While it is clear that as readers we are asked to admire and identify with the deities, the mighty warriors, and above all, the imperial authority, a carnivalesque rupture of this trend toward the hegemonic is occurring throughout the story and in this scene in particular. After all, if the story at its core seeks the reader's moral edification, one cannot help but sympathize with a character that is brought to its ultimate demise through lies and deception. Since in the carnivalesque good and evil coexist in

---

22 In the Shibukawa version, Shuten Dōji is more cautious. But after a while, Shuten Dōji apologizes to the disguised Raikō that he mistook the latter for his archenemy (i.e., Raikō) and tells his minions to entertain Raikō's troop while he sleeps.

23 In Noh's text, Raikō responds to this utterance: "You are lying. If that is true, why are you capturing people in this imperial land and injuring people?" Sanari, 1: 568. The Noh play of the Shuten Dōji story is titled "Ōeyama." For the Japanese Noh text, see Sanari, 1: 553–571. For an English translation, see Horton.

Figure 4. Shuten Dōji's head. Freer Gallery of Art, Smithsonian Institution, Washington D.C.: Purchase—Friends of Asian Art, F1998.26.3 (detail).

grotesque flux, we come to identify not only with that which is heroic but that which is "other" as well.

The carnivalesque voice that emerges in Shuten Dōji's death scene may well be called the voice of the other, which needs a little explanation. The other represents those marginalized persons or groups who are partially or entirely excluded from participation in the political, historical, and cultural affairs of hegemonic society, and who suffer from cultural, intellectual, legal, geographical, and/or physical disadvantages attached to their status. While we see this in the text, we can see it also in the extra-literary context that surrounds the text.

According to Komatsu Kazuhiko, there are four categories of other or "strangers." First, people who visit a community and stay in the community for a brief period of time, such as itinerant priests, artisans, merchants, beggars, travelers, and pilgrims. Second, people who come from outside a community and settle more or less permanently, such as refugees of wars and natural disasters, merchants and priests for their professions, and criminals banished from their homeland. Third are those who are native to the community but shunned by community members; they include ex-convicts, the physically and mentally handicapped, and criminals who are going to be banished from the community or executed. Last, there are strangers who live spatially far away from a community, and are thus known to the community only through their imagination; examples are foreigners who live overseas, and supernatural creatures who live in the other world ("Ijin ron –'ijin' kara 'tasha' e" 177–78).[24] As supernatural creatures, oni are not only firmly ensconced in this fourth group but as embodiments of the carnivalesque they are arguably all of the above.

Shuten Dōji as marginalized other potentially subverts the narrative of political domination in which a central authority commands the brave warriors to eliminate him. The carnivalesque underlies this subversion. Indeed, carnivalesque ambivalence permeates how otherness is transacted throughout the Shuten Dōji texts. Shuten Dōji resided in Mt. Hiei long before Priest Dengyō claimed the area. He is relocated from his native place to another, from where he is again expelled. He even explains that he causes the natural disasters because he bears a grudge against humans whom he views as usurpers of his various homes.[25] There is certainly room for sympathy

---

24   For the discussion of "other" also see Goodich; Dallery and Scott; Huffer.
25   The idea that Shuten Dōji brings disasters to the land and people in Japan because of

in this case where the strong take the possessions of the weak. And again, the reader's sympathy is drawn away from the ideal as it falls victim to carnivalesque ambivalence and as she or he finds her or his sympathy drawn toward a demon.

Amano Fumio conjectures that Shuten Dōji may have originally been a local deity from Mt. Hiei whom Priest Dengyō first encounters when Dengyō enters Mt. Hiei to establish the Tendai sect of Buddhism. This local deity came to be considered an oni, because Mt. Hiei is located away from the capital in the direction of *kimon* where oni are said to reside ("Shuten Dōji kō" 16–27). The Tendai Buddhists were strongly linked to the imperial authority and as such were widely viewed as protectors of the nation.[26] Effectively, Shuten Dōji, the local deity forced to leave Mt. Hiei, is disenfranchised by imperial authority. Baba Akiko takes this a step further surmising that oni are a representation of those suppressed people and/or those who were not a part of the Fujiwara Regency (from the 10th century through the 11th century) (141). The Fujiwara Regency reached its peak with Fujiwara Michinaga (966–1027). Michinaga attained supreme power in court through his position as Emperor Ichijō's regent. Importantly, Emperor Ichijō's reign is the period setting for *Shuten Dōji*. The abducted page Raikō seen in Shuten Dōji's palace is the son of Michinaga. It is not surprising then that the page becomes the target of Shuten Dōji's wrath. And it is probably even less surprising that he is safe, protected by Buddhist deities because he is the page of the head of the Tendai sect. So, even in these historical, extra-literary contexts that surround the production of the text, it is possible to see Shuten Dōji as the marginalized other. But, what then of the carnivalesque?

---

his grudge against humans (including the emperor and influential priests) is similar to what Sugawara no Michizane did, as seen in chapter one. According to *Dōken shōnin meido ki* (Record of Holy Priest Dōken's Travel to the Realm of the Dead), evil deities cause disasters in Japan and good deities protect Japan from disasters. If an evil deity like Michizane intends to destroy Buddhism because of a grudge, then it brings disasters to the land and people of Japan. Imahori Taitsu writes that this view that calamities are caused by evil deities' actions is in accord with *Konkōmyō saishōō kyō* (Golden Splendor Sutra), a scripture for defending a country. *Record of Holy Priest Dōken's Travel to the Realm of the Dead* was produced by the priest(s) of Shingon esoteric Buddhism who were in search of measures against and prevention of disasters based upon the *Golden Splendor Sutra* (26–40).

26   Needless to say, not all the Buddhist sects rejected local deities. The Sōdō sect of Zen Buddhism, for example, recognized local deities to provide religious justification for villagers to support new Zen temples (Bodiford 174).

It is exactly the carnivalesque ambivalence of Shuten Dōji, both the character and story that makes credible the demon's position as marginalized other. As noted above, delineations of ideal and other are placed in flux as either comes to define both, as exemplified by the story's treatment of Shuten Dōji's severed head. We are told that by imperial command it is locked away in the fastness of Uji no hōzō, the treasure house built by Fujiwara no Yorimichi, the eldest son of the regent, Michinaga. Furthermore, for the people in the medieval period, Uji no hōzō was the treasure house which stored invaluable objects such as *busshari* (Buddha's ashes), *nyoi hōju* (wish-completing Jewels) which symbolize imperial authority, and imaginary priceless items including *Genji monogatari*'s "Kumogakure" (Vanished into the Clouds) chapter. The belief in the existence of the treasures increased precisely because the objects were hidden in Uji no hōzō and nobody, except for the Fujiwara regent and a limited number of imperial family members, could see them (see Tanaka, *Gehō to aihō no chūsei* 115–147). Obviously Shuten Dōji's head belongs to the annals of folklore, rather than historical fact, for Uji no hōzō, part of Byōdōin buildings, was built in 1053, thirty-two years after the death of Raikō. Emperor Ichijō, who, in the story, issues the imperial order to store the head at Uji no hōzō, had been dead since 1011, so it is impossible that he could have issued such a command. But the important thing here is the folk nature of this belief; by the time the tale is produced, people *believe* that the severed head of Shuten Dōji, a symbol of anti-imperial resistance, is in Uji no hōzō, protected by the Yorimichi's spirit.[27] This can be viewed as another carnivalesque inversion, just as Shuten Dōji takes in the flesh and blood of the young maidens to maintain his power and vitality, so too the imperial court takes in the head of the demon to do the same. Indeed, Komatsu Kazuhiko interprets *Shuten Dōji* from the perspective of a medieval *Ōken setsuwa* (narrative prose concerning sovereign authority). In medieval *Ōken setsuwa*, the "central" sovereign authority appropriates "outside" power through a symbolic jewel. In the case of the "Shuten Dōji" story, the symbolic jewel is represented by the demon-leader's head. With Shuten Dōji's head coming into the capital, "the outside power" is incorporated into the capital, i.e., to the central authority.[28] The

---

27 Yorimichi, the founder of Uji no hōzō, is said to be transformed to a dragon king to protect the treasures of Uji no hōzō.

28 See Komatsu Kazuhiko, *Shuten Dōji no kubi* 9–55; Abe Yasurō, "'Taishokukan' no seiritsu" 80–195, and "Hōju to ōken" 115–169. Komatsu notes that Raikō's group disguised themselves as mountain priests, who, as mountaineering ascetics live in a

swallowing of the jewel, (the head of Shuten Dōji) into the body of the capital gives a renewed life to the Heian central authority. From the point of view of the oni's attributes, Shuten Dōji gave wealth and prosperity to the Capital of Heian and imperial authority with his own head.

Recognizing oni as the embodiment of the carnivalesque and as the representation of the marginalized other is a key to understanding Shuten Dōji's naiveté as seen in the enigmatic death cry in which he bewails Raikō's lack of honor while extolling the higher values of the demons. Rosemary Jackson asserts: "the fantastic traces the unsaid and the unseen of culture; that which has been silenced, made invisible, covered over and made 'absent'" (4). In this light, Shuten Dōji's exclamation can be seen as the voice of the disenfranchised other—marginalized and preordained for elimination by a powerful and hegemonic culture. Shuten Dōji's body as he lies sleeping is an example of carnivalesque grotesqueness and otherness. Recall that he is described as a fifty-foot tall giant with a red body, five-horned head, fifteen eyes and variously colored limbs. He is the epitome of the carnivalesque. And herein lies the critical efficacy of the carnivalesque: a gross and vulgar parody of the human form. Shuten Dōji is of human form, nevertheless, and thus our sympathy is drawn once again to the demon through its grotesque affinity to the ideal. Just as Shuten Dōji's otherness is manifest in the extra-literary historical context of the legend, it is also found in various theories concerning Shuten Dōji's origins.

Origins of Shuten Dōji

Although he is widely perceived as a supernatural being with extraordinary powers, one popular theory put forward during the medieval period has it that Shuten Dōji and his fellow oni were nothing more than a gang of bandits who lived on Mt. Ōe (see, for example, Takahashi Masaaki; Baba). The Kamakura military government's edict, issued in 1239, was designed to suppress the "villainous robbers" living on Mt. Ōe, and is cited in support of this view. Similarly, Kaibara Ekken (1630–1714), a Confucian scholar,

---

human world, and therefore, belong to the "inside." Yet at the same time, mountaineering ascetics were socially and spatially located on the periphery, and sometimes, they fluxed from "inside" to "outside." From the point of view of the oni, mountaineering ascetics belonged to the "outside." Yet, there were some who broke away from "inside" and became oni. As oni were often based in the mountains, inevitably some would stray into their territories, particularly mountaineering ascetics (boundary beings) who could go back and forth between the two worlds of humans and oni (*Shuten Dōji no kubi* 20–21).

asserts, "Shuten Dōji was originally a robber who donned the appearance of a demon to scare people so that he could steal their wealth and abduct women" (qtd. in Takahashi Masaaki 48).[29] Takahashi Masaaki asserts that the prototype of Shuten Dōji was originally a deity of smallpox (vi). He explains that in and after the Heian period (794–1185) a ceremony of *onmyōdō* (way of yin and yang) called *shikai no matsuri* (ritual at the four demarcations) was held every time an epidemic of smallpox broke out in Kyoto. The ritual was designed to prevent the epidemic deity from entering Kyoto and was held at four locations simultaneously in the suburbs of the capital. A series of magical activities designed to appease these epidemic deities sought to turn the invisible, shapeless spirits into fully formed corporeal beings with a sense of reality, i.e., oni of Mt. Ōe (see Takahashi Masaaki 1–53). At this time, quarantine as a public health measure was widely used to stop the spread of disease. Not surprisingly, a stigma was associated with forced isolation (Lederberg et al. 22). The diseased were effectively disenfranchised, much as the oni were in later mytho-historical treatments.

Another intriguing theory of the origins of Shuten Dōji put forth by several modern-day scholars is that the oni stories were actually based on the unconventional lifestyles of a group of metal or mine workers living in the Ōe Mountains. The metal workers were travelers who were purportedly well versed in magic and medicinal practices. It is because these men led such different lifestyles that they were feared and ultimately regarded as heathens by many of the local townsfolk. There exists ample literary and historical proof that people living in the mountains were often referred to as the descendants of oni. Because the customs and manners of these mountain dwellers were different from those of the people living on the flatlands (Miyamoto Masaaki 10; Wakao 46), they were frequently branded for their otherness. Yet another take on the Shuten Dōji story involves the tale of a Caucasian man who drifted to the shore of Tanba Province, in what is present-day Kyoto (Takahashi Masaaki ii). He apparently hailed from Mt. Ōe and drank red wine, a veritable parallel to Shuten Dōji's predilection for blood *sake*.[30]

---

29   Ekken also remarks that the story of Shuten Dōji resembles fiction of the Tang Dynasty entitled *Hakuenden* (Story of White Monkey). For the relation between *Shuten Dōji* and *Hakuenden*, see Kuroda Akira 374–388.

30   These folk beliefs of Shuten Dōji as a Caucasian and/or bandit living in Mt. Ōe have been actively utilized in modern fiction. One such story is entitled "Oni no matsuei" (Descendants of Oni, 1950), written by Mihashi Kazuo (1908–1995) for young people. In this story, the protagonist is a twenty-year-old Spanish language major who discovers that he is a descendant of Shuten Dōji's cohorts. Shuten Dōji and his cohorts

Although distinct from each other, all these theories share a profound sense of otherness: a sense of someone or something forced to live on the periphery of hegemonic culture being different and feared, so thus vilified and made monstrous. Underlying these various viewpoints is an unspoken yet palpable feeling of sympathy for the otherness of those vanquished by the mighty. These Er-stories—one or the other or perhaps all—get consumed by folk culture swallowed into the carnivalesque, consumed and renewed as the substance of legend.

Ironically, in the legends it is only with *divine* assistance that the warrior-heroes beguile and defeat Shuten Dōji and his minions. Moreover, it is the evil oni who, evincing the ideal value of trust, open their palace up to the deceptive heroes. Shuten Dōji's trusting and thus, weakened, position foreshadows the end of his reign and the success of the "forces of good." It should be noted that the title, "forces of good," is bestowed upon the warriors by the emperor, foreshadowing the emergent power of the warrior class in medieval Japan. The Fujiwara regency boasted of its political power, but when it came to the physical subjugation of its enemies, the warriors were summoned into action. These same warriors eventually gained economic and political power befitting heroes of the imperial authority.

One final twist or irony is that Raikō, the killer of oni, is related to oni himself. Takahashi Masaaki offers an interesting interpretation as to why Raikō was chosen as the conqueror of the demons at Mt. Ōe. He writes that

---

are not "real" oni but bandits living on Mt. Ōe in the eleventh century. They are portrayed as Spanish pirates who drift to Japan—similar to other origin theories of foreigners who inadvertently drift to Japan. After Raikō and his *shitennō*'s attack on their den, an escaped bandit impersonates a Japanese citizen and marries a Japanese woman. The protagonist's father, a renowned educator, turns out to be the murderer-robber who broke into houses and killed thirteen people twenty years earlier. Thirteen small Buddha statues that his father cherishes—the statues that eerily laugh at the beginning of the story—represent the people his father has murdered and for whom he has promised to pray. According to witnesses who escaped from the robbery and murders, the criminal (his father) said before killing, "I have been working hard since young, but I still cannot support my wife. There are many illiterate, shameless, and robber-like people out there leading a luxurious life without making family suffer." The killer explains that he needs money to support his pregnant wife and coming baby. Although the killer's justification that "There are many illiterate, shameless, and robber-like people out there leading a luxurious life without making family suffer" might apply in any society at almost any time, it seems particularly appropriate in the economic realities of Japan in the immediate wake of World War II. Thus the popularity of *Shuten Dōji* remains unchanged throughout Japan's history.

Raikō is associated with *Raikō* 雷公, the thunder god, and notes how the frightening effects of thunder and lightning were often required to eliminate similarly terrifying demons (34–35, 58–62).[31] As seen in chapter one, Kondō finds the genesis of oni in the people's fear of natural phenomena, the destructive power of nature's fury manifest in such forms as thunder and lightning storms and earthquakes. Of all the natural forces, thunder and lightning are most strongly associated with the oni. In the story of Shuten Dōji, right before the appearance of the archfiend, "Suddenly, an odor of rotting fish seemed to carry on the wind and thunder and lightning began to strike." Just as Sugawara no Michizane frightened people with thunder and lightning, Shuten Dōji emerges from a foreboding backdrop of thunder and lightning. In terms of Kondō's theory, Raikō 雷公 is the thunder god who slays and conquers the demons of Mt. Ōe, despite his concurrent role as their progenitor.

The Rise of the Warrior Class and Fall of Oni

The rise of the warrior class correlated with the beginning of the fall of Shuten Dōji's status as king of evil (Chigiri 473) in medieval Japan. A warrior's true essence is to fight; he must engage in battles undaunted even when the enemy is as evil, frightening and seemingly indestructible as oni. The more demonic the opponent in this paradigm, the greater the warrior's fame. In a nod to the carnivalesque we might say that, like Shuten Dōji himself, the warriors consume the oni and in turn, the oni feed the warriors' power. According to Kumasegawa Kyōko, the first appearance of the appellations, oni and warrior (*bushi*), listed (or classified) together is in *Yowa no nezame* (The Tale of Nezame, ca. late 11th century) (210). It is described in *Yowa no nezame* that "*oni-gami, mononofu to iu tomo, namida otosanu wa arumajiki wo*" (Even gods, demons, or warriors would not fail to shed tears);[32] the narrator referred to oni as daring and ruthless beings. Also, the narrator of the *Heike monogatari* (Tale of the Heike) tells that "[Oni-sado of the Hōrin'in] was a warrior worth a thousand, capable of meeting devils or gods with his strength and his forged weapons."[33] Here,

---

31 Kondō Yoshihiro earlier cites an example of 頼光 written as 雷公 (See Kondō 171–72).
32 For the Japanese text, see Sugawara no Takasue no musume 132.
33 The English translation is by McCullough (*The Tale of the Heike* 150). For the Japanese text, see Ichiko, *Heike monogatari* 45: 310–11.

the physical strength of the warriors is considered comparable to the deities and oni. Most intriguingly, one of the warriors, Oni-sado, has oni as part of his name, signifying that he has corporal prowess equivalent to that of the oni. How the warriors should fight in battles is described in contrast to the aristocratic or courtly warriors (i.e., the Heike clan) in *Heike monogatari*:

> Every big landholder can command at least five hundred horsemen. Once a rider mounts, he never loses his seat; ... if a man sees his father or son cut down in battle, he just rides over the body and keeps fighting. In battles fought in the west, a man leaves the field if he loses his father, ... a man who loses a son is too broken up to come back at all.... In summer, they think it's too hot to fight; in winter, they think it's too cold.[34]

The warrior's ideal, a carnivalesque pastiche of the oni, is quite different from that of the aristocratic ruling class of the Heian period bound by sensitivities and taboos. With the warriors' increased mobility in political and economic circles, a concurrent weakening of the oni becomes inevitable, but also a weakening of the imperial authority itself and thus the imperial ideal that, on its surface, *Shuten Dōji* portends.

Shuten Dōji is an exemplary oni story of the medieval period, revealing the textual peak and decline of oni. Shuten Dōji's demise symbolizes the rise of the warrior class and the fall of oni status. As carnivalesque literary figures, through their representation of otherness, the oni not only trouble the sacred and serious customs and manners of the imperial ideal, they also provide the underpinnings of those subversive elements challenging the established order from within. Thus, the Shuten Dōji story frames these moral dilemmas from the perspectives of central authority and the marginalized other. Shuten Dōji's affable gestures during the banquet with Raikō and his exclamation at the moment of his demise are the carnivalesque voice of the disenfranchised. Although Shuten Dōji is preordained for elimination by the will of authority, in the carnivalesque world of the text he becomes entwined with the imperial ideal and thus, textually anyway, invincible. This timeless condition might offer some insight into the popularity and longevity of the Shuten Dōji story.

---

34   The English translation is by McCullough (*The Tale of the Heike* 188–89). For the Japanese text, see Ichiko, *Heike monogatari* 45: 402.

3

Women Spurned, Revenge of Oni Women
Gender and Space

T<small>HE MEDIEVAL TIME PRODUCED A GREAT MALE ONI</small> called Shuten Dōji as we saw in chapter two. Indeed, the medieval period also created an awesome female oni who is as destructive as Shuten Dōji. Named Uji no hashihime (Woman at Uji Bridge) as described in the "Tsurugi no maki" (Swords Chapter) of *Heike monogatari* (Tale of the Heike), this fierce female oni goes on a killing spree. Spurned by her lover, she is turned by her angst and jealousy into an oni while she is still alive, and takes the lives of her husband, his mistress, and many others. The Uji no hashihime story illustrates the Japanese version of "hell hath no fury like a woman scorned." A famous Noh play titled *Kanawa* (Iron Tripod), also a product of the medieval time, is based upon this Uji no hashihime episode, though the heroine of *Kanawa* gives much pathos to the wild image of a jealous woman. I postulate that Uji no hashihime, which predates the Shuten Dōji legend, is a possible literary source for the Shuten Dōji texts. It is intriguing to conjecture that the texts of Shuten Dōji may be related to or even derived from the Uji no hashihime story, underscoring the gender-crossing powers of an oni. While examining the women who turned into oni because of their strong desire for revenge, this chapter also studies the different sociopolitical spaces that male and female oni occupy in the minds of Japanese.

Uji no hashihime (Woman at Uji Bridge)

The Stories of Uji no hashihime

The legend of Uji no hashihime, also mentioned in the *Genji monogatari* (*Tale of Genji*, ca. 1010), existed long before stories of Shuten Dōji emerge. According to a legend known in Heian poetics, a wife suffering from morning sickness asked her husband to get seaweed for her, so the husband went to the sea palace in search of seaweed. At the palace, however, a sea goddess became enamoured of him and he became the sea goddess's husband. His human wife, who had been waiting for his return in vain, felt bitter and threw herself into the Uji River. After her death, the abandoned wife was enshrined at the foot of the Uji Bridge. In folkloric studies, a bridge represents a boundary space where frequently a pair of male and female *dōsojin* (traveler's guardian deities) is enshrined. In the case of hashihime (woman of a bridge), her grudge is deeper because she was enshrined alone without a partner (Tanaka, *Ayakashi kō* 38). The *Heike monogatari* version of Uji no hashihime, the topic of this chapter, is similar in that the woman is abandoned by her husband for another woman and the abandoned woman jumps into Uji River. But instead of killing herself, the woman in the *Heike monogatari* takes revenge aggressively.

The Uji no hashihime episode in the "Swords Chapter" of *Heike monogatari* goes as follows: during the generation of Raikō, people mysteriously began to disappear, and through divination it was discovered that in the reign of Emperor Saga (reign. 809–823) a certain noble woman, overcome by jealousy, goes to the Kibune Shrine. There, she prays for the Kibune deity to change her into an oni while she is still alive so that she can kill the woman with whom her husband has fallen in love. The deity answers her prayer and instructs her to change her appearance and to bathe for twenty-one days in the rapids of the Uji River. Pleased by the oracle, the woman changes her appearance as instructed: she divides her hair into five bunches and fashions them into five horns. She applies vermilion to her face and body, puts an iron tripod (*kanawa*) on her head and carries three torches. Late at night, as she runs out on the Yamato Avenue toward the south, those who see her are so terrified that they swoon and die. Thus she becomes an oni and is also known as Uji no hashihime. As an oni, she seizes the relatives of the woman who is the source of her jealousy, and of the man who rebuffs her, both men and women high and low. To kill the men, she changes into a woman. To kill the women, she changes into a man. As she murders many people, she becomes increasingly terrifying and consequently, after the hours of Monkey (3 p.m. to 5 p.m.) the people of the capital cease to visit each other; they firmly close and bar their doors and stay in their houses.[1]

---

[1] The story of "Uji no hashihime" is found in Asahara, Haruta, and Matsuo 517–19. For the texts of "Swords Chapter," see note 35 of chapter one. A similar story to "Uji no hashihime" appears in *Kankyo no tomo* (Friend of an Idle Life, 1212). A jealous woman becomes an oni, eating her lover who abandoned her, and other innocent people. The

In contrast to the passive Uji no hashihime of the Heian poetics who puts an end to her own life and is later enshrined, the *Heike monogatari*'s Uji no hashihime belligerently kills not only the people involved with her, but innocent people as well. Interestingly, she takes the lives of people in and around the capital, which brings us back to the story of Shuten Dōji.

Uji no hashihime vs. Shuten Dōji

Shuten Dōji's killers, Minamoto no Raikō and his *shitennō* have long been associated with stories about conquering supernatural creatures. In addition to Shuten Dōji, they also subjugate *tsuchigumo* (earth spiders), which are, as we shall see in detail in chapter eight, considered a variant of oni. Watanabe no Tsuna (953–1025), a leader of Raikō's *shitennō*, also features prominently in oni stories. As discussed in chapter one, Tsuna cuts off an oni's arm at Modoribashi Bridge in the Heian capital. Their stories are widely known through Noh, Kabuki, *otogi zōshi,* and *kusa zōshi*. With the exception of Shuten Dōji, it is commonly known that a major source for these stories is the section describing the Raikō's generation in "Swords Chapter" of *Heike monogatari*. Shuten Dōji, who is associated with Abe no Seimei, Raikō and his *shitennō*, does not appear in "Swords Chapter." Indeed, the main source of Shuten Dōji is unknown. Or is it? Close examination of various texts shows some remarkable similarities between the narratives of Shuten Dōji and the "Swords Chapter"—specifically the opening section of Shuten Dōji and that of an Uji no hashihime episode of the "Swords Chapter." In chapter two, we saw a variety of possible origins for Shuten Dōji and the Shuten Dōji legend. Could Uji no hashihime, an abandoned woman who eats people in the capital, be one of the many sources of *Shuten Dōji*? Shuten Dōji could be a twin brother of Uji no hashihime, or Uji no hashihime herself at the beginning.

This conjecture is important in that oni are not only adept transformers but also gender-switchers as well. Uji no hashihime's episode is immediately followed by the Tsuna story in "Swords Chapter." This allegedly happens during the reign of Emperor Saga (reign 809–823) as a related incident of people's disappearance at the time of Minamoto no Raikō (948–1021). One logical interpretation of these two narratives is that the disappearance of people at Raikō's time is caused by the lingering Uji no hashihime's

---

woman uses candy to fashion her hair into five horns. She also wears red trousers and runs away at night. For the text of this episode, see Taira et al. 422.

evil spirit, who has since lingered on earth. This means that the oni who attacked Tsuna was female, although Tsuna's story does not mention oni's gender. The oni's arm Tsuna cut off, which he thought was as white as snow, turns out to be ebony-colored, packed with earth-like white hair. It is a masculine arm. Interestingly, in the Noh play, "Rashōmon," whose foundation is the Tsuna's episode in "Swords Chapter" of *Heike monogatari*, the oni appears as a male. This indicates that an oni can shed its gender, becoming genderless. Of course, oni can also be androgynous. What this speculation highlights is the very issue of oni and gender identity to wit that as spiritual beings that switch readily between male and female, oni have no essential gender and any attempt to assign one is a metaphysical venture at best. The extent to which a particular oni is characterized as masculine or feminine is then largely contextual and says more perhaps about cultural influences on a given narrative than anything particularly inherent in the oni.

Let us look at the opening passages of the Uji no hashihime episode and the texts of Shuten Dōji. They are remarkably similar, using comparable language. First, both episodes begin with the disappearance of people. In both cases, numerous people *strangely* begin to disappear, using the same word, *fushigi* (strange). The backdrop of the time during which the incidents occur is a close match: in the generation of Minamoto no Raikō (948–1021) for *Heike monogatari;* and during the reign of Emperor Ichijō (reign 980–1011) for Shuten Dōji. Second, in both stories, the disappearances during Emperor Ichijō's time are followed by the retrospective description of people vanishing during Emperor Saga's reign (r. 809–823). Among the texts of Shuten Dōji, *Ōeyama Ekotoba* does not have this retrospective section, but by Shuten Dōji's own confession, he was active at the time of Priest Dengyō (d. 822), i.e., during Emperor Saga's reign. In both stories, after having people deliberate on the situation it is discovered that the culprit is an oni—one is Uji no hashihime and the other, Shuten Dōji. Third, Uji no hashihime and Shuten Dōji share an association with the color red and an oni-like appearance. Uji no hashihime divided her hair into five bunches and then put turpentine on them to fashion them into five horns. Then she applied vermilion to her face and cinnabar to her body. She is a horrific five-horned, red oni. Likewise, Shuten Dōji has five horns on his head and a red body.

It is quite possible that these remarkable similarities in setting and language are just a coincidence, or the authors of *Shuten Dōji* refer to the Uji no hashihime episode, adding more elements to Shuten Dōji's passages to give rhetorical flourishes. Yet, if Shuten Dōji has some relationship to the Uji no hashihime's narrative described in "Swords Chapter," it then suggests that an oni's gender is indeed a matter in flux. As mentioned earlier, the episode of Uji no hashihime is immediately followed by the story of Modoribashi Bridge where Tsuna cuts off an oni's arm, indicating that the masculine oni was in fact the lingering evil spirit of Uji no hashihime. As if to confuse the matter more, this "female" oni looking like a male appears in the narrative of Shuten Dōji in the Shibukawa version as one of Shuten Dōji's right-hand "men," Ibaraki Dōji. In the Noh play, "Rashōmon," which is based upon the Tsuna's episode, the oni is a male. While oni can change their gender as they wish, the authors/narrators also contribute to cross gendering to suit their stories, and this is perhaps more telling than anything else. In chapter one, I mentioned that the label oni was applied to the supernatural possession of ordinary household objects brought on by age. Named *tsukumogami*, the abandoned old household objects bear grudges against people.[2] Household objects do not have gender in Japanese. If a gender-less object can become an oni after it ages, it stands to reason that an oni can become gender-less after it ages as well.

Sociopolitical Space for Gendered Oni

What is interesting about the gender switching of oni is the different space and scope that each oni as male or female occupies. Put simply, Shuten Dōji, a masculine oni, occupies public space whereas Uji no hashihime of *Heike monogatari*, a female oni, resides in private and personal space. Shuten Dōji is marginalized by hegemonic authority when he is deprived of his living space. His resentment is both public and political; it is aimed at the court and the Japanese people at large. He does not choose his targets at random, he kidnaps the Kyoto maidens—daughters of the ruling class—albeit for his personal pleasure as well as for his sustenance. From this the arch demon derives his power in the world and because of this the emperor orders the courageous warriors to eliminate him. The head of Shuten Dōji—a symbol of his formidable opposition to the central authority—is stored in the regent treasure house as a status symbol, and importantly, the head becomes a source of nourishing power for the Heian capital. In contrast, a female oni, the Uji no hashihime described in the *Heike monogatari*, is marginalized by

---

2   For a discussion of *tsukumogami*, see Rambelli 211–258; Reider "Animating Objects"; Lillehoj 7–34; Tanaka *Hyakki yakō no mieru toshi*; Komatsu Kazuhiko *Hyōrei shinkō ron*, 326–342.

her husband, a private person. Her jealousy targets individuals—specifically her husband and the mistress to whom her husband's love shifts. Her unleashed fury that results in the killing of numerous innocent people in the capital and has everyone else locking their doors and hiding, is less a public act than a warning against the danger of women entering the public sphere. Also, in spite of her vicious attacks, no public imperial command for her subjugation is issued, as if to emphasize the private origins of her acts.[3] While there it may be true that the Uji no hashihime of Heian poetics is enshrined at the foot of Uji Bridge, this is not so much a public act, as an act of concealment. In any case, it is no match for the treatment of Shuten Dōji whose head becomes a public treasure stored in the prestigious treasure house of Uji. Uji no hashihime occupies private space without political involvement.

Noh *Kanawa*: Lingering Affection of a Spurned Woman

The point of spurned women occupying private space becomes more acute in the story of the Noh play entitled *Kanawa* (attributed to Zeami Motokiyo [1363–1443]), which uses the episode of Uji no hashihime in *Heike monogatari* for its base. Noh's *Kanawa* consists of two acts: with no mention of disappearing people, the first act starts with a woman's nightly visit to the Kibune Shrine. She prays for the Kibune deity to change her into an oni while she is still alive so that she can kill her former husband who abandoned her for a new wife. While the woman professes to still love her husband, she is consumed by grief and jealousy. The deity answers her prayer, and through a shrine attendant, instructs her to change her appearance and fill her heart with anger. She is instructed to apply vermilion to her face and wear red clothing, put an iron tripod on her head and carry three torches. In the second act, her ex-husband visits Abe no Seimei's residence to have his bad dream divined. According to Seimei's oneiromancy, his ex-wife is

---

3   Later in *Kanawa* of the *otogi zōshi* version (the late 16th to early 17th century), an imperial decree to subjugate the female oni is issued almost at the end of the story like an afterthought. Receiving the decree, instead of going out himself, Raikō dispatches his men, Watanabe no Tsuna and Sakata no Kintoki, with his treasured swords. In the face of Raikō's swords, the oni surrenders, promises to protect Japan, and disappears into the water. The same oni appears in a woman's dream later and begs to have a shrine built for her. *Otogi zōshi*'s *Kanawa* is an amalgamation of Noh *Kanawa*, *Taiheiki* and the *Rashōmon* episode of the "Swords Chapter." The complex plot grafts several plots one after another. In this later story, the shrine built for the oni plays a part in the auspicious ending rather than the oni-woman's power. For the text of *Kanawa* of the *otogi zōshi* version, see Yokoyama and Matsumoto, 3: 451–62.

cursing him and he is going to die that night. In response to the man's pleas, Seimei performs a ritual to save his life. Seimei makes two life-size dolls representing the man and his new wife, in an attempt to transfer his former wife's curse to the effigies. When the oni-woman appears in the room to kill her husband, various deities summoned by Seimei prevent her from exacting her revenge. After she fails and proclaims that she will wait for her revenge, she disappears.[4]

It is poignant that, although through divine help the Noh protagonist successfully becomes an oni and plots to kill her husband for abandoning her, she still cannot extinguish her feelings for him. While she is determined to destroy him, she cries, "Why did you abandon me?" She is a pathetic and empathetic figure with uncontrollable passion. Indeed, the very unreasonableness of her action comes to define her agency within the play. Some audiences may find solace or inspiration in the story of an abandoned woman who takes action rather than endure her suffering; some, however, may even prefer Uji no hashihime for her non-discriminatory, all-out killing sprees.

Unlike Uji no hashihime, the woman in the play fails to kill her husband because of the intervention of Abe no Seimei. It should be noted that in the story of Shuten Dōji, Abe no Seimei was at his public residence protecting the Heian capital against Shuten Dōji, whereas in the play, Seimei is at his private residence protecting one man who has had a bad dream because of the abandoned woman's curse. Symbolically, as if to underscore the societally mitigated power of the woman in *Kanawa*, the scene in which she attacks her husband occurs in the private confines of a bedchamber. Thus it is political disappointment, resentment, and rage against a public entity that drives the plot in stories about male oni, while jealousy, shame and grudges involving love affairs that serve as the driving force in stories about female oni. It may be reasonable to speculate then that the reason the female oni of Uji no hashihime becomes the male oni of Shuten Dōji is exactly to maintain this divide between public male role and private female role as the tale evolved over time from the personal to the political.

Uji no hashihime is born of the spite she has towards the man who abandoned her; and in that sense, she is considered a spiritual descendant of Yomotsu-shikome discussed in chapter one. These stories issue warnings to men in the then-polygamous Japanese society not to cheat on their wives.

---

4   For the Japanese text of *Kanawa*, see Sanari, 1: 703–714. For an English translation, see Kato.

Conversely, that living women can turn irreversibly into hideous oni stands as an imperative for women to rein in their unruly emotions and passively accept the *status quo*. In this sense, a female oni may seem little different from evil spirits (*mononoke*) appearing in such classical Japanese literature as *Genji monogatari*. Notably in *Genji monogatari*, the spirit of Rokujō Lady leaves her living body because of her anger, jealousy and/or stress, and attacks and kills her rival mistresses—the cause of her angst. Haruo Shirane writes that "*mononoke* become a dramatic means of expressing a woman's repressed or unconscious emotions, particularly [in expressing] the jealousy and resentment caused by polygamy" (114). A noteworthy difference between Rokujō Lady and Uji no hashihime is, however, that the former is morbidly concerned about her decorum and her spiritual transgressions are quite unintentional. Uji no hashihime is, on the other hand, extremely conscious of her action. She prays to the Kibune deity with great intensity to become an oni; when she is told to change appearance and run down the main avenue of the capital as an oni, she carries the order out without hesitation. Decorum is clearly not her concern. Indeed, when a female becomes an oni, stereotypical feminine decorum goes out the window. Uji no hashihime goes on an all-out killing spree in public space, and yet, as I have shown, her actions remain within the private realm of a marital relationship as presented in the Noh play, *Kanawa*. Whereas the irrational comes to define the interactions of female oni in *Kanawa* and Uji no hashihime, the interplay between male protagonists and male oni in Shuten Dōji is one of political intrigue. On certain levels, in Shuten Dōji it is simply a matter of who deceives and kills whom first and, at least as far as the struggle for political power is concerned, there is little question about the rationality of the struggle itself.

4

Yamauba, the Mountain Ogress
Old Hag to Voluptuous Mother

JEALOUSY AND SHAME ARE OFTEN INTRINSIC CHARACTERISTICS of fierce female oni who exact revenge against the men and/or women causing their undying angst. As we saw in chapter three, Uji no hashihime as described in "Swords Chapter" of *Heike monogatari* and the Noh *Kanawa* are good examples.[1] Yet, some female oni are relatively detached from the jealous emotions stemming from heterosexual relationships, and yamauba (literally mountain old women) are prime examples of this.

The medieval Noh text aptly entitled *Yamamba*[2] describes "yamamba (yamauba) is a female oni living in the mountains."[3] Indeed, even now, to many contemporary Japanese, the word "yamauba" conjures up images of an ugly old woman who lives in the mountains and devours humans. The witch in the Grimm Brothers' *Hansel and Gretel* and Baba Yaga of Russian folklore can be considered Western counterparts of the yamauba figure. The *Konjaku monogatarishū* depicts one such yamauba in the story titled "Sanseru onna minamiyamashina ni yuki oni ni aite nigetaru koto" (How a Woman Who Was Bearing a Child Went to South Yamashina, Encountered

---

1   For the Japanese texts of "Swords Chapter," *Heike monogatari*, see Asahara, Haruta, and Matsuo 3: 514–47; Mizuhara 1: 59–88. For an English translation, see A. L. Sadler, 1921: 325–354. For the Japanese text of *Kanawa*, see Sanari, 1: 703–714. For an English translation, see Kato

2   The same kanji as yamauba, but pronounced as yamamba.

3   See Yokomichi and Omote 279. For the Japanese text of *Yamamba*, see Yokomichi and Omote 275–87. An English translation is found in Brazell 207–25. In Noh, there are five types of plays categorized according to the role of *shite* (the lead actor). These categories are plays that focus on gods, warriors, women, mad persons and demons 鬼. The play *Yamamba* is categorized as a demon play.

an Oni, and Escaped).⁴ A young pregnant woman secretly gives birth in the mountain hut of a seemingly kind old woman, only to discover that the old woman is actually an oni with plans to eat her newborn baby. The image of the yamauba is, however, complex. Commenting on the medieval Noh play, *Yamamba*, Karen Brazell calls the yamamba character "an impossible bundle of contradictions" (207). By the end of the seventeenth century, the oni in the story has come to be considered the mother of Kintarō, a legendary super-child raised in the mountains. Kintarō is the childhood name of Sakata no Kintoki, one of Raikō's *shitennō* who, as we saw in the previous chapter, helps eliminate Shuten Dōji. Also by this time, the theme of motherhood in the yamauba legend comes to the forefront, as exemplified in the Kabuki/Puppet play entitled *Komochi yamauba* (Mountain Ogress with a Child, 1712) (see Chikamatsu, *Chikamatsu jōruri shū* 177–226). And in a complete inversion of imagery, in the late Edo period, yamauba comes to be portrayed as an alluring and seductive woman who, far from contemplating infanticide, is quite attached to her son, as exemplified in the works of Kitagawa Utamaro (1753–1806).⁵

This chapter examines the sea change in the representations of the yamauba from the medieval period through the early modern period. These changes reflect a coterminous change in people's social expectations of oni in general and the yamauba figure in particular. Yet, oddly yamauba's status as marginalized "other" remains the same, strongly associated in particular with the two groups of strangers or others discussed in chapter two, i.e., those "strangers who are native to the community but shunned by community members," and those who "live spatially far away from a community, and are thus known to the community through their imagination" (Komatsu Kazuhiko, "Ijin ron –'ijin' kara 'tasha' e" 177–78).

Cannibalism

Let us return our attention to the medieval yamauba who is described in the Noh text as "a female oni dwelling in the mountains." The archetypal yamauba figure appears in the story from the *Konjaku monogatarishū*. Alone and ashamed of her condition, the young pregnant woman journeys deep

---

4   For the Japanese text, see Mabuchi et al. 38: 54–58. An English translation is found in Ury 161–163.

5   Reproductions of Utamaro's art are found in *Ukiyo-e Masterpieces in European Collections*, vols. 7 and 9; Narazaki and Kikuchi, *Masterworks of Ukiyoe: Utamaro*.

into the heavily wooded mountains to give birth in secret. She comes upon a dilapidated hut where she encounters an elderly, white-haired woman who offers her assistance. Lured by the old woman's kind words, the pregnant woman stays and gives birth in the hut. A few days later, however, she discovers that the old woman is actually an oni with plans to eat her newborn baby. The old woman in the story is termed oni rather than yamauba (the first appearance of the word "yamauba" is in the Muromachi period [1336–1573][6]) but she is considered a prototypical yamauba, because she is an old woman with white hair living in the mountains, ready to devour humans who happen to cross her path. As we have seen, because she is an oni, cannibalism is one of her principal occupations.

The cannibalistic aspect of yamauba is underscored in many folktales including *Ushikata to yamauba* (Ox-Cart Puller and Mountain Ogress). In this tale, a yamauba attempts to devour anything she can obtain. First, she demands fish from a young man carrying fish in his ox-cart. After consuming all the fish in his cart, she demands the ox and after devouring the ox, she sets her sights on eating the man. He flees from her and soon comes upon a lone house in the woods that turns out to be the yamauba's dwelling. Eventually he vanquishes the yamauba with cleverness.[7] Although the yamauba in *Ushikata to yamauba* is portrayed as destructive, these figures are not always entirely negative or destructive. Since, as we have seen, oni are also harbingers of wealth, yamauba have some positive aspects as well. In some versions of this tale, such as one collected in Miyagi prefecture, her corpse turns into carrots ("Ninjin no okori"), thereby bringing some benefit to humans ironically in the form of food.

---

6 The word "yamauba" does not appear in the *Wamyō ruijushō* (Japanese Names for Things Classified and Annotated; ca. 930s) or the first Japanese language dictionary, *Ainōshō* (1446). However, the *Nippo jisho* (*Vocabulario da Ligoa de Iapam com a declaração em Portogues*), compiled by a Jesuit missionary and published 1603–1604, has an entry for *yamauba* which reads "the face of the yamauba is not known. They are believed to live in the mountains" (Doi et al. 809). Komatsu Kazuhiko notes that the first appearance of yamauba in literary materials occurred in the Muromachi period (Kaisetsu, 428). Interestingly, the *Wakan sansai zue* (1713), an encyclopedia, explains the yamauba as an animal that lives in the regions of Guangdong and Guangxi in China, which has only one leg with three toes and three fingers on each hand, and which begs for food from people at night. The author, Terashima Ryōan, mentions nothing about any Japanese yamauba.

7 For a Japanese text, see Yanagita, *Nihon mukashibanashi meii* 109–13; Seki, *Nihon no mukashibanashi* 1: 155–161. For an English translation, see Mayer, *The Yanagita Kunio Guide to Japanese Folk Tales* 107–110; Seki, "Types of Japanese Folktales" 44.

In another folktale entitled *Tentō-san kin no kusari* (Golden Chain from Heaven), a yamauba comes to a house in the mountains to eat children while their mother is away. She eats the baby, but its siblings narrowly escape her by climbing up a golden chain sent from heaven. She pursues them, climbing another rope sent from heaven, but slips and plummets into a field of buckwheat. Her blood turns the buckwheat red.[8] While in this story the death of the yamauba does not produce any specific food, her blood is credited with creating the redness of buckwheat, providing a supernatural connection to a certain aspect of that food.

Yamauba as Great Mother and Nurturer

In stark contrast to yamauba's representation in "Sanseru onna minami-yamashina ni yuki oni ni aite nigetaru koto," other tales represent yamauba as a nurturing character, and actually associate the image with motherhood.[9] Hori Ichiro writes, "In the popular belief of rural areas, the mountain deity is believed to be a goddess who gives birth to twelve children every year. She is therefore called Mrs. Twelve (Jūni-sama), and her twelve children symbolize the twelve months of the year" (*Folk Religion in Japan* 167). According to Ōshima Tatehiko, the mountain deity was probably originally male. The female in the story was there as his subordinate, to serve the mountain god and to give birth to his divine children. Consequently, she came to be revered as a goddess by association ("Yamauba to Kintarō" 52). Indeed, in the fifteenth century, the Zen priest, Zuikei Shūhō (1391–1473), recounts in his diary *Gaun nikkenroku* that a yamauba gave birth to four children. "The reason why the summer of that year had lots of rain was because yamauba gave birth to four children, namely, Haruyoshi (Good Spring), Natsusame (Summer Rain), Akiyoshi (Good Autumn), Fuyusame (Winter Rain)" (125). The year's abundant rainfall, the priest suggests, is the result of yamauba's multiple childbirth. Indeed, the quality of the four seasons is implicit in the children's names and reflects a simultaneous expression of reverence to a higher power and hope for good seasonal weather to come.

---

8 For a Japanese text, see Seki, *Nihon no mukashibanashi* 3: 113–15. An English translation is found in Seki, *Folktales of Japan* 54–57.

9 As Ōshima Tatehiko writes, there are many legends and associated sites that tell of the yamauba giving birth to a child or children and raising him or them ("Yamauba to Kintarō" 51).

An interesting parallel appears in a folktale that describes a yamauba giving birth to a baby boy. In this story titled "Yamauba hōon" (Miyazaki Kazue 428–30), the yamauba comes to a married couple in a village and asks for shelter while giving birth, which the sympathetic couple gives her. After the safe birth of her baby, the yamauba asks the couple to name the baby as well as her other nameless children. The couple feels honored, and names the first child, Natsuyoshikō (Good Summer), the second, Akiyoshikō (Good Autumn), and the third one, Fuyuyoshikō (Good Winter)—names very similar to those in the *Gaun nikkenroku*. The yamauba rewards the couple with two boxes—a magical box that produces abundant gold and a box filled with yarn.[10] Here, the yamauba as an oni-woman is clearly a bringer of wealth. As Yoshida Atsuhiko points out (*Mukashibanashi no kōkogaku* iii, 108–112), the roots of the yamauba can be found in various female deities in Japanese myth such as Ōgetsuhime in *Kojiki* (712) and Ukemochinokami in *Nihongi* (720), who produce food from different parts of their bodies.

The identity of the yamauba is thus complex and contradictory: a dichotomous primordial goddess, the Great Mother, who brings fertility and wealth, as well as death and destruction,[11] similar to other mythico-religious figures such as the Egyptian Isis and the Hindu Kali. In medieval Europe, the pagan archetype of the Great Mother always possessing two aspects is no less complicated as it falls under the hegemony of Christianity: the light side is represented by the officially-worshipped Virgin Mary, and the dark side, excluded from the image of Mary and maintaining much of its pagan influence, degenerates into a witch (Franz, *Shadow and Evil in Fairy Tales* 105, 195).[12] Witches, like oni, are typically known for their propensity for cannibalism (Jacoby et al. 201). This trait is shared with yamauba who is labeled as an oni in the aforementioned story from *Konjaku monogatarishū* as well as in other Japanese folktales.

---

10 Yanagita recounts a story of a family living on a mountain that finds a yamauba's *tsukune* (a ball of hemp yarn [dialect word]), which produces infinite yarn. The *tsukune* makes the family rich, but soon after the young wife gives birth to an oni's child with two horns ("Yama no jinsei" 240).

11 Kawai Hayao regards Kannon as the positive Great Mother, and the yamauba, who appears in fairy tales as an all-devouring mountain witch, as the negative image. See Kawai, *The Japanese Psyche*, particularly chapters two and three.

12 Marie-Louise von Franz interprets the witch in two of the Grimm Brothers' fairy tales, *The Two Brothers* and *The Golden Children*, as an archetypal figure of the Great Mother and an archetype of the unconscious. Franz, *Shadow and Evil in Fairy Tales* 104. Also see Jacoby et al. 205–206.

From the viewpoint of gender studies, Mizuta Noriko considers yamauba as gender transcendent. She contrasts yamauba with the women of the village (*sato*). The *sato* was considered a safe place where people were protected and insulated from the various dangers of the mountains. According to Mizuta, the women of the *sato* are idealized and standardized—they are good mothers, good wives, chaste, humble, and obedient to their fathers and husbands (10–12). Conversely, yamauba is someone who falls distinctly outside the norm. Although she is often excessively fertile, she lacks the feminine traits ascribed to the women of the *sato*, namely, chastity, obedience, and compassion. Yamauba defies the norm for the *sato*'s women, for her essential qualities are so complex, nebulous and multivalent that she nullifies traditional gender roles. In other words, yamauba exists outside the *sato*'s system of gender normativity. She refuses to be assigned a household role such as mother or daughter and will not be territorialized. Mizuta emphasizes that while the women of the *sato* stay in one place, yamauba are comparatively nomadic, moving constantly through the mountains, appearing in an array of locales, often outside or away from a town's territorial boundary (10–15).

An excellent literary example of yamauba living on the periphery or margin of a common boundary appears in the *otogi zōshi*'s "Hanayo no hime" (Blossom Princess, ca. late Muromachi period to the early Edo period; see Yokoyama and Matsumoto 10: 530–31). Here the yamauba, formerly human, has survived her own children. Disliked by her grandchildren, she is subsequently expelled from their house. With nowhere to turn, she goes to live in the mountains. Indeed, this yamauba is the quintessential other, a "native to the community but shunned by the community members," in this case, her very family. Yanagita writes that "yamauba" and "yamahime" (mountain princess) were originally euphemisms used by villagers to explain a mysterious woman living deep in the mountains ("Yama no jinsei" 255). As we saw in chapter one, those who were alienated from mainstream society were sometimes considered oni. Many such outsiders were not actually evil, but, as we have seen, simply differed enough from the hegemonic norm, in appearance, age or lifestyle to rouse suspicion or derision.

The representation of yamauba that exerts the most significant influence on later representations is the medieval Japanese Noh *Yamamba*. Compared with yamauba in *Konjaku monogatarishū* or "Hanayo no hime," the Noh yamamba (yamauba) is more enigmatic and self-reflective. In the play, a courtesan or entertainer (*tsure* or companion) and her troupe, famous for their yamamba dance, meet the real yamamba (*shite* or lead actor) on the mountain. She describes herself to them as being "with birthplace unknown, lodgings uncertain" who, "dragging good and evil [with her], makes her mountain rounds."[13] Baba Akiko considers yamauba legends representative of the downfall of the *kunitsukami* (deities of the land). Popular during the medieval period, the Noh play *Yamamba* is shrouded by overlapping religious and philosophical subtexts such as "the good and evil are not two; right and wrong are the same" (Brazell 207). The core concept of the Noh *Yamamba* is the transcendental philosophy of non-dualism epitomized in the Heart Sutra (*Hannya shinkyō*), perhaps the best-known Wisdom literature of Buddhism. From the point of view of the statement that "form is nothing other than emptiness, emptiness is nothing other than form" (shikisoku zekū, kūsoku zeshiki), the existence of Buddhas, human beings and/or yamauba is miniscule within the vastness of time and space.[14] This yamauba is a seeker of enlightenment, and would wander the mountains until her delusions ceased to exist, in order to escape the wheels of painful rebirth.

The Noh yamamba has supernatural power to darken the sky so that the courtesan or entertainer is forced to spend a night at her lodging and perform a yamamba dance. She is, at the same time, a lonely old woman who helps humans with their chores—assisting woodsmen and weavers by shouldering their work burdens. During the play, the audience learns that yamamba indeed has human feelings; she is very sensitive to her own image—an image created as she lives "spatially far away from a community, and [is] thus known to the community through their imagination." She is ashamed as well of the old tale about an oni eating a maiden in one gulp, and asks a group of entertainers to spread her side of the story to people in the capital. This naïve side is not so surprising, because Zeami (1363–1443), to whom the authorship is generally attributed, considered that the human derivation of demons was important in the portrayal of demons. In the treatise titled *Sandō* (The Three Ways, 1423), one of the *hiden* (secret transmissions) written exclusively for the writer's successor(s), Zeami notes that in composing demon-plays (to which *Yamamba* belongs), the character should have "the form of a demon and the heart of a person."[15] Zeami rejects any

---

13 Translation by Karen Brazell. Brazell 220–221. For the Japanese text, see Yokomichi and Omote, *Yōkyokushū* 284–285.
14 See Baba 284. For the English translation of the *Heart Sutra*, see LaFleur 82–83.
15 Translation by Shelley F. Quinn. Quinn, "How to Write a Noh Play: Zeami's Sandō" 79.

representation of a demon that "has the form of a demon and the heart of a demon," because this type of demon "precludes the possibility of audience empathy" (Quinn, "How to Write a Noh Play: Zeami's Sandō" 80–81). The Noh yamamba seeks to help people in her striving after salvation, and sings, "Let the vibrant strains of your music and dance serve as a Buddhist sacrament for then I, too, will escape from transmigration and return to the blessed state of enlightenment."[16] Zeami's depiction (or endowment) of a humane yamauba seems to have helped pave the way for more sympathetic portrayals of the Japanese mountain ogress.

Image of Yamauba in the Medieval Period

During the medieval period, the yamamba remains, physically, a wrinkled old woman with a huge mouth, round eyes, and (disheveled) white-hair (the *shite* wears a large white headpiece).[17] *Yamamba* was the fourth most frequently performed piece during the period between 1429 and 1600 (Nose 1314). Its popularity suggests that the visual image of the yamauba it portrays could very well have influenced the general image of the yamauba in the medieval period: ugly, old, and often regarded as evil, as in the *Konjaku monogatarishū* story. It is of interest to note that if we relocate the yamauba from the mountain to the *Sanzu* river, which divides this world and the next, she looks very much like the terrifying *datsueba*, a hag who mercilessly strips the clothes off the dead. Similar to the yamauba in the *Konjaku monogatarishū*, the *datsueba* is harmful to human beings, and like the yamauba of "Hanayo no hime," she personifies old age, ugliness and infertility (due to her advanced age). The Noh yamamba is concerned with Buddhist cosmology. While the *datsueba* is referred to as "ōna no oni" (old female oni), Kawamura Kunimitsu writes that she too has a dichotomous aspect—she strips clothes off the dead but gives clothes before the birth of human being—and so is a goddess of birth and death ("Onna no jigoku to sukui" 35–37). This dichotomous nature is also suggestive of the yamauba.

---

16 Translation by Karen Brazell. Brazell 213. For the Japanese text, see Yokomichi and Omote, *Yōkyokushū* 279.

17 The yamauba in "Hanayo no hime" brings wealth to the princess who helped kill the coiling worms in the yamauba's hair, but she also has a grotesque appearance. Her face is square, "her eyes sank deep in her head but her eyeballs protruded nevertheless. She had a big mouth, the ends of which almost touched the edges of her nose. That nose resembled a bird's beak and her forehead was wrinkled up; her hair looked as though she had recently worn a bowl on her head."

Although *datsueba* is not associated with images of a mother of many children, could it be that the representational similarities of these women, popular in the medieval period, become entwined with each other, strengthening the trend toward the yamauba's unfavorable visual representation?

Orikuchi Shinobu writes that the yamauba was originally a virgin consecrated to a mountain deity. The maiden nursed the deity to health and later became his wife. These mountain women tended to live long lives, and so the idea of "nurse" (*uba*) came to be associated with elderly women ("Okina no hassei" 363). By the end of the medieval period the yamauba was widely accepted as a frightening-looking old woman with an affinity for human flesh. In stark contrast, she was also known as a compassionate and caring mother of divine children or ones with supernatural powers.

Yamauba in the Early Modern Period: Mother of Sakata no Kintoki

At the beginning of the ensuing Edo period (1600–1867), the yamauba came to be considered the mother of Kintarō, the child name of Sakata no Kintoki (ca. tenth century).[18] Sakata no Kintoki is one of the famous *shitennō* of Minamoto no Raikō, whose feats are discussed in chapter two. Behind the creation of the fictional childhood account of Kintoki is the popularity of stories and plays about Shuten Dōji. *Shuten Dōji* was recited as jōruri (performances with musical accompaniment) from the beginning of the Edo period when the jōruri repertoire was not yet largely established. The earliest extant jōruri's *Shuten Dōji* was published in 1625, and the entry of 1638 of the *Kabuki nenpyō* (Kabuki Annals) notes that *Shuten Dōji* was popular in Edo society as an auspicious piece (Torii, *Dentō to Geinō* 49–52).[19] The stories of Shuten Dōji in the medieval period describe Raikō as the chief of warriors, but in the jōruri piece of the Edo period, he is elevated to being the "protector of the land" and "head of the force maintaining order in the capital" (see, for example, Muroki, *Kinpira jōruri shōhon shū*, 1: 429). This change in status is probably attributable to the fact that the image of Raikō had been superimposed on that of the Tokugawa shogun, who claimed to be head of the Minamoto clan. It should be noted that the creation of *Kan'ei shoke kakeizu-den* (Genealogy of the Lords of the Kan'ei,

---

18 Regarding the birth of Kintarō and his changing images, see Torii, *Kintarō no tanjō*.

19 For the earliest extant jōruri text, see Yokoyama 1: 456–57.

1643), which linked the Tokugawa genealogy to that of the Minamoto clan, greatly helped heighten interest in the ancestors of that clan. Minamoto no Mitsunaka (or Manjū, 912–997), Raikō's father who had built the base for Minamoto power, was so idealized that it is said Tokugawa Yorinobu (1602–1671), the founder of the Kii branch of the Tokugawa, ordered in his will that his tombstone be placed beside that of Mitsunaka in the inner sanctuary of Mt. Kōya (Itagaki 422, 439). Admiration for Raikō, as a brave warrior and conqueror of supernatural creatures, meant admiration for the Tokugawa shogunate.[20] The theme of *Shuten Dōji*—that of courageous good conquering evil, reinforced by the image of the shogunate eliminating its enemies, was certainly auspicious.

From the narrative of Raikō and his *shitennō* came the jōruri stories of their children, the so-called "Kinpira jōruri." Kinpira jōruri were popular in the 1660s, and extant literary texts reveal that they give some of the earliest Edo literary depictions of yamauba. They describe how Kintoki's fictional son Kinpira and his fellow warriors pacify insurgents through not only brute force, but also intelligence (Torii, *Dentō to Geinō* 6). The first extant play (or piece of literature) in which the children of Raikō's four lieutenants make their appearance is *Shitennō musha shugyō* (Military Training of the Four Lieutenants), dated 1659.[21] In the second play, Tsuna and Kintoki die (the other two were already dead), and their children—the young *shitennō*—play a more active role in the tale. Muroki Yatarō indicates that around 1659 or 1660 there was a dramatic increase in the popularity of youth culture among patrons of jōruri, and Kinpira was probably born out of this trend (*Katarimono no kenkyū* 455).[22]

---

20   See Muroki, *Katarimono no kenkyū* 442–43; Torii, *Dentō to Geinō* 50–51. Regarding censorship, edicts against the treatment of current events in books were issued in 1684. A later edict issued in 1722 prohibited heterodox or pornographic writings. Writings that negatively reflected upon the house of illustrious samurai, or that questioned the authority of the Tokugawa house were similarly banned (Hamada Keisuke 35–37). The effect of these edicts was that any criticism of society, however minor, could be prohibited on the grounds that it was a criticism against the Tokugawa house or the powerful daimyo. It is not difficult to surmise that the writers of jōruri *Shuten Dōji* would have been careful in their descriptions of the ancestors of the Tokugawa family, even though such edicts were not yet issued.

21   See Muroki, *Katarimono no kenkyū* 447, and *Kinpira jōruri shōhon shū* 514.

22   In the Kabuki theater, too, right after the New Year's Kabuki performance in 1660, *shitennō* repertoire became suddenly popular. Kabuki's *shitennō* repertoire focused more on the young *shitennō*, the children of Raikō's original four lieutenants. The basic qualification of Kabuki aesthetics at that time was the physical beauty of the

According to Torii Fumiko, *Kinpira tanjō-ki* (Record of Kinpira's Birth, 1661) is the oldest extant description of Kintoki as the son of yamauba (Torii, *Kintarō no tanjō* 32)—a boy raised in the mountains, who later goes on to become one of Raikō's *shitennō*. It should be noted that the relationship between the yamauba and Kintoki is not established in the earlier *shitennō* (i.e., Raikō's lieutenants) series; rather, it appears that the character of Kinpira was soon so popular it became necessary to clarify his genealogy. *Kinpira tanjō-ki* states, "Kintoki is Yamauba's son. One year Raikō received Kintoki from an oni-woman (i.e. yamauba) in the mountain, and Kintoki entered into the master-vassal relationship" (Muroki, *Kinpira jōruri shōhon shū* 1: 192–211). Similarly in *Kintoki miyako-iri sukune no Akutarō* (Kintoki Entering the Capital, [Struggle of] Akutarō, 1664). Kintoki is said to be the yamauba's son:

> One year, Raikō wrongfully received an imperial remonstration because a high-ranking official, Kiyohara Takafuji, spread lies about him to the emperor. His life in danger, Raikō went into hiding on Mt. Ashigara. There, a yamauba doing her mountain rounds appeared out of nowhere, and gave him her child (Kintoki). Since then, (Kintoki) served Raikō and (Kintoki) became one of his four lieutenants.[23]

Today, the Japanese take it for granted that the yamauba dwells on Mt. Ashigara in Kanagawa prefecture, but it is interesting to note that this was not the case before the early modern period. Examining various jōruri texts, Torii surmises that a folk belief holding Kintoki to be the son of a yamauba must already have existed at the beginning of the Edo period (*Dentō to Geinō* 8). It could be, however, that the narrator or authors connected the two (yamauba and Kintoki) for the purposes of augmenting literary drama and furthering the intergenerational story line. Indeed, Kintoki's birth as the son of a yamauba may have been added for both dramatic and technical reasons—to explain his son Kinpira's unusual physical strength, as well as to ensure a compassionate perspective of Kintoki to draw audience empathy. What is significant about this creation is, however, more than mere literary creation in that Kintoki, an oni's child, helps kill Shuten Dōji and other famous oni. It is an oni that slays other oni. This is the same paradigm we

---

young male, and Muroki writes that the stories of young *shitennō* suited the Kabuki trend well (*Katarimono no kenkyū* 447).

23 Muroki, *Kinpira jōruri shōhon shū* 2: 147. For the text of *Kintoki miyako-iri sukune no Akutarō*, see Muroki, *Kinpira jōruri shōhon shū* 2: 147–75.

saw in chapter two that Minamoto no Raikō, the killer of oni, is related to oni himself through the thunder god.

The *Kinpira tanjō-ki*, announcing Kintoki to be the son of yamauba, goes on to explain how Kinpira's mother was actually a giant serpent disguised as a beautiful woman. This is an interesting twist in Shuten Dōji's birth story. According to one text that describes the birth of Shuten Dōji, he was born of a beautiful human female and a god of Mt. Ibuki, previously a giant serpent.[24] In fact, Kinpira too is described as an oni child when he was born after being in the womb for five years; he had "a red-face, disheveled, upright hair, ... [and] a big mouth slit from ear to ear" (Muroki, *Kinpira jōruri shōhon shū* 1: 194–95). This supernatural portrayal is a fitting foreshadowing and explanation of his extraordinary physical strength, not to mention his single-minded stubbornness. Satake Akihiro notes, giving examples including super-powerful Benkei (1155–1189)[25] as the oni's child in *Benkei monogatari* (Tale of Benkei), that an abandoned oni child growing up by himself on the mountain is a very fitting origin and backdrop for a hero with extraordinary prowess (*Shuten Dōji ibun* 28–34). Although Kinpira is not abandoned on the mountain, he does, by virtue of birthright, possess super physical strength. Since Kintoki is the son of a female oni, Kinpira would likely be an oni as well—a red-skinned one. In the second act of *Kinpira tanjō-ki*, after Kintoki's wife reveals her identity as a serpent and prepares to take her leave, Kintoki implores her to stay because as a son of a "female oni," Kintoki understands her emotional needs. More importantly, Kintoki's human-like emotion and compassion invites empathy (and tears) from the audience. Sakata no Kintoki is known for his red skin color today. I surmise that Kinpira's popularity as an impetuous brave young man could have been a major reason why Kintoki is, in the reverse order, considered to have great strength, a tempestuous childhood in the mountains, and red skin, just like Kinpira in *Kinpira tanjō-ki*.

In the illustrations of the early Kinpira jōruri, *Mida hachiman no yurai* (Origin of Mida Hachiman, 1659 or 1660) the face of Kinpira is portrayed the same way as his fellow lieutenants, without beard or grim features, though Muroki Yatarō notes that Kinpira's countenance becomes increasingly grim and frightening as time passes (*Kinpira jōruri shōhon shū* 1: 527). I suspect

---

24   See "Ibukiyama Shuten Dōji" in Yokoyama and Matsumoto, 2: 358–65.

25   Benkei is a historic monk warrior of great strength from the time of the Genpei wars and a legendary figure.

that before the birth of Kinpira, Kintoki was considered to be simply one of *shitennō*, a man of ordinary birth (or more precisely, nobody cared about his birth). There is hardly any historical evidence of Sakata Kintoki.[26] The lack of an official historical record allowed later playwrights and authors writing about Kintoki greater latitude for imagination. The belief that Kintoki was a yamauba's son was probably established and reinforced through representations of Kinpira, Kintoki's fictional son. Bakhtin suggests:

> The work and the world represented in it enter the real world, enriching it, much as the real world enters the created work and impacts it, as part of the natural process of its creation. Thus, there is a continual renewing of the work through the creative perception of listeners and readers. (*The Dialogic Imagination* 254)

Thus a later fictional representation comes to color an earlier "historical" one, creating its own historical truth in the process.

Regarding the connection between the legends of Raikō and *shitennō*, and those of the yamauba, Minamoto no Raikō and his four lieutenants have long been associated with valor in conquering demons and other supernatural creatures. The belief in their relationship with the supernatural makes more plausible the belief that Kintoki is the son of a mountain god and/or yamauba (Torii, *Kintarō no tanjō* 8). Indeed, for people living in Edo-period Japan, the perceived potency of supernatural beings was widely held and the supernatural was seen as a plausible extension of day-to-day reality. The supernatural was also used to explain or rationalize the extremely gifted. Superhuman abilities were sometimes attributed to birth,[27] though Izawa Banryō (1668–1730) asserts in the 1715 work *Kōeki zokusetsu ben* (A Refutation of Vulgar Legends for the Benefit of the Public) that the widely held belief that Kintoki was the offspring of a union between a mountain god and yamauba was false, fabricated to make Kintoki's birth more mysterious (185). The mere fact that Izawa felt compelled to produce an extended

---

26 Vol. 28 of *Konjaku monogatarishū* tells a story about Sadamichi, Suetake, and Kintoki getting car sick, and vol. 9 of *Kokon chomonjū* (ca. 13th century) mentions Kintoki as a messenger. Other than these, and the stories about Shuten Dōji, there is hardly any mention of him.

27 One example is a story entitled "Sotōba no ko o umu koto" (A Stupa Giving Birth to a Child) in *Otogi monogatari* (Nursery Tales, 1660). The work tells the story of an actor (*waki*) named Hazama who was supposedly born from the *stupa* of his dead mother. Hazama's remarkable acting skills were attributed to his special birth. For the text of "Sotōba no ko o umu koto," see Takada, 1: 82–85.

treatise to argue the falsehood of the literary account of Kintoki's origins reveals the extent to which such beliefs were prevalent and stubbornly held among the masses.

A little more than a decade after *Kinpira tanjō-ki*, the yamauba in *Kiyohara no udaishō* (Kiyohara, General of the Right, 1677) is still described as an "old woman" who asks Raikō to take her son into his service.[28] The yamauba tells her child not to consider her his mother anymore, because she is looking for release from the perpetual cycle of rebirth. Linking the yamauba with the Buddhist concept of rebirth is reminiscent of the Noh yamauba, who does her mountain rounds and then mysteriously disappears into thin air. But unlike the Noh character, the yamauba here is the mother of the super-child, Kintoki, already sixteen or seventeen years old. *Kinpira nyūdō yama-meguri* (Lay-priest, Kinpira's Mountain Round), published in the early 1680s, portrays the yamauba as Kinpira's grandmother, ten-feet tall, with white hair and carrying the oni's signature iron staff, and says she "has received supreme supernatural power, travels through the three-thousand realms and, as she continues her mountain rounds, travels to the sky over the clouds. She is called the oni-woman" (see Muroki, *Kinpira jōruri shōhon shū* 3: 144–62). She also tells Kinpira that when he exerts his extraordinary strength, she is helping him, as his protector. The dialogue of the Noh *Yamamba* influences Kinpira jōruri texts. The yamauba's countenance is still old and scary, but her supernatural power is now used to protect her grandson. She is a family woman, and there is no further mention of her cannibalism. Indeed, there is no trace of the voracious yamauba of the *Konjaku monogatarishū* or spurned women of "Hanayo no hime" in the yamauba of the Kinpira jōruri. While they talk about Buddhist karmic causation in the manner of the Noh yamamba, they are simply mimicking the respected Noh text, without its deep religious meaning. After Kinpira has been rescued and told that the yamauba's support in this *ukiyo* (floating world) is behind his prowess, the story of *Kinpira nyūdō yama-meguri* goes on without further reference to the yamauba. Given the widely held perception in the medieval period that the yamauba was the mother of many children or super-children, it seems logical and unsurprising then to find her conveniently "popping up" in early modern texts as the mother of a strong warrior who conquers demons. Also given the time of the publication, close

---

28 Muroki, *Kinpira jōruri shōhon shū* 1: 494. For the text of *Kiyohara no udaishō*, see Muroki, *Kinpira jōruri shōhon shū* 1: 477–502.

to the vibrant Genroku era (1688–1704) when Ihara Saikaku (1642–1693) wrote "human beings are bewitching apparitions" (19) in his *Saikaku shokoku banashi* (Saikaku's Tales from Various Provinces, 1685), it is not surprising that the jōruri yamauba have been somehow stripped of their religious or philosophical aura.

During the Edo period, many intellectuals attempted to explain supernatural phenomena logically, with, for example, the theory of yin and yang. This helped take the religious aura away from inexplicable events. Yamaoka Genrin (1631–1672), a widely recognized intellectual of his day and author of the work entitled "Kokin hyakumonogatari hyōban" (An Evaluation of One Hundred Strange and Weird Tales of Past and Present, 1686) explains the yamauba as "an evil spirit of mountains and rivers," underscoring the negative side. He goes on, "… but that *uba* is more like what we call tatsutahime (goddess of autumn) and yama-hime (princess of the mountains)" (46). It is interesting to note that this early modern scholar seems to completely conflate the representations of yamauba and *datsueba* that we examined earlier in this chapter. Genrin notes the dichotomous nature of yamauba, and the name yama-hime (Princess of Mountains) does conjure up the image of a youthful woman. This is reminiscent of Yanagita's observation mentioned above that yamauba and yama-hime were originally euphemisms (used by villagers) for a mysterious woman living deep in the mountains. Genrin writes, "Yamauba is narrated in the Noh piece as associating with weaving and spinning" (46). While the influence of Noh is mentioned, he does not refer to the yamauba as the mother of Kintoki.

Several years later, *Zen-taiheiki* (Chronicle of Pre-Grand Pacification, 1692?), a popular historical narrative widely read throughout the Edo period, describes yamauba as an old woman, a little over sixty years of age. She explains to Raikō that about twenty-one years ago, when she was sleeping atop Mt. Ashigara, she dreamt that a red dragon made love to her. Jarred awake by a sudden clap of thunder, she found herself pregnant, and soon after, she bore a supernatural child. Now in the present, Raikō, on his way to the capital, has found the super-child on Mt. Ashigara, named him Sakata Kintoki and made him one of his four lieutenants (*Zen-taiheiki* 325–328). It is worth noting how the yamauba was impregnated. From the descriptions in both the *Zen-taiheiki* and the *Kōeki zokusetsu-ben*, Takasaki Masahide delineates that the birth of Kintoki is based upon a belief in a thunder god, noting that a red dragon is the symbol of the thunder god; Kintoki's red skin color and the axe he carries point to Kintoki's father being a thunder god (13–43). Takasaki also writes that for ancient people, *kami* (deity) meant *kaminari* (thunder). This reminds one of Kondō's theory about the oni's origin being thunder and lightning, and also, as discussed in chapter one, Orikuchi's conjecture that in ancient times there may have been no clear demarcation between an oni and a *kami*. Both were "awesome" beings, although the oni may not have been worshipped. Thus, yamauba is, as are many oni, related to thunder and lightning. Further, *Zen-taiheiki*'s explanation goes along with Orikuchi's explanation of the yamauba being the wife of a mountain deity. Understood by many as a female oni, the yamauba seems to compensate for her evil nature by giving birth to a super-child who ultimately conquers oni.

Zen-taiheiki is also significant in that it places the yamauba in a specific location. As mentioned earlier, Mizuta emphasizes the yamauba's nomadic nature, which refuses to be territorialized as she moves constantly through many mountain regions. Now associated with Mt. Ashigara, she has become more static, and a step closer to the life of the women of the *sato*. In this regard, Yanagita notes:

> Until the appearance of *Zen-taiheiki*, the main habitat of yamauba was not necessarily in Mt. Ashigara. Mt. Kintoki in Shinano province (Nagano prefecture) has caves where yamauba and Kintoki were purported to have lived, ponds where Kintoki took his first bath… and this is in accord to the old tale that the yamauba makes rounds of the mountains. But when the yamauba of Mt. Ashigara became the mother of Kintoki in *Zen-taiheiki*, this place alone became famous as the dwelling-place of the yamauba. ("Yama no jinsei" 248)

While there were precedents for the yamauba at Mt. Ashigara, it could be said that the popularity and wide distribution of *Zen-taiheiki* made the relation between the yamauba and Mt. Ashigara definitive. Further, according to Matsui Toshiaki, Chikamatsu Monzaemon (1653–1724) probably got the idea about the relationship between the yamauba and Sakata no Kintoki for his *Komochi yamauba* from the *Zen-taiheiki* (32–33).

Chikamatsu's *Komochi Yamauba* (Mountain Ogress with a Child)

One of the most important and influential yamauba in the Edo period appears in *Komochi yamauba* (Mountain Ogress with a Child, 1712), authored by Chikamatsu Monzaemon.[29] It is a jōruri/kabuki play with the familiar themes of love, revenge, and the substitution of a child. Its world is drawn from an amalgam of the tales of Minamoto no Raikō and his lieutenants, and of the yamauba. Chikamatsu modernized these tales, incorporating many up-to-date nuances, including a tobacco peddler and the conversational acumen of a famous contemporary *onnagata* (actor of female roles in the Kabuki theater). Such contemporary elements are often woven into Japanese folklore, especially in stories involving the yamauba. Chikamatsu gives us a new and rejuvenated yamauba on stage—the image of a youthful woman now performed by a male. The traditional yamauba, the old hag with disheveled hair, a solitary mountain-dweller who preys on unsuspecting human beings, has now become a youthful, beautiful, devoted wife and the compassionate mother of a super-warrior charged with killing evil demons. One of the oni's attributes is transformation power, and yamauba, therefore, can skillfully change her countenance for an urban audience.

Komochi yamauba is a five-act play. The first act introduces the great warrior Minamoto no Yorimitsu (a.k.a. Raikō) who takes into his protection a young couple, Koito and her lover, the man who avenged her father's death. However, the man whom the couple murdered had been under the protection of Takafuji, a high official, and as a result, Yorimitsu must go into hiding, since it is beneath Takafuji's dignity to have a man under his protection slain by someone in Yorimitsu's camp. To further complicate things, Takafuji is in love with Yorimitsu's fiancée, so framing Yorimitsu seems the best way of getting him out of the picture. While in hiding, Koito's lover becomes one of Yoritmitsu's *shitennō*. The second act, which is also known as "Shaberi yamauba" (Loquacious yamauba) or "Yaegiri kuruwa-banashi" (Story of Yaegiri in the Pleasure Quarters), introduces Sakata Tokiyuki, now in disguise as the tobacco seller Genshichi, and Yaegiri, a former courtesan.[30] Sakata/Genshichi is Koito's elder brother and Yaegiri's husband, but he has left Yaegiri to avenge his father's death. He does not know that Koito has already done so. Sakata/Genshichi and Yaegiri accidentally meet at the residence of Yorimitsu's fiancée. Under the guise of talking about her former life as a courtesan, Yaegiri tells him about Koito's successful strike and accuses

---

29 The play was first performed for *jōruri* in 1712. The first recorded Kabuki performance was 1714. For the text of *Komochi yamauba*, see Chikamatsu, *Chikamatsu jōruri shū* 177–226.

30 The second act is the only act performed today.

Genshichi of spinelessness. Genshichi is deeply ashamed and commits suicide, vowing revenge on Takafuji. As he dies, he swears to Yaegiri that, if he impregnates her, their future son will help Yorimitsu take revenge on Takafuji and also informs her (and the audience) that she will be superhuman from then on. He orders her to leave the worldly life so as to rear their unborn child in the seclusion of the mountains. Yaegiri immediately acquires superhuman power—an attribute of a yamauba—and reveals her prowess before leaving for the mountain by easily repelling encroaching samurai. The third act involves a substitution theme. Takafuji uncovers the location of Yorimitsu's hideout and demands his head from the man hiding him. To save Yorimitsu, the mother of Yorimitsu's stepbrother makes the ultimate sacrifice, killing her own son and giving his head to Takafuji. Subsequently, the mother's husband becomes one of Yorimitsu's four lieutenants. In the fourth act, Yorimitsu and three lieutenants (the original one, Watanabe Tsuna, and two who joined later) encounter the yamauba and her super-child on Mt. Ashigara. Impressed by the superhuman power of the child and well aware of the yamauba's wish, Yorimitsu names the child Sakata Kintoki and makes him one of his lieutenants. In the final act, Yorimitsu and his *shitennō*, including Sakata Kintoki, conquer the demons that were threatening the capital. As a reward, Yorimitsu's fiefdom is restored and he is promoted to be protector of all Japan. At the same time, the truth about Takafuji is revealed and he is finally punished.

Of the five acts, Acts Two and Four deal directly with the yamauba. The former describes the genesis of the yamauba and the conception of Sakata Kintoki, and the latter shows her as a mother of a super-child, a great warrior who helps conquer and vanquish the demons threatening the capital. The yamauba's speech to Raikō about her mountain rounds comes directly from the Noh *Yamamba*, but the story of Kintoki as a child of a yamauba comes from either the *Zen-taiheiki* or the Kinpira jōruri. Probably reflecting the time as well as the genre, Chikamatsu's yamauba carries little philosophical weight; unlike the Noh yamamba who explains the concept of non-dualism to a group of entertainers, Chikamatsu's yamauba simply reveals to Yorimitsu how she came to live on the mountain.

Of particular significance in Chikamatsu's yamauba is her noted previous life as a courtesan. According to Matsui Toshiaki, Chikamatsu made the protagonist of his play a former courtesan because the *tsure* in Noh's *Yamamba* was a courtesan/entertainer (33). Yaegiri is described as being very attractive, and even after she has become yamauba, she is called a "flower among firewood."³¹ Though Chikamatsu's yamauba is a beautiful and voluptuous woman, when the audience hears in the fourth act the word "yamauba," two horns pop up out of her scalp and her eyes sparkle. The sight is frightening but when contrasted with her subsequent behavior it is obvious that the Yaegiri-yamauba is non-threatening. She confesses her past to Raikō, inviting audience sympathy. Instead of eating Raikō, as a typical yamauba would do, she makes herself vulnerable to him. Yet another distinction of Chikamatsu's yamauba is her age. In contrast to the yamauba of *Zen-taiheiki* where she is described as being about sixty years of age, Chikamatsu's yamauba is relatively young. She also appears with Kintoki, who, though five or six years old, clings to her and begs to drink from her breast. The image of a mother humoring a small (super-) child is underscored, and this in turn greatly influences later art portraying the yamauba. Elements of the attractive yamauba may have existed previously, but Chikamatsu should be credited with having selected an attractive image of the yamauba, and disseminating this seductive image through the stage. His attractive motherly yamauba makes a good contrast with the predominantly old-hag image prevalent during the medieval period.

Chikamatsu's yamauba is also a wife. Since the yamauba is represented in folk belief as a mother of super-children, it is not strange that she should be portrayed as a wife. In the aforementioned "Kokin Hyakumonogatari hyōban," a column on the yamauba states: "People say that the yamauba abduct human beings. Sometimes she disguises herself as a wife" (Yamaoka 46). By the seventeenth century then, the idea that yamauba disguise themselves as wives was relatively common.

---

31   Ihara Saikaku also connects a stunning beauty to an old mountain hag in a short tale included in the aforementioned *Saikaku shokoku banashi*. In this case, she is not a real yamauba, but an old woman who *looks like* a yamauba because of her advanced age. When she was young, she was exceptionally beautiful, but her eleven lovers died one after another before she was eighteen years of age. After that, she remained single. Her profession was spinning, which reminds us of the Noh yamauba. As she grew old, she became less attractive and more frightening in appearance. This is probably why Saikaku called her "yamauba." She was shot to death by an arrow while stealing oil from a shrine. When the arrow cut off her head, the head flew in the air and blew fire. After that, anyone who saw the firing head passed out, and some even died (Ihara 142–144). The fire-breathing head is new to yamauba lore, although the character's evil side remains intact; causing men to pass out or die is indeed reminiscent of the older, more negative image of the yamauba.

The folktale "Kuwazu nyōbō" (The Wife Who Doesn't Eat) exemplifies the yamauba as a deceptive wife.[32] The story opens with the mutterings of a man to himself (in some versions, he mutters to a friend) about how he wants a wife who does not eat. Soon after that, a young woman appears at his house and declares that since she does not eat, she would like to be his wife. The man takes her in, and she becomes his wife. But this seemingly ideal woman turns out to be a yamauba who has a second mouth at the back of her head—a mouth with a ravenous appetite. When the man finds out the truth, the yamauba attempts to eat him whole—as yamauba are generally inclined to do. In contrast to this yamauba, Chikamatsu's is full of humility and conscientiousness. In fact, Yaegiri is more destructive before she becomes a yamauba. Instead of eating her husband, which may have been too fantastic for an Edo audience, her weapon of choice is shame; delivered in vitriolic bursts, it destroys her husband's self-esteem and eventually drives him to suicide. Unlike her counterpart in "Kuwazu nyōbō," her real identity is human—a former courtesan and an attractive wife. Further, similar to the Noh yamamba, Yaegiri possesses a human heart even after her transformation into a yamauba. In fact, she becomes a yamauba as a result of her husband's death wish, and by the same wish is impregnated with his child, the super-child—Sakata no Kintoki, destined by birthright to avenge his father's death and become one of Raikō's four lieutenants.

It is worthwhile to note that it is Genshichi's declaration that his soul will be reborn as a child to Yaegiri that impregnates her. Not only do his words transform his human wife into a yamauba, but they also impregnate her with a super-child. Masuda Katsumi points out that in folktales if one would express a wish in words the wish would come true (96). For example, in the aforementioned "Kuwazu nyōbō" when the man states aloud, "I want to have a wife who doesn't eat," a woman who claims not to eat arrives on his doorstep. The utterance of the words and their transformation into reality reveals the power of language. This is in accord with old Japan's *kotodama shinkō*, the reverence of the miraculous power of language (Masuda 96–97).[33] In Chikamatsu's play, Genshichi's declaration is sometimes accompanied by

---

32   For a Japanese text, see Yanagita, *Nihon mukashibanashi meii* 113–17; Seki, *Nihon no mukashibanashi* 1: 162–65. For an English translation, see Mayer, *The Yanagita Kunio Guide to Japanese Folk Tales* 110–114; Seki, "Types of Japanese Folktales" 45.

33 Kawamura Kunimitsu states that what Genshichi did to Yaegiri (entrusting her to avenge his enemy in his dying moment) is based upon *goryō shinkō*, appeasing of the avenging spirits of the dead ("Kintarō no haha" 402).

a green spirit flame coming out of his severed belly and flying into Yaegiri's mouth,[34] and in the later Kabuki version, Genshichi puts his entrails into Yaegiri's mouth.[35] But in either case, it is Genshichi's spoken desire that impregnates Yaegiri:

> Genshichi: Three days after my death, if you feel pain in your womb, know that my spirit has entered [your womb] and you will bear a child after ten months.
> Narrative: My soul will come back to this world again as a miraculous superhuman and destroy Masamori.
> Genshichi: You, too, will become a wondrous woman from today.
> Narrative: Live in deep mountains and raise the child.
> Genshichi: Take my soul into your body.
> Narrative: He pulled out his entrails and drew his wailing wife to his side. As soon as he put them into her mouth, he took his last breath ("Komochi yamauba" 77–78).

Genshichi's utterance endows Yaegiri with superpowers and makes her *komochi yamauba* (yamauba with child). This theme, the utterance of words that become reality, is both fundamental and prevalent in Japanese folklore as seen in *Kuwazu nyōbō*. Genshichi's utterance might be considered reflective of the true nature of performing arts, in that he had to verbalize his wish so the audience would understand it. Yet, this segment could easily have been allotted to the narrator/chanters, and Genshichi could have remained silent.[36] It is the power of language and spirit—an old rule of folklore—that magically renders Yaegiri pregnant with the future Kintoki, and through this single wish, she is transformed into a yamauba.

Meera Viswanathan writes "…in *Komochi yamauba*, the yamamba metamorphoses into an entirely different being, one lacking the awesomeness and alien nature of earlier avatars. Instead, she is first and foremost mother and wife, loving, loyal, and somewhat pathetic. Her demonic nature is not intrinsic to her, but merely an unfortunate outcome of her appropriation of

---

34   See Chikamatsu, *Chikamatsu jōruri shū* 198.
35   For a Kabuki text, see "Komochi yamauba."
36   In *jōruri*, a narrator performs both narration and dialogue. Although there is no strict rule, dialogue tends to be expressed in a more *kotoba* [speech] mode rather than a *ji* [dramatic singing] mode. Genshichi's words, "Three days after my death, if you feel pain in your womb, know that my spirit enters [your womb] and you will bear a child in ten months," is an exemplar of the *kotoba* [speech] mode.

male concerns. She must be sacrificed so that the larger issues of politics and moral justice may be played out" (252). If Yaegiri-yamauba possesses any demonic tendencies, they seem most evident when she is still human; her acts of jealousy and lust are part of her original human makeup. However, as evidenced particularly in Act Four, she does indeed possess a loving and caring nature. She is both maternal and loyal to her husband. This change, or evolution, in the yamauba's character partially reflects some of the social expectations of Japanese women of the time.

The Edo period is often referred to as a dark age for Japanese women (Hayashi 325), and women's social activities were extremely limited throughout the period (Fukuda 257). There are numerous references that support the supposition that Japanese women filled a subservient role to men and were held in low regard. For example, *Onna daigaku takarabako* (Treasure Box for Women's Great Learning, 1716), a popular handbook to educate women about their duties as women, states: "A woman's infirmities include a lack of submission, ill temper, resentfulness, jealousy, slander of others, and stupidity. Seven or eight out of ten women are afflicted with these infirmities" (46). Comparing women to *yin*, the book says, "*yin* is night and dark. In comparison to men, women are ignorant and do not understand things right in front of them" (54). Similarly, Confucian scholar Kaibara Ekken (1630–1714), detailed in the "Joshi o oshiyuru no hō" (Method of Teaching Women)[37] the Three Obediences, a popular maxim of the day regarding women's conduct: "A young woman obeys her father; a married woman obeys her husband; and a widow obeys her son" (12). A man could have a mistress if he wished, and divorce was essentially the unilateral prerogative of the husband. The ease with which a man could generally get a divorce was apparent in the brief divorce letter called a *mikudarihan* (three-and-a-half lines) written by the husband to announce divorce.[38] While a woman could own property, her dowry became her husband's upon marriage.[39] A three-and-a-half line divorce letter is exactly what Yaegiri received from her

---

37 "Joshi o oshiyuru no hō" (Method of Teaching Women) is Volume Five of *Wazoku dōji-kun* (Precepts for Children, 1710).

38 Takagi Tadashi asserts that the legal treatment of divorce among commoners clearly argues against the idea that women's status was vastly inferior to men's (Takagi, "Marriage and Divorce in the Edo Period"). Still, women's status was far from equal to men's.

39 However, upon divorce, money and land related to the dowry had to be returned to the woman, except in cases where the divorce was initiated by the wife or her family. See Nakada Kaoru 99–110, 140.

husband, Genshichi, so that he could avenge his father. Under these circumstances, it was expected that Yaegiri-yamauba be loyal to her husband. The *Onna daigaku takarabako* listed seven reasons for a husband to divorce his wife and one of them was "jealousy" (34). Jealousy caused Genshichi to be disowned, and Yaegiri herself to be thrown out of the pleasure quarters.

Acting on behalf of her dying husband and making his wish her own may have helped compensate for her impetuous behavior. The empowerment of women through verbal tact and supernatural strength only increased female audience appeal. No doubt many Edo-era women secretly yearned to act like Yaegiri but found themselves restricted by social expectations and conventions. Mizuta Noriko writes that, "one reason why yamauba could become a prototype for modern women's pursuance of self is that she inherently annuls such concepts as motherhood versus independence, and family versus work" (21). Thus the yamauba transcends this dichotomous perspective. In this respect, Chikamatsu's Yaegiri-yamauba seems to have melded the two dichotomous concepts into one character/stage persona. Moreover, Chikamatsu accomplished it without bringing the two seemingly opposing perspectives into conflict. In other words, while Yaegiri-yamauba possesses a fantastic prowess to overpower any man to destabilize social order, she is ultimately committed to realize her husband's wish and devotes herself to Kintarō as a woman was expected to behave in the contemporary society. Thus a potential threat to conventional social order is contained to keep equilibrium. In addition to the verbal and acting acumen of the actor who, ironically, would be a man, the audience would have been attracted to this character specifically because of the seeming conflict in her nature.

Another way of looking at the transformation of Yaegiri is spirit possession—Yaegiri becomes a yamauba by means of Genshichi's spiritual possession of her. Doris Bargen describes spirit possession in the *Tale of Genji* as "spring[ing] from a destructive impulse directed against male dominance," and goes on to explain that "appearing suddenly in a culture normally characterized by gentleness and indirection the disturbingly violent phenomenon of spirit possession can best be understood as a disguised form of female protest triggered by the psychological hardships of Heian polygyny" (6–7). An interesting point in Yaegiri-yamauba's case is that although the possessor is a male, the fundamental nature of the possession remains the same. Genshichi's shame and humiliation are triggered by his wife's logical verbal assault, and rather than continuing to live on in humiliation, he chooses to commit suicide. The possessed Yaegiri is, unlike the female role model of the time, an outspoken woman who openly expresses her emotion without any hesitation. In fact, she is not only outspoken but is also physically confrontational in pursuit of her lover in public. It appears that the Yaegiri-Genshichi spirit possession is a kind of *mitate* (allusion, analog), if not a complete parody of spirit possession of the Heian period. As someone possessed, and possessed by a male spirit at that, Yaegiri is not bound to social norms (though it does not mean that she acted according to them previously). Yaegiri-yamauba goes to the mountain where she attends to her child without any concern about social criticism. This may have appealed greatly to the Genroku audience.

The Alluring Yamauba

Chikamatsu's yamauba is extraordinary, for in his modernized tale, he successfully re-engineers yamauba into a seductive courtesan and motherly figure to whom Kintoki clings and cries, "I'm sleepy, Mommy. Give me some milk" (*Chikamatsu jōruri shū* 220). The yamauba's motherly aspect of *Komochi yamauba* gave birth to a Kabuki dance sub-genre called *yamauba-buyō* (*shosagoto*). Torii writes that the yamauba always appears as a beautiful woman in this dance piece (*Kintarō no tanjō* 67). The first yamauba dance piece in the present style is entitled *Shitennō Ōeyama-iri* (Shitennō Enters Ōeyama, 1785) (Kokonoe 257–258). In this work Segawa Jokō (1739–94), the author, amplified the yamauba's motherly affection for her child significantly with such phrases as "he is so dear to me… you may laugh if you want. Everything is for the sake of this child" (332–33).[40] The yamauba was performed by Segawa Kikunojō III (1751–1810), a very popular and well-known *onnagata*. It is easy to imagine how this Kabuki dance in which a beautiful yamauba declares her undying love for her child, performed by a seductive male actor a number of times, could have had some degree of influence on the ensuing ukiyo-e version of the alluring yamauba.[41] Kabuki actors were popular subjects of the ukiyo-e artists, with their images painted on posters much like present-day celebrities.

---

40 Kokonoe Sakon writes that this piece became popular because of its theme of motherly love (258).

41 In regard to the yamauba dance, Torii considers that the image of the beautiful yamauba of the ukiyo-e was reproduced on the stage. However, I suspect it was the other way around. The beautiful image of the *onnagata* dance on the stage is what probably influenced ukiyo-e.

During the Kansei era (1795–1801) yamauba was portrayed in ukiyo-e as an alluring, fully matured mother humoring Kintarō (Kintoki). Utagawa Toyokuni (1769–1825), for example, created *Momiji no sode nagori no nishiki-e* (a theatrical scene showing Yamauba and Kintaro, 1812).[42] The most famous ukiyo-e artist of the yamauba, however, is Kitagawa Utamaro, who produced about forty works on the theme of *Yamauba and Kintarō* (Shimizu Christine 231). His yamauba is loving and voluptuous with long black hair and white skin.[43] Motherly love is amply revealed in such prints as *Yamauba to Kintarō ennenmai* (Yamauba and Kintarō, dance) and *Yamauba to Kintarō genpuku* (Yamauba and Kintarō, coming-of-age).

Torii writes that a *kuro-hon* (picture book; literally "black books")[44] version of Chikamatsu's *Komochi yamauba* entitled *Kintoki osanadachi tsuwamono no majiwari* (Stories of Kintoki's Childhood, 1765) portrays the yamauba as an old woman, and points out that the yamauba in *kusa-zōshi* (illustrated storybooks) is depicted as demonic looking (*Kintarō no tanjō* 74, 87–88). In this light, Utamaro's yamauba is more of a descendant of Yaegiri on the stage rather than from picture books. His yamauba is an idealized woman, tall and slender, just like Yaegiri (an idealized woman performed by a male actor in Kabuki).

One of the reasons behind the production of a sensual, but less controversial yamauba was the need to avoid censorship. Rather than depicting courtesans, Utamaro portrayed the sexual image of idealized motherly figures through the yamauba (Ōkubo 257–58).[45] A mother and her child was a safe topic. But a closer look reveals that Utamaro's yamauba oozes sensuality. For example, in *Yamauba to Kintarō kamisori* (Yamauba and Kintarō, shaving hair), a tall yamauba carefully shaves Kintarō's hair, while her own hair remains unkempt and her breasts are partially revealed to spark sensual reaction in the viewer's imagination. Another example is *Yamauba to Kintarō chibusa* (Yamauba and Kintarō, breastfeeding). Kintarō is sucking his mother's

---

42 The work is found in Tanba (ill. no. 323).

43 Reproductions are found in *Ukiyo-e Masterpieces in European Collections*, vols. 7 and 9; Narazaki and Kikuchi, *Masterworks of Ukiyoe: Utamaro*.

44 Picture books about popular Kabuki/*jōruri* plays. They were called "black books" because of their black cover.

45 Matsudaira Sadanobu, upon becoming the senior shogun councilor, initiated the Kansei Reforms (1787–93) and strictly controlled people's morals and lives. Many novelists and artists who depicted pleasure quarters and/or related topics were punished. Utamaro was one of them; his hands were placed in chains for fifty days and it was probably due to the shock of the punishment that he died within two years.

Figure 5. *Yamauba to Kintarō ennenmai* (Yamauba and Kintarō, dance). Courtesy of the Royal Museums of Art and History—Brussels. Catalog number 116.

Figure 6. *Yamauba to Kintarō genpuku* (Yamauba and Kintarō, coming of age). Courtesy of the Royal Museums of Art and History—Brussels. Catalog number 113.

large breast while touching the other nipple with his hand. Her white skin with long unkempt hair reveals certain unrestrained and erotic beauty.

Utamaro, influenced by Torii Kiyonaga (1752–1815) in the portrayal of beauties, had great success through his creation of bust portraits (*Ōkubi-e*; literally "big-head-pictures"); a scary looking yamauba, advanced in age, would not suit this type of portrayal. His yamauba are women ideally portrayed, with sensuously arranged long black hair, small mouths and white skin. Utamaro has transformed the yamauba into a sensual mother and a commodity. These yamauba are "different" in the sense of their ethereal beauty, and are to be gazed upon and admired. According to Pavel Medvedev, this genre is "a specific way of visualizing a given part of reality. ... new genres reflect changes in real social life. Those changes lead to new views of experience and to different genres of speech, social behavior, and literature" (Morson and Emerson 275–77). It was thus a combination of social, political and commercial forces that helped give birth to the concept of the alluring yamauba. The yamauba as an oni woman is ever transforming.

The impression Utamaro's yamauba gave to the people in Edo society must have been considerable: Torii notes that, pre-Utamaro, the yamauba was portrayed in picture books as a scary looking oni-woman; after him, she came to be depicted as young and beautiful (*Kintarō no tanjō* 61–67). Indeed, there is great contrast between the beautified yamauba portrayed by Utamaro and those that came before him, including his teacher, Toriyama Sekien (1712–1788). Sekien depicts the yamauba in his *Gazu hyakki yagyō* (Pictures of Demons' Nocturnal Stroll) as a tired-looking old creature. Similarly Nagasawa Rosetsu's (1754–1799) yamauba, famous as a treasure of Itsukushima Shrine at Miyajima, is a white-haired old hag who looks suspiciously at the beholder. Their artistic renditions depict a skeptical- (or tired-) looking old woman with disheveled white hair, in other words, the familiar image of the medieval period. On one hand, the yamamba in Noh was performed with the old woman's mask and a white-haired wig, not generally regarded as a sexually attractive visage except in highly stylized Noh art. Also, in the countryside, where urban culture and vogue did not necessarily match the pace of their traditions, the yamauba probably retained much of their indigenous images, the fertile mother, lonely woman, or voracious hag, as local traditions dictated. On the other hand, for commercial appeal and to suggest eroticism without attracting the ire of the government censors, the yamauba in the jōruri/Kabuki theaters and ukiyo-e was portrayed in a sensuous manner, underscoring the sensuality of youth

Figure 7. *Yamauba to Kintarō kamisori* (Yamauba and Kintarō, shaving hair) Courtesy of the Royal Museums of Art and History—Brussels. Catalog number 117.

and motherhood. This urban and urbane type of yamauba was portrayed as sensual, yet, precisely because of her idealized representation, she was at the same time alienated from the audience living in culturally conservative Edo society. Thus, though now beautiful and sensual, yamauba remain nevertheless marginalized others as they "live spatially far away from a community, and are thus known to the community only through their imagination" (Komatsu Kazuhiko, "Ijin ron—'ijin' kara 'tasha' e" 178). The representations of yamauba vary with individual imagination. With the archetypal image of the yamauba as her base, she evolved as time passed.

5

Oni in Urban Culture
De-demonization of Oni

ONI IN EARLY MODERN JAPAN (1600–1867) remained relatively static in their representational attributes and their overall impact on social life, particularly when compared with the medieval period. The oni as a dark, enigmatic force threatening the central authority of the court retreated, by this period, into the cultural background. While the oni may have no longer troubled the councils of the imperial court, they thrived nonetheless in the minds of common people and remained visible in their literary and visual arts. In urban culture in particular, the oni flourished in the literary, visual, and performing arts as entertaining creatures. This chapter examines a general trend of de-demonization of oni in the Early Modern period and looks into an increasing tendency in more recent times toward commercialization and commodification of oni in urban cultures as seen in *Tōkaidō Yotsuya kaidan* (Yotsuya Ghost Stories, 1824), and *Kotō no oni* (Oni of a Solitary Island, 1929–30).

The Edoites' Belief System

The Edo period is an interesting time and space in Japanese culture in which individuals from all walks of life, on some level or other, seem to unite in their belief in the supernatural. Arai Hakuseki (1657–1725), a Confucian scholar, statesman, and rationalist, enumerates supernatural beings and strange phenomena with erudition in "Kishinron" (Theories of Demons and Deities), so much so that Yamagata Bantō (1748–1821), a townsman scholar, writes that "[Arai Hakuseki] believes in the strange and mysterious just as Buddhist priests do." Yamagata further comments, "even an erudite like Arai believes in the supernatural, let alone other people. There is nothing one can do about people's belief in and indulgence with the demons and deities" (516–517).

As late as 1860, at the closing of the Edo period, there is evidence to support the idea that this "supernatural threat" was never too far from the bureaucrats' and governors' minds for they knew the unknown was something they held very little, if any, control over. In preparation for a visit by the fourteenth Tokugawa shogun, Iemochi, officials posted an official warning to supernatural demons at Nikko that read:

> To the *tengu* [flying goblin] and the other demons: Whereas our shogun intends to visit the Nikko mausoleums next April: Now therefore, ye Tengu and other demons inhabiting these mountains must remove elsewhere until the shogun's visit is concluded. (qtd. in Figal 78)

While it is unlikely that all government officials believed in the supernatural, the aforementioned document demonstrates state recognition of the supernatural at the highest level. At the same time, this passage suggests that even demons are subject to the shogun's rule. Soon, the shogunal power yielded to the emperor with the Meiji Restoration. Most noteworthy, the formation of the Meiji Restoration was significantly influenced by an intellectual whose beliefs were strongly rooted in the supernatural. Hirata Atsutane (1776–1843) was an influential scholar of *kokugaku* or "nativism," an institution that began in the seventeenth century for the philological and exegetical study of Japanese classical literature. Atsutane's aim of study was to clarify the cultural and spiritual uniqueness of Japan through his belief in the supernatural. This desire is emphasized in many of his works, including *Kishin shinron* (New Theories of Demons and Deities, 1820) and *Kokon yōmikō* (Strange Creatures of Past and Present, 1821). In another work *Senkyō ibun* (Report from a Different Realm, 1822), Atsutane's firm belief in the supernatural seems to solidify as he recounts his interview with a boy who claims to have met *tengu*.[1]

Nakamura Hiroaki writes that edification of the intellectuals based upon Zhu Xi philosophy's yin and yang rationalism became fairly common in the early modern period, though it did not change the general population's fundamental folk beliefs or superstitions (333–34). For example, Yamaoka Genrin (1631–1672) explains in "Kokin hyakumonogatari hyōban" (An Evaluation of One Hundred Strange and Weird Tales of Past and Present, 1686) about the oni as follows:

---

1   For the texts of *Kishin shinron*, *Kokon yōmikō*, and *Senkyō ibun*, see Hirata 17–60, 71–358, and 361–604 respectively.

> Heaven and earth, mountains and rivers, trees and grasses, water and fire, stones and dirt, all sentient beings are yin-yang. The work of *yang* is called kami, and the work of *yin* is named oni. ... Since all the bad and evil belong to *yin*, the souls of wicked people are called oni. ... their [wicked] souls have nowhere to go and nobody worships them. So they linger in the air and cause various problems [to humans]... Shuten Dōji did not necessarily eat humans, but he is called oni because he overestimates his own prowess, goes against imperial authority and Buddhist teachings, and does evil-doings. ... The oni that ate the lady near the Akuta River was said to have been the Chief Councilor of State, Kunitsune. (13–14)

Genrin attempts to provide an operational definition of what a so-called oni is. To the modern reader, this explanation does not seem to rationalize the existence of the oni because *yin* alone does not explain why oni should linger in the air. Yet, Genrin's students who asked the question seemed to find his answer quite acceptable. With this increasing trend toward intellectualization and rationalism, the awe and fear previously associated with oni seem to have significantly lessened. Not surprisingly, making the supernatural comical, parodying them, and even sexualizing them became fashionable in some circles, especially in urban areas.

De-demonized Oni

By the middle of the seventeenth century, Yamaoka Genrin had already expressed that Shuten Dōji was an evil human rather than a supernatural creature called oni. For the general population, however, perhaps Chikamatsu Monzaemon contributed more significantly to the de-demonization of the awesome chieftain of oni, Shuten Dōji, just as in the case of yamauba. Shuten Dōji had already spoken of his personal life and showed a naïve side in the previous era, as we have seen. But Chikamatsu Monzaemon's Shuten Dōji is quite like a human and becomes a pathetic creature. In the play titled *Shuten Dōji makurakotoba* (Shuten Dōji Pillow Words, 1708), Shuten Dōji confesses:

> My mom's affection was so deep that she nursed me till I was ten years old. As I was sucking her bosom all day long, I couldn't forget the taste of my mom's milk...even after I went into the mountains, I sneaked into the bedroom of the priests' pages to suck their bosoms... eventually I was sucking lifeblood, forgetting the taste of milk... before I knew, my heart turned into the real oni. ...Even a heavenly being's pleasure will be run out once, let alone the oni's. What kind

of suffering will I receive? ...When you return home, please hold memorial services for the thousands of those I murdered. (*Chikamatsu zenshū* 6: 78–80)

Although murdering thousands of people as the legend goes, Shuten Dōji regrets his evil deeds, asking for the salvation of his victims. More remarkably, he misses his mother's milk. As we saw in later yamauba tales, the themes of motherhood and maternity are invoked to make the demon more sympathetic, and arguably, human. It is also interesting to note how this tale, just like the earlier Shuten Dōji tales, bears the stamp of carnival as mother's milk and lifeblood appear in carnivalesque flux. This is a far cry from Shuten Dōji as the great enemy of imperial authority.

Kusa zōshi's *Shuten Dōji kuruwa hinagata* (Shuten Dōji's Model for the Pleasure Quarters) goes further and presents Shuten Dōji and other oni as comical fools (see Saitō Mikihiro 58–69). In this story, Shuten Dōji orders his cohorts to abduct courtesans from the pleasure quarters of Yoshiwara, Shimabara, and Shinmachi[2] to create his own pleasure quarter. In the older *otogi zōshi*'s *Shuten Dōji*, the residence of Shuten Dōji was called the Iron Palace—an imposing azure palace with rows of roofs and bejeweled screens within which the abducted young women served the oni. For the Edo people a gorgeous dwelling with many beautiful women ready to serve men was easily associated with the pleasure quarter, a major fixture in urban culture. Thus, the Iron Palace was smoothly replaced (or *mitateru*/alluded) by the pleasure quarter (Saitō Mikihiro 70–71). Shuten Dōji in the pleasure quarter does not consume human flesh and blood; he just becomes intoxicated with real sake. Instead of Raikō rescuing the abducted ladies, the kidnapped cunning beauties escape by themselves. The oni are completely duped by the women, one even places his tiger-skin loincloth in a pawnshop to pay the courtesan for her service; the oni are a laughing stock.

Oni's de-demonized image eventually became popular as a souvenir, too, as seen in Ōtsu-e (Ōtsu pictures)—folk paintings produced in and around Ōtsu town in the Edo period. Philosopher and the founder of Japan Folk Crafts Museum Yanagi Sōetsu (1889–1961) writes that Ōtsu paintings "represent folk art in its purest form" (qtd. in McArthur 12). The most well-loved figure in the entire Ōtsu-e repertoire is called *oni no nenbutsu* (oni intoning the name of the Buddha), which depicts a praying oni dressed

---

2   Yoshiwara in Edo, Shimabara in Kyoto, and Shinmachi in Osaka were the pleasure quarters designated by the Tokugawa shogunate.

in the Buddhist priest's garb with a gong around his neck, a striker in one hand and a Buddhist subscription list on the other. As McArthur comments, an oni as a Buddhist priest seems contradictory, for the oni who is considered to be evil strives for Buddhahood itself. Some of the "inscription to the paintings warns against superficial appearance of goodness, while others suggest that even the most evil beings can be saved by Buddhism" (30). The depicted image of an oni in Buddhist garb is quite humorous and friendly. Ōtsu town is one of the fifty-three stations of Tōkaidō (Eastern Sea Route) connecting Edo and Kyoto. Undoubtedly, the praying oni were popular souvenirs for the traveler who journeyed on to Tōkaidō. As Juliann Wolfgram notes,

> At a time when the image of *oni no nenbutsu* became an invitation for prospective buyers of Ōtsu-e, it is clear that the original spiritual nature of the demon had been thoroughly transformed by the secular wit and humor of the age. Whereas the belief in oni has never been completely lost in Japan, its fearsome supernatural powers have been superseded by its parody of human frailties. (101)

Some oni receive both eerie and artistic treatment in the fictional world. For example, Ueda Akinari (1734–1809), a poet, scholar, physician, and fiction writer, published the renowned tales of the supernatural entitled *Ugetsu monogatari* (Tales of Moonlight and Rain, 1776). Among the nine short stories, two tales in particular, "Kibitsu no kama" (Cauldron of Kibitsu) and "Aozukin" (Blue Hood) describe oni vividly and frighteningly more in line with a traditional oni image. In "Cauldron of Kibitsu," excessive jealousy transforms an exemplary wife into an oni, causing her to brutally terminate her husband's life and that of his mistress as well. Akinari wove the scenes and diction from the *Tale of Genji* into the "Cauldron of Kibitsu," evoking courtly elegance in the middle of gruesome fate.[3] In "Blue Hood," a revered Buddhist monk falls from grace because he has become a pederast, obsessed with his young catamite. When his catamite dies prematurely, he takes to cannibalism to satiate his terrible loss, and turns into a barbaric oni. Only upon encountering a revered mendicant priest are the pederast's previous carnal obsessions re-directed toward his own salvation. While frightening to the villagers, Akinari's narrative reveals the oni's pathos; Akinari's oni behave as the traditional image of oni would,

---

3   For the analysis of the "Cauldron of Kibitsu," see chapter four of Reider, *Tales of the Supernatural in Early Modern Japan*.

and one should not forget that Akinari was well aware his literary products would be read mostly by urbanites.

Chikamatsu's humanized Shuten Dōji and *oni no nenbutsu* exemplify de-demonized oni, and they both also represent the image of oni as commodities. Indeed, the supernatural becomes increasingly commodified in urban Edo culture, as we have already seen in the portraits of voluptuous yamauba in chapter four.

Commercialization and Urban Culture: Oni as an Example of *Yōkai*

As mentioned in chapter one, oni are the *yōkai* with the most negative associations. Oni in earlier times occupied special, dominant topos of their own. Yet in the Early Modern period oni are just one of many *bakemono* (phantom/shape-shifter/monsters) or in more modern terms, *yōkai* (hobgoblins/monsters).[4] Concerning the bifurcation of the *yōkai* phenomena at the end of the Edo period Adam Kabat observes:

> [T]he major difference between *yōkai* in folk beliefs and those of urban culture is that the latter is purposefully created and sold as a commodity.... The publisher who sold *bakemono* came up with various strategies.... For example, at the time of the carnival side-show if a publisher would print books of related subjects, the book would become an advertisement for the carnival side-show and vice versa.... Those who came to Edo took *bakemono* books back to their hometowns as souvenirs. There certainly would have been a re-importation of *yōkai*, that is, *yōkai* born of a local legend were recreated through urban culture and went back to the countryside as a new form of *yōkai*. The *yōkai* of these media were disseminated widely from urban areas to the countryside. ("'Sōsaku' to shite no yōkai" 146)

Similarly, Melinda Takeuchi notes:

> [A]s the Edo townsmen became more sophisticated and cynical, they became less credulous. Records of supernatural hoaxes perpetrated on the public indicated that in the tough-minded atmosphere of

---

4   Inoue Enryō (1858–1919), a thinker and educator of the modern period, disseminated the term *yōkai* in his attempt to enlighten the Japanese masses about the identities of *yōkai*. The term *bakemono* was used in the early modern period. Komatsu Kazuhiko, "Yomigaeru Kusazōshi no bakemonotachi" 232. For the study of *yōkai*, see Foster, *Pandemonium and Parade*.

nineteenth-century urban life, as opposed to the rural environment…
The carnival side-show atmosphere that often accompanied the Edo-period experience of the supernatural no doubt brought about a certain degree of de-mystification. (12)

Indeed the Edoites' proud saying goes, "Buffoons and *bakemono* live beyond Hakone," (*yabo to bakemono wa Hakone kara saki*) meaning that there is no room for buffoons and *bakemono* in the city of Edo.

In the environment of urban culture, especially in a literary genre called *kibyōshi* (yellow covers),[5] parody becomes full-fledged to entertain its audience. Adam Kabat writes that no writer can surpass Jippensha Ikku (1765–1831) in terms of depicting *bakemono* as entertaining creatures, and adds that his secret is to portray *bakemono* in the "reverse world." For example, in the "reverse world," a groom aims high and wants to marry an ugly woman (*Edo bakemono sōshi* 18). Similarly in "Kaidan mikoshi no matsu" (Ghost Stories of the Long-neck, 1797), a human baby born to a ghost mother and a monster father suffers because of his anomalous appearance from the viewpoint of monsters. His mother wants him to be monstrous both in looks and behavior so that he will be accepted in her world.[6] In another *kibyōshi* by an anonymous author titled "Bakemono chakutō chō" (Record of Various Monsters, 1788), an oni becomes just one of many *bakemono/yōkai*. In this short booklet, a number of *bakemono* appear one after another, and a red oni shows up at the end of all *bakemono* with a caption that reads "red oni, eating a baby." This page is followed by the final page in which the red oni is subdued by Asahina Saburō, a powerful warrior of the early thirteenth century. The caption on the final page states, "there Asahina Saburō jumps in and subjugated various demons, so demons are all eliminated. In this present world, there is no frightening thing. Honorable children, stand firm and please go to tinkle without fear" (48). It has long been a given that oni are certain to be defeated by strong warriors. In *Shuten Dōji makurakotoba*, Chikamatsu Monzaemon even has Hōshō declare:

---

5   Sumie Jones writes that *kibyōshi* is "the most conspicuous case of narrative subversion…. Edoesque subversiveness surfaces in the juxtaposition of word and image. Parodies of an earlier genre of children's books, pictorial and verbal texts in *kibyōshi* interact with each other, mixing classics with contemporary fashion and the blurring of established categories such as the public and the private or the high and low of theme and diction, as well as the collapsing of words into images" (Jones 56).

6   See Kabat, "Bakemono zukushi no kibyōshi no kōsatsu."

It's a business of *yamabushi* to subjugate shape-shifting demons. It is not rare for the Buddhist monks to pray to do the same. The warriors' fame is to destroy the imperial court's enemy, which are more frightening than oni, and to achieve the distinguished service to capture them alive and leave the honor to the posterity. (12–13)

To the warriors then, oni were no longer so frightening because humans—specifically samurai with various regulations, rituals, and privileges—became ever more terrifying to the lives of common people. The rigid class system created by the Tokugawa shogunate limited people's opportunities and places for most activities. Outcasts and performers were confined in certain areas and people's movements and behavior were constantly supervised. Under these circumstances, belief in the existence of oni became increasingly difficult (Aramata and Komatsu 85). For urban residents, oni were the creatures of literature and art, not an immediate threat to their day-to-day existence, whereas samurai with two swords and various political and social benefits could actually endanger their lives and livelihood.

The appeal of "Bakemono chakutō chō" is mirrored in artwork that explores the variety of *yōkai*. Edo artists produced various types of *yōkai hyakutai zu* (pictures of one hundred forms of *yōkai*) and *Hyakki yagyō zu* (pictures of night processions of one hundred demons). The most famous of these is Toriyama Sekien's (1712–1788) *Gazu hyakki yagyō* (1776).[7] Sekien's *Gazu hyakki yagyō* presents various *yōkai* of folk belief as in an encyclopedia. Hence, he portrayed a yamauba in line with a traditional, aged yamauba. Similarly, the caption of oni in *Gazu hyakki yagyō* states "the direction of

---

7 Nakazawa Shin'ichi connects these *yōkai* portrayals to the theme of urban consciousness, specifically, that of natural history. Natural history was born at the time of Europe's Age of Discovery, the era marked by an enormous influx in awareness of new species of plants and animals. People's desire to better understand the natural world was inspired and natural history provided a system of classification for all these new specimens. In the latter half of the eighteenth century, Japanese intellectuals' natural curiosity about the world around them was intensely aroused, in spite of (or perhaps because of) the shogunate's isolationist policies. The Western scientific procedures for collecting, classifying, naming, and exhibiting specimens were soon applied and directed toward the supernatural, and thus, Sekien's *Gazu hyakki yagyō* was born. Nakazawa, "Yōkaiga to hakubutsugaku" 79–81. *Gazu hyakki yagyō* greatly influenced later prints and illustrations of *yōkai*. Kagawa contends that the significance of Sekien's *Gazu hyakki yagyō* as *yōkai* painting is two-fold: first, its encyclopedia-style format introduces each *yōkai* one by one; second, the *yōkai* pictures, which formerly only a select few had been able to see through manual copying, were made available to ordinary people by way of the woodblock prints' mass production (Kagawa 44). For a detailed explanation of Toriyama Sekien's *Gazu hyakkiyagyō*, also see Foster, *Pandemonium and Parade* 55–71.

ushitora [northeast] is called *kimon* [oni's gate]. In portraying the oni now, [I put] the ox's horns on its head and [had it] wear tiger-skin loincloth. It is said that the shape was made by combining an ox and a tiger" (110). The picture portrays the oni as a hairy monster devouring an animal in a cave. The oni has two horns on its head and long claws. A human skull is laid on its side. Somehow, Sekien's oni gives an impression of primitiveness—a creature that can be hunted without much difficulty. It is given the same small space—one page—as any other strange creature. Indeed, an oni becomes just one of the *yōkai* to be gazed at leisurely. It may be inevitable that when something mysterious is given a shape and classified, thus coming under the control of human hands, the enigmatic aura of the supernatural is inevitably deflated. Yet, earlier oni images, as we have seen, present much more imposing and impressive creatures, perhaps reflecting the earlier awe in which the oni were held.

To reiterate what we observed earlier, people of the Edo period were ruled by samurai who, if not stronger than the oni, were at least more realistically present in day-to-day life. Indeed, the samurai-bureaucrats' strict control over people's conduct appears to have been more terrifying than the oni's. Ichiyūsai Kuniyoshi's (1797–1861) portrayal of the well-known theme of Raikō and his four lieutenants conquering the earth spider in *Minamoto no Raikō yakata tsuchigumo yōkai o nasu zu* (Picture of the Earth Spider Doing Mysterious Things at Raikō's Residence, 1841) attests to the fact. In this satirical picture, Raikō represents the ineffectual Shogun Ieyoshi, who is taking a nap in the corner, while his four warriors represent unsympathetic ministers. One of them is assumed, from the family crest he is wearing, to be Mizuno Tadakuni, main mover behind the Tempo Reform. The earth spider and *yōkai* symbolize popular culture repressed during the Reform. Tzvetan Todorov, speculating on the reason for such fantastic stories writes, "For many authors, the supernatural was merely a pretext to describe things they would never have dared mention in realistic terms" (158). *Yōkai* was a good outlet for expression without censorship. As the end of the Edo period approached and the shogunate's control over the people slackened, *yōkai* who were also under the strict supervision began to strike back and flood the storefront. It should be noted, however, that no oni appears in the *Picture of the Earth Spider Doing Mysterious Things at Raikō's Residence*.

Demonic People in Popular Culture of the Early Modern Period

Iconographic oni may not be used as actively as other *yōkai*, but the name is often used to refer to demonic people. As Yamaoka Genrin explained above, "the souls of wicked people are called oni." This motif frequently appears in the Kabuki plays of Tsuruya Nanboku IV (1755–1829). For example, his *Tōkaidō Yotsuya kaidan* (Yotsuya Ghost Stories, 1824) depicts the retaliation of a once-beautiful woman, Oiwa, against her cruel husband, Iemon, a masterless samurai. After killing Oiwa's father who was against Oiwa's marriage to Iemon, Iemon lies to her. Wishing to be with her, he promises that he will avenge Oiwa's father's murder. Being unemployed, Iemon is in dire poverty, but with the prospect of marrying a rich young woman who is madly in love with him, and being employed again through her grandfather's connection, Iemon soon discards Oiwa in a most humiliating way. To speed up his marriage with the young girl and save face at the same time, Iemon kills an innocent man and mentally tortures Oiwa, his wife, to death. Iemon is the personification of evil, yet he is a human being. Again, a human can be more frightening than an oni.

It should be noted the Kabuki play of *Yotsuya Ghost Stories* was a child of the urban culture of the day. The Bunka-Bunsei eras (1804-1830) were times of relative political stability and economic prosperity. This was at the same time a period of decadence. A book of gossip entitled *Seji kenbun-roku* (1816) comments on the decline in the morals of the people as reflected in dramatic productions:

> Up to seventy or eighty years ago the amorous play of men and women was suggested by an exchange of glances; if the man ever took the woman's hand, she would cover her face with her sleeve in embarrassment. That was all there was to it, but even so, old people of the time are said to have been shocked by what they deemed to be an unsightly exhibition. Women in the audience were also very modest, and would blush even at the famous scene in *Chushingura* [The Treasury of Loyal Retainers, 1748] in which Yuranosuke takes Okaru in his arms as he helps her down the ladder. Nowadays sexual intercourse is plainly shown on the stage, and women in the audience watch on, unblushing, taking it in their stride. It is most immoral. (in Keene, *World within Walls* 458)[8]

The inclination of Edoites toward the sensual pleasures was growing fast. Their favorite pastime, Kabuki, was as popular as ever, but theatergoers were not content with ordinary Kabuki plays. Instead, they looked for something more titillating. *Kaidan-mono*, or ghost plays were written in response to

---

8 When *Yotsuya Ghost Stories* was first produced at the Nakamura Theater in Edo in the summer of 1825, it was part of a two-day double bill with *Chūshingura* (Brazell, 456).

such demands. Among the numerous *kaidan-mono* plays, the most famous ghost story is unquestionably *Yotsuya Ghost Stories*. Katō Shūichi comments, "*The Ghost of Yotsuya* [i.e., *Yotsuya Ghost Stories*] takes the bloodlust present in the completely personal sphere of the secular townsmen society to the limits of possibility" (2: 206).

Kotō no Oni (Oni of a Solitary Island): Demonic People in the Erotic-Grotesque-Nonsense Culture

Almost one hundred years later, a story entitled *Kotō no oni* (Oni of a Solitary Island, 1929–30) appears in the literature of the urban culture now known as "erotic-grotesque-nonsense (*ero-guro-nansensu*), the prewar, bourgeois cultural phenomenon that devoted itself to explorations of the deviant, the bizarre, and the ridiculous" (Reichert 114).[9] Reaching its peak in 1930 or 1931, the erotic-grotesque-nonsense culture extolled decadent, ephemeral pleasure. This culture—somewhat similar to the Bunka-Bunsei eras—produced representations of oni as demonic, sadistic, and evil people. *Oni of a Solitary Island* was quite a commercial success, appealing primarily to the urban audience. The main consumers of erotic-grotesque-nonsense were "modern girls" and "modern boys" living on the cutting edge of urban life. The novel's continued success—long after erotic-grotesque-nonsense ceased as a phenomenon—is proven by its repeated publication.

The trend of the oni's commercialization continued in the modern era perhaps because an oni as a supernatural creature was considered imaginary. We can contrast this to ancient—and somewhat Early Modern—times when evil people and oni were two distinctly different beings: the former being mortal while the latter were supernatural. While we have seen, in earlier chapters, instances in which humans became oni, it is important to remember this distinction and what happens representationally when the distinction collapses. Edogawa Ranpo (1894–1965), a leading figure of erotic-grotesque-nonsense and a pioneer of the Japanese detective story in the early Shōwa period (1926–89), made full use of such images of oni, in which the distinction collapses. Ranpo serialized *Oni of a Solitary Island* in

---

9   Reichert's article highlights "the 'freakish' nature of the text itself" with the background of erotic-grotesque-nonsense culture and Social Darwinism of that time. Reichert writes that his "use of this term is influenced by recent theoretical discussions of freak discourse, which (according to Elizabeth Grosz) define 'freakishness' as the quality that fascinates and horrifies by 'blurring identities (sexual, corporeal, personal)' and by 'travers[ing] the very boundaries that secure the "normal" subject in its given identity and sexuality'" (116). Also see Grosz 55–66.

the first and second issues of a popular literature magazine called *Asahi*. It is of interest that Ranpo wrote this story after he came to the conclusion that to live is to compromise; while he did not produce trifling works, he wanted money (by selling what he considered trifling stories), and so he embarked on popular entertainment (Gonda 148).

Oni of a Solitary Island is a mystery-detective story told by the narrator, Minoura, in flashback format. It starts out with the murder of a young woman—Minoura's fiancée—followed by the death of his friend, an amateur investigator. Minoura first suspects another of his male friends, Moroto, who is passionately in love with Minoura. He believes at first that Moroto killed his fiancée out of jealousy. Yet, the case is more complex, and Minoura and Moroto follow its twists and turns to solve the mystery. It turns out that the guilty culprit is Moroto's foster father, Takegorō, the personification of an oni who commits murders to obtain hidden treasures while at the same time creating physically abnormal human beings. Takegorō is unusually short, with a hunched back. He makes and sells physically deformed humans as revenge against physically normal humans.

Moroto, alone with Minoura in a dark cave, tells his friend how Takegorō became an oni—a story of revenge. The master of a wealthy family on a remote island had a one-night affair with an ugly hunchback maid. The baby born to the maid, Takegorō, shares his mother's deformity. Disgusted by the sight, the master gives money to the maid and sends her away with her child. The maid goes into the mountains to live and curses the world. The baby is raised with a curse as his lullaby. When his mother dies, Takegorō returns to the home of his wealthy father. His stepbrother, who is his father's legitimate son, has recently died. Takegorō stays on as a kind of a guardian of the house and falls in love with his late stepbrother's beautiful wife. He proposes to her but she rejects him claiming that she would rather die than be married to such a deformed and grotesque man like him. His jealousy and sense of inferiority toward other humans turn to hatred, and Takegorō becomes the personification of revenge—to curse the world and everyone in it who is not similarly deformed.

The fiction is rife with then-contemporary scientific elements such as eugenics and criminology. Reichert explains that eugenics was one measure to respond to societal concerns about the "deviant" individuals in the 1920s and '30s, and it was closely interwoven with nationalism in its attempt to improve the Japanese race and thus enhance Japan's position in the international arena. Similarly, criminology of the time was based upon the Social Darwinist belief that society is categorized into the "fit"—law-abiding citizens, and the "unfit"—criminals (Reichert 134–41). Countering the eugenics theories of contemporaneous Japanese society, Takegorō in fiction uses imaginary modern medical science to create unhealthy, "unfit" Japanese with an ultimate goal of filling Japan full of deformed Japanese. Takegorō attempts to turn a marginalized group of his kind into the mainstream Japanese.

While the text exploits various scientific disciplines of the day, when it comes to Takegorō's oni himself, the representation appears to be remarkably conventional. Although he does not have horns on his head, he occupies the subject position of the traditional oni as "other." The oni in *Oni of a Solitary Island* is a human whose evil doings and determination for revenge transform him into an oni. While his cruelty resembles that of Iemon, the personification of evil determination, Takegorō is reminiscent of the holy man of Mt. Katsuragi mentioned in chapter one. Recall that the holy man dies obsessed by carnal craving for the emperor's beautiful consort—a daughter of the prime minister, Fujiwara Yoshifusa. In the holy man's case, his extraordinary determination to realize his sexual desire makes him an oni. While the holy man appears with a typical oni appearance in public and behaves monstrously, Takegorō avoids public appearances and his evil doings are carried out in secret. There are many elements of traditional oni that are associated with Takegorō's otherness. His anomalous appearance as a hunchback, and isolation in the mountains are certainly familiar from those early stories. His ugly appearance, which is disliked by villagers, is similar to oni stories, such as those involving Zenki (literally anterior demon) and Goki (literally posterior demon), En no gyōja's disciples, discussed in chapter one.[10] Takegorō is not fortunate enough to encounter En no gyōja; instead, his mother, equally hunchbacked, raises him with cursed lullabies.

The situation of Takegorō's mother appears to be quite conventional as well and is similar to that of a yamauba—especially that of "Hanayo no hime" mentioned in chapter four. "Hanayo no hime" was formerly human, but having survived her own children she came to be disliked by her grandchildren and was consequently expelled from their house. With nowhere to turn, she went to live in the mountains. Likewise, Takegorō's mother is sent away by a normal-looking father, and she too chooses to lead a solitary life in the mountains with her baby. She does not have any supernatural

---

10   See the section "*The Other: The Oppressed, Alienated, and Isolated*" in chapter one.

power, but her cursing lullaby has a lasting effect on her equally cursed son. Both Takegorō and his mother are maltreated because of their physical deformities. Their height and hunched backs deviate from the cultural and physical norm making them a target of contempt and disrespect. Needless to say, Takegorō's life on a solitary island makes him a foreigner with different customs living at a distance from society at large, another element of his otherness and his terribly marginalized life. But it is important at this point to remember the distinction we drew earlier between modern and current era representations of oni and their antecedents. The older tales reflect the views of a society where the firm belief in the physical existence of oni and other supernatural beings was an integral part of everyday life. The newer tales, however, reflect a society in which representations of oni are considered a product of commercialized urban cultures, be it "Bunka-Bunsei eras" or "erotic-grotesque-nonsense."

The oni of the Early Modern period are said to survive deep in the mountains, by remote rivers, and are still feared by country folks. While the oni did find a place in art, literature, and folktales, their existence seems to have been dramatically reduced. In the meantime, oni or *yōkai* as a commodity appeared in urban life of Early Modern Japan. Books about *yōkai* would were sold at carnival sideshows to complement the physical "freak shows" trotted out for the entertainment of Edoites. That tendency continued to modern times as we saw in *Oni of a Solitary Island*. The protagonist of *Oni of a Solitary Island*, if he physically existed in the Early Modern period, could have been part of a carnival show of urban life; and Edoites may have thought that Takegorō was born as such because of some sins in his previous life. On the other hand, if he were a real human in the 1920s, he may have become an experiment for a study of medical science. Fortunately he is a fictional character born out of the urban culture. The popularity of *Yotsuya Ghost Stories* and *Oni of a Solitary Island* seem to testify that a Japanese taste for something strange and weird as symbolized in the oni was and is indispensable for urban Japanese entertainment, and this tendency was further escalated in modern Japan.

6

Oni and Japanese Identity
Enemies of the Japanese Empire in and out of the Imperial Army

IN THE PREVIOUS CHAPTER, WE SAW THAT THE EDOITES, on some level or other, seem to unite in their belief in the supernatural. While in urban life, oni were fictitious, existing purely for the carnival sideshow-like entertainment of city dwellers, it is noteworthy that at the highest levels of government, officials paid due respect to select types of the supernatural. With the coming of the Meiji period (1868–1912), Japan imported and adapted many Western cultural and political institutions, as well as scientific and military technologies, in its attempt to build a modern nation and catch up with the West. Railroads were laid and gaslights erected in rapid succession. Belief in the supernatural looked to be quashed in the wave of modernization; but as Gerald Figal contends, it was re-conceptualized with the return of the emperor. Figal writes, "The Meiji emperor, who as a manifest deity was perhaps the most fantastic creature of all in Japan, became a kind of ideological lightning rod to rechannel, focus, galvanize, and control the outlet of worldly thoughts and sentiments as well as otherworldly fantasies and desires that coursed through Japanese bodies" (5). As the emperor—with his supernatural status—was restored to the position of power, the labeling of those who had "different customs or lived beyond the reach of the emperor's control" as oni was back in use, both metaphorically on real people and for imaginary creatures in a fictional world. Throughout Japanese history oni have been employed to describe Japan's military enemies. In the face of foreigners, the idea of outsider or other promotes a sense of unity among the Japanese.[1] This became especially true during the ongoing wars of modern times when Japan had been established as a nation-state. The oni foregrounds the mentality of "us" versus "other." Native Japanese look

---

1 See an interesting article by Nakar about visual representation of the other.

upon the non-Japanese races as "different," and when the non-Japanese defied the Japanese imperial authority, the foreign force became a certified oni. If the wars had ended with Japan on the victorious side, the labeling of oni may have stayed as it was. Yet, as it turned out, the Japanese learned that they were the oni from the viewpoints of enemy forces. This problematized the naming of oni: the concept of oni essentially came to define how a Japanese identifies him- or herself. This identification of oni became a focal point in some postwar fiction such as *Teito monogatari* (Tale of the Imperial Capital, 1983–89).

Reconfiguration of the Supernatural in Modern Japan

Lafcadio Hearn (1850–1904) writes in Matsue, Shimane prefecture, of the Japanese belief in "Ghosts and Goblins" (1894):

> "Kinjurō, those goblins of which we the ningyō have seen—do folk believe in the reality thereof?" "Not any more," answered Kinjurō— "not at least among the people of the city. Perhaps in the country it may not be so. We believe in the Lord Buddha; we believe in the ancient gods; and there be many who believe the dead sometimes return to avenge a cruelty or to compel an act of justice. But we do not now believe all that was believed in ancient time. (*Glimpses of Unfamiliar Japan* 643–644)

It is noteworthy that while Japanese city folk of 1894 did "not now believe all that was believed in ancient time," they did continue to believe in select supernatural beings such as the "Lord Buddha ... ancient gods" and avengers of injustice. Indeed, talking of avengers of injustice, on the day following Emperor Meiji's enthronement in 1867, the emperor invited the vengeful soul of the Retired Emperor Sutoku (1119–64) from Shiromine in Kagawa prefecture to Kyoto (Tanigawa, *Ma no keifu* 21). More than seven hundred years before, the Retired Emperor Sutoku and his supporters revolted in their attempt to depose Emperor Goshirakawa from the throne, causing the Hōgen disturbance in 1156. Sutoku and his supporters lost the battle and, according to the legend, he was transformed into an evil spirit while he was still alive and became a King of Darkness to avenge his enemy. The dramatic life (and afterlife) of the vengeful spirit of Retired Emperor Sutoku is familiar to many Japanese in both oral and print traditions.[2] Sutoku's

---

2   As early as the thirteenth century, Sutoku's lonely life in exile and his obsession with revenge were described in a war tale entitled *Hōgen monogatari* (Tale of Hōgen). *Hōgen monogatari* is a historical prose narrative that describes *Hōgen no ran* (Hōgen Rebellion)

spirit influenced not only literary and performing art, but also real court life and the central government. Seven hundred and five years later the Emperor Meiji's invitation letter to Sutoku's soul is written as if to curry Sutoku's favor and in the process affirms not only his predecessor's supernatural status but, by extension, his own as well. Thus, at the beginning of the modern era, Emperor Meiji seeks to pacify the angry spirit of his own clan (Tanigawa, *Ma no keifu* 41–43).

Japan's hierarchical system goes beyond this world. The system is applied to the realm of the supernatural, or one might say that the hierarchical order of the supernatural world has always been reflected in this world. In modern Japan, the emperor's supernatural status was publicly asserted, and with the imperial court once again at its center, the status of various supernatural beings was (re)examined; some were affirmed and others were simply dropped from the cosmic map.

San'yūtei Enchō (1839–1900), a famous storyteller of the modern age, lamented over these teachers of the Age of Enlightenment because many "thought that the supernatural was the product of the mind, a neurological pathology, and *kaidan* or ghost stories, an extension of that neuropathy" (7). His lamentation reveals a pensive discontent with the denial of the (selected) supernatural advocated by Meiji intellectuals. While the modern nation with heavy industry was rapidly established, many folk beliefs, some of which had been undoubtedly exploited by swindlers, were considered by the central government and progressive intellectuals as a hindrance to civilized thought, superstitions, the product of an unenlightened mind, or simply a form of mental disorder. While laws and regulations may change relatively quickly, manners and customs are slow to alter. Various thinkers and educators such as Inoue Enryō (1858–1919) made a concerted effort to convince the Japanese populace that, by and large, *yōkai* did not exist and that they were simply the products of imagination. It is important to note, however, that they did not deny the supernatural in its entirety.

Figal writes, "When necessary, modern reason had its imaginary allies. While officials and public intellectuals worked to center a modern national

---

with Minamoto no Tametomo (a samurai on Sutoku's side) as its center. Recited by the blind musicians called *biwa hōshi*, *Hōgen monogatari* had a large following during the medieval period. Continuing into the Edo period, professional storytellers frequently narrated Sutoku's legend, and it was also performed in both the kabuki and puppet theaters. For the text of *Hōgen monogatari*, see Yanase et al. 205–405. For an English translation, see Wilson.

citizenry on a supernatural emperor, folklorists were sympathetically studying 'outmoded' forms of supernatural beliefs throughout the Japanese populace" (15). Ishibashi Gaha, a folklorist of modern times, writes that there are no physically existing oni, but the belief in such has, itself, been long in existence. Based upon this belief, Ishibashi enumerates the literary incidents of oni of the past "in order to learn the essence of Japanese culture, i.e., the reverse side or background of overt cultural activities such as politics, economics, literature and art" (2). Indeed, studying the oni reveals an interesting flow of Japanese thought and also reveals much about the human psyche.

Oni as Foreign Enemy in the Second World War

It is common knowledge among Japanese that during the Second World War the appellation oni was used to describe the Japanese enemies: the American, British, Russian, and Chinese leaders of the allied forces. As the war intensified, government censorship tightened. Even cartoonists and caricaturists were having their works scrutinized. In fact, various organizations of cartoonists were forced to reorganize to suit the needs of the government. Backed by the government, *Shin Nippon mangaka kyōkai* (New Association of Japanese Cartoonists) published the monthly, *Manga*, the only cartoon magazine that existed during the war. The editor, Kondō Hidezō (1908–1979), depicted evil demons Roosevelt, Churchill, and Stalin (Lent 227). Addressing the cultural function of *Manga*, writer Kobayashi Nobuhiko says:

> There is hardly any other magazine which expresses the Japanese popular culture during World War II [than *Manga*]. Writers and thinkers cooperated during the War, but none were more vocal than cartoonist, Kondō Hidezō, who instigated the populace [to support the War]. His simple style and his ability to connect with ordinary people were truly outstanding. (179)

One of *Manga's* cartoonists, Fujii Tomu (1912–1943) depicts Roosevelt with horns on his scalp.[3] The caption reads "oni wa washi, oni wa washi" (I'm the oni, I'm the oni), which is a play on the phrase "oni wa soto, fuku wa uchi" (Demons out, Fortune in), the customary expression uttered on the day of the *setsubun*. In this cartoon, a super-sized Roosevelt in a western shirt and traditional samurai upper-garb is scattering bullets on Japanese towns. In another cartoon, Sugiura Yukio (1911–2004) draws an attractive

---

3   Reprinted in Shimizu Isao, *Taiheiyō sensō ki no manga* 29.

Japanese wife, holding a pocket book, looking to buy materials for clothes in a store window. The materials have three faces embroidered on them, those of Roosevelt, Churchill, and Chiang Kai-shek. Each man is drawn with horns, the primary feature of oni. The caption reads, "The Spirit of Saving" (6). This was a powerful juxtaposition of imagery. Similarly, the slogan, "Luxury is enemy," speaks to the theme of saving encouraged by the Japanese government. In this cartoon, the ordinary housewife is smiling because instead of buying materials for new clothes, she decides to save her money. The small caption reads, "My saving spirit is quite something. Even things started to look like this [oni]." This certainly encouraged many wives to save, while subtly reinforcing the image of the Allied forces as demons and true enemies of Japan, and by association the cartoon demonizes wasteful luxury as well.

The oni's adaptability becomes increasingly apparent when one examines how they were used in the Japanese war effort when applied to the "evil allied forces." A good example of this appears in the folktale, "Momotarō," or "Peach Boy." Momotarō is so named because he was born from a peach, which was divinely sent or which floated down a stream. As the boy grows older, he begins to demonstrate miraculous strength. At that time, oni from a distant island frequent the capital, looting treasures and abducting people. A young Momotarō decides to confront and subjugate the oni. His elderly parents provide him with dumplings for food. En route, Momotarō meets a dog, a monkey, and a pheasant which all become his vassals in exchange for his remarkably delicious dumplings. Momotarō and his three vassals go to the oni's island, defeat the oni, and take back all the island treasures with them. Momotarō's goodness, affection, and filial piety toward his elderly parents, provide the perfect model for good conduct for young Japanese.

To explain how the seemingly innocuous story of "Momotarō" could be exploited during wartime requires some background information. Named as one of the five most famous folktales in Japan in the pre-war period, one would be hard-pressed to find a Japanese youngster not familiar with Momotarō's story, most probably because it was included in the textbooks for elementary language instruction issued by the Ministry of Education. The Momotarō story was first adopted in the elementary language text during the Meiji period—in 1887 to be precise—and was continuously printed until the end of World War II (Namekawa ii).[4] Also,

---

4   The Momotarō story disappeared from textbooks after the Second World War.

Iwaya Sazanami (1870–1933), an author and a scholar of children's literature, wrote an immensely popular and financially successful children's literature series titled *Nihon mukashibanashi* (Japanese Fairy Tales, 1894–96); "Momotarō" is the first in the series.[5] After a phase of almost indiscriminate adoption of Western technologies, medicine, literature, etc., there was a tendency in the latter part of the 1890s to reconsider Japan's traditions, a response, no doubt, to unchecked westernization and a string of unequal treaties imposed by Western powers. Iwaya began writing *Japanese Fairy Tales* amidst this trend (Ueda Nobumichi 474). The traditional folktale "Momotarō," from which Iwaya derives his *Nihon mukashibanashi,* originated sometime between 1550 and 1630, but Momotarō's imagery, shared by contemporary Japanese, is relatively new, set in the eighteenth century (Namekawa 2–3, 206). Namekawa notes that in older texts, there is no explanation given for Momotarō's subjugation of oni on the Oni's Island (*Oni ga shima*). They were subjugated simply because they were oni. In earlier eras oni as a symbol of all that is evil sufficed as excuse enough for their elimination. However, as Momotarō increasingly became a symbol of the ideal Japanese boy in the Meiji period, educators started to ascribe more contemporary moral reasons for the oni's extermination (17–18). The ideal hero just does not exterminate someone without any good reason; or more to the point, a reason that does not reflect the values of the period. Thus in Iwaya Sazanami's *Nihon mukashibanashi,* oni are eliminated not simply because they are wicked, but because "they don't obey the benevolent rule of imperial Japan and do harm in Japan. They take people and eat them, seize their valuable property, and they are the most hateful creatures in the world" (*Nihon mukashibanashi* 19).

Given the time of the texts' production—the Sino-Japanese War (1894–95) in which Japan emerged as an industrial nation in the eyes of Western powers—one is tempted to read Momotarō's description as an allegory for Japanese imperialism. Note how Momotarō's first and foremost reason for destroying the oni is that they are the enemy of imperial Japan. Using the term "oni" as an appellation for a different race that is to be subjugated, or to single out people with different traditions and manners, is an old custom as we have seen. In this instance, one might argue, this custom is brought to the foreground by the geopolitical events of the era, as Iwaya Sazanami's

---

5   For the text of Iwaya's "Momotarō," see Iwaya, *Nippon mukashibanashi* 15–30. For an English translation of "Momotarō," see Iwaya, *Iwaya's Fairy Tales of Old Japan* vol. 1.

"Momotarō" reflects the spirit of the Japanese Empire. Momotarō claims that the oni have snatched away treasures from the people; however, he also declares before he embarks upon the adventure that he is going to take all the oni's treasure. Recall from chapter one, that an oni's treasure includes a straw raincoat of invisibility, a hat of invisibility, and a mallet of fortune (*uchide no kozuchi*). Those magical items certainly do not belong to people. Needless to say, Momotarō as a victor confiscates every single one of the treasures from the oni, but Iwaya Sazanami's Momotarō remains silent about what to do with them after returning to Japan. (It is expected that Momotarō will dispense them fairly.) In any case, Momotarō becomes a Japanese hero partly because of his enterprising, adventurous spirit. An examination of this spirit reveals not only his brave willingness to go to unknown places to subdue evil supernatural creatures, but an imperialistic mind as well to take (loot) someone's prized property.

Thus Momotarō was used as an instrument to promote nationalism during the Meiji period, but as John Dower explains, the message was taken to the extreme during the Second World War. Momotarō's divine appearance on Earth symbolizes Japan, a divine country. His animal vassals, a dog, monkey, and a pheasant, symbolize other Asian countries under the umbrella of Japan's ambitious Greater East Asia Co-Prosperity Sphere. The cartoons, magazines, and animated films for the Momotarō story were made to help support the Japanese cause and encourage nationalism (Dower, *War without Mercy* 250–258).[6] The concept of an oni Allied force was spoon fed to Japanese youth, quickly disseminating into the larger populace. Unlike the medieval period when the anti-establishment oni took shape gradually over hundreds of years, the oni as enemy during wartime in Japan was quickly and artificially created by Japanese leaders and enthusiastic nationalists. Far from an image that evolved over time, this use of oni was a ploy that exploited fearful associations and thus advanced the Japanese wartime ultra-nationalist agenda. In the case of the war, the oni's evolution was entirely a product of machination. While the Japanese propaganda machine was projecting the image of oni onto the enemy camp, the Japanese army was acting like oni in various Asian countries, their acts exemplified in the atrocities of Nanking in 1937 and the Bataan Death March in 1942.

---

6   For the detailed account of how the *oni*'s island is identified as an uncultivated, barbaric land far from the center of Japan, see Antoni.

From the Allied viewpoint, Japan was itself a "disenfranchised" oni, deemed an emergent threat to Asia and the West, "… a 'racial menace' as well as a cultural and religious one" (Dower, *War without Mercy* 7). For Americans (who as citizens of a relatively young nation had much less colonial experience than their European allies), Japan was indeed foreign—its people and customs, different. To Japanese at the time, however, the perception was completely reversed. Americans were the evil oni: an elite, imperialistic cultural and economic invasion force with interests already firmly wedged in Asia. Americans were "people who had different customs or lived beyond the reach of the emperor's control."

Notwithstanding this blindness to one's own imperialistic tendencies (which was, unfortunately, all too common among all parties in this period) Momotarō became a Japanese hero by virtue of an enterprising, adventurous spirit that enabled and inspired him to seek and seize the oni's treasure. In this instance one can read Momotarō as the very personification of Japanese imperialism exemplified by Japanese aggression in Manchuria in 1931, China in 1937, and continuing on to the Pacific War of 1941. Japan had hoped to take control of China swiftly, but met with unexpectedly strong resistance from Chiang Kai-shek's Kuomingtang army.

Japan soon found itself depleting its already strained natural resources on two simultaneous fronts—domestically, as well as in the war effort in China. With many essential imports from the West decreasing, particularly oil, Japan began to eye with increasing appetite the rich raw materials in the southeastern colonies of the Dutch East Indies. One may compare these raw materials to an oni's prized treasure of a straw raincoat of invisibility, a hat of invisibility, and a mallet of fortune. Japan, to justify aggressive moves throughout Asia, aimed at replacing Western control of Asian countries with its own system of colonial control, and advocated the Greater East Asia Co-Prosperity Sphere. In Japan's plan for the acquisition of resources, the Army wanted to acquire the resource-rich regions of Northern Asia while the Japanese Navy wanted to appropriate the resource-rich territories of Southeast Asia. Machines of war are dependent on technology, processed raw materials and fuel (Dyer 39). The greater the population of any given territory, the greater the strain placed on its natural resources. In September 1940, Japan joined Germany and Italy in signing the Tripartite Alliance Pact. The Pact stipulated (Article One), "Japan recognizes and respects the leadership of Germany and Italy in the establishment of a new order in Europe," and (Article Two), "Germany and Italy recognize and respect the leadership of Japan in the establishment of a new order in Greater East Asia" (Morley 298). Japan had defined its territorial spoil—Asia. In 1941, Japan's Navy required 2,000,000 tons of oil, the Army, 500,000 tons and the civilian population 1,000,000 tons (Stinnett 121). The American embargo of 1940 originally allowed sales of oil to Japan. In 1941, however, the United States placed a full embargo on the sale of oil to Japan. It was an ultimatum. Japan was appropriating other nations' natural resources and knew this would result in conflict with the United States. As Emperor Hirohito (Showa emperor) wrote in retrospect, "the war against the United States would be started with oil and ended with oil" (112). Oil, an oni's most prized treasure, was not Japan's or Momotarō's. An unsuccessful enterprise of appropriation thus ended in disaster, making one reconsider what an oni is.

It is perhaps not so ironic, given the oni's power and predilection to transform, that the American oni would turn into Japan's strongest strategic ally and economic partner in the postwar period, showing its kind side immediately after the war by providing much needed food and democratic guidance. In this light, the oni enemy was transformed into a liberator from Japanese militarism and fascism; as "gifts from heaven," democratic revolution was given to the Japanese from the American occupation force (Dower, *Embracing Defeat* 65–84).

Labeling another person or group as oni could be easily exploited to create and enhance a unity within to defeat a targeted group as we have seen repeatedly in history. But the Japanese experience of wars in modern times, especially the Second World War, makes one think, "who are/were the 'people who had different customs or lived beyond the reach of the emperor's control'"? The use of oni as a label thus becomes problematic. It becomes a matter of perspective.

After the War, the emperor declared himself a human being, and the whole supernatural paradigm of the Japanese Empire collapsed. The branding as oni of those against the establishment or the imperial authority lost its physical target in the real world, but the war experience and its memories offered fertile ground for fiction—again, as entertainment to arouse people's nostalgic imagination. We have seen the entertainment value of oni in the previous chapter, and will see it in the following chapters as well; among recent examples, the novel entitled *Teito monogatari* (Tale of the Imperial Capital, 1983–89) stands out because it exemplifies the theme of "naming of oni is a matter of perspective" by insinuating that the fictional Showa emperor is also an oni. In addition, the protagonist of the story is an oni who is an officer of the imperial army. Further it summarises the modern theory of oni in the form of a novel, and brings back some weight to oni albeit in a fictional world.

Teito Monogatari (Tale of the Imperial Capital)

It has been quite a while since Abe no Seimei (921?–1005), an *onmyōji* or official yin and yang diviner of the Heian court, became an icon in Japanese pop-culture. While various things, no doubt, have contributed to the recent boom in interest in the oni, Aramata Hiroshi's work *Tale of the Imperial Capital* (1983–89)[7] is widely credited as the beginning.[8] *Tale of the Imperial Capital* is a science fiction involving science, magic, grudges, incest, and eroticism. The work is remarkable in its skilful weaving of the supernatural into both modern and contemporary Japanese historical landscapes. The backdrop of time for *Tale of the Imperial Capital* ranges from the late Meiji through 1998, 73rd year of the Showa period. *Tale of the Imperial Capital* gives an excellent explanation of what oni are in the context of the novel, and is important for the study of oni in that it establishes the oni as a major serious character/creature in Japan's popular culture.

The story's main character, Katō Yasunori, is a mysterious human with formidable supernatural powers that enable him to manipulate oni. An oni himself, Katō is bent on destroying the imperial capital of Tokyo with help from Taira no Masakado (903–940). Taira no Masakado, a descendant of the Emperor Kammu (reign 781–806), is a historical figure. He was a rebel leader who, after gaining control of the Kanto region in central Japan, proclaimed himself the new emperor. He meets a violent death at the hands of the imperial army sent from Kyoto.[9] Needless to say, Masakado—

---

7   *Tale of the Imperial Capital*, which has sold 350 million copies, received the Japan Science Fiction Award in 1987.

8   The prominent contributors to the boom include all of the following works. Aramata Hiroshi's *Teito monogatari*, Yumemakura Baku's *Onmyōji* and Kyōgoku Natsuhiko's *Kyōgokudō* series are enormously popular. Then Okano Reiko's graphic novel, *Onmyōji*, based upon Yumemakura's series, ignited the explosive boom. Riding the popularity of *Onmyōji* and Abe no Seimei, the film of the same title was created. Regarding scholarly activities, Komatsu Kazuhiko's various works on the supernatural of the dark side influenced various fiction writers. See Komatsu Kazuhiko, *Abe no Seimei "yami" no denshō* 204–5; *Seimei jinja* 28–61.

9   This incident is called *Tengyō no ran* (Tengyō Disturbance). For Masakado's story, see *Shōmonki* (Story of Masakado's Rebellion) in Yanase et al. 13–94. For an English translation, see Rabinovitch.

who went against imperial authority—is considered a major oni both by the narrator and in the context of Japanese history. In *Tale of the Imperial Capital*, Masakado's head is buried in central Tokyo. Katō seeks to awaken Masakado's spirit from its deep sleep to use his wrath to destroy the capital of Japan.

It is symbolic that the narrator in the prologue, entitled "Oni is Coming," comments on a carnival show in which the monsters at the show cannot break from their confinement, so citizens can enjoy them without fear (Aramata 1: 17).[10] This effectively sets the novel at the beginning of modern times, when the oni's existence was primarily confined to the carnival show as we saw in the previous chapter. The narrator then warns that the citizens (and readers) do not realize that an uncontrollably atrocious oni strides freely in the imperial capital of Tokyo (Aramata 1: 17). This oni is Katō Yasunori, who is tall and has an unusually elongated face. Instead of an old-fashioned tiger skin, he wears the crisp uniform of the imperial Army—he is a first lieutenant. Katō Yasunori is directly referred to as an oni in various places of the main text. For example, when Katō wants to use Yukari, an attractive young woman with strong mystic abilities, to awaken Masakado's wrath, Kōda Rohan, whose character is based upon the historical writer and scholar with the same name, says "she is targeted by an oni" (Aramata 1: 20). Further evidence comes from the fact that many of Katō's actions are derived from a number of familiar oni stories. For instance, Aramata incorporates a Kabuki version of Rashōmon entitled "Modoribashi" (Modori Bridge, 1890)[11] into his story. To recap the familiar story, according to "Modoribashi," Watanabe no Tsuna is sent by his master, Minamoto no Raikō, on an errand. At Modoribashi Bridge in the capital Tsuna encounters a beautiful young woman—a theme that should be quite familiar to us by now. She says that she is going to Fifth Avenue, but she has become separated from her servants on the way. Tsuna offers to accompany her. Looking at her lovely face in the moonlight, he is charmed by her beauty. But then he realizes from her shadow reflected on the water that she is in fact an oni. In the course of conversation, Tsuna points out her real identity. The oni

---

10   The prologue does not appear in the 1985 version of the text.
11   Authored by Kawatake Mokuami (1816–93), "Modoribashi" is a dance piece first performed in 1890 by Onoe Kikugorō V (1844–1903). It has a subtitle, "Rashōmon, Meiji period version." The story is based upon the sword chapter of *Heike monogatari*. Interestingly, the supernatural creature referred to as oni in *Heike monogatari* and Noh is labeled as *yōkai* in this 1890 text.

grabs Tsuna's topknot and flies off into the air, but Tsuna manages to cut off one of the oni's arms causing the oni to fly off leaving Tsuna and the oni's severed arm behind (Kawatake 141–51). In Aramata's work, when Kōda Rohan attempts to challenge Katō's attack to protect Yukari, the description of their encounter brings the reader back to the familiar story of Tsuna at Modoribashi Bridge. Grabbing Yukari, Katō tries to fly away, but Kōda jumps to stop him. As Katō keeps flying higher, however, now with Kōda attached to him, Kōda takes a dagger and cuts off Katō's arm to free himself (Aramata 1: 280). Kōda is equated with Tsuna, and Katō is oni.

Importantly, while Katō is human, he has an oni's appetite for human organs. In order to obtain a passport for his lover and secure her safety, he performs an esoteric magic act of rejuvenating himself at Shanghai. However, to recuperate and nourish himself after the magical performance, he eats human organs. In this story, human organs are an important ingredient to prolong an oni's life—a familiar trait of oni that is described in the story of *Shuten Dōji* in chapter two. Unlike the description in *Shuten Dōji*, however, Katō's diet is more selective, limited to organs while Shuten Dōji drinks blook and eats the meat of human thighs. Katō's diet is presented in an analytical manner. This macabre diet is enjoyed by another character in the story as well, Narutaki.

Katō is described as the personification of the avenging oni, born from the grudge of one thousand five hundred years of Japan's hidden history (Aramata 1: 377). Masakado is later explained as a collective entity rather than an individual person. Apparently, those who rebel against the ancestors of the contemporary ruler are uniformly called Taira no Masakado (Aramata 5: 242). Further, Masakado's grudge is not his personal grudge, but the curse of the entire earth (6: 480). In the end, Katō is identified as Masakado himself. This is predictable since, again, anyone who goes against the present ruler is considered Masakado. Katō, by virtue of his burning desire to destroy the imperial capital, thus is also identified as Masakado. Interestingly, however, some characters in the novel consider Taira no Masakado as the guardian spirit of Tokyo, a gracious deity. Some believe that Masakado has already transformed from a cursing deity into a salvation oni (1: 166). As in the case of *yōkai* in general, when humans worship an oni, the oni becomes a deity. The negative association turns into a positive one.

Enshrined in Kanda district of Tokyo, Masakado becomes a guarding spirit of Tokyo. In *Tale of the Imperial Capital*, the meaning of oni is completely a matter of perspective that the author uses at his convenience—a theme familiar from history as described above. Perhaps what is most intriguing is that the head of Masakado turns out to be enshrined within the compound of the imperial palace, and the narrator suggests the Great Chief Priest of Masakado's shrine is the Showa emperor (i.e., Emperor Hirohito). The people surrounding the aged and frail emperor keep him alive with the help of a life-prolonging nostrum, the indispensable ingredient of which is a human organ; logically it follows that both oni and the emperor equally practice cannibalism, or more to the point, both Katō and the emperor qualify as oni. Just as Minamoto no Raikō, the killer of Shuten Dōji and his cohorts, is related to an oni,[12] the emperor and oni are related. Or, as it is insinuated, the emperor is a chief oni, which makes the labeling of oni problematic. Who calls an oni "oni" and when is an oni NOT an oni? Again, the story makes the naming of oni a matter of perspective.

While Katō is an oni himself, he is simultaneously an *onmyōji* who manipulates oni. The author, Aramata Hiroshi (b. 1947), explains that he wanted Katō to symbolize the mysterious group of *onmyōji*, encompassing both the official and heretical ones (Seimei jinja 32). In the story, Katō practices heretical magic from the viewpoint of the official, legitimate *onmyōdō* that is practiced by Hirai Yasumasa, the head of the Tsuchimikado clan. Historically the Tsuchimikado clan, which traditionally practiced official *onmyōdō* at the imperial court until the middle of the nineteenth century, had Abe no Seimei, the great yin and yang diviner at the Heian court, as their founder. Yasumasa is the direct descendant of Abe no Seimei and his action is based on one of Abe no Seimei's stories. In a story that appears in *Uji shūi monogatari* (A Collection of Tales from Uji, ca. 13th century), old Seimei sees a handsome young chamberlain cursed by a crow-shaped genie. The genie is sent by an enemy yin and yang diviner and the young man's life is in danger. "After sunset Seimei kept his arms tight around the chamberlain and laid protective spells. He spent the night in endless, unintelligible muttering."[13] Seimei's protection is so strong that the genie is sent back to the enemy diviner and kills him instead. In *Tale of the Imperial Capital*, old Yasumasa protects young Yukari, holding her like a parent crane and praying the magical words to keep her from the enemy diviner, Katō. Unlike Seimei's story, however, the genies Yasumasa sent previously were

---

12 See "Origins of Shuten Dōji" in chapter two.

13 Translation by Tyler. *Japanese Tales* 82–83. The original text is found in Kobayashi and Masuko 83–85. Another English translation is found in Mills.

defeated by Katō, and Katō's genies in the shape of birds would attack them in return. Yasumasa, the official diviner, lost to Katō, the heretic diviner (Aramata 1: 272–73). Intriguingly, although Katō is described as a heretical *onmyōji*, his handkerchief has a pentagram, the hallmark of Abe no Seimei, on it. Later in the novel Katō is considered part of Abe no Seimei's clan and is described as Great *onmyōji*. Indeed, Yasunori in Katō Yasunori coincides with the name of Abe no Seimei's master, Kamo no Yasunori (917–77). Considering these descriptions, Katō may be a descendant of a marginalized line of the Abe no Seimei clan, that is nonetheless considered pedigreed.

Aramata Hiroshi, a critic, commentator, and writer, explains that while he was taking part in the project of *Heibonsha World Encyclopedia*, he was in constant touch with Komatsu Kazuhiko, an anthropologist. Komatsu Kazuhiko told Aramata about many sources of the strange and mysterious, and Aramata wanted to share that knowledge with general readers as a form of fiction. That is how he started his career as a writer (Seimei jinja 30). Hence various concepts of oni, many of them familiar, are introduced throughout his text. For example, Kadokawa Gen'yoshi, a character based upon a historical figure of the same name who founded Kadokawa Publishing Company, says:

> Oni were, in short, inhabitants of remote regions. They were different from Yamato people and those who were labeled as water people, mountain people, and earth spiders. By the end of the Heian period, rebels like Masakado, vengeful spirits like Sugawara no Michizane, and in fact all those oppressed by the central government came to be called oni, and, over time, came to be regarded as Night species. (Aramata 5: 122)

As the introduction of the characters preceding the novel explains, Kadokawa Gen'yoshi studied Japanese folklore under Orikuchi Shinobu and revered Yanagita Kunio (Aramata 5: 10);[14] this explanation comes as no surprise. Similarly, the character of Hirai Yasumasa, head of the Tsuchimikado clan of *onmyōji* who has lost the battle against Katō, writes about Katō and oni:

> From the viewpoint of *onmyōdō* of the Tsuchimikado line, an oni is a transparent genie that *onmyōji* manipulates. The term oni means the indigenous people of the water or mountain. It could be a descendant of Chinese, Korean or naturalized Japanese who did not worship

---

14 Kadokawa says himself, "what I call my teachers are, first Orikuchi Shinobu, then, Yanagita Kunio in the area of folklore" (Aramata 5: 121).

the imperial court. He is a descendant of those who rebelled against the imperial court in ancient times. Katō is a villain who inherited the grudge and heresy from them, and will endanger the unbroken Japanese imperial line. He is probably not a Japanese subject. (1: 368–76)

The tone becomes somewhat nationalistic, perhaps reflective of the official imperial court's pride. Again, one sees that anyone who goes against the emperor bears the name of oni. The assignment of the name oni shifts as the story progresses.

In its kaleidoscopic presentation of oni, *Tale of the Imperial Capital* evinces what Michel Foucault calls "heterotopia." In contrast to utopia, heterotopic sites are something like "counter-sites, a kind of effectively enacted utopia in which the real sites, all the other real sites that can be found within the culture, are simultaneously represented, contested, and inverted" (Foucault 24). Foucault gives a mirror as an example of a heterotopia: "it makes the place that I occupy at the moment when I look at myself in the glass at once absolutely real, connected with all the space that surrounds it, and absolutely unreal, since in order to be perceived it has to pass through the virtual point which is over there" (24). We see this in the heterotopic relationship between Katō and the emperor, but it also occurs on several levels of significance throughout the novel. In the *Tale of the Imperial Capital*, heterotopic space is created in the basement of Narutaki Jun'ichi's mansion. It is a little Ginza, which mirrors the time and space of Ginza in 1923. Narutaki is in love with Yukari whose normal life is mercilessly taken away by Katō. Through the entanglement with Katō, Narutaki creates the nostrum that prolongs life, and amasses enormous wealth by selling it to the Showa emperor. In the 1970s, Narutaki is over one hundred years old, and obsessed by the idea of having young Yukari back from the other world. To satisfy his wish, he pours out his wealth to reconstruct, in his basement, the time-space at the end of the Taisho period (1912–26), before the Great Earthquake of Kanto hits Tokyo at noon of September 1, 1923. As a result of the earthquake, the rubble of Ginza city sank to the bottom of Tokyo Bay. Narutaki collects the rubble to reconstruct the Ginza, and the carefully collected materials take the wall of dimension away, and bring back not only the space but also the time of a little before noon of September 1, 1923.

Heterotopia creates "a space of illusion that exposes every real space, all the sites inside of which human life is partitioned, as still more illusory" (Foucault 27). Narutaki's Ginza in the basement is one quarter of what it used to be. It occupies real space and it exists, but it is illusory.

As a heterotopic site is "linked to slices in time" (Foucault 26), Narutaki's Ginza is strictly bound to that brief slice of time in 1923. Indeed, the time restriction contributes to catastrophe in Tokyo. Since different times cannot exist simultaneously, whenever Narutaki finds a new piece of Ginza's rubble and places it in his basement, that part of the real Ginza falls (Aramata 6: 37), constantly causing accidents in the Ginza of 1970s Showa. Just as "the heterotopic site is not freely accessible like a public place" (Foucault 26), Narutaki's private residence is not freely accessible. As the project progresses, Yukari is prematurely summoned back from the other world, and is trapped in the heterotopic site where oni also attack.

Aramata's novel, while an entertaining work, is in itself a heterotopic site where its contemporary representations of oni reflect past representations, where oni of the past are not simply superimposed upon the present but where both act as extensions of each other in an odd continuum. From the interstices of past and present emerges a narrative that not only highlights the machinations and actions of the mysterious contemporary *onmyōji* and the dark magic from the past with which they deal, but arguably paves the way for another equally successful work of contemporary fiction replete with oni entitled *Onmyōji*, which will be discussed in the next chapter.

The end of the Second World War brought the collapse of the reconfiguration of the supernatural with Japan's emperor as its center. World War II made clear to many mainstream Japanese that the branding of oni is arbitrary and could be easily used for war propaganda. While the physical enemies of the Japanese Empire with their oni label may have disappeared, the terrain of the imaginary oni remains rich—one may even say that the Japanese Empire has given more room for the oni to play. *Tale of the Imperial Capital* is an exemplary work of fiction that utilizes imperial Japan for its backdrop with a sub-theme of the emperor-oni paradigm. Freedom of speech brought about after World War II allows contemporary authors to connect the emperor directly to oni as part of an entertaining and complex plot. Now that the oni are entirely fictitious figures without leverage in real day-to-day life, their commodification (described in the previous chapter) peppered with sex and violence thrives all the more, as we will see in the next chapter.

7

Sex, Violence, and Victimization
Modern Oni and Lonely Japanese

The commercialization and commodification of the supernatural that we have witnessed in earlier chapters have followed the oni for most of their literary existence. This trend has seemingly reached its apotheosis in current Japanese culture. Thus, oni now flourish in Japanese people's nostalgic as well as futuristic imaginations. While the traditional oni breathe within the newly reimagined oni, the oni of the present age reflect and express contemporary Japanese thoughts and beliefs. Modern authors build upon and modify earlier images of oni and adapt them to new systems of belief. When employing imaginary oni, writers pepper their stories with sex and violence to attract a larger audience. Particularly noteworthy in modern times is the portrayal of oni as victims rather than as victimizers or evil-doers. It appears almost fashionable to see oni from the oni's perspective. Often, the oni of modern fiction are lonesome creatures looking for companions. By portraying oni from the oni's viewpoint and oni as victims of mainstream society, some modern authors essentially seem to probe the Japanese psyche of new generations that, stripped of the traditional communal base such as the village community or extended family system, look for some connections to the collective past. This chapter examines oni representations that evince these trends through Nakagami Kenji's "Oni no hanashi" ("A Tale of a Demon") and Yumemakura Baku's extremely popular series entitled *Onmyōji* (The Yin-Yang Master). Nakagami Kenji's oni is a lonesome creature, looking for a companion. The disenfranchised oni in "A Tale of a Demon" could be an allegory for a community of Nakagami's roots, *buraku* (area of outcast group). Yumemakura's oni are also forlorn, but sensible. Yumemakura seems to gauge what the oni must have felt in the Japanese society of that particular time he describes, but through a contemporary lens. The changes the authors make reflect and express contemporary Japanese attitudes toward the supernatural, and by extension, give the reader a glimpse into historical and contemporary Japanese thoughts on religion and demonology.

Nakagami Kenji's "Oni no hanashi" ("A Tale of a Demon")

Nakagami Kenji (1946–1992) is an Akutagawa Prize winner who declared that he was from the outcast quarter a year after he had received the Akutagawa Award in 1979. His portrayal of oni in his "Oni no hanashi" ("A Tale of a Demon," 1981)[1] is enigmatic and sexual. Kitagawa Utamaro portrayed an erotic yamauba or oni-woman in his illustrations as noted in chapter four. Unlike Utamaro's yamauba, the dedicated mother of Kintarō, however, Nakagami Kenji's oni-woman is a solitary and lonesome creature, looking for a companion. In that sense, she may be akin to the earlier yamauba of the medieval period, especially Noh's yamamba. Like Noh's yamamba who wants people to know her side of the story, Nakagami Kenji's oni-woman insists that oni are misunderstood creatures. Yet, while Noh's yamamba aspires for spiritual awakening and recognizes loneliness as part of her path to enlightenment, Nakagami Kenji's oni has no ambition for enlightenment, and her solitude is similar to the loneliness felt by modern people who are searching for friendship or a bond with others. Indeed, while retaining many traits of oni including cannibalism, Nakagami Kenji's oni is perhaps reflecting the author's own belief; his disenfranchised oni could be an allegory for *burakumin* or outcasts, Nakagami's roots.

"A Tale of a Demon" is based upon a story from *Konjaku monogatarishū* (Tales of Times Now Past), incorporating character elements from Ueda Akinari's "The Lust of the White Serpent" and "Hankai." Born in the *buraku* community (outcast quarters) of Shingū, Wakayama prefecture, Nakagami intimately understood discrimination by mainstream Japanese society and its government, which, the oni, as outcasts of society, also symbolize. In his work, Nakagami appears to treat the oni sympathetically, yet a close examination of the story reveals that Nakagami is not an unreserved champion of the oni's condition. Rather, Nakagami's perception of oni is oblique,

---

[1] For the Japanese text of "Oni no hanashi," see Nakagami, *Nakagami Kenji zenshū* 5: 315–26. For an English translation, see Nakagami, "A Tale of a Demon."

sometimes double layered, and certainly enigmatic. Nakagami incorporates the beliefs, mythology, and imagery of the oni into his text. In doing so, "A Tale of a Demon" may have been Nakagami's challenge to the hegemony of Japanese written language and its recorded historical accounts—a vehicle historically *alien* to a majority of Japan's socially and economically displaced.

Japan is often thought of as a homogeneous society, but a number of minority groups exist and have historically faced discrimination by mainstream Japanese. *Burakumin* are one of these groups, centered on professions considered "unclean," such as tanners, butchers, or day laborers. Before the Second World War, they lived their lives with virtually no formal schooling, leaving most of them illiterate. Nakagami Kenji was born in such a *buraku* of Shingū, Wakayama prefecture. Under the postwar equal education system, Nakagami, the youngest of his siblings, was the only one to attend school. Nakagami recalls, "I was treated like a prodigy because I could read my own name" (*Nakagami Kenji hatsugen shūsei* 6: 338–39).[2] About Nakagami's narrative, Nina Cornyetz comments: "Following the political unrest of the 1960s, an ethnic boom and consumption of multiculturalism enjoyed by middle-class Japanese in the late 1970s and 1980s and the search for original nativities and the exotic within the Japanese heartland became the cultural backdrop for Nakagami's violent narrative attacks on the myths of Japanese homogeneity" (17–18).

"A Tale of a Demon" follows a man who vows to kill an oni that is rumored to be eating people at Tatsumi Bridge in Ōmi province. Nicknamed Hankai, the man is proud of his physical strength. On the bridge, he meets a beautiful young woman with a broken statue of Kannon Bodhisattva that she is taking to be fixed. She says that she suddenly feels sick; he immediately falls in love with the woman, and after he fails to find the oni, he goes to her house. The house is called the House of Demons and belongs to Chūnagon (Middle Councilor) Asanari; the vengeful spirit of Asanari became an oni because of the unfortunate events of his human life. The fair young woman is also an oni, a maid to Asanari's little daughter. The ersatz

---

2 Also, see Zimmerman 1999. Although they are no different ethnically and racially than other Japanese, discrimination against outcasts continues as evidenced by the fact that the area of their domicile is still referred to as *buraku*. This discrimination is pervasive: *buraku* still face prejudice in all areas of Japanese society. The topos of outcast communities termed *roji* by Nakagami is the landscape of his fiction including his novella *Misaki* (The Cape) for which he won the prestigious Akutagawa Prize in 1976 as the first postwar generation writer. See Nakagami, *Nakagami Kenji hatsugen shūsei* 4: 330–34.

maiden tells Hankai that oni are not always out eating people as everyone seems to think, rather it's the oni-hunters who, by bragging of their killing, render the oni's reputation more vicious. The girl cares for her new love so much that she decides to let the man kill her. While lying in bed together, she asks the man if he would love her if she were an oni. Even though he says yes, he quickly realizes her true identity, backs away and draws his sword. In the end, the young oni-woman kills Hankai.

The oni-woman's master is Fujiwara no Asanari (917–974), a historical character who is also recognized as Sanjō no Chūnagon (Middle Councilor on the Third Avenue). In classical Japanese literature,[3] Asanari is known as a man who became an oni as a result of a quarrel with his kinsman Fujiwara no Koretada (924–972) regarding promotion. According to *Ōkagami* (The Great Mirror, ca. 1085–1125), despite Koretada's promise to Asanari that he would not seek the position of *Kuraudo no kami* (the Head Chamberlain)[4] so that Asanari himself may have it, Koretada takes the position. Asanari becomes infuriated by Koretada's thoughtless and duplicitous actions. In his rage, he turns into an oni, swearing to curse Koretada and his descendants and to terminate Koretada's line. He further threatens that anyone who sympathizes with the family will also pay the price.[5] *Hōbutsushū* (Collection of Jewels, ca. 1178) recounts that Emperor Kazan's (Koretada's grandson) early retirement at the age of nineteen was also Asanari's doing. Moreover, *Jikkinshō* (A Miscellany of Ten Maxims, 1252) tells that after being humiliated by Koretada about the promotion, Asanari became *ikiryō* or a living vengeful spirit to torment Koretada.[6]

---

3   See for example, *Ōkagami* (The Great Mirror, ca. 1085–1125); *Hōbutsushū* (A Collection of Treasures, ca. 1178); *Kojidan* (Stories of Ancient Events, ca. 1215). For the respective stories, see Tachibana and Katō 183–88; Taira et al. 98; and Minamoto Akikane 126–127.

4   *Kojidan* writes about the position of *Sangi* (Consultant). Asanari, however, became Consultant two years ahead of Koretada. According to *Jikkinshō* (1252), the argument is about the status of Chūnagon (Middle Councilor) that Asanari became many years after Koretada.

5   From the historical viewpoint, this information is not correct because both Asanari and Koretada become the Head Chamberlain at the same time. The *Ōkagami*'s narrator is not concerned about the historical fact. *Ōkagami* is written primarily from the point of view of the successful and victorious family of the Fujiwara clan, and while the narrator is sympathetic to Asanari, calling him superior in letters as well as worldly reputation, he does not concern himself much about a minor Fujiwara kinsman being placed in a negative light.

6   For the text, see Asami 372–74. In *Jikkinshō*, Asanari desired the position of *dainagon* (Major Councilor).

Asanari's residence, located on the corners of the Third Avenue was called *Oni den* (Demon's House).

According to the heroine of "A Tale of a Demon," who, as we have seen is Asanari's female servant, Asanari's circumstance is explained quite differently. She explains:

> My master is not nearly as bad as the townspeople would have him be. He quarrelled at court with his rival, Fujiwara Koretada, who had formed a regency of his own while Chunagon remained at his former rank. When Chunagon requested promotion to the new regency himself, Fujiwara refused him. Chance had it that Fujiwara died shortly afterward, causing people in the Capital to suspect that Chunagon had sent a vengeful ghost[7] to torment Fujiwara and lead him to his death. But my master was not of such a hostile nature. Indeed, as evidence of that, two years later he literally wasted away, unable to bear the vicious slanders they spread about regarding his conduct. Thus Chunagon himself became a vengeful ghost and has been living here in the House of Demons ever since. …after Chunagon died, he turned into a ghost and then a demon. He haunted the streets at night and there were even sightings of him at court. *That* is what demons are like. They are not forever gobbling people up, only men like *you* who go galloping around in broad daylight, waving their sword and shouting and threatening to kill them. ("A Tale of a Demon" 113–15)[8]

Watanabe Eri observes that the oni-woman's voice denies the story of the historical tale, *Ōkagami*, which describes the prosperity of the Fujiwara Regency's male history recorded in written text, and re-narrates the story in a female voice (143–44). What is most interesting to me about the oni-woman's explanation of Asanari is that Asanari's story is, itself, narrated by an oni; this is an oni's story told from an oni's point of view.

Nakagami, who clearly sympathizes with the oni, seems to want to decode and debunk the oni myth handed down and so readily accepted by mainstream Japanese culture. The story of a vengeful spirit, a doer of malicious deeds, is probably not unlike the fiction about outcasts narrated by such writers as Shimazaki Tōson who wrote *Hakai* (Broken Commandment). Nakagami considers the outcast figures described by Kawabata Yasunari and Mishima Yukio, whom Nakagami believes were born in outcast villages, as powerfully aesthetic and moving (*Nakagami Kenji hatsugen shūsei*

---

7   To be accurate, Asanari had become a vengeful living spirit.
8   For the original Japanese text, see Nakagami, *Nakagami Kenji zenshū* 5: 323–24.

6: 341).⁹ So it is plausible to speculate that Nakagami wants to claim that one has to hear the voice of the people and characters actually living in the surroundings in order to accurately recount them. According to Nakagami's oni-woman, whose existence is also shrouded in social stigma, oni are harmless to people who are not involved in any grudges or feuds. She further asserts that not all oni are human-eaters, and that not all of them are representatives of pure, unadulterated evil; oni can display a wide variety of emotions and feeling and are thus complex characters with motivations and attributes similar to those of humans. To the oni-woman, the oni are just misunderstood because of the words and phrases uttered by the people in power.

Having said this, however, Nakagami's oni-woman destroys that very humane, sympathetic oni image with her barbaric actions at the end of the story. The act of eating the man completely undermines her earlier lamentation. She

> …slashed open his belly with claws as hard as steel and tore off his arms with two sets of sharp fangs which had sprouted above and below her mouth. …He lay there helpless, gasping and groaning as the demon wrenched off his legs and gobbled them down and licked and slurped and munched at his entrails. Finally, she picks up his head, severed from the torso. ("A Tale of a Demon" 119)¹⁰

How can the perpetrator of such gruesome acts make successful claims on the readers' sympathy? In order to understand this seemingly paradoxical incongruity of words and actions, one might usefully examine this complex oni-woman figure in juxtaposition to an oni described in *Konjaku monogatarishū*, "The Lust of the White Serpent" in *Tales of Moonlight and Rain* (1776), and folk legends.

The basic plot and core framework of "A Tale of a Demon" follows the story entitled "About an Oni at Agi Bridge at Ōmi that Eats Humans" in *Konjaku monogatarishū*. As mentioned in chapter one, the story goes as follows: a man who bragged about his prowess goes to Agi Bridge in Ōmi province in his attempt to exterminate an oni that has been haunting the area. At the bridge, the oni lies in waiting, about to demonstrate another of the oni's supernatural traits—transformative ability. With his greenish skin,

---

9 Nakagami says that nobody talks about it, but it is clear that Kawabata Yasunari and Mishima Yukio were born in outcast communities (*Nakagami Kenji hatsugen shūsei 2*: 37).
10 For the original Japanese text, see Nakagami, *Nakagami Kenji zenshū* 5: 325.

an imposing nine-foot-tall stature, dishevelled hair and three-fingered claws for hands, the mere sight of him would send most running. But, disguised as a beautiful young woman, he easily plays on the wits of his unsuspecting victim, though in the end, he fails to kill the man, who narrowly escapes. Later, the oni, now disguised as the man's younger brother, visits his house and finally murders him. Similar to *Konjaku monogatarishū*, the man in "A Tale of a Demon" brags about his prowess, meets a beautiful woman on the bridge, the woman turns out to be an oni, and at the end of the story, the oni murders the man. While somewhat mirroring the story of *Konjaku monogatarishū*, the oni-woman in "A Tale of a Demon" reflects other elements—she is a sexually active female,[11] echoing the supernatural creature of Ueda Akinari's "The Lust of the White Serpent."[12]

It is commonly known that Nakagami admires Ueda Akinari (1734–1809), the author of the *Tales of Moonlight and Rain*. Among the *Tales of Moonlight and Rain*, Nakagami especially likes "Jasei no in" (Lust of the White Serpent) in which Shingū, his birthplace, is a backdrop. He comments that, unlike the *Genji monogatari* (Tale of Genji, ca. 1010), sexuality is exposed in "Lust of the White Serpent" (*Nakagami Kenji zenshū* 15: 176).[13] The protagonist of "Lust of the White Serpent" is a young woman driven to keep her man's affections at all costs.[14] Her name is Manago, and she is in fact, a white serpent. Graceful-looking Manago is so in love with a dreamy, gentle-looking man, Toyoo, that she follows him everywhere in total disregard of his wishes. In creating "Lust of the White Serpent," Akinari heavily adapted the two Chinese vernacular tales, "Madam Bai Eternally Buried under Thunder Peak Pagoda" and "Strange Tale of Thunder Pagoda,"[15] both based upon a Chinese legend. Akinari also used a well-known Japanese

---

11   The gender of the oni of *Konjaku monogatarishū* is not specified; probably it was not considered very important.

12   For the Japanese text, see Nakamura Yukihiko, Takada, and Nakamura Hiroyasu 357–87. For an English translation, see Zolbrod 161–84; Ueda, *Tales of Moonlight and Rain* 155–85.

13   Nakagami named one of his major stories, "Jain," or "Snake Lust," after "Lust of the White Serpent," and its female protagonist is full of sexuality and has a lustful nature.

14   In the end, Manago threatens him, "If you believe what other people say and recklessly try to abandon me, I shall seek vengeance, and tall though the peaks of the mountains of the Kii High Road may be, your blood will drain from the ridges into the valleys. You must not be so rash as to throw away your life in vain." The translation is by Zolbrod (179).

15   For the translation of the Chinese text, see Ma and Lau 355–78.

serpent folk legend, Dōjōji, popular in Noh, puppet theatre, and Kabuki.[16] In Dōjōji, a woman whose passion is rejected by a handsome monk transforms into a serpent while in pursuit of the man. As he hides in the bell of Dōjōji temple, she coils around the bell and burns him to death. In the Buddhist belief, a woman is compared to a poisonous serpent because of her lustful nature. When her passion is not accepted, it is with jealousy and enmity she avenges herself upon the man and murders him.[17] Akinari enhances the montage of both legends by setting the "Lust of The White Serpent" in the same courtly atmosphere as the *Tale of Genji*. Thus, "Lust of The White Serpent" resounds with the exotic appeal of the past of both China and Japan past.[18]

Toyoo returns Manago's affections, but later, a priest informs Toyoo of Manago's identity and the possible danger to his life, warning him that his lack of *ōshisa* (manliness) is what has allowed him to be possessed by Manago. Toyoo then marries Tomiko, a beauty who has served in the palace. Taken with Tomiko's refined manner and appearance, Toyoo lets down his guard against Manago and Manago possesses Tomiko, much like Lady Rokujō possessed Aoi in the *Tale of Genji*.[19] Having discovered his *ōshisa*, he follows the instructions from a revered Dōjōji priest to put an end to Manago's reign of terror. Manago's demise at the end of the tale follows the Chinese stories: the white serpent/Manago is buried deep in the ground, never to appear again.

16   The Dōjōji legend appears in such works as *Dainihonkoku hokke genki* (Miraculous Efficacy of Lotus Sutra in Great Japan, 1043), *Konjaku monogatarishū*, *Dōjōji engi* (History of Dōjōji, ca. late 15th century). For the respective stories, see Inoue and Ōsone 217–19; Mabuchi, Kunisaki, and Inagaki, 35: 406–12; and Komatsu Shigemi, Yoshida, Shimatani, Uchida, and Oshita, 61–120, 189–94.

17   The Noh mask "ja" (snake), used for the Noh play *Dōjōji* expresses that fury with a pair of horns on the forehead, bare golden eyes, enlarged nostrils and split mouth with fangs. It is not human, but possesses evil dragon or snake attributes (Nogami 288–89).

18   Yamaguchi Takeshi contends that there is no work in which Chinese sources and Japanese sources are as beautifully mixed and crafted (49).

19   When slightly intoxicated Toyoo playfully talks to Tomiko who is facing down on the bed, she lifts her face and replies, "it is more hateful of you to treasure this common creature" in the voice of Manago. This sentence immediately recalls scenes from "Yūgao" and "Aoi" of the *Tale of Genji*. When the evil spirit, believed to be that of Lady Rokujō, is about to kill Yūgao, the spirit utters the same lines. Also, when the spirit of Lady Rokujō is attacking Aoi, Aoi becomes unusually gentle, and there the spirit speaks to Genji in Lady Rokujō"s voice. From this allusion, the reader can anticipate the fate of Tomiko; she is destined to die just as Aoi did. Allusions in Akinari's text are thus interwoven with the world of the original text. For English translations of *Genji monogatari*, see Murasaki, *The Tale of Genji*.

The oni-woman's surroundings in "A Tale of a Demon" recall Manago's territory in that a supernatural creature follows a man, the target of her passion. The oni-woman-serpent paradigm is indicated at the very beginning of the story from the name of the bridge, Tatsumi.[20] *Tatsumi* is a directional word meaning Southeast, but *tatsu* in *tatsumi* means "dragon," according to the twelve signs of the Chinese zodiac, the fifth animal. *Mi* in *tatsumi* means snake, interestingly, the first animal of the Chinese zodiac. The woman who appears at Tatsumi Bridge signifies the snake of "The Lust of the White Serpent" as well as those serpents of old Japan—like Dōjōji—that transform into oni-serpents/dragons. The narrator of "A Tale of a Demon" also points to a snake-dragon-oni continuum as "the girl [i.e., oni-woman] knew that if she were to reveal her true form to him, his heart would be turned inside out, much as a stagnant swamp is burst asunder by a dragon rising from its bed" (117).

Like Manago, the oni-woman feels for the man and like Toyoo, the man called Hankai is charmed by what he perceives is a beautiful girl from the capital. They are enchanted by emotion-driven lust and sexuality, especially in Nakagami's story where physical contact, raw sexual passion and themes of sexuality are highlighted. In both stories, after the first encounter when they confirm their mutual lust for each other, the man has difficulty finding the woman's residence. In "A Tale of a Demon," the man looks for her house in the capital and asks around about Chūnagon's residence on the Third Avenue, but nobody knows where she resides. Similarly, in the "Lust of the White Serpent," when Toyoo looks for Manago's house, nobody seems to know its location. The oni-woman in "A Tale of a Demon" explains that the house the man finally finds on the Third Avenue of the capital is called a "House of Demons," and the master, Asanari, is in fact, an oni. In the "Lust of the White Serpent," after Toyoo believes he has been tricked by Manago, he calls her "oni" and the place where she lives, "a house where oni would live."

Manago is so infatuated with Toyoo that when he falsely proclaims he will become hers, she happily believes his words and comes to his side, transforming into her original shape. As for the oni-woman, she asks whether he would love her even if she was an oni, and he replies, "even if she was an oni." Mellowed by his words, she reveals a hint of her true form. Both supernatural beings believe their respective men's promises of love, resulting in their revealing their true forms. In the end, both men do not carry out

---

20   In *Konjaku monogatarishū*, the name of the bridge is Agi.

their promises. Unlike Toyoo, who knows Manago's true identity and is prepared to sacrifice himself to save his new bride, Hankai, in "A Tale of a Demon" does not know the oni-woman's true identity nor, as it turns out, is he prepared to sacrifice his life for anyone else. The man is attracted only to the woman's beautiful human form and has no interest in getting involved with an oni. So when the man sees her true oni form, for lack of a better phrase, "he wants out."

Apparently Nakagami sympathized with Hankai, the male protagonist of "A Tale of a Demon." While Hankai is based upon the main character of "About an Oni at Agi Bridge at Ōmi that Eats Humans" of *Konjaku monogatarishū* as noted earlier, he also reflects Taizō, the main character of Akinari's "Hankai"[21] from *Tales of Spring Rain* (1809). Taizō is a roughneck with unrivalled strength and is nicknamed Hankai as well. Taizō becomes a bandit after inadvertently killing his father and elder brother, and scaring a widow away with his excessive drinking. Similarly the man of "A Tale of a Demon" seriously considers becoming a bandit if he fails to kill the oni. Akinari's Hankai (Taizō) is no moral paragon; he takes a shrine's offertory box, gambles, drinks heavily and steals, and kills his father and brother as well as several other innocents. He is a wild boy who does not give much thought to things in general.[22] Nakagami comments, "the protagonist of 'Hankai' [Taizō] is like a child (*yōjiteki*), for Akinari has kept nullifying the oppression of law and system by the protagonist's positive impulse, which is symbolized by his repeated question of, "So what!?" (*Nakagami Kenji zenshū* 15: 161). The oni-woman in "A Tale of a Demon" describes the face of the man who sleeps with his mouth pouted *like a child*, and feels dear about the man who cries that he would rather die than not meet an oni. "If only he could love her as a demon, she felt, she would be glad to fulfil his dream [of killing an oni] by letting him strike her down." She wants the man to love

---

21 For the Japanese text, see Nakamura Yukihiko, Takada, and Nakamura Hiroyasu 519–62. For an English translation, see Ueda, *Tales of the Spring Rain*.

22 Interestingly, Nakagami considers "Hankai" as the best villain fiction (*akkan shōsetsu*). Taizō is, however, enlightened and became a revered Buddhist priest. Akinari writes that Taizō is a good example of how "A restrained mind originates the Buddha's nature, yielding to the desires creates a monster" (Nakamura Yukihiko, Takada, and Nakamura Hiroyasu 562). Incidentally, this phrase appears in *Tsūzoku saiyūki* (*Xi you ji*) and describes the character of Songokū (or *Sun Wukong*) in *Saiyūki*. Songokū, a wild boy, causes a stir in heaven when he yields to earthly desires. But when he realizes the power of Buddha and restrains his mind, he becomes a disciple of Sanzō hōshi (*Sanzang fashi*), and attains Buddhahood. See Yan.

her for what she is, an oni, a creature largely misunderstood and according to her, misrepresented by those in the mainstream.

The oni-woman earlier explains that it was people's vicious *rumors* that made her master Asanari turn into an oni, not his grudge against Koretada. Clearly for this oni-woman words have power. The man *says* he would love her "even if she was an oni." So she slowly and cautiously reveals the true self she believes he is capable of loving. It is perhaps understandable that she tears him to shreds when the man reacts so differently from his word. However, it is not easy for an ordinary man to love a woman whose "eyes glitter as though the sockets were two golden bowls… [whose] huge mouth is filled with sabre-like teeth, [and whose] tusks grow above and below," let alone a man who does not think much—just like the protagonist of "Hankai."

Indeed, it seems naïve for the oni-woman to take the man at his word that he would still love her, even in her true oni form. But as is often *told*, there is nothing false in the words of demons.[23] The narrator *says* that she would indeed give up her life. But then again, did she really resolve to sacrifice herself to satisfy his desire or was there something more profound at work here? These questions undermine the text's reliability, and in the end, nobody can definitively know the truth. In the end, the oni ends up gobbling up the man, thus further propagating its mythical concept. Interestingly, in this story, both human and oni are left thinking they are misunderstood. For the man, to kill a strange and ominous creature lying right beside him is an instinctive act without premeditation. When the oni-woman attacks and devours Hankai, she is committing an act of preservation and instinct as well. Eventually the oni-woman does what she has warned earlier, which is attack "only men like *you* who go galloping around in broad daylight, waving their swords while shouting and threatening to kill them."

"A Tale of a Demon" also emulates *Konjaku monogatarishū* through its use of continuous, long sentences. A compound or complex sentence in "A Tale of a Demon" frequently lasts more than fifteen lines using subordinating conjunctions with a number of independent as well as dependent clauses, probably to make the sentences sound a little more formal. Nakagami often employs the stem form of a verb rather than the more colloquial te-form of a verb: For example, he uses "osowareta to *ii*" (says

---

23 The idea that demons are honest and not manipulative is not novel. See the section on "Prosperity" in chapter one.

that she was attacked) instead of "osowareta to *itte*," and so, the sentence continues almost endlessly. Further, like *Konjaku monogatarishū*, there are no paragraphs in the entire story; the story appears and reads like one gigantic paragraph. A page is filled with letters without a space. One may say that there are many other instances when Nakagami continuously uses long sentences, refusing to make paragraphs. But in "A Tale of a Demon," he uses absolutely no paragraphs or even quotation marks for conversations.[24]

The written texts were historically alien to a majority of outcasts. Commenting on his Japanese language, Nakagami states, "some Japanese writers point out that my Japanese expressions are strange… the opinion that my written Japanese language which came from the world totally unrelated to written language, is strange… That indication causes me anxiety, and this causes me incomparable anger" (*Nakagami Kenji hatsugen shūsei*, 6: 345). "A Tale of a Demon" may have been Nakagami's challenge to the heritage of Japanese written language and traditional literary pieces such as *Konjaku monogatarishū*, "The Lust of the White Serpent" and "Hankai."

Also, Nakagami may have wanted to express the oni-woman's loneliness, a trait of oni not entirely known to humans. Arguably the oni-woman's all too human loneliness makes her vulnerable to Hankai's promise. In the end, despite what the oni-woman has *said* to the Hankai about the nature of oni, the oni's cannibalistic instincts prevail, and the image of oni remains unchanged.

The story's poignant aftermath lingers for a while, but eventually too, dissipates in the air, and the oni's myth continues, as does the myth of *burakumin*. Using the old tales of oni, Nakagami's oni becomes an allegory of *burakumin*.

Yumemakura Baku's *Onmyōji* (The Yin-Yang Master)

In Yumemakura Baku's (born 1951) series *Onmyōji*, Abe no Seimei, a legendary *onmyōji* known for his skills of divination, magic, and sorcery teams up with aristocratic Minamoto no Hiromasa (918–?). Together they solve mysteries and crimes of supernatural origin. The popular series, which first appeared in 1988, has been adapted as an equally successful manga (graphic novel) and a television series of the same title. In writing *Onmyōji*,

---

24 Nakagami's admiration for *Konjaku monogatarishū* is revealed from such a statement as "Frankly speaking, neither *Tales of Moonlight and Rain* or *Tales of Spring Rain* surpasses *Konjaku monogatarishū*" (*Nakagami Kenji zenshū* 15: 163).

Yumemakura remarks that he has always wanted to write about stories of the Heian period when darkness and oni still reside in the living space of people (*Onmyōji* 331).²⁵ While *Onmyōji*'s setting is indeed the Heian period, Yumemakura's representations of oni and the development of his human characters are quite contemporary. Similar to Nakagami Kenji's oni, Yumemakura's oni are lonely, misunderstood beings. But while Nakagami's oni—stigmatized supernatural beings—are perhaps a projection of his personal experience, community, and anger, Yumemakura's oni are primarily for the entertainment of a mass audience as well as the author himself. Yumemakura is quite skilled at touching a chord of empathy with Japanese readers and viewers.

Just as Nakagami did, Yumemakura builds upon or modifies earlier images of oni and historical characters to make his series appeal to a contemporary audience. Regarding the protagonist, Abe no Seimei, the historical Seimei's youthful years correspond to the period of Engi-Tenryaku (901–947), a time of prosperity for *onmyōdō*, during which excellent practitioners of *onmyōdō* arose. In this time, practitioners of *onmyōdō*, which included *onmyōji*, were recognized imperial servants. Their primary duties were to observe and examine almanacs, the heavens, and astrological charts for use in divination.²⁶ As noted in chapter one, the Engi-Tenryaku era was a time when the official practitioners of *onmyōdō* were consolidating their own power by serving the Fujiwara (Murayama, *Nihon onmyōdō sōsetsu* 112, 172). These court practitioners of *onmyōdō* came to be known as the aristocracy's private "cat's paws" (Murayama, "Kyūtei onmyōdō no seiritsu" 378, 385).

One anecdote often used to prove Seimei's prescient ability concerns Emperor Kazan's (968–1008) abdication. According to *Ōkagami*, in 986 Emperor Kazan was set to renounce his throne as the result of the political machinations of Fujiwara no Kaneie (929–990). Kazan's abdication would allow Kaneie to rule as regent when Kaneie's six-year-old grandson, Crown Prince Yasuhito, ascended the throne. When Emperor Kazan's entourage, on its way to a temple, passed Abe no Seimei's house "they [heard] the diviner clap his [Seimei's] hands and exclaim: 'The heavens foretold His Majesty's abdication, and now it seems to have happened.'"²⁷ Suwa Haruo, however,

---

25 Yumemakura's fictional Seimei claims that his profession will be lost without oni.

26 See the section on "The *Onmyōdō* Line" in chapter one.

27 Translation by McCullough. *Ōkagami: The Great Mirror* 81. For the original text, see Tachibana and Katō 46.

writes that for Seimei who served Kazan closely, it would not have been difficult to predict Kazan's abdication (20). Some, including Shibusawa Tatsuhiko, even hypothesize that Seimei most likely knew the political circumstance in court and took part in Fujiwara Kaneie's family plot to depose Emperor Kazan (see Shibusawa, "Mittsu no dokuro" 175). This incident happened when Seimei was in his mid-sixties. Be it through psychic powers or political connections, Abe no Seimei became larger than life soon after his death.[28]

Before Yumemakura's *Onmyōji*, Abe no Seimei was traditionally depicted either as an old man, as he sporadically appears in the classical Japanese literature, or a young boy as portrayed in plays of the early modern period. In the current Heisei era, Yumemakura's Seimei is a beautiful, good-looking adult with thin red lips. He is a sophisticated, handsome hero endowed with supernatural powers, solving the mysterious crimes of the nostalgic Heian period and facing his demonic adversary.

The world of *Onmyōji* is frequently that of *Konjaku monogatarishū*, Noh plays such as *Kanawa*, *Ugetsu monogatari*, and other classical literature. Yumemakura's approach to the classical text is simple and direct. Yumemakura substantiates the contexts and explanations left unexplained in the original stories so that the readers do not have to read between the lines. Filling the gaps, Yumemakura presents the oni's perspective. This important feature differs from classical literature where the oni's stance is overlooked by authors and readers. Yumemakura often portrays oni in a sympathetic light, enabling readers to identify with these marginalized creatures. At the same time Yumemakura peppers the plots of these old stories with a mixture of sex, pathos, and grotesque imagery involving the oni and their emotions. Many of his oni are the marginalized spirits of humans trapped in the world of the living by the overpowering force of unrequited love.

One example is "Genjō to iu biwa, oni no tameni toraruru koto" (A *Biwa* [Pipa] called Genjō is Stolen by an Oni)[29] which is based upon the story of the same title in *Konjaku monogatarishū*.[30] The episode in *Konjaku*

---

28 For more information about *onmyōdō* and Abe no Seimei's descendants in English, see Butler.

29 The text is found in Yumemakura, *Onmyōji* 7–78. For an English translation, see McGillicuddy 1–57.

30 For the text of "Genjō to iu biwa, oni ni toraruru koto" in *Konjaku monogatarishū*, see Mabuchi, Kunisaki, and Inagaki 37: 308–11. For an English translation, see Ury 146–49.

monogatarishū is a straightforward narrative; a prized *biwa* called Genjō disappears from the imperial palace. While the emperor deeply laments the loss, an enchanting melody of Genjō is heard from the direction of Rashō Gate. Minamoto no Hiromasa, an excellent musician, follows the tune, and discovers an oni at the gate playing the missing *biwa*. (The reader is never quite sure who this oni is, let alone why the oni steals the Genjō and is playing it at Rashō Gate.) Hiromasa asks the oni to return the *biwa*, an imperial treasure, and the oni obeys. Ever after, the *biwa* acts like a living being—it plays if it feels like it.

Yumemakura's *Onmyōji*, in contrast to the original, gives background information and flavor to the tale, fleshing it out in the process. The narrative is much more detailed. To begin with, the oni is the spirit of a foreign *biwa* maker who created the Genjō and died years before—one hundred twenty-eight years to be precise. That the oni is a spirit of the dead follows a Chinese interpretation discussed in chapter one. Further, this oni is identified as foreign born, thus reinforcing the view that the oni is the marginalized other. Thus, Yumemakura uses a conventional image of oni in his text. The oni does not rest peacefully because of his attachment to his homeland (India) and his wife, so he steals the *biwa* he made to console himself with music. Yumemakura creates a story behind the story and the oni is no longer so mysterious.

While the oni in *Konjaku monogatarishū* obeys a command to return the instrument to the emperor, *Onmyōji*'s oni requests a woman in trade. The oni explains to Abe no Seimei, who does not appear in the original episode of the *Konjaku monogatarishū*, that while strolling in the imperial palace, he has fallen in love with someone who bears a remarkable resemblance to his wife. The oni agrees to return the *biwa* in exchange for a night spent with the woman. Thus, the oni is endowed with human feelings and desires, filling the episode with sex and violence.[31] Abe no Seimei accedes

---

31 In *Onmyōji*, the idea that the oni recognized the heavenly power of the emperor and returned the Genjō is absent. Obviously simply returning the *biwa* would not be exciting. However, it is also possible that the change is a conscious or unconscious reaction to something deeper—perhaps the admission that Emperor Hirohito (Showa Emperor) is not a god, and thus would be unable to command the oni. Yumemakura has Seimei regularly refer to the emperor as "that man." To call the emperor "that man" was unthinkable in those days—even today it does not sound very respectful. This phraseology may reflect the author's (and perhaps many readers') attitude toward the emperor or royal family in contemporary society.

to the oni's request and the two agree that there will be no tricks during the one-night affair. But the woman's brother told his sister to take the oni's head with a hidden knife, and as she tried to do so, she was torn asunder and eaten by the oni.

The grotesque appearance of the oni is in accord with convention and so is its cannibalism. Yet, it is important to note that instead of being outwardly violent or antagonistic towards the other characters, the oni first reveals his weaknesses. He shows sadness and remorse for losing his wife and having to live as an oni. Yumemakura casts the oni in a pitiable light as the reader is informed of his love for his wife and his tragic death. While the fact that he stole the *biwa* remains unchanged, the fact that he is a creator of the very same *biwa* makes him more sympathetic. It is the human who has broken the promise that caused the oni to revert to his evil nature and thus prey on innocent humans (i.e., the woman who resembles his late wife). In the process of devouring the woman, the oni says "how sad..." (73). It sounds rather comical for a devouring oni to lament, "how sad..." but since the woman's state of mind is never described, there is not much opportunity for the reader to feel empathy or sympathy for her or for her brother who intervened in Seimei's plan and foiled it. If one pauses a moment and gives it some thought, it seems quite natural for the woman's brother to botch the plan. As the brother says, it would ruin the reputation of the family if a rumor that his sister made love with an oni spreads. (It is noteworthy that how his sister must have felt is completely absent from anybody's thoughts). Yet, the reader is asked to sympathize with the oni rather than the woman or her brother because the oni's loneliness is the focal point of the story.

In the end it is revealed that the spirit of the *biwa* maker possessed a dying dog earlier and transformed into the conventional masculine oni image. After the oni-dog is killed by the brother, the soul of the *biwa* maker comes to possess the royal *biwa* itself. That is why, Yumemakura writes, Genjō acts like a living creature—an explanation absent from the *Konjaku monogatarishū*.

Another example of Yumemakura's gap bridging is "Kanawa" (Iron Tripod), which is based upon the Noh play, *Kanawa*.[32] In fact, *Onmyōji*'s "Kanawa" follows the Noh text so closely that it even utilizes the language conventions of the Noh play—for example, he inserts narratives between the lines of the lyrics to explicate the Noh's ornate diction. Yumemakura

---

32   For the gist of Noh *Kanawa*, see the section "Noh Kanawa" in chapter three.

comments that the Noh play *Kanawa* does not sufficiently describe the woman who turned into an oni, especially the play's closing, so he wrote his "Kanawa" to offer a clear ending or explanation of that oni-woman (*Onmyōji: Namanari-hime* 385–86). At the end of the Noh text, the oni-woman proclaims that she will wait for her revenge, and the chorus recites, "Only her voice is clearly heard; the demon now is invisible. She has passed beyond the sight of men, an evil spirit beyond the sight of men" (Eileen Kato 204). Yumemakura explains what is meant by the "invisible oni" and what happens to the woman. In comparison with the Noh play, Yumemakura's characters are more nuanced, as are their dealings with each other and the events they encounter. Like the mortal characters, Yumemakura's oni are nuanced as well. By presenting the woman-turned-oni as the victim of a philandering husband, Yumemakura presents an oni whose actions are at least understandable, if not necessarily deserving of the reader's sympathy.

In his work, Yumemakura gives the man and his former wife names for the sake of convenience and adds other personal touches. The man's name is Fujiwara no Tameyoshi, and the woman, Tokuko. Yumemakura makes a significant change in the treatment of oni in Tokuko's attack scene. In the Noh play, the woman has already become an oni when she appears in the room to attack her former husband—this is the beginning of the second act and the woman appears on the stage wearing either a *hannya* (she-demon) mask or a *namanari* mask.[33] Furthermore she does not realize that she is tormenting a doll throughout the play. In contrast, Tokuko is still a human shape when she comes to Tameyoshi's residence—she is wearing a tripod, but she is a human. Importantly, she realizes that she is assaulting a doll when Hiromasa, the musician mentioned above, utters a sound of surprised disgust. When she becomes aware that Hiromasa, Seimei, and Tameyoshi have seen her grotesque appearance and violent behavior, she turns into an oni. Tokuko says, "Did you see me? You looked at this wretched appearance, didn't you? ... how shameful, my miserable appearance" (*Onmyōji: Tsukumogami no maki* 79–80). Then, for the first time, the horns start to grow on her forehead and she begins to transform to an oni.[34] As seen in chapter one, Yomotsu-shikome, an origin of Japanese oni, was born out of a woman's feeling of shame about her repulsive appearance and being

---

33   A *namanari* mask represents a being in the process of becoming a full-fledged oni. This is symbolized by small horns on its forehead (See Nogami 299).

34   This is literally visualized in Takita Yōji's film of the same title, *Onmyōji*. Part of the film version of *Onmyōji* follows the plot of "Kanawa."

watched by a man; Tokuko follows this pattern in which shame and anger turn a woman into an oni. For a woman who tries to maintain decorum, to be watched in a shameful act is powerful enough motivation to transform her into a different being. As her respectability is broken in the eyes of others, her jealousy and anger surface. This motivation follows convention, but while the classical literature omits the transformation completely, Yumemakura graphically describes its process, capturing the reader's attention with a gripping portrayal of *oni*fication. Failing to kill Tameyoshi, and overcome by shame, Tokuko commits suicide. In her dying moment, she asks Hiromasa to play the flute whenever she is overwhelmed by her desire to eat Tameyoshi. She says that his flute will appease her anger. Since then when the oni appears beside Hiromasa, Hiromasa plays the flute. The oni listens to the flute without saying a word and disappears. This is Yumemakura's explanation of what happens to, or what is meant by the "invisible oni."

It is important to notice that while Tokuko-oni is still possessed by anger and has a predilection for cannibalism, she offers a solution to her own problem and therefore causes no harm to anyone. In that respect, she is sensible, conscientious and restrained. Tokuko-oni is also more self-reflective. She blames herself for having fallen in love with Tameyoshi. She says, "it is I who fell in love with you. Nobody told me to do so. ... Not understanding that you play double, I pledged and shared a bed with you. ... I know it's all my fault, but..." (*Onmyōji: Tsukumogami no maki* 76).

Tokuko-oni's assault is quite vicious, but as her environment and feelings are amply explained by both the omniscient narrator and Tokuko-oni herself, the reader can sympathize with her. In Yumemakura's *Namanarihime* (2003), which further expands the story of "Kanawa," Tokuko's situation becomes more pitiful and deserving of sympathy, for she is framed by her husband, belittled by his new wife, and thus marginalized by society in general. (At the same time, her violence becomes more escalated and graphic.) Notwithstanding their violence, Yumemakura's female oni are portrayed as sensible and understanding.

The heroine-oni in "Oni no michiyuki" (Oni's Journey [to the Palace]) is also sensible, understanding, and patient. The oni's identity is the unsaved spirit of a neglected woman.[35] Unlike the previous examples, this story appears to be unique to Yumemakura. Fifteen years before her death, the emperor visits her, promising that he will come back to take her to the palace.

---

35 For the text, see Yumemakura, *Onmyōji* 233–96.

She clings to his promise, but the emperor never returns. Upon her death, she starts her journey to the palace at night to realize the unfulfilled trust. She appears as a beautiful woman of about twenty-eight years of age with a pleasant fragrance. Challenged by people on the street, however, she changes into a blue-skinned oni with a masculine hairy arm, killing and eating those who challenge her. The sudden transformation from a beautiful woman to a masculine oni is reminiscent of the oni in *Konjaku monagatarishū*, particularly the one in the familiar story of Watanabe Tsuna and an oni at Modoribashi Bridge.[36] The oni in "Oni no michiyuki" is a victim of the emperor's utter neglect. Unlike the fierce oni of classical literature, however, she happily goes to the other world upon the emperor's acknowledgement of his neglect and his sincere remorse. Before her disappearance, the oni's anguish and marginalization serve to engender the reader's sympathy. In the end, the oni is not an evil creature bent on harming people, but someone who simply wants acknowledgement after fifteen long years of abandonment.

Yumemakura's view of oni is replicated in the dialogs of Seimei and Hiromasa, which in turn seem to mirror the concept of oni-*yōkai* delineated by the folklorists and anthropologists. Yumemakura's Seimei claims that *kami* and oni are essentially the same, and their naming depends upon human perception. When a phenomenon is perceived as beneficial, it is considered the act of a *kami* whereas negative occurrences are labelled as those of an oni. Thus, Seimei claims that "oni and *kami* don't exist without involving humans," and further explains that "be it *kami* or oni, human minds produce them" (*Onmyōji: Hōō no maki* 57). Commenting on the water deities enshrined in the Kibune Shrine, Seimei says, "Originally, water is just water. People call it good or evil because both good and evil lie on the side of humans." Hiromasa responds, "You mean, oni is a product of humans" (*Onmyōji: Tsukumogami no maki* 86–87). Further, Seimei and Hiromasa discuss that oni hide and live in human *kokoro* (hearts or souls) (*Onmyōji: Ryūteki no maki* 133). The expression "kokoro no oni" first appeared in the *Kagerō nikki* (The Gossamer Years, ca. late 10th century) and became a topic of discussion in the Heian women's literature (Knecht et al., "'Oni' to 'mushi'" 286). Through its symbolism it provides a psychological explanation for the discord and conflict of emotions in one's heart that sometimes accompany marital relationships and relations between men and women

---

36 See the section "Transformation Power" in chapter one.

in general.[37] The discord caused by unhappy marital relationships ripples in the hearts of women, described symbolically as oni in the Heian literature. When women are overwhelmed by this discord they show the physical appearance of oni. This occurs in the Noh play as well as in Yumemakura's "Kanawa." In the latter case, as noted before, the graphic description of her transformation, tantamount to horror fiction, becomes a major focal point.

The view of oni as a product of the human psyche and the difference between oni and *kami* as one of human perspective become more prominent in the film, *Onmyōji* II (2003). In the film the oni is a human boy named Susa. Against his will, he is transformed into an oni in order to carry out the wishes of his father, the chieftain of the Izumo clan. Susa-oni devours various people to obtain great power. When Susa says, "I don't want to be an oni," his father corrects him by claiming that "No, you are going to be a *kami*." Throughout the film, the other characters who know Susa realize his humanity, and rather than trying to defeat him, set about to help him, even when he is beyond control and attacking innocent victims. His sister knows that he is transformed and out to kill her, but even so she ventures into harm's way to help him. This film turns the oni into a victim. This victimization of oni is a modern tendency; modern interpretations go deeper into the oni's motivations and feelings, creating a more complex view of these creatures by humanizing them. At his core, Susa is a young man capable of evoking a powerful sympathetic emotional response from the audience of the film. The audience sympathizes with the oni as an outsider or loner who is unable to belong to society at large.

This sympathy and even empathy for oni seem to reflect modern people's affinity for the oni-like existence. In other words, modern authors take the oni as a being tantamount to a human and attempt to understand their behavior and feelings—in doing this the authors attempt to pry out their own human motivations and needs. Contemporary Japanese consciously or unconsciously view themselves as lonely individuals or marginalized creatures like oni. They are perhaps trying to find a niche in society, just as the oni are trying to do.

Onmyōji has been a driving force in a recent "Abe no Seimei boom" that has spawned a number of books on Seimei as well as on *onmyōdō*. The shrines endowed with the name of Abe no Seimei are popularly visited

---

37 For various meanings of "kokoro no oni" and its origin, see Knecht et al., "'Oni' to 'mushi'."

by countless young female *Onmyōji* fans.[38] Indeed, just a decade ago, the Seimei Shrine in Kyoto was quite obscure and hard to locate. But the popularity of Abe no Seimei has brought numerous visitors to the shrine, and the shrine has added new offices, renovated the buildings, and is now a tourist spot in Kyoto (Seimei jinja 47). Whether or not this represents a renewed interest in the religious aspect of these shrines, Abe no Seimei supposedly brings material wealth with him, and oni are heavily involved as harbingers of wealth. Be it Abe no Seimei or oni, the reality is that both are commodities sold for their entertainment value. Perhaps people visit the shrines associated with Seimei looking to buy access to the scenes of the stories and to immerse themselves in that time and space—to experience in the three dimensional physical space what they had imagined from the stories written on two dimensional paper—and get in touch with some romantic time and space that they imagine existed in Japan's past, much as people visit a theme park like Disney World to immerse themselves in the Disney stories. Make no mistake, *Onmyōji* offers all the classic features of a good action film: magic, music, fighting, demons, royalty, heroic men and beautiful women, and a few nice twists in the middle and at the end of the tale.

While readers sympathize with oni or idolize Seimei, perhaps the popularity of Seimei and oni simultaneously reveals people's continued interest in something unknown and inexplicable about life, if not in an established religion proper. As fantastic and outrageous as Yumemakura's stories may be, the reader must consider the existence or evil doings of oni somehow as an extension of reality, whether it is reality of the imagined past or of the present. The notion that this could happen to someone who exhibits similar behavior makes the reader feel close to the stories and makes the stories more exciting. It may be likened to "rubbernecking," not in the sense of traffic accident, but as a human trait of morbid curiosity. What is it that makes the mysterious (and shocking) events of *Onmyōji* somehow believable? People's affinity for doomed souls who cannot go to the other world—an oni's fate—could be a possible answer. Iwasaka and Toelken write:

> [D]eath is not only a common subject in Japanese folklore but seems indeed to be the *principal* topic in Japanese tradition; nearly every festival, every ritual, every custom is bound up in some way with relationships between the living and the dead, …the hypothesis that death is

---

38 A manga version of *Onmyōji* authored by Okano Reiko (based upon Yumemakura's *Onmyōji*) increased Abe no Seimei's popularity among female readers.

the prototypical Japanese topic, not only because it relates living people to their ongoing heritage, but also... because death brings into focus a number of other very important elements in the Japanese worldview: obligation, duty, debt, honor, and personal responsibility. (6)

Indeed, complex Japanese funeral rituals and year-round ceremonies for the dead speak of how important the dead and their memories are for family and community. The bereaved family wishes the dead to go on to the other world peacefully. Souls lingering on earth after *shijū kunichi* (forty-nine days)—the limit according to Buddhism, when the dead are supposed to go to the other world—are believed to be dangerous to the living. Yumemakura's *Onmyōji* often describes violent death, and the culprit of the mysterious crimes is often an oni unable to go to the other world peacefully. The oni in "Genjō," for example, is a soul who lingers on earth because of his attachment to the musical instrument. In "Kanawa," the invisible oni remains on earth still wanting to kill Tameyoshi. The oni in "Oni no michiyuki" stays on earth to realize her wish (while crushing those who meet her on her way to the palace). The concept of the dead lingering on earth for unfinished business is familiar among Japanese, deeply rooted in the mixture of Buddhist and Shinto beliefs. If something unfortunate happens to someone, is it because an evil entity—like an oni—is working to cause it? If this is the case, wouldn't it be nice if a person like Abe no Seimei could solve the mystery?

Shimo Yoshiko (b. 1952) is a medium and healer who practices a line of *onmyōdō*, speaks on TV, and publishes how-to books about improving the individual lives of Japanese people. Her books, such as *Ryūseimei* (Flow Life, 2002–),[39] and interviews answer questions about what happens to one after death, or why certain (unfortunate) things happen. She explains that there is a higher force working in the universe and that it controls one's destiny. She attempts to explain how one works within the web of destiny. These concerns and questions fall within a religious field of thought. Diviners, many of them fortunetellers or prognosticators, continue to do good business, such as the contemporary figures Shinjuku no haha (mother in Shinjuku) and Ōizumi no haha (mother in Ōizumi).[40] The fact that there are still quite a number of people who live on the profession of exorcism or

---

39 Her books about *Ryūseimei* (Flow Life) have been published every year since 2002.
40 Some use the date and time of a birth while others may use tools such as tarot cards, crystal balls, or an abacus in the practice. Many of the visitors appear to be females who wish to know about their marriage prospects and the future of their working situations.

healing suggests that numerous people still believe in exorcists, healers, and religious workers. Among interesting news of Japanese religious belief in recent years was that unlawful dumping of garbage ceased as soon as a small (imitation) *torii* (Shinto shrine gate) was placed on the area.[41] It seems that while contemporary Japanese may not necessarily claim to be familiar with religious doctrine, or firmly believe in established religions, they do believe in things inexplicable and supernatural.[42] Japanese are curious about spiritual or supernatural occurrences and manifestations so they seek some information or guidance from healers, mediums, diviners or religious leaders.

In a wider interpretation, this *Onmyōji* boom seems to manifest people's desire to understand why and how certain things happen that cannot be explained logically or scientifically. While *Onmyōji* readers may seek tales of mystery, sex, violence, romance, etc., perhaps they also feel good about some causal relationships being explained. Many young Japanese women would doubtless look at Abe no Seimei as some kind of Prince Charming. But some Japanese may view the character Abe no Seimei as they view healers, mediums, or diviners. Abe no Seimei solves supernatural mysteries by explaining the inexplicable just as a medium, healer, or religious leader explains the working of misfortune as a causal relationship. In this paradigm, evil happenings are tantamount to an oni. There is a reason for an oni to act in a certain way and one must look at the situation from the oni's point of view as well. After all, one must feel sympathetic for the marginalized oni, as there is a chance for all of us to become an oni after death. In the final analysis, the humanization of oni portrayed in *Onmyōji*

---

41 In January 2003, a major Japanese newspaper reported that a Japanese company manufactured products to dissuade people from dumping garbage at unapproved sites. The product in many ways resembles a *torii*. When the product that resembles a *torii* was placed on a site where unlawful dumping of garbage had occurred, illegal waste dumping immediately ceased. The construction workers who had placed the simulated *torii* just as a test were amazed by its remarkable efficacy. Indications suggest, according to Japan's official Shrine Agency, that many Japanese respect religious sites and perhaps fear divine retribution for dumping garbage on hallowed ground. See "Torii tachi gomi tōki yamu." Six years later, in January 2009, another major Japanese newspaper reported similar news. It described the cases of success and failure of the past, as well as the spreading phenomenon of placing the miniature *torii* in illegal garbage dumping sites. This time, a spokesman of Japan's official Shrine Agency expressed his concern for or puzzlement at the connection of *torii* and garbage. See "Gomisute bōshi ni 'jintsūriki' kitai."

42 As Reader and Tanabe assert, Japanese people are "Practically Religious" and they are heavily engaged in *genze riyaku* (this-worldly benefits), an important aspect of religion. See Reader and Tanabe.

is a reflection and expression of contemporary Japanese thoughts and attitudes toward themselves—and by extension, the uncertainty of their lives.

As we have seen, some modern authors treat the oni as a being tantamount to human and attempt to explain oni behaviors and feelings in an effort to better understand our own motivations and needs. Needless to say, oni as a commodity, highly sought after for its entertainment value, remains unchanged. Riding on a high tide of commercialism, a number of contemporary oni are characterized by sex, violence or horror to satisfy the readers' appetite for entertainment. The entertainment values appear to have a close connection to people's interest in or anxieties over the idea of an afterlife and other supernatural phenomena.

8

Oni in Manga, Anime, and Film

IN CONTEMPORARY JAPAN, A VIRTUAL WORLD OF ANIME (Japanese animation), film, and games offers oni and other *yōkai* unlimited potential. Manga (graphic novels)—a close relative of anime and an essential component in contemporary Japanese pop culture—is also fertile soil for oni. Japanese manga were popular in the pre-war period, but it was only after the war that the industry fully recognized its potential, most notably with the publication of Osamu Tezuka's (1928–1989) *Tetsuwan Atomu* (*Astro Boy*).[1] In 1995, comic books were a billion-dollar industry in Japan accounting for 40 percent of all books and magazines sold (Schodt 19). Overseas as well, a San Francisco-based Japanese manga and anime company that translates Japanese work into the English language was a four- or five-man operation in 1986; by 2007 it had grown to a staff of 130.[2] Many anime are based on stories that appeared first in manga. Indeed, Japan's first animated television series was the aforementioned Osamu Tezuka's *Astro Boy* in 1963.

Susan Napier writes, "anime, with its enormous breadth of subject material, is … a useful mirror on contemporary Japanese society, offering an array of insights into the significant issues, dreams, and nightmares of the day" (*Anime* 8). In the various array of subject materials, oni and *yōkai* are important ingredients to help understand the Japanese, as well as the broader human psyche.

As human knowledge of earth expands, and as the world becomes smaller, oni's trope moves beyond this planet. Perhaps because it is less believable today that oni would inhabit far-distant mountains and rivers in Japan, a contemporary oni in these media is often portrayed as a creature from a

---

1 Tezuka is widely regarded as the godfather of manga.
2 See "Are Made-in-Japan Manga and Animation About to Be Blindsided?" 15.

different time and/or space. An oni is an alien, a hybrid of earthlings and some different species, or simply a different species on earth from the very long past, the future, or, if from the present then from a different temporal dimension. An oni's existence has also become entwined with cutting-edge technologies such as electronics, mechanics, and robotics. In cyberspace, oni often cohabit with humans as urban dwellers. Geopolitics may change; but the oni is still an alienated "other." Some oni are looking for a companion just as we saw in the previous chapter, and others exist as allegories or social commentaries. Just as the subject matters of the contemporary representative pop cultural media vary greatly, the oni's representation varies widely.

Apocalyptic and Elegiac Oni

Nagai Gō's Oni

According to Susan Napier, the most significant modes of anime are those of apocalypse, festival, and elegy; and distinctively Japanese in the Japanese vision of apocalypse is the sense of the elegiac (Napier, *Anime* 32, 199). She writes specifically the "Japanese vision of apocalypse" because the end of the world in the Judeo-Christian tradition, i.e., the final battle between the binary concept of righteous forces against evil, with a select few going to Heaven and the rest falling into Hell does not exist in the Japanese tradition.[3] Still, "while Buddhist and Shinto scriptures do not contain visions of good frightening evil at the end of the world, the Buddhist doctrine of mappō or 'the latter days of the Law' does revolve around the notion of a fallen world saved by a religious figure, the Maitreya Buddha" (Napier, *Anime* 196).

Apocalyptic fiction became quite popular in the late 1960s and 70s as rapid economic growth came to Japan, and with it came pollution, and societal anxieties. Even though the Cold War was over and the nuclear threat had receded, various apocalyptic fictions were created with a background of societal intransparency and other disasters facing mankind.

---

3   Napier writes, "What sets Europe and America apart from Japan, however, is that they share the common tradition of the biblical Book of Revelation, the themes and imagery of which have become the fundamental version of the apocalyptic narrative: a final battle between the forces of the righteous and the forces of Satan, the wholesale destruction of the world with the evil side being cast into hell, and the ultimate happy ending with the evildoers condemned and the righteous believers ascending to the kingdom of heaven. Traditional Japanese culture has never shared in this vision" (*Anime* 194).

One of the pioneering artists portraying apocalyptic and elegiac modes of manga through the utilization of oni and demonic creatures is Nagai Gō (born 1945). Nagai often depicts oni as members of a different tribe from the mainstream Japanese race or as creatures born out of grudge, enmity, and suffering. For example, the oni in "Oni—2889 nen no hanran" (Oni—The Rebellion in 2889), which appeared in December 1969, is a synthetic human—a creation of human technology. Similar to "replicants" in the film *Blade Runner* (1982), the oni are absolutely supposed to obey the humans. But the oni rebel against the humans and their cruel treatment.[4] While the setting is literally futuristic, the core concept of an oni as a marginalized being borne out of grudge, enmity, and suffering remains unchanged. In the following I have chosen two of Nagai's representative works whose protagonists are oni, *Debiruman* (Devilman, 1972–73) and *Shuten Dōji* (1976–78).

Debiruman (Devilman)

Debiruman (Devilman, 1972–73) is one of Nagai's most influential and popular works. This oni, as the name Devilman itself indicates, is definitely more akin to the Judeo-Christian "devil" than to Japanese oni. The author uses the translation of "*akuma ningen*" for Devilman rather than something like "oni *bito*," and the architectural framework of Devilman is predominantly Christendom. Indeed, when Nagai's representative works are compiled, *Devilman* is often categorized by itself, separate from his "oni series" that include "Oni—The Rebellion in 2889" and *Shuten Dōji*.[5] Yet, various oni aspects that appear in *Devilman* make this story part of oni as we shall see later. *Devilman* ran as serials of manga and TV anime almost simultaneously, but the manga serial is much more violent and cruel with many atrocious scenes typified in the dismembering of Miki's body (Miki, a main character, is the protagonist's love).[6]

The basic plot of the manga version of *Devilman* is as follows: a long time ago, demons, an indigenous race, had ruled the earth, but a cataclysm

---

4 See Nagai, *Nagai Gō kaiki tanpenshū* 1–112.

5 See for example, Nagai's *Debiruman wa dare nano ka*. When Nagai's work is classified according to genre, both *Devilman* and *Shuten Dōji* are categorized under *denki* (strange stories, romance) with an English subtitle, "legend."

6 Nagai has a broad spectrum of subjects. While he is celebrated for violent manga, he is also famous for comical, sexy, and/or erotic manga such as *Harenchi gakuen* (Shameless School, 1968–1972) and *Kyūtī Hanī* (Cuty Honey 1973–74). In fact the *Devilman* serial comes almost in between *Shameless School* and *Cutie Honey*. For an insightful observation on *Cutie Honey*, see Napier, *Anime* 73–76.

imprisoned demons in ice. The demons are skilled transformers, or more precisely, amalgamators (*gattai*) who combine with other beings, and their pleasure is to kill sentient beings. The time moves to the present day and the place is Japan. The protagonist is Fudō Akira, a gentle, righteous, but timid teenager. Ryō, Akira's best friend, one day tells Akira that the demons that had been imprisoned in the glacier are resurrected and will destroy humans to have the earth back. In order to save mankind, Akira transforms into Devilman by allowing himself to be possessed by one of the most powerful demon warriors called Amon. As Devilman, Akira has a human heart and the demonic power of Amon; he is not shy any more. Devilman battles against various demons to protect humans, but then demons begin indiscriminate amalgamation (*gattai*), murdering countless humans. Examining this mysterious phenomenon, a Nobel Prize winner of Biology, Professor Rainuma, concludes that the demons are actually humans. In a plot twist resembling a medieval witchunt, humans, who have heard the professor's statement, start to torture and kill suspicious people and those who may turn into demons. To complicate the story, Ryō turns out to be Satan, whom the demons worship as their god. Akira/Devilman decides to form the Devilman Army to counter the demons' indiscriminate attack on humans. Eventually the humans all kill each other out of distrust. With no humans left on earth, the final campaign of Armageddon begins, with the Demons' Army led by Ryō/Satan against Devilman's Army. After twenty years when the final battle is over, Ryō/Satan speaks to Akira/Devilman. He explains that long ago, God tried to destroy the demons that were ruling the Earth. Satan went against God's will, and stood on the side of the demons. Victorious demons went into a long sleep in the ice—they were not encaved in the ice against their will—but when they woke up, humans were devastating earth, so the demons decided to destroy humans. Satan realized that what the demons did was exactly the same as what God had tried to do to the demons earlier. After Ryō/Satan's confession, he apologizes for his action to Akira/Devilman, but Akira/Devilman dies of his battle wounds.

Devilman's appearance resembles the devil named Mephistopheles that appears in the legend of Faust lithograph by French artist, Eugène Delacroix (1798–1863) or Lucifer, King of Hell, an illustration to the Divine Comedy by Gustave Doré (1832–1883). As the term "Armageddon" suggests, the framework of the story is based upon Biblical literature, especially the Revelation of St. John the Divine. Indeed, when Akira declares that he is going to form the Devilman Army that could battle against demons, Ryō compares Akira's idea to the Armageddon, explaining,

> It's in the Revelation of St. John the Divine. God tells His prophesy to John who was on Patmos and told him to write the prophecy down. Satan, who was encased in the ice by God's desire, will be resurrected after the time of eternity and will bring calamities with his army. God's Army will meet Satan's Army. All the beings on earth will be divided into two groups: good and evil. This battle is called "Armageddon." (Nagai, *Debiruman* 4: 186–87)

It should be noted that a part of Ryō's statement above, "Satan, who was encased in the ice by God's desire," comes from the *Divine Comedy* by Dante Alighieri (1264–1321). In *Divine Comedy*, Satan is bound in the ice to his mid-point in the place just past the last circle of Cocytus, the ninth and final circle of Hell called Judecca. The Revelation of St. John the Divine simply states that Satan is chained and thrown into an abyss to be sealed for a thousand years. Nagai freely adapts famous descriptions from the work of Christian literature and mixes them to meet his needs, making the work more appealing to a wide audience.

Interestingly, in response to Ryō's statement, Akira believes that his Army, i.e., the Devilman's Army, corresponds to God's Army in the Revelation of St. John the Divine. But his Army loses the campaign at the end the story. The term and meaning of Armageddon is widely known among contemporary Japanese mainly as a result of an incident in 1995 in which, a religious/cult group called the AUM Shinrikyō attempted to force Armageddon by planting sarin gas in Tokyo subways in 1995, killing twelve commuters and injuring many others. But when *Devilman* was serialized in the mid-70s, the notion of Armageddon, let alone its term, was unfamiliar to majority of Japanese. It was in that sense a fresh concept in the manga world.

So why is the Devilman story considered an oni story in spite of its overwhelmingly Judeo-Christian theme? To begin with, there is no "good" or "evil" in support of just one religious belief in this story. As mentioned earlier, oni and the Judeo-Christian devil are distinctly different. The devil or Satan as evil exists in opposition to God, without whom the devil does not exist. But even in the sense of "good" in terms of righteousness against "evil," there is no absolute "good" against absolute "evil" in Debiruman. Neither Satan's Army nor Devilman's Army is the completely righteous one. While Akira is Devilman, he has the virtuous Akira's heart and soul.

He is more akin to an oni with its own righteousness in his heart.[7] As we have seen, oni have both positive and negative aspects, and the demons in *Devilman* also possess both positive and negative sides. Despite Ryō's explanation that "the demon's purpose in life is to kill. The demon does not possess 'love.' They are indeed devils" (Nagai, *Debiruman* 1:114), some major demon characters such as Serene and Kaimu do understand love. In fact, the death scene of Serene and Kaimu who offered his life to Serene is quite elegiac. In the anime version of Devilman, Akira dies at the very beginning and it is the brave demon warrior Devilman who is protecting Miki and her family against other demons. Indeed, Ryō tells Akira, "Devils existed. The legends of *yōkai* that exist all over the world such as devils, oni, werewolves, vampires, *tengu, kappa* (water imps)—aren't they demons?" To this, Akira responds, "come to think of it, Japanese oni look like an amalgamation of humans and oxen" (Nagai, Debiruman 1: 100–101). I should mention that in Japan in the 1970s the word, "gattai" (amalgamation) was a very popular, catchy word, especially among children. While shouting, "gattai!" children would pretend to transform into something different; one transforms into something else, into something more powerful, by amalgamating with another being. It is human to desire to transform oneself into a more desirable or powerful being.

Fighting a lonely fight, Devilman is a marginalized being. He is of a different species. He is the "other." I should note that the protagonist's name, Fudō Akira, is written in *kanji* characters 不動明. If one adds the character 王 (ō, king), it becomes Fudō myōō 不動明王 (Ācala Vidyārāja, Immovable Protector of Dharma),[8] the most venerable and best known of the Five Wisdom Kings (godai myōō), who represent the luminescent wisdom of the Buddha. Fudō myōō 不動明王 is a manifestation of Mahavairocana—the fundamental, universal Buddha of esoteric Buddhism, and has a fearsome countenance as he destroys the delusions and material desires of humans in exchange for the salvation of mankind. He is a conqueror of the evil. As we have seen in chapters two and four, it is an oni and oni's progenitor who

---

7   This reminds me of a group of folktales called "Oni no ko Kozuna" (Kozuna, Oni's Child) in which the protagonist, Kozuna, is kind to humans. Kozuna is a half-oni and half-human child, and it is implied that the kind side is his human side. His cannibal oni side is latent but Kozuna asks to be killed whenever he feels an urge to eat humans. Kozuna is an oni with a human heart.

8   Fudō or Ācala, i.e., immovability, refers to his ability to remain unmoved by carnal temptations.

conquer the very oni. Thus, while the Devilman's world is futuristic and set partly within the Judeo-Christian mode, an influence of Hindu-Buddhist art and concept is undeniable. The gravity of the oni brings Devilman into their terrain. In that sense, although *Devilman*'s world is Christian-oriented, Devilman himself is deeply rooted in the traditional Japanese world view.

As the story develops, such familiar motifs as "demonic people" become foregrounded. For example, in one episode, American cavalry possessed by demons massacre a Native American tribe. When Devilman arrives on the scene of murder, the cavalrymen look at Devilman and cry, "it's a devil!" But Devilman shouts at them, "No, the devils are within you!" (Nagai, *Debiruman* 3: 186–87). So readers may predict Professor Rainuma's statement, "The true identity of demons is humans." The professor's explanation for the cause of human's demonization, however, reveals a contemporary societal tendency. He explains, "The humans' strong desire has changed the biological cells of human bodies and has transformed themselves into demons. … The accumulation of contemporary men's pent-up frustrations turned them into demons" (Nagai, *Debiruman* 4: 254–55). In other words, it is the angry, frustrated human psyche that takes the shape of demons. This is an interesting theory when one considers the country's situation then: Japan was just starting to enter an affluent phase, and yet, there were various societal anxieties such as the political unrest of the 1960s and the pollution that came with the rapid adoption of modern conveniences. Aggravation and uneasiness toward the present and future, and an identity crisis for that matter, took the physical form of demon. The professor's statement triggers the "human-hunt" similar to "witch-hunt" of the medieval period of western civilization. "Suspicion will raise bogies" is repeated throughout human history.

Devilman's influence has been enormous on later manga and anime works, including the *Neon Genesis Evangerion* (*Shin seiki Evangerion*, 1995–96), a spectacularly successful manga and anime serial (see Ōizumi 97–100). *Devilman*, which essentially portrays a series of great battles for hegemony over the earth, may be taken as an allegorical war story. Nagai writes, "I started to look at Devilman as a symbolic story of wars. For example, Miki is Akira's fiancée who waits for Akira's return at home, the members of the Devilman Army are combatants, and humans are civilians." But then, he quickly adds,

> …sometimes there are some people who swallow my story [at face value]. So I will clearly declare here. This symbolism is just one result

of a 'simulation game' ... *Devilman* is not a prophecy—it is a simple manga that I created. Don't ever think that Japan is planning wars, and don't be deceived by weird cult groups! (Nagai, *Debiruman way dare nana ka* 48–51)

Nagai is saying that *Devilman* is a creation for entertainment, and understandably he does not want *Devilman* to be an inspiration for an ideologue or a cult group that may become dangerous to the public. This statement, in turn, speaks to how manga and/or his creation may influence modern readers' ways of thinking and acting so much so that the author has to draw the readers back to its pure entertainment value.

Shuten Dōji (A Child Handed from Heaven)

While *Devilman*'s oni is written in the framework of Christendom, *Shuten Dōji* is clearly cut from Japanese oni cloth, right down to the oni's traditional masculine appearance with horns. Serialized in *Shōnen Magajin* (Boy's Magazine) from 1976 to 1978, *Shuten Dōji* is a story whose time and space span the tenth through the twenty-first centuries, from the Earth to the universe, to the realm of oni. Although the title, *Shuten Dōji*, is pronounced the same as the medieval Shuten Dōji 酒顛童子 or 酒吞童子 as "Drunken Demon," Nagai Go uses different characters for his Shuten Dōji 手天童子, which literally means, "a child handed from heaven." Indeed, the protagonist, Shutendō Jirō, is so named because "the child was handed [to the couple] from heaven," and his name also reflects the most famous oni, Shuten Dōji (Nagai, *Shuten Dōji* 1:41). Nagai's *Shuten Dōji* is roughly divided into three parts: the first is a school-horror in the present Japan; the middle part is a psychic action story that depicts Shutendō Jirō and his friends fighting against a dark religious group that worships Daiankoku shiyajarai (Great Evil Deity of Darkness and Death); and the third part is written totally in science fiction mode—with spaceship, cyborg, time machine, etc.—in which Shutendō Jirō travels through time and space.

The story starts with the sudden appearance of a gigantic oni handing out a baby to a couple, Mr. and Mrs. Shiba, who are visiting Mr. Shiba's ancestral grave to report their marriage. The oni leaves the baby with the couple, saying that he will come back to retrieve him after 15 years. The baby is named Shutendō Jirō after the famous oni, Shuten Dōji. Fifteen years later, Jirō notices his supernatural powers, and two horns grow on his head. Then, strange creatures start to attack him, and Jirō realizes that he must be an oni, but he does not know where he came from or why he exists.

In order to find out who he is and also to follow his destiny, he sets off to the *ongokukai,* the oni's realm. Shutendō Jirō is accompanied by Goki (literally protector of the oni),[9] an oni who exists solely to protect him. The manga sequences span the tenth century to the future world of 2100.

Like *Devilman,* the oni in *Shuten Dōji* are endowed with the ability to copy the shapes, characters, and memories of any sentient beings (Nagai, *Shuten Dōji* 1: 382). Nagai's oni—both the demons in *Devilman* and the oni in *Shuten Dōji* portrayed in the mode of Science Fiction—are more sophisticated and multi-talented than the traditional oni representations. As in *Devilman,* an apocalyptic thought rises up ominously in *Shuten Dōji* as a delinquent says, "the future of humankind is limited. Only gods or demons survive in the end. Weak humans are destined to perish. ... we saw an *akuma* (devil), a being of the evil realm. Its appearance terribly resembled a legendary oni!" (Nagai, *Shuten Dōji* 1: 370–72). This is a tangent point of *Devilman* and *Shuten Dōji*. Further, an army of oni that attacks Shutendō Jirō when he is about to enter the realm of oni is in fact composed of demons similar to those that appear in *Devilman*.[10] As Devilman cries out to the humans, "the devils are within you," their mental state then creates the oni within their minds. Indeed, the basic premise of *Shuten Dōji* is that negative human emotions such as anger and spite, which essentially do not hold mass, create an oni that has physical mass in this world.

It turns out that the *ongokukai* was within Mrs. Shiba's mind. Mrs. Shiba subconsciously created *ongokukai* out of her anger and grudge against the oni who took Shutendō Jirō away from her. Mr. Shiba explains, "*On*gokukai, the realm of oni, is the realm of grudge (the same pronunciation of *on*gokukai, but the first character is now replaced by a character meaning "grudge"). The mind bearing "grudge" phenomenolized the shape of oni. Ongokukai is the world of grudge that Kyoko [Mrs. Shiba] created when the oni took Jirō away from her" (Nagai, *Shuten Dōji* 6: 238–39). Mrs. Shiba also created Goki, and Senki, another super-strong oni who protects Shutendō Jirō from vicious oni. As we saw in chapters two and four, it is usually an oni that slays other oni.

---

9   Like many other manga artists, Nagai creates interesting names for the characters. This Goki, for example, is pronounced the same as En no gyōja's Goki (literally posterior demon. Regarding En no gyōja's Goki, see the section of chapter one "The Other: The Oppressed, Alienated, and Isolated"), but written in a different character that makes the name mean, a "protector of the oni."

10 See Nagai, *Shuten Dōji* 3: 332–348.

Mrs. Shiba had always known that Jirō would be taken away from her, but when Jirō was physically removed after 15 years, she was so shocked that she was diagnosed with typical *yūkaku kannen* or Over Valued Ideation. According to Mrs. Shiba's psychiatrist, Over Valued Ideation happens to ordinary people when they receive an enormous mental shock. The shock is so traumatizing that a patient does not respond to any outside stimuli. Thus, Mrs. Shiba's mind stopped at the time of Jirō's disappearance and she can only think of her grudge against the oni who has taken her boy away (Nagai, *Shuten Dōji* 3: 293–94). This traumatic experience created Daiankoku shiyajarai (Great Evil Deity of Darkness and Death) who exists to draw the universe into the world of darkness (Nagai, *Shuten Dōji* 2: 167–68) and that is worshipped by an evil religious cult. Mrs. Shiba is the Daiankoku shiyajarai. As the time moves back and forth rather casually in *Shuten Dōji*, what happens in the present affects the past, i.e., the causal relationship is reversed. Goki explains that the oni's world was created suddenly in meta-dimensional space from nothingness (Nagai, *Shuten Dōji* 4: 167–68). This is because the oni world was created in Mrs. Shiba's mind when Jirō was taken, and her state of mind has affected what had happened before: that is, the creation of Daiankoku shiyajarai, fighting against strange creatures, etc. Nagai Gō writes:

> I started to write the story as an adventure fantasy with a motif of oni, … but a structure changed in the middle… I think the oni's accumulated grudges over the millennia made the story change. Originally an oni was something that the authorities considered non-human and punished arbitrarily. … *Shuten Dōji* eventually made me think what an oni is, how an oni affects human mind, and the violence of love and hate. (Nagai, *Nagai Gō SAGA* 206)

According to Nagai, a person with a grudge becomes an oni. He believes that the oni really existed—not as a different species of beings, but that a human being is the oni's true identity (Nagai, *Debiruman wa dare nano ka* 103).

The ending of *Shuten Dōji* is literally full of lights, with a happy reunion scene of Jirō and Mr. and Mrs. Shiba. It is seemingly a happy ending. But is it? What about those who died for Shutendō Jirō, or to be more precise, those who were physically killed in the world that Mrs. Shiba created? Mrs. Shiba's angst and spite triggered the killing spree, which is tantamount to the indiscriminate violence we saw Uji no hashihime in chapter three. Yet, Mrs. Shiba's case seems more frightening because the grudge stems from "motherhood"—a supposedly nurturing nature. As we saw in chapter four, the Great Mother has two aspects, and Mrs. Shiba's Daiankoku shiyajarai personifies the destructive aspect. The relationship between mother and son is said to be strong in Japan. While Nagai does not mention anything about the destructive power of motherhood, the *Shuten Dōji* story can be interpreted as a sharp criticism of the mother-son relationship. If motherly love turns vicious, for any reason, it creates an oni. While the mother's instinct to protect her child is strong, if it becomes excessive "motherhood" can destroy its surroundings, taking the many characters involved with it. Whether it is intended or not, this is a message that may touch one's heartstrings.

Akira Kurosawa's "The Weeping Demon"

It has been quite a while since Japan experienced the atomic bombs on its land, but its memories of the almost end-of-the-world devastation still continue. When it comes to apocalyptic thought, probably the atomic bombings of Hiroshima and Nagasaki are the most obvious cataclysms for Japanese. "The Weeping Demon," the seventh episode of a recent film entitled *Dreams* (1990) by Akira Kurosawa, deals with the danger of nuclear technology. Kurosawa heavily relies on conventional images to gain the desired cinematic effects: the oni gather at a bleak place with blood-colored ponds—the landscape resembles Japanese scrolls of Buddhist Hell in the medieval period. "The Weeping Demon" begins with ominous white clouds drifting on the bleak ground, representing the results of the nuclear disaster. The earth is devastated: a hellish place where the purple nuclear clouds caused mutations and monstrosities—giant dandelions and human survivors with horns on their heads.[11] These oni wail over the pain coming from their horn(s), which makes this place all the more infernal.

Though the landscape of "The Weeping Demon" resembles the painting scrolls of the medieval period, there is a great difference between the two portrayals: in the hell scroll of the medieval painting, oni punish humans—they are the inflictors; in the film, however, the oni are both the inflictors and the recipients of suffering. Kurosawa's oni were humans who turn into oni as a result of a nuclear weapon's blast. The oni are used as an expedient to criticize nuclear technology. Furthermore, the horns, a feature of oni, symbolize the hierarchical order of Japan in the film. Japan is a vertical society (Nakane). Where vertical relations such as senior-junior rankings

---

11   Goodwin notes that "[d]andelions have grown taller than a human being and they appear as a grotesque distortion of the passionate intensity of the sunflowers in the famous van Gogh canvas, seen in episode five" (136).

are strong and strictly prescribed, people in the lower social ranks work for (and obey the orders of) those in the higher echelons. In return, the senior members advise and take care of the junior members. A main character of "The Weeping Demon" is a one-horned oni. He laments that even after becoming an oni, the hierarchy exists: the more horns an oni has, the stronger it is. In a realm where the oni eat each other, the weak, one-horned oni serve the stronger oni as a food source. Here, oni are being used as a social criticism—the underlying message being that the well-off of society should help the lesser advantaged, not eat them as was common practice in the oni underworld. Stephen Prince considers "The Weeping Demon" the weakest segment in the film (314). With a perspective on the film's Japanese elements, however, this segment is very interesting in that the episode is replete with Japanese societal phenomena and folk tradition.

Modern Female Oni: Powerful, yet Compromised

Urusei Yatsura: The Cute Sexy Oni

We saw above one devastatingly evil female oni called Daiankoku shiyajarai living in the mind of Mrs. Shiba, a mother. The evilness of Daiankoku shiyajarai may be compared to a black hole of the universe in its darkness. On the other hand, a completely lovable oni, a sexy ogress named Lum, appears in the manga series entitled *Urusei Yatsura* (Those Obnoxious Aliens). When Takahashi Rumiko, the author, created Urusei Yatsura, she combined the aliens of science fiction with the traditional Japanese oni. Her protagonist is Lum, a modern, non-terrestrial version of Japanese oni. The series first appeared in 1978 in a boy's weekly manga magazine called *Shōnen Sunday* (Boys' Sunday), *Urusei Yatsura* was such a phenomenal success that it ran over nine years and was also turned into a TV series from 1981 to 1987. After the TV series had ended, six feature-length movies and eleven OVA (Original Video Animations) were made. Just as any other successful manga, the *Urusei Yatsura* was also released in book form, counting thirty-four volumes altogether, and later the series was also published in the *bunkobon* (pocket edition) format. Abroad, *Urusei Yatsura* was published in North America from 1989 through 1998, and has been translated into Italian, Spanish, and Cantonese (Cavallaro, *The Cinema of Mamoru Oshii* 48-49, 51, 55).

Both manga and anime series of *Urusei Yatsura* open with a fleet of technologically super-advanced oni-invaders arriving on Earth. The invaders challenge earthlings to fight a one-on-one battle of oni-*gokko* (a game of tag) for the destiny of humankind. For humans to be saved, the randomly selected challenger Moroboshi Ataru, a lecherous teenage Japanese boy, enters the battle. If Ataru can hold the ogress Lum's horns in his hands, he wins the game. Lum turns out to be cute and overflowing with sex appeal, but after a series of mishaps, Ataru wins the game, and Lum declares that she is his loving and devoted wife.

The ogress Lum is replete with the traditional oni's attributes discussed in chapter one. She wears a traditional oni outfit of tiger-skin. She has two horns on her head. Instead of a big mouth to eat humans in one gulp, she has cute canine teeth, indicating a sexual appetite. Her mouth becomes conspicuously large when she finds out about Ataru's lecherous actions. She acts as if she is going to devour Ataru—demonstrating a trace of cannibalistic background. Lum can fly, just like the oni at Modoribashi Bridge is reported to do. Although Lum herself does not transform into any non-recognisable creature, her former fiancé, Rei, who is still so enamoured of her that he comes after her from his home planet, transforms himself into a huge tiger- or ox-like monster when excited. Ordinarily, Rei is an oni with an incredibly good-looking human appearance (with two horns and a tiger-skin outfit). Hailing from a different planet and intent on invading the earth, Lum's oni cohorts are obviously beyond the reach of the emperor's control. The alien oni also have many different customs from the human Earth dwellers. Electricity like lightning that Lum's body emits—a traditional oni power—is her weapon. When she becomes jealous or angry, she uses her electric power most effectively to injure her target. As oni can also bring wealth, Lum brought wealth to her creator (the author and the companies who published her manga, made the TV shows and films in which her popular character was featured).

Born in 1957 and one of Japan's most popular manga artists, the author, Takahashi Rumiko, has rendered an oni that is entirely modern. Lum is an alien-oni, who is capable of piloting an advanced spaceship. She is also a sexy oni, cute and coquettish with a curvaceous figure and huge eyes. Lum often wears a tiger-skin *bikini*, showing her attractive figure most effectively. Lum's image is not unlike a teen-age version of ukiyo-e's *yamauba*, although she does not exactly look like a Japanese or for that matter, any specific race.[12]

---

12   Susan Napier's comment is insightful about the anime figure. She notes that "a number

Lum is portrayed as a lovable and devoted (self-claimed) wife. Timothy J. Craig writes that one of the features of "Japan's popular culture is its closeness to the ordinary, everyday lives of its audience" (13). Lum-oni's likeability increases all the more because she behaves just like ordinary human women—in spite of her supernatural electric powers and flying ability—she becomes jealous, cries, laughs, and gets mad, so the mainstream audience can automatically relate to her. Interestingly, her likeability partially comes from conforming to societal norms while she simultaneously creates social tension. Susan Napier writes that *Urusei Yatsura* reflects an aspect of contemporary Japanese society in that increasingly empowered Japanese women in the 70s and 80s are contained through comfort contrivances. Napier notes:

> The chaotic world that Lum often unwittingly creates is an amusing one when confined to the theatre of fantasy, but the subtext has a threatening quality to it, suggesting that in the real world women are increasingly uncontrollable as well. The inherent threat of Lum's powers… is ultimately mitigated by the essentially traditional relationship she has with Ataru. Lum's (women's) destabilizing power is contained through her total commitment to her man, suggesting that, no matter how independent and aggressive she may become, she is still profoundly tied to a traditional male-female dynamic. … her emotional subordination to him ultimately guarantees that she will occupy the traditional (i.e., comforting) female subject position. (Napier, *Anime* 147)

The reader of this book may feel that Napier's statement above can be applied to Yaegiri-yamauba of Chikamatsu Monzaemon's *Komochi yamauba* that we discussed in chapter four. In the case of Hercurian Yaegiri-yamauba, she was totally committed to realizing her late husband's wish and to motherhood. Perhaps to be appealing to the masses or to be widely accepted in

---

of Japanese commentators have chosen to describe anime with the word '*mukokuseki*,' meaning 'stateless' or essentially without a national identity. Anime is indeed 'exotic' to the West in that it is made in Japan, but the world of anime itself occupies its own space that is not necessarily coincident with that of Japan. … another aspect of anime's *mukokuseki* quality in many eyes is the extremely 'non-Japanese' depiction of human characters in virtually all anime texts. This is an issue among American audiences new to anime as well, who want to know why the characters look 'Western.' In fact, while many anime texts do include figures with blond hair, it is perhaps more correct to say that rather than a 'Western' style of figuration, the characters are drawn in what might be called 'anime' style. … This style ranges from the broadly grotesque drawings of characters with shrunken torsos and oversize heads of some anime comedy to the elongated figures with huge eyes and endless flowing hair that populate many romance and adventure stories. While many of them are blond or light brunette, many have more bizarre hair colorings such as pink, green, or blue" (*Anime* 24–25).

the mainstream society, female oni have to become slightly compromised. As *Urusei Yatsura* is quite popular with female audiences as well, one may also say that the expectation for the traditional role for women is strongly supported by women as well. Lum, though modern in appearance, seems to be a tamed oni.

With a popular following in various media, Lum is a tribute to the modern-cosmopolitan age. With the show's catchy theme song, and copious spin-off marketing efforts, the oni Lum has proven to be a true economic commodity to Japan. She is a veritable entertainment franchise that ultimately celebrates the capitalistic and commercial accomplishments of the modern era.

Bigheaded Yamauba in *Spirited Away*

Released in 2001, Miyazaki Hayao's (born 1941) animated film entitled *Sen to Chihiro no kamikakushi* (*Spirited Away*) became the highest-grossing film of all time in Japan. It won a number of awards, including a 2003 Academy Award for Best Animated Feature Film and a Golden Bear at the Berlin International Festival in 2002. With the success of this work "Japanese animation finally began to receive the support of the mass audience" in the U.S. market.[13] Derek Elley, a reviewer, writes, "It's almost impossible to do justice in words either to the visual richness of the movie, which mélanges traditional Japanese clothes and architecture with both Victorian and modern-day artefacts, or to the character-filled storyline with human figures, harpies and grotesque creatures" (72). Miyazaki considers *Spirited Away* to be a fairy tale, a direct descendant of Japanese fairy tales such as "Suzume no oyado" (The Sparrow's Inn) or "Nezumi no goten" (The Mouse's Palace).[14]

---

13   "Are Made-in-Japan Manga and Animation About to Be Blindsided?" 17. "The Japanese animated film market reached 233.9 billion yen in 2005, 1.2 times the size of non-animated Japanese films" (Ibid., 16).

14   See Saitō Ryōichi et al. 74. In "Suzume no oyado," a sparrow that a kind old man has cared for disappears after his wicked wife cut its tongue. With much trouble and hardship, the grandpa finds the sparrow's house. There he is entertained with good food and dance by many sparrows. They give him a souvenir box, which contains great treasures. His wife follows suit and visits the sparrow's house too. She picks a large souvenir box which turns out to be full of snakes, bugs, and monsters. "Nezumi no goten," popularly known as "Nezumi jōdo" (The Mouse's Paradise) or "Omusubi kororin" (The Rolling Rice-ball) is a similar story to "Suzume no oyado." One day a good old man goes to the mountains to cut wood. When he eats his lunch, one of his rice-balls (or dumplings) falls and rolls into a hole in the ground. The old man tries to reach it, but the earth gives way and he tumbles down the hole. Following the rice-ball,

As a domain of Japanese tradition and folktale, it contains oni or oni-like characters. The most remarkable oni figure—and one of the most memorable characters to me—is Yubaba, the owner of the bathhouse in the world of spirits.

Spirited Away is an adventure and coming-of-age film in which the main character, a young girl by the name of Chihiro, embarks on a quest to save her family from a supernatural spell. The film opens with Chihiro's family moving to a new town, making Chihiro uneasy and sulky. On their way to their new house, the family unwittingly enters into a supernatural realm, where Chihiro's parents are turned into pigs. While Chihiro is in a panic, a mysterious boy named Haku appears and offers his help. Chihiro learns that the only way to break the spell and re-enter the "human world" is to find work at the bathhouse (of the supernatural). There, through various challenges and pitfalls, Chihiro finds friendship, she finds a way to help her family, and most importantly, she finds herself.

Miyazaki's portrayals of the spirit-characters are rich, multi-faceted entities replete with cultural memories and histories. Among them, the unforgettable Yubaba is the old witch who owns the bathhouse. She is avaricious and quite strict with her workers. Many critics have pointed out the similarity between Yubaba and the Queen of Hearts in *Alice in Wonderland*. Indeed, Andō Masashi, the art director of *Spirited Away*, states, "In our previous project, ... Yubaba... was drawn as a grotesque character, the kind that might appear in the illustrations of *Alice in Wonderland*" (qtd. in Yu 104). Yubaba's appearance and demeanor, and the very way she commands her workers, may indeed be reminiscent of Lewis Carroll's Queen of Hearts character. But Yubaba, who is also seen excessively pampering her gigantic spoiled baby boy named Bō, strikes me most as a descendant of a yamauba (discussed in detail in chapter four). Indeed, Yubaba is an old woman with white hair who controls her employees through the power of language and magic. She can freely transform humans into animals and eat them, which is entirely in accord with yamauba's cannibalism.

As seen in chapter four, an example of the yamauba's motherhood appears in legends of yamauba being the mother of Kintarō. The legend goes that

---

he reaches the mouse's mansion. There he is entertained with good food and songs. In appreciation of the old man's rice-ball, the mice give him treasures. A neighboring wicked old man hears the good old man's story and attempts to do the same. But the neighbor makes a mistake in the process, and instead of getting treasures, he is punished by the mice.

a mountain yamauba gave birth to and raised a son possessing Herculean strength, named Kintarō. Kintarō was then discovered by a great warrior, Minamoto no Raikō, changed his name to Sakata no Kintoki, and became one of Raikō's *shitennō*. Kintarō is portrayed as full of energy and currently often identified with his red *harakake* (bib or apron) on which the character 金 (*kin* from *Kin*tarō) is printed. Yamauba's motherly attitude toward her son is further emphasized through a series of *yamauba-buyō* or yamauba dances in Kabuki, which appear in the late eighteenth-early nineteenth century. In the dance pieces, yamauba's doting motherhood is amplified as she speaks of him, "it's been seven years since… Day and night, my pleasure is my only son, Kaidōmaru [i.e., Kintarō]" (Tsuruya, "Hakone ashigarayama no ba" 61).

In *Spirited Away*, Yubaba is the mother of super-baby, Bō. Just like Kintarō, Bō wears a red *harakake* on which a big character 坊 *Bō* is written. Similar to Kintarō, Bō has prowess in accordance with his gigantic size—he can easily break Chihiro's arm if he wishes. In contrast to her strictness with her employees, Yubaba dotes on Bō and protects him almost to excess, confining him in a germ-free playroom full of germ-free toys. In this detail, the director may be hinting at an aspect of present-day Japanese parenting; the tendency to spoil or shelter children while depriving them of negative experiences, some feel, prevents children from developing their full potential. Perhaps most strikingly, this same image of over-protecting one's offspring is portrayed by yamauba in Kabuki's dance pieces as discussed.

The visual juxtaposition of a white-haired elderly mother bearing a baby boy has precedents, too. As mentioned in chapter four, one notable example is a votive painting of *Yamauba and Kintarō* created by Nagasawa Rosetsu (1754–1799), a treasure of Itsukushima Shrine in Miyajima. In Rosetsu's painting, yamauba looks like a distrustful old woman—what Robert Moes calls "a caricature of geriatric non-beauty." Moes, however, also comments, "there is a sympathetic humor in the way the mythical old hag stares out suspiciously at the beholder" (28).[15] Yubaba does, on occasion, have a humorous look embedded into her suspicious character. Indeed, Yubaba and Bō may be looked at as a pumped-up, well-fed version of Nagasawa Rosetsu's *Yamauba and Kintarō*. Further similarity is found in the absence of Yubaba's male partner. When yamauba first appeared as the mother of Kintarō in the seventeenth century text, her partner was never mentioned. Likewise, Yubaba's husband is non-existent in the film.

---

15 For the Rosetsu's paintings, see Nagasawa Rosetsu.

Moreover, while Yubaba is avaricious and strict toward her workforce, she also has the ability to observe diligence in her workers. When Stink Spirit (*okusare-sama*) visits the bathhouse, for example, Yubaba notes how hard Chihiro works, and decides to give her a helping hand. Similarly, yamauba also help humans that are helpful to them. The yamauba in "Hanayo no hime," for instance, brings wealth to the princess who helped kill coiling worms in her hair.[16]

From the spatial point of view, too, there is a parallel between the yamauba and Yubaba. Komatsu Kazuhiko writes that "[t]he concept of mountains, as a mountainous realm where oni and *yōkai* reside, is better understood as the 'spatial other world.'"[17] Indeed, the mountains are often the entry-point to the realm where the oni and *yōkai* live along with other mountain deities and deceased ancestors. Yamauba is also a resident of the mountains. Likewise, the environment where Yubaba's bathhouse is situated is a locus of the other world where all the supernatural beings come to relax and unwind. Pertinent to the spatial aspect, a further parallel is seen in the altitude where yamauba and Yubaba live. The mountain where yamauba lives is higher than ordinary flatland. Likewise, Yubaba lives on the top floor of the bathhouse—higher than anyone else, a command center from which she controls her operation and gives orders to her employees. Yubaba-yamauba is the authority of the supernatural world, powerful and rich. She is literally and figuratively bigheaded; also she does not conform to social norms. Within the film, however, social equilibrium destabilized by Yubaba is somewhat returned with the appearance of her twin-sister, Zeniba who is a comforting, self-assured, good, old grandma figure. Yubaba, who

---

16   See note 17 of chapter four. One of the works that influenced Miyazaki in creating the film is Kashiwaba Sachiko's *Kiri no mukō no fushigina machi* (A Mysterious Town beyond the Mist). Aunt Picot, a major character of *Kiri no mukō no fushigina machi*, is an elderly owner of an apartment house. Her motto is "those who don't work should not eat," and like Yubaba, she appreciates and rewards a good worker.

17   According to Komatsu Kazuhiko, the term "the other world" can be understood from two levels: one is to look at the world from a temporal point of view, or time axis; and the other is the spatial viewpoint, or space axis. The temporal view considers the world of time from birth to death as "this world," and the time before birth and after death as "the other world." From the spatial viewpoint, the space where everyday life exists is regarded as "this world" and the space outside of everyday life (the meta-everyday life realm) is regarded as "the other world." Heaven, oceans, rivers, underground, and strange land are understood as "the other world" from the spatial point of view. The "spatial other world" cannot be visited easily, but unlike the "temporal other world," if the conditions are met, one can enter without undergoing death (*Shinpen oni no tamatebako* 57–58).

appears transcendent to the expectation of gender role, in spite of her excessive motherhood, is thus contained within the world of *Spirited Away*. The portrayal of modern female oni is still as "other" yet tamed by the expectation of the mainstream consciousness.

Yōkai and Oni Variants

In chapter five, the tendency of oni to become simply one of many *yōkai* was discussed. The *Tale of the Imperial Capital* has raised the oni's status and popularity greatly in modern times, but the general perception of oni as one of the *yōkai* is undeniable. In cyberspace, one may say oni variants of *yōkai* such as *tsuchigumo* (earth spiders) and *yasha* (yaksa) are probably more active than the traditional iconography of oni. Indeed, there has been a steadfast "*yōkai* boom" in contemporary Japan.[18] The vanishing darkness from night due to modern lighting technology probably contributed to the disappearance of *yōkai* from this physical world. The bright light of urban areas deprived *yōkai* of their traditional living space (Komatsu Kazuhiko, *Yōkaigaku shinkō* 284). Kagawa Masanobu comments on this *yōkai* boom, "[f]ormerly, *yōkai* certainly existed as a real entity. In contemporary Japan, especially in urban areas, *yōkai* do not exist in daily-life. *Yōkai* are creatures in the world of fiction. We mustn't forget that the present '*yōkai* boom' is a phenomenon in that environment" (32). *Yōkai* live in the world of imagination mainly as an entertainment, but they speak to us of what we have forgotten or ignored.

Although touched upon in chapters one and five, the term *yōkai*, given its politico-literary connotations, requires a little more explanation.[19] According to the dictionary, *Keitai shin kanwa jiten*, a *yōkai* is "*bakemono, mononoke*" (shape-shifter, vengeful spirit) (Nagasawa 340). In the early twentieth century, Ema Tsutomu, a folklorist and Kyoto scholar, defined *yōkai* as "mysterious, strange creatures" (*etai no shirenai fushigina mono*) (2). Yanagita Kunio distinguished *yōkai* from ghosts by stating that the former appear only at certain places whereas the latter appear anywhere without spatial limitation. On the other hand, while *yōkai* appear at anytime during the day or night, ghosts appear exclusively at night, especially around midnight.

---

18 As Michael Foster notes, one of the important writers/artists who triggered the recent *yōkai* boom is Mizuki Shigeru's (born 1924). For the study of Mizuki Shigeru and his work, see Foster, *Pandemonium and Parade* 164–82.

19 For the study of *yōkai*, see Foster, *Pandemonium and Parade*.

Furthermore, whereas *yōkai* encounter anyone without distinction, ghosts have some specific person or people to meet ("Yōkai dangi" 292–93). These distinctions are, however, refuted by Komatsu Kazuhiko, an anthropologist, who defines *yōkai* as follows: "People in an ethnic society, who desire to understand and systematize all the phenomena and beings in the world, have their explanation system. When phenomena or beings which cannot be fully explained by that system of thought appear, those incomprehensible or disorderly things are termed *yōkai*" ("Ma to yōkai" 346). Thus, Komatsu employs a broader definition for *yōkai*, one that encompasses anything labelled "strange" or "bizarre" (*Nihon yōkai taizen* 10). Thus, oni are *yōkai* with mostly negative associations.

Yasha and Dog in *InuYasha*

While traditional oni with horns on their scalps are visible, *yamauba* and such oni variants as *yasha* (*yaksha*) and *tsuchigumo* (earth spiders) appear to be taking active roles in cyberspace. As mentioned in chapter one, *yasha* is an Indian-originated Buddhist oni. A good example of *yasha* in pop culture is *InuYasha* (dog-demon), an extremely popular Japanese manga for teens of various countries including the U.S. Appearing first in Japan in 1997, the manga was so successful that it was made into a television anime series and it inspired three feature length films. The author is none other than Takahashi Rumiko, the creator of *Urusei Yatsura*. InuYasha, which literally means "dog-*yasha*," is the male protagonist of the series, and a half-*yōkai*. InuYasha was born of a human mother, and sired by a full-fledged *yōkai*. He yearns to be a full-fledged *yōkai*. At the beginning of the *InuYasha* series, a heroine, Kagome, a fifteen-year-old girl living in present-day Tokyo, is sent to the past by a *yōkai* through an ancient well in her family's compound. There in the sixteenth-century Warring States of Japan Kagome discovers that she is the reincarnation of Kikyo, a deceased priestess who guarded the miraculous Shikon jewel. The Shikon jewel has the power to fulfill any ambition of man or *yōkai*. Fifty years before, InuYasha tried to steal the jewel to become a thoroughbred *yōkai*, but Kikyo prevented it and put InuYasha into a deep sleep by shooting him with a sacred arrow. Now the Shikon jewel is reborn into Kagome's body, and InuYasha has awakened. *Yōkai* of various kinds also start to fight for the jewel, and during the clash the jewel is shattered and its shards scattered across Japan. Kagome and InuYasha team up to retrieve the shards before they fall into the hands of their archenemy Naraku, who manipulates various *yōkai* to try to obtain the shards.

Abe Masamichi comments in his study of *yōkai* that "all *yōkai* are the ruins of humans. *Yōkai* continue to exist both inside and outside humans. They wish to return to a human form, but are unable to do so. They live in fields, mountains, seas, grasses and trees, full of sadness at not being able to return to a human form" (7). Ironically, both InuYasha and Naraku (half-*yōkai*) desire to be full-fledged *yōkai*, knowing that this will increase their powers and strength. Likewise, all the *yōkai* characters in *InuYasha* look down on humans as weaklings. This may simply be a contemporary story element, or it could be a social satire or commentary on humankind's preoccupation with the acquisition of strength and power. These are contemporary *yōkai*.

InuYasha's name reveals the characteristics of his *yōkai* side. He has a keen sense of smell, dog-like ears, claws, and a white mane. Kuroda Hideo notes that during the medieval period, a dog was kept as a pet or a hunting animal. At the same time, dogs were also looked upon as a form of public hygiene because they ate food scraps and corpses or carrion. Consequently, the dog became a symbol of the graveyard and the cities. He further points out that a dog plays a role as a guide to the other world. In *Kōbō daishi gyōjō ekotoba* (Pictorial History of Priest Kōbō, the 14th century) for example, a white dog and a black one are depicted beside a deity who guides Priest Kōbō Daishi into sacred Mt. Kōya.[20] Also, the story from *Uji shūi monogatari* (A Collection of Tales from Uji) entitled "About an uncanny incident involving Seimei and a dog belonging to the Chancellor of the Buddha Hall" reveals how a white dog saved his master's life with its supernatural power.[21] Thus Kuroda concludes that a dog was considered to have supernatural power and was like a trans-boundary animal, between this world and the other world (*Zōho sugata to shigusa no chūsei-shi* 236). InuYasha's father was a powerful *yōkai* of a huge white dog. After his demise, his carcass—a gigantic white skull and bones—served as a demarcation realm between this world and the nether land, which is his graveyard. InuYasha also goes to his father's burial ground on two occasions: once, on a mission to find a

---

20 See Kuroda Hideo, *Zōho sugata to shigusa no chūsei-shi* 210–35.

21 "[Fujiwara Michinaga] had a particular pet, a white dog, which would go along with him and never leave his side. One day it was with him as usual, and just as he was about to go through the gate it ran round and round in front of his carriage, blocking his path and refusing to allow him in.... Michinaga asked Abe Seimei what the dog's behavior meant. Seimei replied, 'If you pass over it, you will suffer harm. The dog possesses supernatural powers and was warning you.'" Translation by Mills (411–12). For the original Japanese text, see Kobayashi and Masuko 450–51.

special sword made from his father's fangs; and next, in search of a Shikon shard. On the first occasion, the key leading to the boundary realm where his father's corpse resides was hidden in InuYasha's body. In this sense, one may say that InuYasha, a white dog, led a team to the different realm, just like the white dog did for Priest Kōbō.

The term *yasha*, conjures up something violent and ferocious, and this is what InuYasha becomes when his *yōkai* side dominates; he acts like a wild animal without knowing what is good or bad. As mentioned in chapter two, in Buddhist mythology, *yasha* was subdued by Bishamonten (*Vaisravans*), one of the Buddhist Guardians of the four cardinal directions, and became Bishamonten's kin to protect the true law of Buddha (Aramata and Komatsu 40). Interestingly, in InuYasha this side, as a protector of the good, is becoming increasingly visible, particularly when he protects Kagome, who purifies the Shikon shards on behalf of good. He feels for Kagome, but he cannot forget Kikyo who urged him to become a human being with the power of the Shikon jewel, and who died fifty years before, protecting it. InuYasha's character develops from a loner to a team player, and he has a hidden desire for companions. The theme that he is no longer a lonely individual appears in one of his theme songs as well. As we saw in chapter seven, modern fiction reflects the present-day societal phenomenon of individuals' desire for connections or relationships. Manga and anime also capitalize on this longing to identify the audience with the characters. While yearning for power, people long for some lasting relationship, and this holds true in the world of *yōkai* or *yasha*, perhaps all the more so because an oni and its variants are marginalized to begin with.

Tsuchigumo (Earth Spider) in *InuYasha*

InuYasha's archenemy is called Naraku, and he too is after the Shikon shards to garner greater demonic power. The name Naraku (*naraka*) is a Japanese term for hell. As the name suggests, Naraku is an entirely hellish character and the central force of malevolence in the story. Like InuYasha, he is a half-*yōkai* who wants to become the most powerful thoroughbred *yōkai*, a fate achievable only through the power of the shards. Naraku was formerly a human being named Onigumo (oni spider). In the manga version, Onigumo appears in the story as a horribly disfigured man with terrible burns. It is explained in the anime version that Onigumo was a wicked bandit with a large spider mark on his back. He had attempted to obtain the Shikon jewel under Kikyo's protection by manipulating his boss, the bandit leader. But his plan failed and the infuriated boss threw a bomb at him, disfiguring his whole body. Onigumo was left to die of his burns, but ironically Kikyo found him and saved his life. While Kikyo was tending Onigumo's wounds, his base desire for Kikyo consumed him and he gave up his body to *yōkai* to realize his lustful wish. *Yōkai* devoured Onigumo's body and soul, but Onigumo's wish was never realized. He was later reborn as Naraku with a latent lust for Kikyo. Onigumo in Naraku is represented by the spider's mark on Naraku's back. Naraku despises Onigumo's weakness, specifically his feelings for Kikyo, and attempts to get rid of him in various ways. Yet, the mark always reappears or re-surfaces on Naraku's back. The oni in Onigumo certainly represents his demonic character, and the symbolic spider reveals cultural memories.

Those cultural memories are *tsuchigumo*, earth spiders. It is commonly accepted among scholars that an earth spider refers to less cultivated indigenous people who lived before the Heavenly descendants claimed their authority. *Tsuchigumo*, an earth spider, is an appellation used derogatorily in ancient Japanese literature for those who defied imperial (central) authority.[22] For example, in *Kojiki* on Emperor Jimmu's eastward expedition to claim his Heavenly authority, he and his men smite a great number of resisting indigenous pit-dwelling tribe-men described as earth spiders.[23] An overwhelming majority of earth spiders had fought and been eliminated in bloody battles; only a few survived by apologizing profusely and escaping capital punishment.[24] An earth spider defies central authority, has different customs and manners, and different physiological features from the mainstream body culture. In that sense, the earth spider is considered to be one of the most ancient types of oni (Baba 170).[25] As for the origin of

---

22 See, for example, Tsuda 188–95.

23 See Kurano and Takeda 157. For an English translation, see Philippi 174–75. Also see Sakamoto et al. 1: 210. Its English translation is found in Aston 129–130.

24 For example, one *tsuchigumo* named Ōmimi in the district of Matsuura of Hizen Province promised to give food to the emperor as a tribute (Uegaki 335–336). Another *tsuchigumo* called Utsuhiomaro in the Sonoki district of the same province even saved an imperial ship (Uegaki 345).

25 In the picture scroll entitled *Tsuchigumo sōshi* (Story of the Earth Spiders, early 14th century), a gigantic oni, sixty feet tall with many legs, which lives in a cave, turns out to be the enormous spider. I should add that the accompanying painting to the *Story of the Earth Spiders*, however, portrays two gigantic oni with only two legs. For the narrative of *Story of the Earth Spiders*, see Komatsu Shigemi, Ueno, Sakakibara, and Shimatani 162, and for the painting, see ibid. 7. Further, in Tsukioka Yoshitoshi (1839–1892)'s picture entitled *Minamoto no Yorimitsu tsuchigumo wo kiru-zu* (Minamoto Yorimitsu

the term, *Itsubun Settsu Fudoki* (a missing writing from the *Topography of Settsu Province*, known from other literary sources) notes that, "In the reign of Emperor Jimmu, there was a villain called *tsuchigumo*—he was given the disdainful name of earth spider because this person always dwelled in a pit" (Uegaki 437). Pit dwelling is strongly associated with *tsuchigumo*.

This also applies to the aforementioned *InuYasha*'s Onigumo who lived in a dark cave below the cliff—a form of pit dwelling. As an abandoned outlaw, terribly disfigured from burns, Onigumo was already socially, culturally, and even physically marginalized when he was in the cave. As the manga series continues, the image of an earth spider as a marginalized being persists in the minds of young readers, and without reading Japanese classical literature or related research materials, cultural memory surrounding earth spiders is thus carried on to new generations.

Tsuchigumo in *Spirited Away*

A reminiscent of *tsuchigumo* also appears in *Spirited Away* in the form of Kamaji who lives in the basement of the bathhouse—a form of pit dwelling. Unlike Onigumo of *InuYasha*, however, Kamaji is a much more likable figure. Kamaji is one of Yubaba's employees, and from the viewpoint of the architectural structure, his dwelling is reflective of vertical, hierarchical Japanese society. As mentioned earlier, Japan is a vertical society where vertical relations such as senior-junior rankings are strong and strictly prescribed. Junior-ranking members may be assigned monotonous and basic work, but the work is vital to the promotion of teamwork. The relationship between bosses and junior members is not without tension. Kamaji lives on the lower end of this vertical relationship—steadfastly resisting Yubaba, but still providing vital work to the bathhouse.

Kamaji is an old man who controls a boiler room. He has six long arms and two ordinary length legs. At first sight he looks scary, but in reality he is a kind and understanding man (Uekusa 10). From all angles including the way he sits and manipulates his unusually long limbs Kamaji resembles a spider or the spirit of a spider.[26] On the symbolic significance of the spider, Merrily Baird writes, "…with the importation of Chinese traditions, the Japanese adopted the view of the spider as an emblem of industry and

---

Striking the Earth Spider, 1892), the earth spider has three claws, which is reminiscent of oni.

26 Sugii Gisaburō, an animation director, writes, "I wonder whether a spider is Kamaji's model. Miyazaki likes (a creature with) many hands" (qtd. in Uekusa, 51).

ability" (Baird 120). As evident in the film, Kamaji is a diligent worker who makes full use of all his extra limbs and his helpers, sootballs (*susuwatari*). Yet as we saw above, as *tsuchigumo*, spiders have a cultural baggage. While Kamaji does not openly battle with Yubaba, he does not always go along with her either; sometimes, he outright resists Yubaba's wishes. The most evident example of this occurs when Kamaji protects not only Chihiro but also Haku, abandoned and left for dead by Yubaba. And yet, Kamaji works for Yubaba, as some ancient earth spiders obeyed the central authority.

Kamaji is a warm being that understands human feelings. However, as we saw earlier, the descriptions in the ancient chronicles hardly express anything that encourages the readers to empathize with earth spiders. After all, from a viewpoint of the editors of *Nihongi*, an earth spider is an enemy of the central government. Interestingly, though, the sympathetic descriptions of earth spiders appear in later texts, specifically in the Noh text entitled *Tsuchigumo* (Earth Spider, ca. late Muromachi Period).[27] According to the Noh's *Tsuchigumo*, the mighty imperial warrior, Minamoto no Raikō is attacked by an unknown illness. One night, a strange priest appears at Raikō's bedside and begins casting silken threads across Raikō. Surprised, Raikō strikes that creature with his renowned sword and the being disappears, dripping its blood behind. It turns out that Raikō's illness was caused by this strange creature, whose real identity is the spirit of the spider who had been killed by the emperor's army at Mt. Katsuragi. Raikō's vassal follows the blood trail and kills the spirit of the spider. The earth spider cries at the moment of his death, "[F]or here the spider's spirit stands Who in the mountain many years did dwell. To trouble the sooreign's reign I hoped, And so I approached Raiko. Alas! Is this to be my end?"[28] This statement does shed a sympathetic light on the earth spider as a victim of the central government. Perhaps he had lived peacefully before the advance of the heavenly imperial army to his district. From the earth spiders' point of view, the imperial army not only disturbed their way of living, it eliminated their tribe without legitimate reason. The earth spider's statement is just a few lines, but it reveals his pent-up emotions.

Likewise, in *Spirited Away* Kamaji is a man of few words and he helps those who no longer interest Yubaba. In this sense, Kamaji is reminiscent of

---

27 For the Noh text of *Tsuchigumo*, see Sanari 3: 2055–67. For an English translation, see Suzuki, Beatrice 87–92. The Noh text of *Tsuchigumo* is based on the *tsuchigumo* narrative of *Nihongi*, the "Swords Chapter" of *Heike monogatari*, and *Tsuchigumo sōshi*.

28 Suzuki, Beatrice 91. For the Japanese text, see Sanari 3: 2065.

the earth spiders' narratives of the past. Kamaji has cherished train tickets for forty years, implying that he has a desire to be away from the bathhouse someday. Yet, he gives them up to help Chihiro save Haku. Kamaji is a spirit that understands the meaning of "love" and an important pillar of the film. One may say that Kamaji may represent an ancient earth spider portrayed from *tsuchigumo*'s point of view—the perspective of the "other."

As we survey the fertile terrain of cyberspace and manga in search of oni and oni variants, indeed quite a number of them pop up on the radar screen, among which only a select few are discussed. As an entity of pure imagination, the oni's habitat is often of a different realm both temporally and spatially. Many characters such as Devilman, Shutendō Jirō, and InuYasha, go freely between different times and spaces; some exist in a completely different realm such as Yubaba and Kamaji in *Spirited Away*. Others' imaginary reality is set here and now but the creatures are from a different planet, as in *Urusei Yatsura*. One noticeable phenomenon is that of the Judeo-Christian devil-like character advancing to what used to be Japanese oni territory. Terms such as Satan and Armageddon are not Japanese-born. While the apocalyptic mode is deeply affected by societal phenomena such as Aum's incident, one may say that the modern Japanese creators of anime, manga or film who are familiar with western thought feel comfortable with non-Japanese elements, and aggressively utilize non-Japanese entitities such as devils in the Judeo-Christian tradition in order to create something novel and artistic. Still, the devils or the world of devils become somewhat Japanized or *oni*ficated as we have seen. Whether it is a representation of the spiteful anger of the human mind or an idealized teenage figure, the oni concept remains strong in the mind of Japanese artists and readers alike.

9

Oni without Negatives
Selfless and Surrealistic Oni

Oɴɪ ᴡɪᴛʜᴏᴜᴛ ɴᴇɢᴀᴛɪᴠᴇs ᴅᴏ ɴᴏᴛ sᴛʀɪᴋᴇ ᴏɴᴇ ᴀs ᴏɴɪ. Yet, modern times have witnessed the birth of an utterly kind and selfless oni. He appears in the children's story, now widely considered a classic, titled *Naita Akaoni* (Red Oni Who Cried). Its author, Hamada Hirosuke (1893–1973), says that he created a kind oni, hoping to spread compassion among modern people. Another oni without harm or evil comes from a famous, authoritative literary figure of the twentieth-century, Inoue Yasushi (1907–1992). Inoue Yasushi's oni is a deceased person, and in that sense, his oni is heavily based upon Chinese ideas of oni discussed in chapter one. The Chinese line of thought from Inoue Yasushi is not surprising when one considers his erudition on Chinese cultural history. His portrayal of oni is keenly personal, and their imagery, surreal. Although these oni themselves do not have negative ambiance, the stories revolve around the basic notion of the stigmatic oni that carries cultural baggage. The modern creation of oni without negativity gives a fresh breeze to the somewhat stereotyped oni world, i.e., a dark, violent and/or sexy image from pop culture. While this reveals the oni's lasting flexibility and elasticity, it also raises a question, "What are oni?"—the very question we asked in chapter one.

Kind and Thoughtful Oni: *Naita Akaoni* (Red Oni Who Cried)

The earliest depictions of utterly kind, selfless oni seem to have come from a noted author of children's literature, Hamada Hirosuke (1893–1973). Kitajima Harunobu's comment on *Naita Akaoni* says that an "oni is a frightening creature. There are many stories about scary and evil oni in Japan. Oni are widely perceived as frightful and evil, so it is quite understandable that the Japanese dislike them. *Naita akaoni* is unique, for it describes the oni as a good creature" (199–200).

In his *Naita Akaoni* (Red Oni Who Cried, 1933), the kind red oni is determined to be good. The red oni wants to befriend mankind, but humans are afraid of oni and want no association with them. Knowing the red oni's desire, the blue oni (the red oni's friend, and also a good oni) makes the major sacrifice: he plans an elaborate ruse that calls for the red oni to conveniently jump to the rescue of humans while the blue oni destroys their homes. The blue oni is willing to come across as the evil one so that his friend, the red oni, can be seen as the good one. His plan is successful and as a result, the red oni comes to have many human friends. One day, when the red oni visits the blue oni's house, he finds that the blue oni has gone away so as not to disturb the red oni's good relationship with the humans. The red oni cries, touched and moved by the blue oni's thoughtfulness, friendship, and self-sacrifice.

Written at a time of change, an era of fast-paced modernization, Hamada's stories would serve to help children and adults come to terms with this new age. The dehumanizing effect of modernization and particularly industrialization raised a number of questions about what it means to be human. As industrialism spread and more people began to feel the marginalizing effects of being cogs in the industrial machine, many began to ask themselves these very pertinent questions. When asked about his motivations, the author states, "I felt that I should like to bestow a good intention on an oni. If the reader pities the well-intended oni and feels compassion towards him, then such a sentiment would undoubtedly be extended to thoughtfulness and compassion for other people's feelings" (Hamada 200). It certainly helped open a path for later oni fiction that treat oni as an alter ego of humans. The red oni was friendly enough to prepare tea and homemade cakes for the humans, while his counterpart, the blue oni, espoused qualities of self-sacrifice, putting the needs of others ahead of his own. The blue oni was considerate enough to leave the area so as not to interfere with his friend's newfound acceptance. This piece served to illustrate the benefits of self-sacrifice, righteousness, and upright behaviour. Hamada succeeds in drawing empathy from his readership by emphasising the more compassionate side of humankind, producing in the process kind-hearted and benevolent oni. Hamada's oni are different from the de-demonized oni we have seen in earlier chapters in that they are not parodied beings; they have no evilness, no ulterior motives or underlining machinations. While Hamada's oni are positive, it should be noted that humans in Hamada's story have the cultural baggage to deny the oni's friendship simply because the red oni is an oni. In other words, the background of *Naita Akaoni* is actually the strongly held belief of oni as wicked.

The roots of this humane oni may be found in the protagonist of the Noh play, *Yamamba*, whose authorship is attributed to Zeami (1363–1443). As discussed in chapter four, folk belief portrays yamauba as a mysterious old woman living on the mountain and feasting on travellers who happen upon her path. Unlike the yamauba of folk tradition, Zeami's character is an invisible, lonely old woman who altruistically helps humans with their chores. She tells a group of entertainers to spread her side of the story to the public. Popular during the medieval period, Zeami's *Yamamba* is heavy with Buddhist philosophical precepts such as "the good and evil are not two; right and wrong are the same" (Brazell 207). Zeami's yamauba is laden with spiritual burdens, forever making the mountain rounds, forever disenfranchised by ordinary people. In contrast, Hamada's oni has no darkness within, therefore no philosophical weight. When one considers the genre of children's literature for which this story was written, having a kind oni becomes more understandable, for it is parents', educators', and for that matter, all adults' hope that children grow up to be kind and considerate. Indeed, oni can be used to teach such moral lessons as "appearance is deceiving"—even an oni that everyone considers evil turns out to be good—or to show the importance of self-sacrifice and true friendship, even among oni.

The oni's compassionate side is not typically an emphasized characteristic. As a purely fictional character, a product of the imagination unburdened by any attendant religious dogma, it is possible for Hamada's oni to be befriended by others, and become a source of hope to expand human compassion. As the story of *Naita Akaoni* has grown in popularity to become a classic of children's literature,[1] the kind oni has become less "anomalous."

I have just used the word, "anomalous." But is the oni without negativity really an anomaly? The reader of this book is familiar with a positive side of oni—the oni as harbingers of wealth and fortune. As mentioned in chapter one, Orikuchi writes that the oni concept before the introduction

---

1   The story is broadcast on the radio and television, and adapted to movies, ballet and opera (Hamada Rumi 117).

of Buddhism was a variation of *tokoyo-kami* (*kami* who live in the other land or the land of the dead) or *marebito* (foreign travelers, *kami* who visit villages) who give blessings on the lunar New Year's Eve and/or New Year's Day for the coming year. Further, demons were believed to be honest and not manipulative in ancient and medieval times. Again, as we saw in chapter one, in one tale of *Konjaku monogatarishū*, Minister Miyoshi no Kiyotsura (847–918) says "real demons know right from wrong and are perfectly straight about it. That's what makes them frightening."[2] Shuten Dōji, who is considered an archfiend, also cries out when he was deceived by humans and is to be killed, "How sad, you priests! You said you don't lie. There is nothing false in the words of demons." He even offers lodging to a group of strangers out of compassion. After all, the multifaceted oni has a role as an attendant of Buddhist protectors, and a duty (as a variation of *marebito*) to be more honest and righteous than normal human beings. The kind oni are not anomalies, but the evil, murderous behavior, and notorious killing sprees that typify most oni stories are carved in human memory much more deeply than any positive elements; the oni as "other" has given unknown fear to ordinary Japanese lives. The oni's general appearance—large mouth with fangs and horns on its head—does not help promote the oni's light side, either. Hamada's oni is remarkable in that the author sheds full light on the oni's positive aspect, which tends to be forgotten. Various aspects of oni are drawn to people's attention according to human needs. Hamada's achievement was in rediscovering a positive aspect of what had been long considered dark and evil, and focusing entirely on that bright side against a harsh backdrop of societal changes and dehumanizing mechanization.

Oni Go to Heaven: Inoue Yasushi's Surrealistic "Oni no hanashi" (A Story of Oni)

Oni can be utilized not only by the authors of pop culture and children's literature, but also by Japan's masterful novelists. Indeed, a nostalgic and personal account of oni comes to us from the hand of Inoue Yasushi (1907–1992). The description of oni by Inoue Yasushi is quite ethereal. Inoue Yasushi, one of Japan's finest novelists (Richie 339), produced serious historical novels as well as semi-autobiographical novels and short fiction of

---

2 The English translation is by Tyler (*Japanese Tales* 123). The Japanese text is found in Mabuchi et al. 38: 97–101.

humor and wisdom. "Oni no hanashi" (Story of Oni, 1970) is one of his autobiographical short stories in which he describes his deceased friends and relatives as oni. Oni in the *Story of Oni* are not frightening or marginalized, they are simply deceased people. Inoue's narrator writes that "it is said that when one passes away, *kiseki ni iru* (one's name is recorded in the roster of the dead or ghosts). Indeed, my uncle died and became an oni" (162). The expression, *kiseki ni iru*, comes from a Chinese expression. As mentioned in chapter one, 鬼 in Chinese indicates an invisible soul or spirit of the dead, both ancestral and evil. When one dies it is believed that his or her name is recorded in King Yama's roster; hence, *kiseki ni iru* means that someone is deceased. Unlike the Chinese concept of death, however, horns are an important element in the narrator's discussion of oni. What convinces the narrator that his late uncle has become an oni are the horns, which have inexplicably grown on his uncle's forehead in an image.

Inoue's oni might be considered the product of mental illness because the narrator encounters them while he is suffering from neurosis and insomnia. The narrator persistently sees the images of his late uncle at night when he is still awake. One night, the narrator notes quite casually that he has noticed two horns on his uncle's forehead. Yet, he quickly adds that his "uncle's face with two horns was not gloomy or eerie in the least. Despite the two horns on his head, his face has become more like his real face" (162). He is sympathetic to his oni, not because they are dead and thus became oni, but because he has mostly fond memories of the deceased while they were alive.

During the course of sleepless nights, the narrator reflects upon the images of his late family members, relatives, friends, and acquaintances one after another. He puts horns on their heads to check whether the horns fit their faces or not. Some of the faces do not accept the horns. He concludes that even if the deceased are called oni, there are some with horns and some without. Further, he notices that a number of characters that contain the shape of the "oni" character, i.e., 鬼, are the names of the stars, and it strikes him that the oni without horns are probably stars in the sky. The narrator explains that when one passes away, one becomes either an oni in heaven as a star (without horns) or an oni on earth (with horns). Indeed, many of his oni are innocent and benevolent. The narrator describes his late baby girl who passes away only seven days after her birth as an "enchantingly lovely oni," and an "innocent oni-child" (164). Of his maternal aunt, who dies at the age of twenty-three or twenty-four, the narrator says, "Her face with horns made me feel that I could trust my baby daughter in her care, and I was much relieved" (164–65). Sabauchi, his friend of college days who took good care of a bed-ridden wife throughout his life, is also an oni with horns.

Naturally the question is raised: "On what kind of persons do horns grow, and on what kind of persons do horns not grow?" The narrator asks Sabauchi, and the answer is intriguing. Sabauchi replies, "Horns grow on the head of a saint who has never sinned. Horns don't grow on the head of a similar saint. Some villains have horns and others don't. The situation is terrible in your world. Sometimes several hundreds of horns of several hundreds of kinds grow on humans' foreheads, and sometimes they don't grow at all. It's just you can't see the horns" (186). Inoue's oni is surreal. Clearly the horns, which initially made the narrator believe that people become oni when they die, are not an indication of one's morality. Yet, if a horn, regardless of its meaning, still indicates an element of oni, the living humans who have horns in great numbers are also oni, but with more variety. Or conversely, if humans have hundreds of them on their heads, then horns do not indicate death, either. There appears to be no demarcation between oni and human and perhaps this is Inoue's point. But one thing seems clear from Sabauchi's further comments: the "realm of death is filled with sadness from separation. There is nothing else. No anger, no joy, no hatred nor jealousy. Only sadness of separation from the loved ones exists. …The realm of the dead is not as dirty as a world of the living. The place is clear" (187). That the living world is dirty and murky is a familiar Buddhist concept. Humans' existence and thought processes are probably much murkier than those of oni's. Inoue's oni, whose images appear to him like a kaleidoscope, are serene and philosophical.

The oni without negatives described by Hamada Hirosuke and Inoue Yasushi highlight the oni's complexities: Hamada draws kindness and compassion, and Inoue illustrates oni as innocent and benevolent who reside in the "other" world. They are not entirely new, but they strike us as something different, something surprisingly fresh because oni have been long associated with the "dark side" or "otherness" of this human world or human psyche. When this unfamiliar "other" is totally kind and benevolent, the degree of fears toward the "other" decreases, though it does not disappear. Most obviously the difference in appearance or behavior remains unchanged. Thus, the oni, regardless of good or evil, seem to remain as "other."

It should be noted that these kind oni have, like other modern oni, a yearning for human relationships. As we saw in chapter seven, by and large, the modern oni are looking for some connections with others. Hamada's red oni wanted to be a friend of humans. Inoue's oni's world is filled with sadness from separation from their loved ones. While Inoue's explanation of the oni's appearance during his neurosis and insomnia keenly describes the situation in which a modern oni exists—it exists only in one's imagination—the loneliness the oni feels, yearning for relationship with others, someone they can love or someone who will love them, reveals the fragmented society of modern times.

Conclusion

As the reader has witnessed in the course of this monograph, oni emerge, take shape and derive substance from Buddhist cosmology, yin and yang beliefs, Chinese literature, and popular Japanese imagination. Through the ebb and flow of Japanese history oni are sustained by and feed upon not just human flesh but human creativity and the seemingly overriding human need to make sense of and bring order to their world. Thus, the Japanese have cast legends about and built praxis around oni according to the exegeses of their particular historical moment and their given beliefs and commitments.

For ancient and medieval Japanese cultures, oni had *real* efficacy. They were accorded the status of *real* entities having *real* physical substance. As objects of fear and awe oni were integral parts, and had important roles, not only within the ancient and medieval Buddhist cosmos, but also in the everyday lives of Japanese people. In these periods, oni were believed to be the very substance of thunder and lightning. Oni were the cause behind epidemics that killed people by the tens of thousands; conversely, these demons were also the harbingers of wealth and good fortune. Importantly, during the time period in question, oni pragmatically influenced the everyday spatial and temporal lives of people. Recall that during the Heian period, when oni were said to stroll at night in groups, people would carefully choose the day and direction of outings in order to avoid mishaps in encountering oni and being devoured.

Oni, throughout their long history, and on many levels of significance, have borne their great burden as repositories of much that is interesting about human emotions and the human psyche. Witness, as we have, what occurs when humans with huge political clout fall out of favor, and are demoted or disfranchised: they become angry, and such chagrin literally turns them into oni. Members of the imperial court, people on the victorious side of a particular political intrigue, and/or the guilty parties in instances of romantic trysts would, at their given historical moments, worship the vengeful spirit in their attempts to appease the wrath of the angry oni that may have come in the form of natural disaster, or as the cause of unnatural death of people around them. Buddhist monks, *onmyōdō* practitioners, and Shinto priests were all summoned to quell the anger of formidable oni as we have seen in the case of Sugawara Michizane. Likewise, jealousy, infidelity, overpowering lust, and unrequited love all had the ability to turn people into oni. What is important for us to recall here is not the actuality of this phenomenon; that is, it is not important that the reader believe oni once walked the earth and derive meaning from the phenomenon. Rather, it is what this very pragmatic and widespread belief meant to, and says about, the historical culture from which it emerges. Most important, however, is what this system of belief *does*, and how it functions in the sociopolitical and physical lives of Japanese people in any particular historical period.

If one accepts the tenet that oni impact the physical everyday lives of people in the culture from which they emerge, then it is relatively easy to make sense of the oni's functions within and influences upon the political events that drive Japanese history. We have seen this happen in the course of this book—recall the warrior class and the shogun's rise to power. As those warriors who pride themselves on their physical prowess and skill at arms appear in the political arena, the oni's status gradually falls from that of an all-powerful and awe-inspiring entity that is to be avoided at all costs, to something to be challenged and subdued on behalf of the "forces of good." In this we witness the rather interesting carnivalesque flux in the relationship between self and other, and the ways that the various transactions of these ideas come to influence historical events. The imperial authority, its court, and recorders of such authority view themselves as the force of good, and label any enemy individual or force as oni, dispatching brave warriors to squash their existence.

As we have seen, this seemingly simple dichotomy of good and evil is much more complex since ostensibly one derives its "essence" from the other. Shuten Dōji is a good example. Recall that Shuten Dōji, the counterforce to the imperial court, lives in the jewelled palace in the mountains where nobody can easily approach. When he becomes hungry, he flies to the capital and even foreign countries to sate his enormous appetite for human flesh and blood. He causes natural calamities. In all aspects, he is the evil creature we associate with the term oni. Yet in closer examination of his origins, Shuten Dōji appears as a politically and socially marginalized being. Originally, he might have been an indigenous deity of the mountains before the official Buddhist sect opened the mountains for Buddhism, depriving him of his residence. He could have been a metal worker, or a bandit. What is important here is that whatever he was, he was outside the sanction of the dominant and hegemonic culture of the court. He is other, something to be subdued and destroyed, an enemy, and this is the exact thing that makes this story, and the rise of the warrior class for that matter, so carnivalesque. The images that surround the scenes of Shuten Dōji and his court of oni (as shown in the picture scrolls) are presented as carnivalesque inversions of scenes of the warriors and the imperial court. That these images and the dichotomous relationships that they imply are indeed in flux, we see in the degree to which warriors' prowess derives directly from the tenaciousness and evil ferocity of the enemy they oppose. Since one comes to be defined in terms of the other, the distinctions between them begin to weaken and become blurred. If we look at the way this juxtaposition of self and other functions in more modern times, we see yet another example of flux. Recall that during the Second World War the state as well as the willing populace projected the image of oni onto the enemy camp, while the imperial Japanese army was acting like oni in various Asian countries, a prime example being the atrocities of Nanking committed in 1937. Who the oni is and who labels one an oni is a matter of perspective, and a blurred perspective at that. It remains a perpetual question.

The carnivalesque flux that characterizes the dichotomy of self and other extends as well to the dichotomy of natural and supernatural. As we have seen, this is indeed a complex relationship since it functions not only on a spiritual level but a spatial one as well. Thus we witness how Michizane is promoted from oni to kami because of abundant worship by the imperial household. We witness the spatial side of the equation in the public space that Michizane occupies nationwide vis-à-vis the Kitano Shrine dedicated in his honor, with numerous branch shrines all over Japan. We have also seen how this same interrelationship attends the Shuten Dōji stories. Recall that Shuten Dōji's severed head is said to be stored in Uji no hōzō. Shuten Dōji's head, physically present in the Fujiwara family's treasure house signifies the Fujiwara's high status as well as the regeneration of imperial authority in the Heian capital as carnivalesque ambivalence dictates. Shuten Dōji's violent death by the hands of the famous warriors, especially Minamoto no Raikō, gives material reward to the involved characters but also leads to the rise of the warriors' status—the severed head that so symbolizes Fujiwara power is won by Raikō, not the regent. Thus, even symbolically, the demise of Shuten Dōji influences events in the public arena.

If Shuten Dōji is a formidable force to threaten the lives of people in Heian capital, so then is Uji no hashihime who indiscriminately kidnaps and kills men and women of the capital. Yet in comparison to male oni, female oni such as Uji no hashihime as described in *Heike monogatari* occupy a private as opposed to a public space. This may be understandable when we consider the Japanese political landscape of that time. Women rarely publicly participated in government affairs—their political machinations were often concocted in private and executed by male relatives. In the Heian polygamous society and the societies of the ensuing periods it was permitted and common for a man to have concubines in addition to a legal wife. While women in this period were taught not to be jealous when their husbands had mistresses, a woman's anger, jealousy, and resentment were directed nevertheless to her husband and his mistresses. The fierce female oni are often born out of jealousy, misery, and anger. Juxtapose these "private" emotions with the more public emotions that characterize men turned into oni by thwarted political ambitions. One might also note that in the private sphere, while women are turned into oni because of thwarted *love*, it is thwarted *lust* that turns men to demons, so even in the private sphere these matters are to some significant degree gendered. It can also be argued that oni, both male and female, act to balance gender relations. The possibility that a woman will be made monstrous by her jealousy acts to curb her emotional response to her philandering husband. The existence of ferocious female oni in turn becomes a warning against a man's amorous behavior. Thus, Uji no hashihime is utterly marginalized by her lover and her jealousy and angst turn her into a living oni.

As we see throughout this survey of Japanese literature, one noticeable common denominator of oni is the stigma of "other" that they seem to have carried about them from the start. We have seen this otherness transacted in many ways throughout this book so it is perhaps proper as we draw our conclusions to revisit some of the socio-cultural ramifications this otherness implies. The other represents those marginalized individuals or groups who, either voluntarily or because of force, are partially or entirely excluded from participation in the political, historical, and cultural affairs of hegemonic society. People's reactions to this otherness range from avoidance, ostracism, or complete subjugation to total elimination. When occasionally oni are welcomed as bringers of prosperity, they are still expected to leave soon after giving the fortune and/or blessing. As seen in the oni character of the *kyōgen* play, *Setsubun*, the oni is expelled as soon as his treasures are obtained.

We have seen how those of different ethnic and cultural backgrounds and/or customs are frequently branded oni. Recall that yamauba is categorized as an oni-woman for very similar reasons. Yamauba, living in the mountains, are said to eat unsuspecting passers-by. But some of them, as we have seen, are simply old women disenfranchised by the mainstream villagers of the flatland. With nowhere else to go, they are forced to live in the mountains. As aged humans, they become viewed as unsightly (yet another form of marginalization), further compelling them to avoid the public space. That negative visual image of yamauba in the medieval period, however, is transformed to an exotic, beautiful nymph-like woman full of sexuality in the hands of skilled ukiyo-e artists and Kabuki performers. A young and beautiful yamauba becomes an object of the "gaze" in the Early Modern period. Again, they bring material profit to the sellers/authors/creators.

Interestingly, yamauba may still exist in contemporary society. In 1979, an urban legend known as "kuchisake onna" (a slit-mouthed woman) swept all over Japan. "Kuchisake onna" was a young woman who covered her mouth with a surgical mask. She asked an unsuspecting person a question, "Am I beautiful?" The usual response would be positive. Then she took off the mask, revealing her slit-mouth, and asked the same question again. If the response was positive, the person (as well as the kuchisake onna) was said to rest in peace. But if the person screamed with fear and ran away, she chased after him or her, leading to the victim's tragic end. The inception of "kuchisake onna" was deep in the mountains of Gifu prefecture (Komatsu Kazuhiko, *Shinpen oni no tamatebako* 254–255), and some scholars, including Miyata Noboru and Komatsu Kazuhiko, consider "kuchisake onna" a type of yamauba (Miyata, *Yōkai no minzokugaku* 19–22).[1]

Young yet unique-looking yamauba then popped up some years ago among high school-aged girls. They painted their faces brown, brushed their lips white, penciled their eyes white, and had disheveled hair dyed gold or silver. These girls were labeled "yamamba" by the Japanese masses and mainstream media; columnist Izumi Asato believes that it was probably some magazine's editorial staff (rather than the girls themselves) that first labeled them "yamamba." He writes that the teenage girls could not possibly have known that the word originated in a Noh play, let alone how to write its kanji, 山姥. Their fashion was considered "heretical" (Izumi 5). Indeed, these girls had quite a distinct appearance. They were not old women but

---

1 For an insightful discussion on "kuchisake onna," see Foster, 182–203.

teenagers who looked and behaved differently from established societal, cultural, and religious norms. Their youth combined with their unusual appearance certainly portrayed quaintness, and at the same time, some sort of exotic sensuality. Just as in old times, these contemporary yamauba had white hair, but they could also be young and exotic. A tradition of yamauba thus continues in our modern age. The young and exotic yamamba seem to beg to see and to be seen.

As society becomes more secular and religion's influence recedes, the oni's power and influence wane. With the development of mass printing in the early modern period, people looked at oni in a book form. Oni thus became something catchable, i.e., a reader could see and examine them in an encyclopedia format. What was once awesome and terrifying became an entertainment and commodity in urban areas. In some cases, oni became a convenient souvenir of travel—like *oni no nenbutsu*. The commoditification of early modern times continues and has been accelerated in the present. In the contemporary landscape, it is not what oni will do to us humans, but what we humans can make out of them. This works on two valences: one is the idea of oni as a pure commodity seen solely for their entertainment value and the financial gains they produce for those who manipulate and control their imagery (a modern twist on oni as harbingers of wealth). The other, which is intricately intertwined with the first, is modern people's curiosity in trying to understand what oni are and why oni do what they do. A modern trend treats oni as an extension of the human psyche, and tries to understand their motivation—often from the oni's point of view. A good example, as we have seen, is the depiction of oni in popular fiction series like *Onmyōji*. In the present age, people now enjoy oni as entertainment, frightening but not threatening to their daily lives. People can open and close the doors to their living spaces to oni just as they open or close their books and/or turn on and off their television sets and video games.

In the realm of virtual reality, oni may take central stage as in the case of cute and sexy Lum in *Urusei yatsura* or righteous Shutendō Jirō in (Nagai Gō's) *Shuten Dōji*. But in many cases, oni have become just one of many *yōkai*, and appear on the screen with some modern-day additives to the original images, whether *tsuchigumo* or *yasha*. The images are evolutionary rather than set in stone. Oni have always been known for their shape-shifting power, and continue to morph into different shapes with new trappings. Indeed, they could appear as hybrids with western devils and succeed, as in Devilman.

Conclusion 183

Figure 8. Oni on the Kamaishi Line, part of East Japan Railway Company's July through September 2007 campaign, titled "Another Japan North East North: Aomori, Iwate, and Akita," to attract more passengers and tourists to northern Japan. Photo by the author.

Outside the world of virtual reality, oni are involved in people's lives and society. In fact, the oni's involvement in bringing some profit to society is exemplified in the movement of *machi-okoshi* (town revitalisation) in such towns as Ōe-machi in Kyoto. Ōe-machi is a town at the foot of Mt. Ōe, known for being the setting of the legend of Shuten Dōji. Once rich with rice, wood, and copper, Ōe-machi is now facing a depopulation crisis. Currently 6,000 people live there and many of those residents are elderly. In attempts to ward off its own extinction, the townspeople decided to make the town rich and comfortable again, employing the theme of the oni legend by "borrowing the strong power of oni to bring happiness" (Nihon no oni kōryū hakubutsukan). The area is rich in oni-related legends and sites and the townspeople decided to capitalize on this. The town has a museum called Nihon no oni kōryū hakubutsukan (The Japanese Oni Exchange Museum), and hopes to be a Mecca of oni in Japan to attract many tourists.

Similarly, there is another oni museum (*Oni no yakata*) in Kitakami City of Iwate Prefecture. Opened in 1994, the municipal museum collects and exhibits materials concerning the oni. The museum was founded as a symbol of the project "to create a town—[former] Waga town, now part of Kitakami City—for oni and peace" to revitalize the town. The museum is, however, located relatively far from the city; it was built where a traditional prayer dance, *oni kenbai*, was born and subsequently transmitted to the people of the surrounding area. The bus runs only four times a day, and it looks sadly isolated. For the people of Kitakami city though, "oni are ancestors who protect the townspeople and good deities who bring happiness" (Kitakami shiritsu oni no yakata 3). The hope is that the oni will become a financial resource, and the locals will preserve folk traditions and pursue the knowledge of oni's roots.

Baba Akiko writes that "in and after the early modern period, oni, as represented on the night of *setsubun*, have been depicted as beings easily chased away by mere beans" (288). But oni are tenacious, flexible, and seemingly ever transmutable. Through the hands of artists, writers, and commercial interests, oni have survived and transformed into more humanlike and commercially profitable entities. Currently, one can find a wide array of oni in the popular media—from the gentle and cute to the sexual and grotesque. The oni's transformation is highly reflective of and inextricably intertwined with Japan's own history and societal change. Still the oni's cannibalism, powers of transformation, enmity towards a central authority, isolation, ostracization because of different customs, ability to emit lightning, as well as their positive attributes (as sources of treasure or bringers of wealth) remain ever-present as the beings' major features. Some aspects of oni may be more emphasized than others to facilitate their use as art objects or political weapons, but whatever they mean, the oni have been an important part of the Japanese psyche for well over a thousand years.

Appendix A
A Translation of Shibukawa's Version of Shuten Dōji

A LONG TIME AGO IN JAPAN, A DIVINE COUNTRY from the time heaven and earth were divided, and where Buddhism thrived, imperial rule from the time of the first emperor[1] to the Engi era (901–923)[2] was endowed with righteous authority, sincere honesty and compassion for the people in ways unsurpassed by the Chinese emperors, Yao and Shun.[3]

Then, strange events began to take place.[4] Demons living in Mt. Ōe of Tanba province[5] began to abduct numerous people at night from throughout the land. In the capital, many people, particularly comely maidens of seventeen or eighteen years of age, were kidnapped.

Of all the recorded tales of demonic abduction, the one that affected the retired emperor's middle councilor Ikeda Kunitaka was especially heart wrenching. Kunitaka enjoyed the retired emperor's favor, and had a home filled with treasures. He also had a daughter of divine beauty.[6] It was said that anyone who encountered this girl's charms, either in person or through another's account, fell in love with her. The parents' love for the princess was most extraordinary. One evening, the graceful princess disappeared. Kunitaka's anguish, not to mention the grief of his wife, was indescribable.[7]

---

1 Emperor Jinmu. The first emperor of Japan who is, according to the ancient literatures, purported to have been enthroned in 660 BCE.
2 The sixtieth emperor, Daigo, reigned during the Engi era (901–923).
3 The reigns of the ancient Chinese emperors, Yao and Shun, were regarded by the Chinese as ideal.
4 The legend does not specify the time frame or historical context. However, the appearance of well-known characters in the story suggests the late tenth century or early eleventh century.
5 Present-day Kyoto.
6 *Sanjū-ni sō no katachi o uke.* These are the thirty-two attributes of Buddha that are used to compare beautiful women.
7 Kunitaka's reaction is not detailed, other than to confirm it was indescribable.

Nurses, maids, and all who happened to be in the dwelling were thrown into calamitous pandemonium.

Overcome with grief, Kunitaka summoned his servant Sakon and said, "I have heard recently that there is a reputable diviner named Muraoka no Masatoki[8] in the capital. Bring him here." Sakon at once went to fetch Masatoki to bring him to Kunitaka's mansion. Pitiable and without concern for his reputation, Kunitaka and his wife received Masatoki immediately.[9] "Hear me Masatoki," Kunitaka spoke, "Parents with even five or ten children would not neglect any one of them [let alone me with only one child]. Last night, my only child was abducted and we know nothing of her whereabouts. She is thirteen years old this year and since she was born, my wife and I have doted on her. We even have nurse chaperones standing guard when she descends from her veranda to protect her from strong winds. If this is an act of a demon, why did the demon not take me, too?" Kunitaka pressed his face to his sleeve [to catch his tears]. Kunitaka piled up tens of thousands of coins in front of the fortune teller, pleading with him: "Seer of fortunes, please tell me where my daughter is and I'll reward you with great treasures. Please divine carefully." The masterly Masatoki took out a scroll. After consulting the text, the seer triumphantly clapped his hands together, certain he had ascertained the princess's whereabouts. "Your princess's disappearance is the work of demons living in Mt. Ōe of Tanba Province. Her life is safe. In proper measure, I will pray for her safety, so please rest assured. After careful examination, the divination indicates to me that this abduction occurred because you failed to keep a promise to Kannon when you sought her blessing for the birth of the child. If you appeal to Kannon now with the appropriate prayers, your daughter will return to the capital soon," and with that clairvoyant revelation, Masatoki took his leave from the Kunitaka mansion.

Kunitaka and his wife were overcome with woe after hearing Masatoki's prognostications. Still in tears, Kunitaka went to the imperial palace to report to the Throne. In the assembly of the emperor, with court nobles and ministers gathered, palace officials discussed Kunitaka's plight, but could offer no definitive consensus on a course of action. Among them, the chief imperial advisor reminded those gathered that, "during the reign of Emperor Saga

---

8   In some versions such as *Ōeyama ekotoba*, the diviner is Abe no Seimei (?– 1005?), a famed specialist of *onmyōdō* during the middle of the Heian period (794–1185).

9   According to the custom of the time, it was not considered suitable that a person of a higher social rank would give an immediate audience to a person of lower rank, in this case, the diviner.

(reign 809–823), a similar incident happened. The Great Priest Kōbō[10] subdued the demon with his magical powers, expelling the demon from our land. If your majesty would summon Minamoto no Raikō to the palace and command him to subjugate the demon, the demon will surely be frightened of Raikō and his lieutenants, Sadamitsu,[11] Suetake,[12] Tsuna,[13] Kintoki,[14] and Hōshō.[15] The emperor agreed, issuing an imperial proclamation charging Raikō with the task of defeating the evil demons. Raikō immediately came to the palace and was granted an audience. "Hear ye Raikō, demons dwell in Mt. Ōe of Tanba province. They are doing wrong. In my divine country it is inconceivable that demons would inhabit even the most remote region to cause distress, let alone in the vicinity of the capital. Crush them."

The warrior Raikō was very moved to receive the imperial command but was also alarmed, reasoning, "Demons are transformers. If they learn that some punitive force is coming, they will turn into dust and leaves, and it will be hard for us ordinary humans to find them. Yet, how can I disobey an imperial order?" Hurrying home, Raikō called his men to his house. At their gathering, Raikō warned them all, "We won't be a match for the mighty demons. Let us pray to the deities and Buddhas for their help. That will be the best." And with that suggestion, Raikō and Hōshō proceeded to Yahata Shrine,[16]

---

10 Kūkai (774–835). The founder of the Shingon sect of Buddhism; he founded Kongōbu-ji on Mt. Kōya in present-day Wakayama prefecture.
11 Usui Sadamitsu (954–1021). A warrior of the mid-Heian period, and one of the *shitennō* (the four heavenly guardians/ lieutenants) of Minamoto no Raikō.
12 Urabe Suetake (?–1022). A warrior of the mid-Heian period and one of the *shitennō* of Minamoto no Raikō.
13 Watanabe Tsuna (953–1025). A warrior of the mid-Heian period and one of the *shitennō* of Minamoto no Raikō. As we have seen in the section on *Transformation Power* in chapter one, Watanabe no Tsuna encountered a beautiful woman of about twenty years of age at Modoribashi-bridge on Kyoto's First Avenue. Her (or probably his) real identity turns out to be an oni. This oni appears as Ibaraki Dōji in the story of "Shuten Dōji."
14 Sakata Kintoki (ca. 10th century). A warrior of the mid-Heian period and one of the *shitennō* of Minamoto no Raikō. As we saw in chapter four, as a child, his name was Kintarō, and his mother was a *yamauba*.
15 Fujiwara no Hōshō or Yasumasa (957–1036). A warrior who was good at both literary and martial arts. He became the governor of several provinces. His wife is Izumi Shikibu, a famous poet of the Heian period.
16 Iwashimizu Hachimangū. Located in present-day Kyoto, the god of battle and/or the deity for the Minamoto family was worshipped at this shrine by samurai warriors.

Tsuna and Kintoki went to Sumiyoshi Shrine,[17] while Sadamitsu and Suetake prayed at the Kumano Shrine.[18] All offered fervent prayers, and since Japan was a divine country where Buddhism thrived, each deity listened to their prayers. Nothing can be more joyous than the reception of their prayers, they thought, and they all went home content. Later Raikō and his lieutenants gathered to discuss plans for dealing with the Mt. Ōe demons, but the discussion ended without a solution.

Raikō took charge of the mission's tactical planning, recommending that the six warriors disguise themselves as mountain ascetics and pretend to be lost. He reasoned that if only they could locate the demon's base in Tanba province, defeating the demons would be easy, whatever military strategy they would employ. To that end, Raikō suggested, "Each of us must fabricate an ascetic's pannier in which to conceal our armor. What do you think?" With his men in agreement, the warriors set out to make their panniers. Concealed within Raikō's pannier was his vermilion armor called *randen gusari*, a helmet of the same vermilion thread named Lion King, and his splendid sword Chisui, which was two-foot-one in length. Hidden in Hōshō's pannier was his purple armor, a helmet of the same color, and his two-foot-long halberd, dubbed Cutting Rocks. Tsuna's pannier held his yellow-green armor with matching helmet and a sword called Cutting Demon.[19] Likewise, Sadamitsu, Suetake, and Kintoki used their panniers to hide their battle armor that was identifiable by color, helmets, and swords. In each pannier, sake, flint, and oilpaper were put atop the battle vestments.[20] Accordingly, each of the men donned the attire of a mountain ascetic: each had a round cap [*tokin*], and dressed in humble linen clothes, each carried a conch shell, a stick, and a striking sword.[21] While in concentrated prayer to the deities and Buddhas of Japan, the party left the capital for Tanba province. The warriors' resolve would terrify any dark force.[22]

---

17   Sumiyoshi Myōjin. The god of navigation as well as the god of battle.

18   Kumano Gongen. One of the strongholds of mountain asceticism (*shugendō*).

19   The origins of the names of the battle equipment are not known. However, other literature such as *Taiheiki* (Chronicle of Grand Pacification) indicates that the name Cutting Demon was given to the sword for it had cut an oni's arm in times past.

20   Flint is used to spark a fire; oilpaper is used as a waterproof cover.

21   A sword with a blade primarily designed to cut as it strikes as opposed to a blade chiefly intended to pierce or puncture.

22   Tenmahajun. A force bent on undermining the Buddhist Way and its universal wisdom.

Raikō's party hurriedly pressed onward, soon arriving at the foot of Mt. Ōe, in Tanba province. There they encountered a woodcutter. "Excuse me, woodcutter," asked Raikō, "Where is the mountain Senjōdake in this province? And, please tell us in detail where the demons dwell." The woodcutter replied, "Pass this peak and the valleys, and peaks that lay beyond, then you will reach the demons' lair, where humans never approach." "I see," said Raikō and to his men enjoined, "Let's pass beyond this peak," and in so saying, Raikō and his followers proceeded to cross the valleys and climb the peaks. While on the trail, Raikō and his men came upon three old men in a brushwood hut concealed inside a cavern. Peering into the makeshift dwelling, Raikō asked the occupants, "What sort of strange beings could you be?" One of the old men replied back, "We are not strange creatures. One is from Kakenokōri of Tsu province,[23] another is from Otonashisato of Ki province,[24] and the other is from Yamashiro,[25] close to the capital. Our wives and children have been stolen by the demon named Shuten Dōji who lives over this mountain. We recently arrived ourselves, seeking revenge for our wives and children being taken away, but in looking at you closely, you don't appear to be ordinary priests. I understand that you are here by imperial command to subjugate Shuten Dōji. By all means, we three old men will show you the way. Put down your panniers, relax, and rest from your journey."

Raikō accepted the old men's welcome. "As you said, we are lost in the mountain and are quite fatigued. We shall then take a rest." Raikō and his party put down their satchels, unpacked the sake and presented it to the three men. One of the old men then advised Raikō, "You must enter the demons dwelling stealthily, by any way possible. The chief demon always drinks sake, and so he is called Shuten Dōji [Drunken Demon]. After he becomes intoxicated and lies down, he becomes oblivious to the goings-on around him. We have in our possession a special kind of sake known as *jinben kidoku* (a divine elixir, poisonous to demons).[26] If demons drink this sake, they lose their supernatural flying powers and become disoriented. But if you drink this sake, it is medicinal. That is why for generations it has been recognized as a divine elixir, poisonous to demons. Now this sake will

---

23 Present-day Osaka, near Sumiyoshi.
24 Present-day Wakayama prefecture, where Kumano Gongen is located. See note 18.
25 Southeast area of present-day Kyoto.
26 It is a play on words of *jinben kidoku*, which means "unfathomable change."

prove its wonders again." Then, the old men produced a hobnailed helmet and handed it to Raikō, "Please put on this helmet when you decapitate the demon. It will protect you." Assessing the situation, Raikō's troop was convinced that the three old men were deities representing the three shrines they had visited before embarking on their mission. Overwhelmed, the six men shed tears of gratitude, their appreciation beyond words.

Emerging from the cave, the deities invited the warriors to follow them, "We shall show you the way." The group proceeded to climb the treacherous mountain Senjōdake. The deities then guided Raikō and his men through a thirty-meter-long dark cave, which opened up into a free-flowing mountain brook. They then directed the warriors, "Follow this waterway upstream and you will encounter a lady of seventeen or eighteen years of age, she can tell you more. When you are ready to strike, we, the deities of Sumiyoshi, Yahata, and Kumano, will again help you." With that promise to return, the elders vanished into thin air.

The six warriors fell to their knees humbled and honored by the deities' presence. Then they pressed upstream as instructed. Just as the deities had foretold, the group came upon a maiden of seventeen or eighteen years of age. The young girl seemed to be crying while washing what appeared to be blood-stained garments. Approaching her, Raikō inquired, "May I ask who you are?"[27] The young lady replied, "I am from the capital. One night, the demon took me away and brought me here. I can see neither my dear parents nor my nurses. Please pity me for I am in such a miserable state," she cried bitterly. Trying to hold back her tears, she sobbed, "Alas, how terrible! This place is called Demon's Cavern, and no human can approach. How could you priests have come here? Please let me return to the capital any way possible." And no sooner had she finished talking than the young maiden burst into tears again. Having heard the girl's plea, Raikō asked, "Who are your parents in the capital?" "I am the only daughter of the middle councilor Hanazono," she replied. "But I am not the only captive here. There are more than ten of us. Recently the princess of the middle councilor Ikeda Kunitaka was abducted and brought here. After taking good care of us, the demons wring the blood from our bodies, which they then consume as their sake. They consume our flesh as banquet condiments. It is so pitiable to look at the sight nearby of the blood-drained captives. This morning, the demons

---

27   Even though the deities suggested that there would be a maiden, the query is reasonable because a lone maiden high in Mt. Ōe would be highly unusual.

drank the blood of the princess of the middle councilor Horikawa. It's so sad that I now wash her blood-stained garments, indeed, it is pathetic," she lamented. The hardened warriors were so moved by the young maiden's distress, they broke into tears alongside her.

"We are here to exterminate the demons and return you all to the capital. Please, tell us about the demons' dwelling in detail." "Is this dream or reality?" she queried. "I shall tell you about the demons' place. You must follow this river upstream. There, you will see the iron gate, guarded by Shuten Dōji's doting demons. Use stealth to enter through the gate, by any means possible. Once you are inside, you will see an imposing azure palace with rows of roofs and bejeweled screens. The living quarters of the palace are adorned to represent the four seasons. They are built of iron, hence the name, the Iron Palace. At night, we are summoned to the demons' living quarters where we perform menial duties, including massaging their bodies. Shuten Dōji has four lieutenants who guard the entrance of the living quarters: Hoshikuma Dōji [Star-Bear Demon], Kuma Dōji [Bear Demon], Torakuma Dōji [Tiger-Bear Demon], and Kane Dōji [Iron Demon]. I have heard that the four demons are powerful beyond mortal comprehension. As for the appearance of Shuten Dōji, he has light-red skin and is tall with disheveled short hair. He has a human appearance during the day but at night he transforms into a ten-foot tall demon whose countenance is truly horrible. He always drinks sake. Once he becomes intoxicated, he forgets everything. So please enter the palace—by any means possible—and serve him sake. When he lies down intoxicated, strike him with a vengeance. The devil's luck will have run out for Shuten Dōji. And he will finally be conquered. Please plan carefully, priests."

The warriors pressed on upstream, toward the Iron Palace. Seeing Raikō and his men approaching, the demons at the gate wondered amongst themselves, "Who are these men? This is indeed rare!" Not having eaten humans for a while the demons at the gate had come to miss the taste. "Like 'moths to a flame' they've delivered themselves to their death. Let's tear them into morsels." Vying to be the first to reach Raikō and his men, the demons were about to sprint forward. Raikō and his men would surely have been eaten had there not been one among this overzealous band of flesh-hungry demons who warned, "Haste makes waste! We should not hasten forward for our own personal gratification. We should first check with our master and at his instruction we'll tear them apart." The rest of the demons agreed and proceeded to the inner palace to report to Shuten Dōji. Upon hearing the report of the priests' arrival, Shuten Dōji declared, "That's strange. At any rate I shall meet with them. Bring them here!" Compliantly, the demons showed the disguised priests to a veranda within the palace complex where they would meet with the oni leader Shuten Dōji. Suddenly, an odour of rotting fish seemed to be carried in by the wind, and thunder and lightning began to strike. In the mayhem of these supernatural calamities, Shuten Dōji appeared. A towering human form with pale red skin and dishevelled short hair, clenching an iron staff, adorned in a checkered kimono with a crimson hakama, looked down on Raikō and his men.

Then, a voice challenged Raikō and his band: "The mountain I live on is no ordinary mountain—the boulders and rocks are towering and the gorges are deep with no passage. Neither birds of flight nor beasts that run on earth can approach this summit, for there is no passageway for them, let alone humans. Did you, despite being humans, fly here? Speak. I will listen."

Raikō responded, "This is normal in our training. Long ago, when an acetic named En no gyōja[28] pushed his way through impassable terrains, he encountered three demons that called themselves Goki, Zenki, and Akki. En no gyōja gave them food and incantations. Since then, every year En has continuously given these demons food and compassion. We priests follow in En no gyōja's wake, and we are from Mt. Haguro of Dewa province.[29] We confined ourselves to Mt. Ōmine[30] during the New Year [from New Year's Eve to the New Year's Day], and now, since spring has arrived, we set out from Mt. Ōmine late last night for sightseeing in Kyoto. But along Sen'non dō,[31] we became lost and we arrived here in search of passage. It must be En's guidance that has led to our fortuitous meeting here and now. There is no other joy than this. It is said that to stay a night under the same tree and to drink from the same river is predestined from a previous life. Please give us lodging tonight. Because I carry sake, we humbly offer to share it with you. We, too, would like to enjoy sake and revel here this night."

---

28   En no gyōja was born in Mt. Katsuragi in present-day Nara prefecture. He was a devout Buddhist and a skilled magician. During the reign of Emperor Mommu (697–707) he was exiled to Izu, present-day Shizuoka prefecture, for the crime of misguiding the public with magic. He was later pardoned. He is considered to be the father of mountain asceticism.

29   Mt. Haguro of Dewa province, present-day Yamagata prefecture, is renowned as a center for mountain asceticism.

30   A main training field of mountain asceticism.

31   Present-day Kyoto, Hyōgo prefecture, Tottori prefecture, and Shimane prefecture all face the Japan Sea.

Hearing Raikō's explanations, Shuten Dōji judged the priests to be of no immediate threat, and so invited them to his inner sanctum to learn more of their journey and their intentions. Once there, the suspicious demon further tested Raikō's sincerity by offering him some of the demon's sake, "You brought sake, I heard. We, too, want to offer sake to you, priests." Shuten Dōji gestured the oni to bring forth the sake. The demons hurried off to obtain the maiden's blood to put into the sake container, placing it in front of Shuten Dōji, alongside his cup. Shuten Dōji then passed the chalice to Raikō and poured him some of the demon's blood sake. Raikō drank his entire portion with apparent zeal and upon seeing this, Shuten Dōji commanded: "Pass it on to the next person." The demon then poured sake for Tsuna. Tsuna received the cup and likewise, drank it all. Shuten Dōji asked his servants, "Are there not condiments?" In response, the demons immediately brought forth human arms and legs that appeared to have been recently severed. The dismembered body parts were carefully put in front of Shuten Dōji. "Prepare them for the priests," he ordered one of his subjects, but before the demon could comply, Raikō volunteered, "I shall do it." He then unsheathed his small sword, cutting the human flesh into five-inch pieces, once again, consuming them with apparent gusto. Looking on, Tsuna quickly followed suit, declaring, "I'm much obliged for your consideration, I will have some, too," and after similarly cutting the flesh into five-inch long pieces, he joined in the feast. Looking at them, Shuten Dōji asked, "What kind of mountains do you live among? It is strange to eat this kind of rare sake and condiments." Raikō replied, "Your suspicion is reasonable. According to our discipline, we do not reject anything if it is given in compassion—even if we do not desire it from our hearts. While I was relishing this sake and these condiments, something came to mind. To defeat or be defeated is but a dream. I am not, yet I am and there are no two tastes in eating. We all attain Buddhahood. Praise be to Buddha," and Raikō prayed. It is said that the world of demons is without deception. In veneration of Raikō's words, Shuten Dōji expressed his admiration for him, opening his heart and saying, "It's sad that we offered something disagreeable to you. It is not necessary for the rest of you to eat it."

In the spirit of this camaraderie, Raikō then took out his own sake, "I have brought this sake from the capital. Most humbly, I would like to offer it to you. I shall taste it first to make sure it is not poisonous." Raikō drank first, before giving the cup to Shuten Dōji who was all too eager to drink. The divine sake was indeed exceptional. It tasted like honeydew—simply beyond description. Delighted, Shuten Dōji then announced, "I have two women who are very dear to me. I shall summon them to have them taste this sake." With that, he called Kunitaka's daughter and Hanazono's daughter to his drawing room. "I shall pour sake for the ladies from the capital," Raikō stood up.

Nearing a state of intoxicated bliss, Shuten Dōji confessed to Raikō, "I will tell you about my past: I was born in Echigo province,[32] and brought up in a mountain temple. But since I bore a grudge against the priests, I stabbed many of them to death and in flight, arrived at Mt. Hiei, thinking that the mountain would become my home. But the Priest Dengyō, in league with the Buddhas, expelled me from there by reciting a holy "blessing on the mountain."[33] Overpowered, I left Mt. Hiei for this Mt. Ōe. Later, an impostor named Priest Kōbō confined me with his magic, and it was beyond me. But now there is no such priest. Priest Kōbō is dead on Mt. Kōya. I returned to this mountain and have had no problems. I abduct ladies of my liking from the capital to use and enjoy as I wish. Look at this place. My azure palace with bejeweled screens has many rows of roofs and before me are trees and grasses in the tens of thousands, representing the four seasons. Within this palace is a living quarter made of iron called the Iron Palace. At night, I summon my maidens within and have them massage my arms and legs. How could any heavenly guardians surpass this? Yet, there is a man who concerns me—his name is Raikō, a great villain. His renown as a mighty warrior is well known in the capital and his power is without rival in all of Japan. Raikō's vassals—Sadamitsu, Suetake, Kintoki, Tsuna, and Hōshō—are all accomplished masters in the arts of pen and sword. It is these six warriors who bother me. The reason for my concern is that on an errand to the capital this past spring, my man, Ibaraki Dōji, met and fought with Tsuna at the crossing of Horikawa and Seventh Avenue. Without compunction, Ibaraki Dōji wisely changed into a woman with the intent of gaining access to Tsuna. His plan was to abduct Tsuna and bring him here, but just as Ibaraki Dōji grabbed Tsuna's topknot, Tsuna unsheathed his sword and cut off Ibaraki Dōji's arm in one swift and seamless stroke. It was only later that Ibaraki Dōji successfully

---

32   Present-day Niigata prefecture.

33   In Book 20 of *Shin kokin wakashū*, the eighth imperial anthology (ca. 1205), Priest Dengyō's poem is written as "*Anokutara sanmiyaku sannbodai no hotoketachi waga tatsu soma ni myōga arase tamae*" (The omniscient Buddhas, please bless this mountain, and the temple I am about to build).

retrieved his severed arm. But I no longer go to the capital myself because Raikō and his men are troublesome."

Shuten Dōji glared at Raikō with a penetrating gaze. "Nevertheless, what strange people you are! When I look at your eyes well, you are Raikō and with you is Tsuna who severed Ibaraki Dōji's arm. And the men that accompany you appear to be Sadamitsu, Suetake, Kintoki, and Hōshō. There is no mistake in my eyes. How hateful. Leave, priests! Demons, be alert, don't get injured. We shall also leave here." Shuten Dōji became enraged and the color of his face changed. Raikō quickly surveyed the situation and knew it would have been a grave affair if he failed to construct a viable explanation immediately. Distinguished in both the literary and martial arts, Raikō's first instinct was to remain calm in the wake of Shuten Dōji's challenge. Raikō erupted into fits of laughter. "What compliments you give me! We, mountain priests, resemble the most powerful warriors in Japan? I have never heard of Raikō or Suetake, let alone seen them. Listening to your story, I understand that they are atrocious. How awful, how wretched! It is disgusting that we even resemble such creatures. It is our custom that in our training we make our lodging in a mountain pass where sometimes we give our lives to tigers and wolves to save the lives of both sentient and non-sentient beings. Shakyamuni,[34] whose name was Shiufū in his previous life, set out to undertake an ascetic life. One day while making his way through a mountain pass, he heard the voice of an unidentified being call out in verse from somewhere deep in the valley, 'All things are transient.'[35] Shiufū then descended into the valley only to discover a frightening-looking demon with eight heads and nine legs. Shiufū approached the demon and asked, 'Please teach me the rest of the verse.' The demon replied, 'It would be easy to tell you but I am overwhelmed with hunger. I might be persuaded to recite it for you, if I could sate my hunger with human flesh.' Hearing this, Shiufū stated, 'That is extremely easy. If you can recite the rest of the verse, I shall be your food.'[36] The demon was delighted to hear Shiufū's offer and proceeded to recite the rest of the verse: 'Transition is the law of birth

---

34 Gotama Buddha (ca. 566–485 BCE), the founder of Buddhism. He was born to a noble family of the ruling class in Lumbini, present-day Nepal. He abandoned material life in pursuit of spiritual tranquility. When he was awakened to the truth about life, he became the Buddha, the enlightened one, and shared his teaching with others.

35 *shogyō mujō*.

36 These are stories of Buddha's previous lives. They are recorded in such collections of prose narrative as *Sanpōe* (ca. 10th century) and *Hōbutsushū* (ca. 13th century).

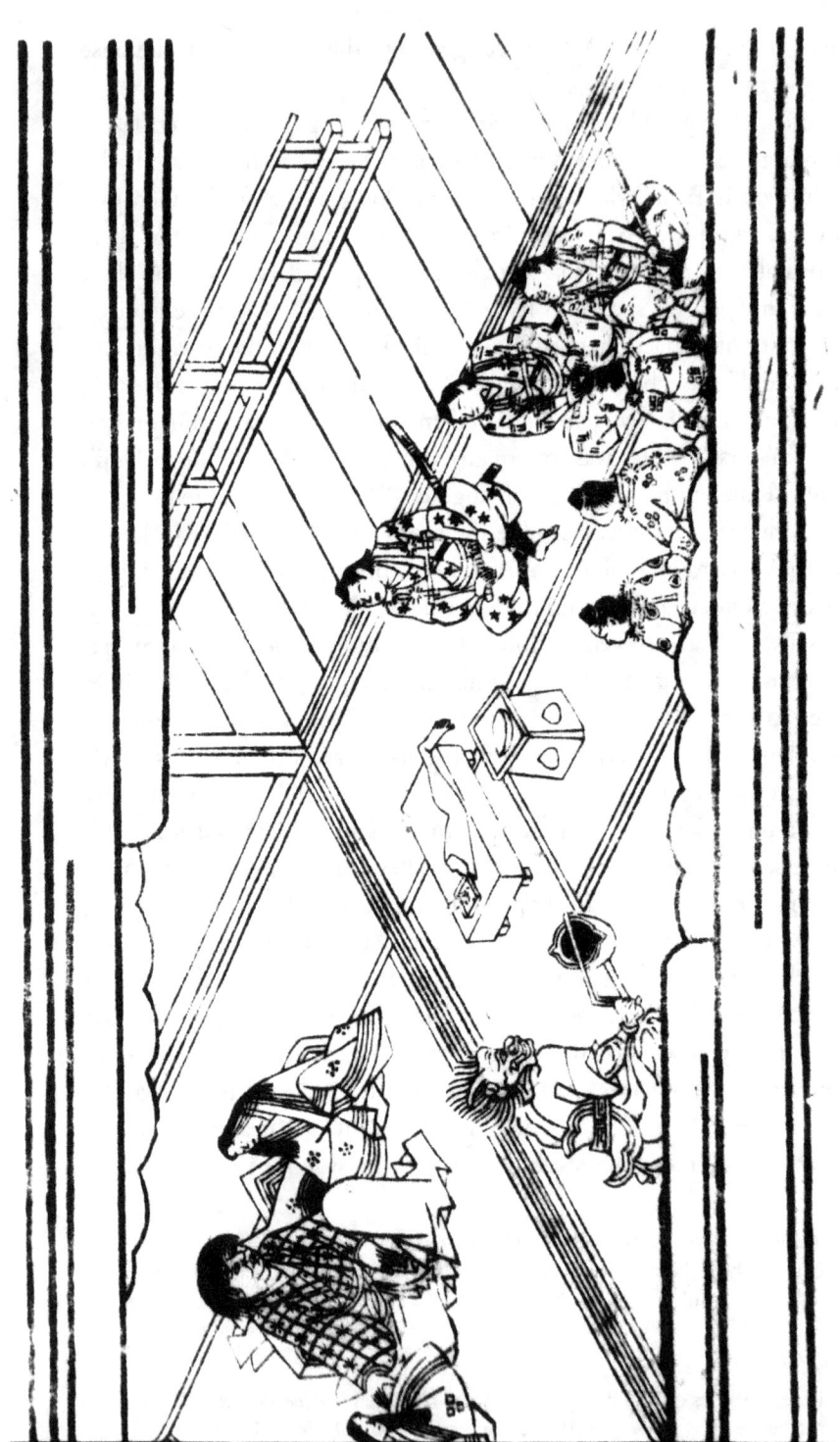

Figure 9. Shuten Dōji entertains Raikō and his vassals with human flesh. Courtesy of Tokyo daigaku kokubungaku kenkyushitsu (The University of Tokyo).

and extinction, all things alive are destined to expire. Detach yourself from the transient world and you will attain the joy of Nirvana.'[37] After receiving the verse, Shiufū thanked the demon. No sooner had Shiufū entered the demon's mouth than the demon transformed into Vairocana[38] and Shiufū became Shakyamuni.[39] On another occasion, Buddha saved the life of a pigeon by cutting off from his own thigh a piece of flesh.[40] The mountain priests here practice the same principles. So please make an incantation and take our lives. Our lives mean nothing to us."

Deceived by Raikō's story, Shuten Dōji's hospitable demeanor gradually restored. "Hearing your stories, I am very grateful. Surely those rogues won't dare come here, but as they are always in mind, it is true to my nature to be on guard, even when I'm intoxicated." He continued, "Please consider it simply my idle complaint under the influence of your sake. My face is red because I'm drunk. Don't think of me as a demon. To me, your appearance looks frightening at a glance, but once one gets used to it, a mountain priest looks quite cute." Singing, dancing, and drinking, he grew increasingly more at ease with Raikō and his men. As the sake was a divine elixir, its poison saturated Shuten Dōji's body, clouding his mind and further dishevelling his appearance. Overcome in drunkenness, Shuten Dōji commanded his demonic minions, "Attention all demons present, drink a cup of this most rare sake before our guests and entertain them. Dance!" The demons complied with the wishes of their master, and as they were about to rise to dance, Raikō offered to fill their cups with the special sake, "First, let me pour some sake for you," and he disseminated the sake to all the demons around him. The sake infused the bodies of the demons quickly, rendering them all disoriented. Amidst this drunken delirium, the demon named Ishikuma Dōji rose to sing out, "From the capital what kind of people lost their way to become condiments of sake. How interesting," for a couple of times. With careful attention, Ishikuma Dōji's song is

---

37 *Zeshō meppō, shōmetsu metsui, jakumetsu iraku.* This verse appears in the *Nirvana sūtra* (*Nehankyō*).

38 A Buddha who sheds light all over the universe. In esoteric Buddhism, Vairocana is most revered.

39 See note 34 above.

40 When Shakyamuni was incarnated as King Sivi, Visvakarman, disguised as a pigeon, flew under King Sivi's armpit. Taishakuten (Sakra), trying to measure the wisdom of Shakyamuni, changed himself into a hawk and demanded the king give him the pigeon. In order to save the life of the pigeon, the king cut off his flesh from his thigh, measuring it out on a scale to weigh the same as the pigeon, and gave it to the hawk.

Figure 10. Shuten Dōji's severed head lunges at Raikō. Courtesy of Tokyo daigaku kokubungaku kenkyushitsu (The University of Tokyo).

understood to suggest that the demons should make condiments and sake out of the mountain priests.

Soon, Raikō stood to serve up more of the intoxicating sake to Shuten Dōji. Making certain Shuten Dōji received the cup, Tsuna rose to dance, singing: "After a passage of time, spring came to the demons' cavern. Wind invites the flowers to fall. How interesting," for a couple of times. This song was foreshadowing how the priests would cut down the demons like the strewn petals of a flower cut down by a storm. But the demons did not catch on to the song's hidden message. Rejoicing in drink and entertainment, the demons continued sinking deeper into their drunken stupors. Shuten Dōji then rose, commanding his demon servants, "Entertain these guest priests well! In my place, I will leave these two princesses. Priests, please rest here for a while. I will see you tomorrow," and with that, Shuten Dōji retired to his bedchamber. After seeing Shuten Dōji leave, the remaining demons lay down in disarray, overcome in drunken slumber.

Raikō beckoned the two princesses, asking them, "In the capital, whose daughters are you?" One of the two maidens responded, crying: "I am the only daughter of the middle councilor Ikeda Kunitaka. Recently I was abducted here and I can see neither my dear parents nor my nurses. Please pity me for I am in such a miserable state." "And you, Lady?" Raikō asked of the other princess. "I am the younger daughter of Yoshida, a state councilor. How hateful that I am still alive," and both princesses cried with such emotion that it appeared both might faint. "Indeed, your sadness is reasonable," Raikō said, "However, I shall conquer the demons tonight, accompany you on your return to the capital and reunite you with your dear parents. So, please, show us the way to Shuten Dōji's bedroom." Hearing this, "Is this a dream or reality?" the princesses inquired. "If this is true, we shall show you the way to the demon's bedroom." And the maidens led the way. Raikō was delighted and turned to his lieutenants ordering them, "Take up your arms" and the men moved into the shadows to don their arms. Then, Raikō advanced in his vermilion armor called *randen-gusari* with the hobnailed helmet given to him by the three deities and another helmet called Lion King of the same vermilion thread on top of the first helmet. He was carrying his splendid sword, Chisui, and recited in mind, "Hail, Great Bodhisattva Hachiman." The rest of his band wore their armor and carried their swords, and led by the ladies, all proceeded in stealth. Passing through large rooms and crossing a stone bridge, they peered inside a huge room where they saw more demons lying in drunken stupors. Not one challenged the warriors by asking, "Who are you?" Walking over the bodies of the demons, the warriors came upon an iron room encased in a large room, the door, also iron, was bolted shut. It appeared very difficult for humans to gain entry. Peering through a crevice, the men could see lights held high in the four corners with iron bars and upside-down halberds against the wall. Inside, Shuten Dōji lay, looking quite different from the figure the warriors had seen earlier. He was now over twenty feet tall,[41] his horns were now protruding through the spiked red bristles on his scalp, his beard had become wildly shaggy, and his eyebrows were overgrown. His limbs had become heavy and thick like those of a bear. He lay sprawled out, his arms and legs spread in all directions. [Unable to enter the demon's bedchamber, the warriors seemed hopeless.] At that moment, the three deities reappeared to help the warriors once more. "You have done well to have come this far. Now you can rest assured. We have chained the demon's limbs to pillars so that he will not move. Raikō, you cut off his head. The rest of you position yourselves to dismember him, it should not be difficult." Upon dispensing these instructions, the deities pushed open the iron door, then once again vanished into thin air. The warriors were moved to tears, knowing that the three deities had appeared to help them. As instructed, Raikō positioned himself at Shuten Dōji's side, smoothly unsheathing his Chisui in preparation for the final act. After praying three times, "Hail the Deities of the three shrines, please give me your helping hands," Raikō stood ready to slaughter Shuten Dōji with his Chisui, when the drunken demon opened his eyes widely, crying out, "How sad, you priests! You said you do not lie. There is nothing false in the words of demons." The bound Shuten Dōji tried in vain to escape from his chains. Then, as if tapping a colossal inner reservoir of strength, Shuten Dōji let out a final reverberating roar causing both heaven and earth to rumble in an unrelenting, thunderous quake.

With blows from the warriors' swords, Shuten Dōji's severed head hurled through the air. But the demon's life force took a few seconds to extinguish and the flying cranium lunged directly at Raikō in one final effort to kill him. Were it not for the hobnailed helmet provided him by the deities, Raikō would have surely perished.

After dismembering Shuten Dōji, the six warriors headed toward the main courtyard. Once outside, they encountered several of Shuten Dōji's demon guards. One demon in particular, Ibaraki Dōji, ferociously moved

---

41   Previously, Shuten Dōji was described as ten feet high.

to attack the six men crying out, "I will let you know my power, the enemies of my master!" Tsuna countered Ibaraki Dōji as he charged, "You should know my strength. You will have to pay for this!" For a while, the ensuing battle seemed to be yielding no victor because as they grappled, Ibaraki at times had the advantage while at other times, Tsuna was dominant. Tsuna's power was said to be equivalent to that of three hundred men combined, but Ibaraki Dōji's strength may have even been stronger, for as time passed, Ibaraki Dōji was able to wrestle Tsuna down to the ground. At that moment, Raikō intervened, [entering the fray] and decapitated Ibaraki Dōji. Ishikuma Dōji, Kane Dōji, and about ten more demons guarding the gate, then engaged the warriors yelling, "Now that Dōji is gone, we have no place to call home. We will go down fighting!" The six warriors responded, "How praiseworthy of these demons. We shall now show our skill." Summoning and employing every one of the possible techniques of military art they had long practiced, the warriors drove the demons to a position of no escape, before cutting them all down with their swords and mettle. After a brief respite from the killing, Raikō announced, "Now ladies, please come out quickly. You won't have to worry now." No sooner they heard his voice than the captive ladies ran from their confinement, one after another. The maidens cried, "Is this a dream or reality? Please help me, too." In so saying, the captives all folded their hands together in prayer. The sight of the maidens' grief would be indeed likened to that of the sinful criminals who were saved from Hell[42] by the Bodhisattva Jizō[43] with his staff[44] and recitation of "onkaakamisensaisowaka."[45]

Then, led by the ladies, the six warriors pressed deeper into the interior of the complex to find a magnificent palace with rows of roofs and bejeweled screens—the quarters were adorned to represent the four seasons. It was beyond imagination, beyond description. Yet, turning their eyes to the other side, the scene—skeletons and bodies of the dead and dying including human flesh pickled with vinegar—was too miserable to witness. Amidst the carnage, a young lady of seventeen or eighteen years of age, half dead and missing an arm and half-a-leg below the thigh, shed tears of

---

42 Avīci hell, *Mugen jigoku*. The worst hell in which beings suffer incessantly.
43 Bodhisattva Ksitigarbha. A bodhisattva who vowed to deliver all people from this world of suffering. He enters hell to save the sinful criminals. His image is like that of a monk.
44 Shakujō. One of the eighteen possessions of a monk.
45 This is probably an incantation.

grief. Raikō asked the princesses, "Whose princess is she in the capital?" The ladies replied, "Yes, that is the daughter of the middle councilor, Horikawa," and they ran to her. "How pitiful, princess. The priests eliminated all the demons and are going to take us back to the capital. But how can we return leaving you behind. How sad. Even in this horrible hell, we feel reluctant to go because of you," the ladies stroked her hair soothingly. "If you have something on your mind, whatever it is, please tell us. When we return to the capital, we shall relay your message to your father and mother, princess." Hearing this, Horikawa's daughter sobbed bitterly, "How envious I am. My condition—short-lived, like a dew drop—is so miserable, yet I still linger in this world. I am so ashamed. When you return to the capital and my parents learn about me, it makes me sad to think that they will lament all the worse for me. Though a keepsake may distress my father and mother, please cut a lock of my hair and give it to them in my remembrance. And this robe, please tell my mother that I was wearing it up until the end. Wrap the hair in this robe and please give them to my mother. Make sure, would you please, to ask her to pray for me in the afterlife. The priests over there, please put a quick end to my life before you return." Hearing her, Raikō said, "Indeed it is reasonable for you to ask. However, when I return to the capital, I shall report to your parents appropriately and will send people back for you. But in the meantime, I bid farewell to you." Raikō and his troupe of warriors and liberated captives left the repugnant grotto. They hurried through the mountains and valleys and before long they arrived at the country village of Shimomura at the foot of Mt. Ōe.

Upon entering the village, Raikō commanded, "Now, villagers, send a swift horse to the capital to announce our return and send the ladies back to the capital. What do you think?" Raikō's request was put into motion immediately. The governor of Tanba Province, also known as the Minister of Ōmiya, heard the auspicious news and quickly brought food and wine to Raikō and his men, while the freed captives were safely en route back to the capital, via horse and palanquin.

In the capital, the anticipation of Raikō's arrival induced a commotion from the jubilant inhabitants. Among those waiting in the crowd were the middle councilor Ikeda and his wife, who came out in person to greet their daughter. Finding Raikō, Kunitaka beckoned, "Hey, here!" The princess caught glimpse of this brief exchange and cried out, "Mother!" Hearing the voice of her daughter, the mother ran to her and embraced her in tears. Kunitaka said, "We are so happy that we could again see our daughter, who was separated from us," and they hurried home. Raikō proceeded on to the palace for an audience with the emperor. The emperor was so impressed with the warrior's report that he bestowed on Raikō and his men tremendous rewards. From that day forward, the land remained safe and the emperor's reign remained peaceful. Raikō's feat and reputation as an invaluable warrior impressed all, from the emperor down to the commoner.

Appendix B
Japanese and Chinese Names and Terms

A
Abe no Seimei 安倍晴明
Adachigahara 安達ヶ原
Agi 安義
Ainōshō 壒囊鈔
Akiyoshi 秋好
Akiyoshikō 秋よしこう
akkan shōsetsu 悪漢小説
akuma 悪魔
Ame-no-hitotsu-kami 天目一命
Anokutara sanmiyaku sannbodai no hotoketachi waga tatsu soma ni myōga arase tamae 阿耨多羅三藐三菩提の仏たちわが立つ杣に冥加あらせたまへ
Aooni no se ni noritaru otoko no tan 青鬼の背に乗りたる男の譚
Aozukin 青頭巾
Aramata Hiroshi 荒俣宏
Arai Hakuseki 新井白石
Asahina Saburō 朝日奈三郎
Asakurayama 朝倉山
Ashigarayama 足柄山
Atagoyama 愛宕山
Azuma kagami 吾妻鏡

B
Bakemono 化物
Bakemono chakutō chō 夭怪着到牒
Benkei 弁慶
Benkei monogatari 弁慶物語
binzasara 編木
Bishamonten 毘沙門天
biwa 琵琶
biwa hōshi 琵琶法師
Bō 坊
Bonten 梵天
Bungo fudoki 豊後風土記
bunkobon 文庫本
buraku 部落
burakumin 部落民

bushi 武士
busshari 仏舎利
Butokuden 武徳殿
Byōdōin 平等院

C
Chikamatsu Monzaemon 近松門左衛門
Chūnagon 中納言

D
Daiankoku shiyajarai 大暗黒死夜邪来
Daigo 醍醐
Daiitoku 大威徳
Daijō-itokuten 太政威徳天
Daikokuten 大黒天
Dainihonkoku hokke genki 大日本国法華験記
dairokuten no maō 第六天の魔王
datsueba 奪衣婆
Debiruman デビルマン
dengaku 田楽
denki 伝奇
Dengyō Daishi 伝教大師
Dōjōji 道成寺
Dōken shōnin meido ki 道賢上人冥土記
dōsojin 道祖神

E
Edo 江戸
Edogawa Ranpo 江戸川乱歩
Eichō ōdengaku 永長大田楽
Ema Tsutomu 江馬務
Emperor Goshirakawa 後白河天皇
Emperor Hirohito 裕仁 (Showa emperor 昭和天皇)
Emperor Ichijō 一条天皇
Emperor Jimmu 神武天皇
Emperor Kammu 桓武天皇
Emperor Kazan 花山天皇
Emperor Keikō 景行天皇
Emperor Kinmei 欽明天皇

Emperor Mommu 文武天皇
Emperor Montoku 文徳天皇
Emperor Saga 嵯峨天皇
Emperor Shōmu 聖武天皇
Emperor Sutoku 崇徳天皇
Empress Saimei 斉明天皇
En no gyōja 役の行者
Engi-Tenryaku 延喜天暦
Enkyō bon 延慶本
Enmaten 閻魔天
ero-guro-nansensu エログロナンセンス

F

Fujiwara no Asanari 藤原朝成
Fujiwara no Hōshō (Yasumasa) 藤原保昌
Fujiwara no Kaneie 藤原兼家
Fujiwara no Koretada 藤原伊尹
Fujiwara no Michinaga 藤原道長
Fujiwara no Senshi 藤原詮子
Fujiwara no Tokihira 藤原時平
Fujiwara no Yorimichi 藤原頼通
Fujiwara no Yoshifusa 藤原良房
Fūten 風天
Fuyusame 冬雨
Fuyuyoshikō 冬よしこう

G

Gaki sōshi 餓鬼草紙
Gatten 月天
Gaun nikkenroku 臥雲日件録
Gazu hyakki yagyō 画図百鬼夜行
Gegege no Kitarō ゲゲゲの鬼太郎
geinō 芸能
Genji monogatari 源氏物語
Genjō to iu biwa oni no tame ni toraruru koto 玄象という琵琶鬼のためにとらるること
Genkō 元弘
Genpei jōsuiki 源平盛衰記
geshin jigoku 解身地獄
Gion nyogo 祇園の女御
Ginza 銀座
Goki 後鬼 (for Nagai Gō's Goki) 護鬼
goryō 御霊
goryō shinkō 御霊信仰
Goshūgen otogi bunko 御祝言御伽文庫
gozu 牛頭
gui-shen 鬼神

H

Hachiman 八幡
Hakaba no Kitarō 墓場の鬼太郎
Hakai 破壊
Hamada Hirosuke 浜田廣介
Hanayo no hime 花世の姫
Hankai 樊噲
hannya 般若
Hannya shinkyō 般若心経
harakake 腹掛け
Harenchi gakuen ハレンチ学園
Harima no kuni no oni hito no ie ni kite iraruru koto 播磨国鬼来人家被射語
Haruyoshi 春好
Haseo sōshi 長谷雄雙紙
Heian 平安
Heike monogatari 平家物語
hiden 秘伝
Higashiyama ōrai 東山往来
Hirata Atsutane 平田篤胤
hitogata 人形
Hizen fudoki 肥前風土記
hokke 北家
honji 本地
Hōbutsushū 宝物集
Hōgen no ran 保元の乱
Hōjō Takatoki 北条高時
hōrai 蓬莱
Hōryū-ji 法隆寺
Hyakki yagyō 百鬼夜行
Hyakki yagyō zu 百鬼夜行図

I

Ibaraki Dōji 茨木童子
Ibuki-yama 伊吹山
Ichiyūsai Kuniyoshi 一勇斉国芳
Ieyoshi 家慶 (Tokugawa Ieyoshi 徳川家慶)
Ihara Saikaku 井原西鶴
ikiryō 生霊
Ikuhōmon'in 郁芳門院
Inoue Enryō 井上円了
Inoue Yasushi 井上靖
InuYasha 犬夜叉
Ishibashi Gaha 石橋臥波
Ishanaten 伊舎那天
Issun-bōshi 一寸法師
Itsubun Settsu Fudoki 逸文摂津風土記
Itsukushima jinja 厳島神社
Iwashimizu Hachimangū 岩清水八幡宮
Iwaya Sazanami 巌谷小波
Izawa Banryō 伊沢幡竜

J

jakumetsu iraku 寂滅為楽
jaki 邪鬼

Jasei no in 邪性の婬
Jikkinshō 十訓抄
Jigoku sōshi 地獄草紙
Jikokuten 持国天
jinben kidoku 神便鬼毒, 神変奇特
Jippensha Ikku 十返舎一九
Jiten 地天
Jizō 地蔵
Jōjin 定深
jōruri 浄瑠璃
Joshi o oshiyuru no hō 女子を教ゆるの法
Jūni-sama 十二様
Jūniten 十二天

K

Kabuki 歌舞伎
Kabuki nenpyō 歌舞伎年表
Kadokawa Gen'yoshi 角川源義
Kagerō nikki 蜻蛉日記
Kagura 神楽
Kaibara Ekken 貝原益軒
Kaidan mikoshi no matsu 化物見越松
Kakuichi bon 覚一本
Kamakura bon 鎌倉本
kami 神
kaminari 雷
Kanawa 鐵輪
Kan'ei 寛永
Kan'ei shoke kakeizu-den 寛永諸家系図伝
Kankyo no tomo 閑居友
Kanmon nikki 看聞日記
Kanō Motonobu 狩野元信
Kanze Kojirō Nobumitsu 観世小次郎信光
Kashiwaba Sachiko 柏葉幸子
kataribon kei 語り本系
Katen 火天
Katori-bon 香取本
Katsuragisan 葛城山
Kawabata Yasunari 川端康成
Kawatake Mokuami 河竹黙阿弥
Kazan 花山
Keitai shin kanwa jiten 携帯新漢和辞典
Kibi daijin nittō emaki 吉備大臣入唐絵巻
kibyōshi 黄表紙
Kibune Shrine 貴船神社
kimon 鬼門
kin 金
Kibitsu no kama 吉備津の釜
Ki no Haseo 紀長谷雄
Kinpira jōruri 金平浄瑠璃
Kinpira nyūdō yama-meguri 公平入道山めぐり

Kinpira tanjō-ki 公平たんじょうき
Kintarō 金太郎
Kintoki miyako-iri sukune no Akutarō 金時都いりすくねの悪太郎
Kintoki osanadachi tsuwamono no majiwari 金時稚立剛士雑
Kiri no mukō no fushigina machi 霧のむこうのふしぎな町
Kiseki ni iru 鬼籍に入る
Kishinron 鬼神論
Kishin shinron 鬼神新論
Kitagawa Utamaro 喜多川歌麿
Kitano tenjin engi emaki 北野天神縁起絵巻
Kiyohara no udaishō 清原右大将
Kobutori 瘤取り
Kojidan 古事談
Kojiki 古事記
Kokin hyakumonogatari hyōban 古今百物語評判
Kokon chomon-jū 古今著聞集
Kokon yōmikō 古今妖魅考
Kokugaku 国学
Komochi yamauba 嫗山姥
Konjaku monogatarishū 今昔物語集
Kōbō Daishi 弘法大師
Kōda Rohan 幸田露伴
Kōeki zokusetsu ben 広益俗説弁
Kōfukuji 興福寺
Kōmokuten 広目天
Kondō Hidezō 近藤日出造
Konkōmyō saishō ōkyō 金光明最勝王経
Kotō no oni 孤島の鬼
kotodama shinkō 言霊信仰
Kōyasan 高野山
kuchisake onna 口裂女
Kūkai 空海
Kumano Gongen 熊野権現
Kumogakure 雲隠れ
kunitsukami 国津神
Kuraudo no kami 蔵人守
kuro-hon 黒本
kusa-zōshi 草双紙
Kuwazu nyōbō 食わず女房
kyōgen 狂言
Kyūtī Hanī キューティーハニー

M

machi-okoshi 町おこし
manga 漫画
marebito まれびと
Meiji 明治
mezu 馬頭

Mida hachiman no yurai 三田八幡之由来
Mihashi Kazuo 三橋一夫
mikudarihan 三行半
Minamoto no Hiromasa 源博雅
Minamoto no Mitsunaka (or Manjū) 源満仲
Minamoto no Raikō (or Yorimitsu) 源頼光
Minamoto no Raikō yakata tuchigumo yōkai o nasu zu 源頼光館土蜘蛛作妖怪図
Minamoto no Tametomo 源為朝
Minamoto no Yorimitsu tsuchigumo wo kiru-zu 源頼光土蜘蛛ヲ切ル図
minokasa 蓑かさ
Miroku 弥勒
Mishima Yukio 三島由紀夫
mitate 見立て
Mitsuneshū 躬恒集
Miyajima 宮島
Miyoshi no Kiyotsura no saishō no ie-watari no koto 三善清行の宰相の家渡りの語
Mizuno Tadakuni 水野忠邦
Modoribashi 戻橋
Momijigari 紅葉狩
Momiji no sode nagori no nishiki-e 紅葉袖名残錦絵
mononoke 物の怪
Mugen jigoku 無間地獄
Muromachi 室町

N

Nagasawa Rosetsu 長沢芦雪
Nagai Gō 永井豪
Naita Akaoni 泣いた赤鬼
Nakabami Kenji 中上健次
namanari 生成
Namanarihime 生成姫
Nanto bon 南都本
Naraku 奈落
Natsusame 夏雨
Natsuyoshikō 夏よしこう
Nehankyō 涅槃経
Nezumi no Goten 鼠の御殿
Nihongi 日本紀
Nihon mukashibanashi 日本昔噺
Nihon no oni kōryū hakubutsukan 日本の鬼交流博物館
Nihon sandai jisuroku 日本三代実録
Nihonshoki 日本書紀
Nijō gawara 二条河原
Nikko 日光
ningyō 人形
Ninjin no okori 人参の起こり
Nippo jisho 日葡辞書

Nitten 日天
Noh 能
nyoi hōju 如意宝珠
Nyonin akuki ni kegasarete kurawareshi en 女人の悪鬼に点されて食喰はれし縁

O

Ōeyama 大江山
Ōeyama ekotoba 大江山絵詞
Ōgetsuhime 大気都比売
Ogiwara Shigehide 荻原重秀
Ōizumi no haha 大泉の母
Ōkagami 大鏡
Ōken setsuwa 王権説話
Ōkubi-e 大首絵
Ōkuninushi no mikoto 大国主命
Ōmi 近江
ōna no oni 嫗の鬼
ongokukai 鬼獄界, 怨獄界
oni 鬼
Oni den 鬼殿
Oni ga shima 鬼が島
Oni-*gokko* 鬼ごっこ
oni hitokuchi 鬼一口
oni kenbai 鬼剣舞
Oni no matsuei 鬼の末裔
Oni no michiyuki 鬼のみちゆき
oni no nenbutsu 鬼の念仏
Oni no yakata 鬼の館
Oni-sado 鬼佐渡
oni wa soto, fuku wa uchi 鬼は外、福は内
onmyōdō 陰陽道
Onmyōji 陰陽師
Onmyōryō 陰陽寮
Onna daigaku takarabako 女大学宝箱
onnagata 女形
Onoe Kikugorō 尾上菊五郎
Orikuchi Shinobu 折口信夫
Oritaku shiba no ki 折りたく柴の記
Ōshikōchi no Mitsune 凡河内躬恒
ōshisa 雄々しさ
Otogi monogatari 御伽物語
otogi zōshi 御伽草子, お伽草子
Ōtsu-e 大津絵

R

Raikō 雷公 (a thunder god)
Rasetsuten 羅刹天
Rashōmon 羅生門
roji 路地
Ryōju bosatsu 龍樹菩薩
ryūgū 竜宮

Ryūseimei 流生命

S

Saichō 最澄
Saikaku shokoku banashi 西鶴諸国噺
Saiyūki 西遊記
Sakata no Kintoki 坂田金時
Sandō 三道
Sanjū-ni sō no katachi o uke 三十二相のかたちをうけ
Sanpōe 三宝絵
Sanseru onna minamiyamashina ni yuki oni ni aite nigetaru koto 産女行南山科値鬼逃語
San'yūtei Enchō 三遊亭円朝
Sanzō hōshi 三蔵法師
Saru-muko dono 猿聟殿
sato 里
Segawa Jokō 瀬川如皐
Segawa Kikunojō III 瀬川菊之丞三世
Seii taishōgun 西夷大将軍
Senjōdake 千丈嶽
Senkyō ibun 仙境異聞
Sen'non dō 山陰道
Sen to Chihiro no kamikakushi 千と千尋の神隠し
setsubun 節分
Shaberi yamauba しゃべり山姥
Shakujō 錫杖
Shibu gassenjō bon 四部合戦状本
Shibukawa Seiemon 渋川清右衛門
shichifukujin 七福神
Shijō gawara 四条河原
shijū kunichi 四十九日
shikai no matsuri 四堺祭
shikisoku zekū, kūsoku zeshiki 色即是空、空即是色
shikigami 式神
shikon 四魂
Shimazaki Tōson 島崎藤村
Shimo Yoshiko 下ヨシ子
Shingon 真言
Shinjuku no haha 新宿の母
Shin kokin wakashū 新古今和歌集
Shin Nippon mangaka kyōkai 新日本漫画家協会
Shinzei 真済
Shiromine 白峰
shite シテ
shitennō 四天王
Shitennō Ōeyama-iri 四天王大江山入
Shitennō musha shugyō 四天王むしゃ執行
Shogyō mujō 諸行無常
shōmetsu metsui 生滅滅己
shomin 庶民
Shōmon ki 将門記
Shōnen Sunday 少年サンデー
shosagoto 所作事
Shōwa 昭和
shugendō 修験道
Shuten Dōji 酒顚童子, 酒呑童子, (for Nagai Gō's Shuten Dōji) 手天童子
Shuten Dōji emaki 酒伝童子絵巻
Shuten Dōji kuruwa hinagata 酒呑童子廓雛形
Shuten Dōji makurakotoba 酒呑童子枕詞
Six Dynasties 六朝
Sonshō Dhāranī 尊勝陀羅尼
Sōdō sect of Zen 曹洞禅
Sotoba no ko o umu koto 卒塔婆の子をうむ事
Sugawara Michizane 菅原道真
Sugiura Yukio 杉浦幸雄
sugoroku 双六
Suiten 水天
Sugawara no Takasue no musume 菅原孝標女
Sukuyōkyō 宿曜経
Sumiyoshi Myōjin 住吉明神
Suzume no Oyado 雀のお宿

T

Taiheiki 太平記
Taira no Koreshige 平維茂
Taira no Masakado 平将門
Taishakuten 帝釈天
Takahashi Rumiko 高橋留美子
Takamimusuhi 高皇産霊
takara 宝
ta kara 田から
Tamonten 多聞天
Tanba 丹波
tankōbon 単行本
tanroku-bon 丹緑本
Tatsumi 辰巳
Tatsuta-hime 龍田姫
Tawaraya Sōtatsu 俵屋宗達
Teito monogatari 帝都物語
Tengu 天狗
Tengyō no ran 天慶の乱
tenma 天魔
Tenmahajun 天魔波旬
Tentō-san kin no kusari 天道さん金の鎖
Terashima Ryōan 寺島良安
Tetsuwan Atomu 鉄腕アトム

Tezuka Osamu 手塚治虫
Togakushiyama 戸隠山
Tokoyo-kami 常世神
Tokugawa Iemochi 徳川家茂
Tokugawa Shogun 徳川将軍
Tokugawa Yorinobu 徳川頼宣
Tōi taishōgun 東夷大将軍
Tōkaidō 東海道
Tōkaidō Yotsuya kaidan 東海道四谷怪談
torii 鳥居
Torii Kiyonaga 鳥居清長
Toriyama Sekien 鳥山石燕
tsuchigumo 土蜘蛛
Tsuchimikado 土御門
Tsukioka Yoshitoshi 月岡芳年
tsukumogami 付喪神
tsukune つくね
tsure ツレ
Tsurezure nagusamigusa 徒然慰草
Tsurugi no maki 剣巻
Tsuruya Nanboku 鶴屋南北
Tsūzoku saiyūki 通俗西遊記

U

uba うば
uchide no kozuchi 打ち出の小槌
Ueda Akinari 上田秋成
Ugetsu monogatari 雨月物語
Uji no hashihime 宇治の橋姫
Uji no hōzō 宇治の宝蔵
Uji shūi monogatari 宇治拾遺物語
ukiyo 浮世
Ukemochinokami 保食神
Urabe Suetake 卜部季武
Urusei yatsura うる星やつら
Ushikata to yamauba 牛方と山姥
ushitora 丑寅
Usui Sadamitsu 碓井貞光
Utagawa Toyokuni 歌川豊国
yūkaku kannen 優格観念

W

Wakan sansai zue 和漢三才図会
Wamyō ruijushō 倭名類聚抄
Watanabe Tsuna 渡辺綱
Wazoku dōji-kun 和俗童子訓

X

Xiuyaojing 宿曜経

Y

Yaegiri kuruwa-banashi 八重桐郭話
Yahata Shrine 八幡神社
yamabushi 山伏
Yamagata Bantō 山片蟠桃
yama-hime 山姫
Yama no jinsei 山の人生
Yamato Takeru 日本武尊
yamauba (*Yamamba*) 山姥
yamauba-buyō 山姥舞踊
yamauba hōon 山姥報恩
Yamauba to Kintarō chibusa 山姥と金太郎乳房
Yamauba to Kintarō ennenmai 山姥と金太郎延年舞い
Yamauba to Kintarō genpuku 山姥と金太郎元服
Yamauba to Kintarō kamisori 山姥と金太郎剃刀
Yanagi Sōetsu 柳宗悦
Yanagita Kunio 柳田国男
yasha 夜叉
Yashiro-bon Heike monogatari 屋代本平家物語
Yasuhito 懐仁
Yin Dynasty 殷代
yōkai 妖怪
Yōkai dangi 妖怪談義
yōkai hyakutai zu 妖怪百態図
yomihon kei 読本系
Yomotsu-shikome 予母都志許売, 泉津醜女
yōjiteki 幼児的
Yowa no nezame 夜半の寝覚め
Yumemakura Baku 夢枕獏

Z

Zeami 世阿弥
Zen-taiheiki 前太平記
Zenki 前鬼
Zeshō meppō 是生滅法
Zhu Xi 朱子
Zōchōten 増長天
Zuikei Shūhō 瑞谿周鳳

Bibliography

Abbreviations:
HJAS—*Harvard Journal of Asiatic Studies*
MN—*Monumenta Nipponica*
NKBT—*Nihon koten bungaku taikei*
SNKBT—*Shin nihon koten bungaku taikei*
SNKBZ—*Shinpen nihon koten bungaku zenshū*
NST—*Nihon shisō taikei*

Abe Masamichi. *Nihon no yōkaitachi*. Tokyo: Tokyo Shoseki, 1981.
Abe Yasurō. "Hōju to ōken." *Nihon shisō*. Ed. Nagao Masato et al. Vol. 16 of *Iwanami kōza tōyō shisō*. Tokyo: Iwanami Shoten, 1989. 115–69.
———. "'Taishokukan' no seiritsu." *Kōwaka bukyoku kenkyū*. Ed. Agō Toranoshin and Fukuda Akira. Vol. 4. Tokyo: Miyai Shoten, 1986. 80–195.
———. *Yuya no kōgō: chūsei no sei to seinaru mono*. Nagoya: Nagoya Daigaku Shuppankai, 1998.
Addiss, Stephen, ed. *Japanese Ghosts & Demons: Art of the Supernatural*. New York: George Braziller, Inc., 1985.
Adorno, Theodor. "Aesthetic Theory." *Continental Aesthetics: Romanticism to Postmodernism An Anthology*. Ed. Richard Kearney and David Rasmussen. Massachusetts: Blackwell Publishers Inc., 2001. 242–53.
Akimoto Kichirō, ed. *Fudoki*. Vol. 2 of *NKBT*. Tokyo: Iwanami Shoten, 1958.
Akutagawa Ryūnosuke. *Kappa*. Tokyo: Shūeisha (Shūeisha bunko), 1992.
———. *Kappa*. Trans. Geoffrey Bownas. Boston: Tuttle Publishing, 2000.
Amano Fumio. "Shuten Dōji—Nihon kānibarizumu no keifu no nakade." *Kokubungaku kaishaku to kanshō* 22. 16 (1977): 104–105.
———. "Shuten Dōji kō." *Nō kenkyū to hyōron* 8 (1979): 16–27.
Amino Yoshihiko. *Igyō no ōken*. Tokyo: Heibonsha, 1986.
Anesaki Masaharu and J. C. Ferguson. [Chinese myth by J. C. Ferguson, Japanese myth by Masaharu Anesaki.] Vol. 8 of *Mythology of All Races*. Ed. J. A. MacCulloch and G. F. Moore. Boston: Archaeological Institute of America. 1928.
ANIMEIGO. *Urusei Yatsura*. Web. February 2001.
Anno Hideaki. *Shin seiki Evangerion*. Tokyo: Telebi Tokyo, 1995–96. T.V. anime.
Antoni, Klaus. "Momotarō (The Peach Boy) and the Spirit of Japan: Concerning the Function of a Fairy Tale in Japanese Nationalism of the Early Shōwa Age." *Asian Folklore Studies* 50. 1 (1991): 155–188.
Aoki Masaji. *Ugetsu monogatari*. 2 vols. Tokyo: Kōdansha, 1981.
Aoki, Michiko Yamaguchi, trans. *Izumo Fudoki*. Tokyo: Sophia UP, 1971.
Arai Hakuseki. "Kishinron." Ed. Washio Junkei. Vol. 3 of *Nihon shisō tōsō shiryō*. Tokyo: Meicho Kankōkai, 1969. 1–42.
———. *Oritaku shiba no ki*. Tokyo: Iwanami Shoten, 1975.

Araki, James T. "Otogi-zōshi and Nara-ehon: A Field of Study in Flux." *MN* 36. 1 (1981): 1–20.
Aramata Hiroshi. *Teito monogatari*. 7 vols. Tokyo: Kadokawa Shoten, 1995.
Aramata Hiroshi and Komatsu Kazuhiko. *Yōkai sōshi*. Tokyo: Kōsakusha, 1987.
"Are Made-in-Japan Manga and Animation About to Be Blindsided?" *Japan Close-up* (June 2007): 13–18.
Asahara Yoshiko, Haruta Akira, and Matsuo Ashie, eds. *Yashiro-bon kōya-bon taishō Heike monogatari*. 3 vols. Tokyo: Shinten-sha, 1990–93.
Asakura Musei. *Misemono kenkyū*. Kyoto: Shibunkaku Shuppan, 1977.
Asakura Musei, Nobuhiro Shinji, and Kawazoe Yū. *Misemono kenkyū: shimai-hen*. Tokyo: Heibonsha, 1992.
Asami Kazuhiko, ed. *Jikkinshō*. Vol. 51 of *SNKBZ*. Tokyo: Shōgakukan, 1997.
Aston, W. G., trans. *Nihongi: Chronicles of Japan from the Earliest Times to A. D. 697*. London: Kegan Paul, Trench, Trubner & Co. Ltd, 1896. Rpt. London: George Allen & Unwin Ltd. 1956.
Averbuch, Irit. *The Gods Come Dancing: A Study of the Japanese Ritual Dance of Yamabushi Kagura*. Ithaca: Cornell U East Asia Program, 1995.
Baba Akiko. *Oni no kenkyū*. Tokyo: San'ichi Shobō, 1971. Rpt. Tokyo: Chikuma Shobō, 1988.
Baird, Merrily C. *Symbols of Japan: Thematic Motifs in Art and Design*. New York: Rizzoli International Publications, Inc., 2001.
"Bakemono chakutō chō." Illust. Kitao Masami. *Edo bakemono sōshi*. Ed. Adam Kabat. Tokyo: Shōgakukan, 1999. 27–48.
Bakhtin, Mikhail M. *The Dialogic Imagination*. Trans. Caryl Emerson and Michael Holquist. Austin: U of Texas Press, 1981.
———. *Rabelais and His World*. Trans. Helene Iswolsky. Bloomington: Indiana UP, 1984.
Barbaro, Federico, tr. *Shin'yaku seisho*. Tokyo: Kōdansha, 1975.
Bargen, Doris G. *A Woman's Weapon: Spirit Possession in the Tale of Genji*. Honolulu: U of Hawai'i Press, 1997.
Bathgate, Michael. *The Fox's Craft in Japanese Religion and Folklore: Shapeshifters, Transformations, and Duplicities*. New York: Routledge, 2004.
Bender, Mark. *Plum and Bamboo: China's Suzhou Chantefable Tradition*. Urbana: U of Illinois Press, 2003.
Benjamin, Walter. "The Work of Art in the Age of Mechanical Reproduction." *Continental Aesthetics: Romanticism to Postmodernism An Anthology*. Ed. Richard Kearney and David Rasmussen. Massachusetts: Blackwell Publishers Inc., 2001. 166–181.
Bennett, Gillian. *Alas, Poor Ghost!: Traditions of Belief in Story and Discourse*. Utah:Utah State UP, 1999.
Beth Monica and Karen Brazell. *Nō as Performance: An Analysis of the Kuse Scene of Yamamba*. Ithaca: Cornell U East Asia Papers No. 16, 1978.
Bettelheim, Bruno. *The Uses of Enchantment*. New York: Alfred A. Knopf. 1977.
Bix, Herbert P. *Hirohito and the Making of Modern Japan*. New York: Perennial, 2000.
Blade Runner. Dir. Ridley Scott. Perf. Harrison Ford. Warner Bros. 1982. Film.
Bodiford, William M. *Sōtō Zen in Medieval Japan*. Honolulu: U of Hawai'i Press, 1993.
Botting, Fred. "In Gothic Darkly: Heterotopia, History, Culture." *A Companion to the Gothic*. Ed. David Punter. Oxford: Blackwell Publisher Ltd., 2000. 3–14.
Bowring, Richard John. *The Religious Traditions of Japan, 500–1600*. Cambridge: U of Cambridge Press, 2005.

Brazell, Karen, ed. *Traditional Japanese Theater: An Anthology of Plays.* New York: Columbia UP, 1998.
Burns, Susan L. *Before the Nation: Kokugaku and the Imagining of Community in Early Modern Japan.* Durham: Duke UP, 2003.
Butler, Lee A. "The Way of Yin and Yang. A Tradition Revived, Sold, Adopted." *MN* 51. 2 (1996): 189–217.
Casal, U. A. "The Goblin Fox and Badger and Other Witch Animals of Japan." *Folklore Studies* 17 (1959): 1–91.
Cavallaro, Dani. *The Anime Art of Hayao Miyazaki.* Jefferson, N.C.: McFarland & Co., 2006.
———. *The Cinema of Mamoru Oshii: Fantasy, Technology, and Politics.* Jefferson, N.C.: McFarland & Co., 2006.
Chigiri Kōsai. *Oni no kenkyū.* Tokyo: Tairiku Shobō, 1978.
Chikamatsu Monzaemon. *Chikamatsu jōruri shū.* Ed. Shuzui Kenji and Ōkubo Tadakuni. Vol. 50 of *NKBT.* Tokyo: Iwanami Shoten, 1959.
———. *Chikamatsu Monzaemon shū.* Ed. Torigoe Bunzō, Yamane Tameo, Nagatomo Chiyoji, Ōhashi Tadayoshi, and Sakaguchi Hiroyuki. Vol. 75 of *SNKBZ.* Tokyo: Shōgakukan, 1998.
———. *Chikamatsu zenshū.* Ed. Chikamatsu zenshū kankōkai. 17 vols. Tokyo: Iwanami Shoten, 1985–94.
Childs, Margaret H. "Didacticism in Medieval Short Stories: Hatsuse Monogatari and Akimichi." *MN* 42. 3 (1987): 253–88.
Chuang Tzu. *The Complete Works of Chuang Tzu.* Trans. Burton Watson. New York: Columbia UP, 1968.
Clark, Timothy. *Demon of Painting: the Art of Kawanabe Kyōsai.* London: Published for the Trustees of the British Museum by the British Museum Press, 1993.
Coomaraswamy, Ananda K. *Yaksas: Essays in the Water Cosmology.* Indira Gandhi National Centre for the Arts: New Delhi, 1993.
Copeland, Rebecca L., and Esperanza Ramirez-Christensen, eds. *The Father-Daughter Plot: Japanese Literary Women and the Law of the Father.* Honolulu: U of Hawai'i Press, 2001.
Cornyetz, Nina, *Dangerous Women, Deadly Words: Phallic Fantasy and Modernity in Three Japanese Writers.* Stanford: Stanford UP, 1999.
Craig, Timothy J. *Japan Pop!* New York: M.E. Sharpe, 2000.
Dallery, Arleen B. and Charles E. Scott, eds. *The Question of the Other.* New York: State U of New York Press, 1989.
Davidson, Hilda Ellis, and Anna Chaudhri. *Supernatural Enemies.* North Carolina: Carolina Academic Press, 2001.
De Visser, Marinus Willem. "The Fox and Badger in Japanese Folklore." *Transactions of the Asiatic Society of Japan* 36. 3 (1964): 1–159.
Dix, Monika. "Hachikazuki: Revealing Kannon's Crowning Compassion in Muromachi Fiction." *Japanese Journal of Religious Studies* 36. 2 (2009): 279-293.
Doi Tadao, Morita Takeshi, Chōnan Minoru, eds. *Hōyaku Nippo jisho.* Tokyo: Iwanami Shoten, 1980.
Dorson, Richard M., ed. *Folk Legends of Japan.* Rutland, Vermont: Charles Tuttle, 1962.
———. *Japanese Folklore.* New York: Arno Press, 1980.
Dower, John D. *Embracing Defeat: Japan in the Wake of World War II.* New York: W. W. Norton & Company, 1999.
———. *War Without Mercy: Race and Power in the Pacific War.* New York: Pantheon Books, 1986.
Dyer, Gwynne. *War.* New York: Crown Publishers, Inc., 1985.

Earhart, H. Byron. Introduction. *Shugendō: Essays on the Structure of Japanese Folk Religion.* By Miyake Hitoshi. Ann Arbor: Center for Japanese Studies The U of Michigan, 2001. 1–7
Edogawa Ranpo. *Kotō no oni.* Vol. 4 of *Edogawa Ranpo zenshū.* Tokyo: Kodansha, 1978.
Elley, Derek. "Spirited Away." *Variety* 25 Feb. 2002: 72.
Ema Tsutomu. *Nihon yōkai henge-shi.* Kyoto: Chūgai Shuppan, 1923.
Farris, William Wayne. *Japan's Medieval Population.* Honolulu: U of Hawai'i Press, 2006.
Figal, Gerald. *Civilization and Monsters: Sprits of Modernity in Meiji Japan.* Durham: Duke UP, 1999.
Fisher, Robert E. *Buddhist Art and Architecture.* New York: Thames & Hudson Inc., 1993.
Foster, Michael Dylan. *Pandemonium and Parade: Japanese Monsters and the Culture of Yōkai.* Berkeley: U. of California P., 2009.
———. "Strange Games and Enchanted Science: The Mystery of Kokkuri." *The Journal of Asian Studies* 65. 2 (2006): 251–75.
Foucault, Michel. "Of Other Spaces." *Diacritics* 16. 1 (1986): 22–27.
Franz, Marie-Louise von. "The Problem of Evil in Fairy Tales." *Evil.* Ed. The Curatorium of the C. G. Jung Institute, Zürich. Evanston [Ill.]: Northwestern UP, 1967. 83–119.
———. *Shadow and Evil in Fairy Tales.* Zurich: Spring Publications, 1974.
Frazer, James George. *The Fear of the Dead in Primitive Religion.* 1933. Rpt. New York: Biblo and Tannen, 1966.
Fujii Masao. "Sorei shinkō no kannen." *Kami kannen to minzoku.* Ed. Gorai Shigeru. Vol. 3 of *Kōza nihon no minzoku shūkyō.* Tokyo: Kōbundō, 1979. 68–93.
Fujii Takashi, ed. *Otogi-zōshi kenkyū sho.* 9 vols. Tokyo: Kuresu Shuppan, 2003.
Fujioka Tadaharu and Tokuhara Shigemi, eds. *Mitsuneshū chūshaku.* Tokyo: Kichōbon Kankōkai, 2003.
Fujiwara Tokihira et al. *Sandai jitsuroku.* Ed. Saeki Ariyoshi. Vols. 9 and 10 of *Rikkokushi.* Tokyo: Asahi Shinbunsha, 1940–41.
Fukuda Mitsuko. "Ie to kon'in no kisō o saguru—dai nibu no hajime ni." *Ranjukusuru onna to otoko: kinsei.* Ed. Fukuda. Vol. 4 of *Onna to otoko no jikū: nihon josei-shi saikō.* Tokyo: Fujiwara Shoten, 1995. 255–75.
Genshin. *Ōjōyōshū.* Trans. Ishida Mizumaro. 2 vols. Tokyo: Heibonsha [Tōyō Bunko], 1963–64.
Gerstle, Andrew C. *Circles of Fantasy: Convention in the Plays of Chikamatsu.* Cambridge: Harvard UP, 1986.
Glassman, Hank. "'Show Me the Place Where My Mother is!' Chūjōhime, Preaching, and Relics in Late Medieval and Early Modern Japan." *Approaching the Land of Bliss: Religious Praxis in the Cult of Amitāba.* Eds. Richard K. Payne and Kenneth K. Tanaka. Honolulu: U of Hawai'i Press, 2004. 139–68.
"Gomisute bōshi ni 'jintsūriki' kitai: kakuchi ni minichua torii." *Asahi.com.* Asahi Shinbunsha, 1 Jan. 2009. Web. 1 Jan. 2009.
Gonda Manji. "Tojikomerareta yume." *Edogawa Ranpo: hyōron to kenkyū.* Ed. Nakajima Kawatarō. Tokyo: Kodansha, 1980. 140–55.
Goodich, Michael. *Other Middle Ages: Witnesses at the Margins of Medieval Society.* Philadelphia: U of Pennsylvania Press, 1998
Goodwin, James. *Perspectives on Akira Kurosawa.* New York: G.K. Hall & Co., 1994.
Gorai Shigeru. *Oni mukashi.* Tokyo: Kadokawa Shoten, 1984.
Gosukō-in. *Kanmon nikki.* 3 vols. Tokyo: Kunaichō shoryōbu, 2002–2006.
Gotō Tanji, Kamada Kizaburō, and Okami Masao, eds. *Taiheiki.* Vol. 34 of *NKBT.* Tokyo: Iwanami Shoten, 1960.

Grosz, Elizabeth. "Intolerable Ambiguity: Freaks as/at the Limit." *Freakery: Cultural Spectacles of the Extraordinary Body*. Ed. Rosemarie Garland Thompson. New York: New York UP, 1996. 55–68.
Gyōyo. *Ainōshō*. Ed. Hamada Atsushi and Satake Akihiro. Kyoto: Nozomikawa Shoten, 1968.
Hamada Hirosuke. *Naita akaoni*. Tokyo: Popurasha, 1978.
Hamada Keisuke. "Shuppan jānarizumu tanjō." *Bunka ryōran*. Ed. Nakamura Yukihiko and Nishiyama Matsunosuke. Vol. 8 of *Nihon bungaku no rekishi*. Tokyo: Kadokawa Shoten, 1967. 30–67.
Hamada Rumi. *Hirosuke dōwa o tsukutta Hamada Hirosuke: Chichi Hamada Hirosuke no shōgai*. Tokyo: Yumani Shobō, 1998.
Hanada Kiyoteru. "Gajinden." *Muromachi shōsetsu shū*. Vol. 15 of *Hanada Kiyoteru zenshū*. Tokyo: Kōdansha, 1978. 418–68.
Hanawa Hokinoichi, ed. *Gunsho ruijū*. Vol. 25. Tokyo: Zoku gunsho ruijū kanseikai, 1987.
Hasegawa Tadashi, ed. *Taiheiki*. 4 vols. Vols. 54 to 57 of *SNKBZ*. Tokyo: Shōgakukan, 1994-98.
Hashimoto Hiroyuki. "Oni ga enjiru sairei geinō." *Oni*. Ed. Komatsu Kazuhiko. Vol. 4 of *Kaii no minzokugaku*. Tokyo: Kawade Shobō, 2000. 425–33.
Hashimoto Naoki. "Shuten Dōji no kohanbon ni tsuite—otogi zōshi-bon kaimei ni yosete." *Kokubungaku* 60 (1983): 22–39.
Hattori Kunio. *Oni no fudoki*. Tokyo: Seikyūsha, 1989.
Hayashi Reiko. Henshū kōki. *Kinsei*. Ed. Joseishi sōgō kenkyū-kai. Vol. 3 of *Nihon joseishi*. Tokyo: Tokyo daigaku shuppankai, 1982. 325–34.
Hearn, Lafcadio. *Glimpses of Unfamiliar Japan*. Boston: Houghton, Mifflin and Company, 1894. Rpt. Tokyo: Charles E. Tuttle Co., Inc., 1976.
———. *Japanese Fairy Tales*. New York: The Peter Pauper Press, 1948.
Heibonsha World Encyclopedia. 36 vols. Tokyo: Heibonsha, 1981.
Higashi Masao, intro. and Robert Weinberg, forward. *Kaiki: Uncanny Tales from Japan*. Vol. 1. Fukuoka: Kurodahan Press, 2009.
Higashino Hōmei. "Kikai to nansensu-hyakki yagyōzu." *Sansai* 96 (1958): 34–45.
Hirabayashi Hatsunosuke. "Nihon no kindaiteki tantei shōsetsu: toku ni Edogawa Ranposhi ni tsuite." *Edogawa Ranpo: hyōron to kenkyū*. Ed. Nakajima Kawatarō. Tokyo: Kodansha, 1980. 9–13.
Hirano Imao. *Inoue Enryō yōkaigaku kōgi*. Tokyo: Riburopōto, 1983.
Hirata Atsutane. *Shinshū Hirata Atsutane zenshū*. Ed. Hirata Atsutane zenshū kankōkai. Vol. 9. Tokyo: Meicho Shuppan, 1976.
Hirohito. "Shōwa tennō no dokuhaku hachijikan—taiheiyō sensō no zenbō o kataru." Comment. Handō Kazutoshi. *Bungei shunjū* 68. 13 (1990): 94–145.
Hisamatsu Sen'ichi and Nishio Minoru, eds. *Karon-shū, Noh gakuron-shū*. Vol. 65 of *NKBT*. Tokyo: Iwanami Shoten, 1961.
Hisamatsu Sen'ichi, Yamazaki Toshio, and Gotō Shiteo, eds. *Shin kokin wakashū*. Vol. 28 of *NKBT*. Iwanami Shoten, 1958.
Honda Yasuji. "Dengaku." *Sekai daihyakka jiten*. Ed. Shimonaka Kunihiko. Vol. 21. Tokyo: Heibonsha, 1972. 359.
Honko, Lauri. *Textualising The Siri Epic*. Helsinki: Academia Scientiarum Fennica, 1998.
Honma Masahiko. *Oni no jinruigaku*. Tokyo: Takashi Shoten, 1997.
Hori Ichirō. *Folk Religion in Japan: Continuity and Change*. Chicago: U of Chicago Press, 1968.
———. *Wagakuni minkan shinkōshi no kenkyū*. Vol. 2. Tokyo: Sōgensha, 1953.

Horton, H. Mack, trans. "Ōeyama." *Twelve Plays of the Noh and Kyogen Theaters*. Ed. Karen Brazell. Ithaca: Cornell U East Asia Program, 1988. 147–67.
Hudson, Mark J. *Ruins of Identity: Ethnogenesis in the Japanese Islands*. Honolulu: U of Hawai'i Press, 1999.
Huffer, Lynne. *Another Look, Another Woman: Retranslations of French Feminism*. New York: Yale UP, 1995.
Ichiko Teiji. *Chūsei shōsetsu no kenkyū*. Tokyo: Tokyo Daigaku Shuppan, 1955.
———, ed. *Heike monogatari*. Vols. 45 and 46 of *SNKBZ*. Tokyo: Shōgakukan, 1994.
———, ed. *Otogi zōshi*. Vol. 38 of *NKBT*. Tokyo: Iwanami Shoten, 1958.
Ichiko Teiji and Noma Kōshin, eds. *Otogi zōshi, Kana zōshi*. Vol. 16 of *Nihon koten kanshō kōza*. Tokyo: Kadokawa Shoten, 1963.
Ienaga Saburō. *Taiheiyō sensō*. Tokyo: Iwanami Shoten, 2002.
Iguchi Kazuki. *Nichiro sensō no jidai*. Tokyo: Yoshikawa Kōbunkan, 1998.
Ihara Saikaku. *Saikaku shokoku hanashi*. Ed. Munemasa Isoo, Teruoka Yasutaka, and Matsuda Osamu. Vol. 67 of *SNKBZ*. Tokyo: Shōgakukan, 1994.
Iida Masami. "Denshō no naka no majo to yamauba." *Tsukushi jogakuen tanki daigaku kiyō* 33 (1997): 61–73.
Iijima Yoshiharu, ed. *Minwa no sekai: jōmin no enerugī*. Vol. 10 of *Nihon bungaku kenkyū shiryō shinshū*. Tokyo: Yūseidō Shuppan, 1990.
Iizawa, Tadasu. "Oni no shinsō." *Kokubungaku kaishaku to kanshō* 17. 11 (1971): 142-153.
Ikeda Yuriko. "Oni or Ogres in Japanese Literature." *Waseda Journal of Asian Studies* 1 (1978): 34–47.
Ikegame Kazuo. *Yamauba no genryū*. Niigata: Niigata Nippō jigyōsha, 1978.
Imahori Taitsu. *Gonja no kegen—Tenjin · Kūya · Hōnen*. Tokyo: Shibunkaku Shuppan, 2006.
Inokuchi Shōji. "Yōkai to shinkō." *Nihon minzokugaku kaihō* 34 (1964): 1–6.
Inoue Enryō. *Inoue Enryō yōkai zenshū*. 6 vols. Tokyo: Kashiwa Shobō, 1999–2001.
Inoue Mitsusada and Ōsone Shōsuke, eds. *Ōjōden, Hokke genki*. Vol. 7 of *NST*. Tokyo: Iwanami Shoten, 1974.
Inoue Yasushi. "Oni no hanashi." Vol. 6 of *Inoue Yasushi tanpenshū*. Tokyo: Iwanami Shoten, 1999. 157-88.
Ishibashi Gaha. *Oni*. Ed. Shimura Kunihiro. Vol. 1 of *Shomin shūkyō minzokugaku sōsho*. Tokyo: Bensei Shuppan, 1998. Rept. from Tokyo: Shōkabō, 1909.
Ishiguro Kichijirō and Shimura Arihiro, eds. *Ōeyama emaki: Chester Bītī Raiburari shozō*. Tokyo: Benseisha, 2006.
Ishii Kendō. *Tenpō kaikaku kidan*. Tokyo: Shun'yōdo, 1926.
Ishikawa Tomohiko and Ozawa Hiroshi. *Zusetsu En no gyōja: Shugendō to En no gyōja emaki*. Tokyo: Kawade Shobō shinsha, 2000.
Ishizawa Saeko. "*Iwaya's Fairy Tales of Old Japan* ni tsuite." *Baika jidō bungaku* 11. 6 (2003): 1–21.
Itagaki Shun'ichi, ed. *Zen-taiheiki*, vol. 1. Vol. 3 of *Sōsho Edo bunko*. Tokyo: Tosho Kankōkai, 1988.
Ivy, Marilyn. *Discourses of the Vanishing: Modernity, Phantasm, Japan*. Chicago: U of Chicago Press, 1995.
Iwasaka, Michiko and Barre Toelken. *Ghosts and the Japanese: Cultural Expressions in Japanese Death Legends*. Logan, Utah: Utah State UP, 1994.
Iwaya Sazanami. *Iwaya's Fairy Tales of Old Japan*. Trans. Hannah Riddell and Ume Tsuda. 12 vols. Tokyo: The Hokuseido Press, 1938.
———. *Nihon mukashibanashi*. Ed. Ueda Nobumichi. Tokyo: Heibonsha (Tōyō bunko), 2001.

Izawa Banryō. *Kōeki zokusetsu ben*. Tokyo: Heibonsha, 1989.
Izumi Asahito. "Yamamba." *Asahi shinbun*. 27 Nov. 1999, evening ed.: 5.
Izushi Yoshihiko. *Shina shinwa densetsu no kenkyū*. 1943. Rpt. and Expanded ed. Tokyo: Chūō Kōronsha, 1973.
Jackson, Rosemary. *Fantasy: The Literature of Subversion*. London: Methuen and Co., 1981.
Jacoby, Mario, Verena Kast, and Ingrid Diedel. *Witches, Ogres, and the Devil's Daughter: Encounters with Evil in Fairy Tales*. Trans. Michael H. Kohn. Boston: Shambhala, 1992.
James, T. H., trans. *The Ogres of Oyeyama*. Vol. 19 of the *Japanese Fairy Tale Series*. Tokyo: Hasegawa, 1889.
Joly, Henri L. *Legend in Japanese Art: A Description of Historical Episodes, Legendary Characters, Folk-Lore, Myths, Religious Symbolism. Illustrated in the Arts of Old Japan*. Vermont: Charles E. Tuttle, 1967.
Jones, Sumie. "The Other Side of the Hakone: Ghosts, Demons, and Desire for Narrative in Edo Literature." *The Desire for Monogatari: Proceedings of the Second Midwest Research/Pedagogy Seminar on Japanese Literature*. Indiana: Purdue U, 1994.
Joseishi sōgō kenkyū-kai, ed. *Nihon joseishi*. Tokyo: Tokyo daigaku shuppankai, 1982.
Kabat, Adam. "Bakemono zukushi no kibyōshi no kōsatsu: Bakemono no gainen o megutte." *Yōkai*. Ed. Komatsu Kazuhiko. Vol. 2 of *Kaii no minzokugaku*. Tokyo: Kawade Shobō, 2000. 141–64.
———. *Edo bakemono sōshi*. Tokyo: Shōgakukan, 1999.
———. "'Sōsaku' to shite no yōkai." *Nihon yōkai taizen*. Ed. Komatsu Kazuhiko. Tokyo: Shōgakukan, 2003. 145–78.
Kagawa Masanobu. "Asobi no naka no yōkai-tachi." *Nihon yōkai taizen*. Ed. Komatsu Kazuhiko. Tokyo: Shōgakukan, 2003. 31–64.
Kaibara Ekken. "Joshi o oshiyuru no hō." *Onna daigaku-shū*. Ed. Ishikawa Matsutarō. Tokyo: Heibonsha, 1977. 1–26.
Kanai Kiyomitsu. "Fukujin kyōgen no keisei." *Shichifukujin shinkō jiten*. Ed. Miyata Noboru. Tokyo: Ebisu Kōshō Shuppan, 1998. 327–361.
Kanaya Osamu. *Sōji*. Vol. 1. Tokyo: Iwanami Shoten, 1971.
Kanda Tatsumi and Nishizawa Masashi. *Chūsei ōchō monogatari, otogi zōshi jiten*. Tokyo: Benseisha Shuppan, 2002.
Kanzaki Mitsuharu. "'Nōe hōshi ekotoba' no kotobagaki." *Nōe Hōshi ekotoba, Fukutomi sōshii, Hyakki yagyō emaki*. Ed. Komatsu Shigemi. Tokyo: Chūō Kōronsha, 1993. 100–108.
Kashiwaba Sachiko. *Kiri no mukō no fushigina machi*. Tokyo: Kodansha, 2003.
Katagiri Yōichi et al., eds. *Taketori monogatari, Ise monogatari, Yamato monogatari, Heichū monogatari*. Vol. 12 of *SNKBZ*. Tokyo: Shōgakukan, 1994.
Kato, Eileen, trans. "Kanawa." *Twenty Plays of the No Theatre*. Ed. Donald Keene. New York: Columbia UP, 1970. 193–205.
Katō Shūichi. *A History of Japanese Literature*. 3 vols. Tokyo: Kodansha International, 1979.
Kawai Hayao. *The Japanese Psyche*. Connecticut: Spring Publications, 1996.
———. *Mukashibanashi to nihonjin no kokoro*. Tokyo: Iwanami Shoten, 1982.
Kawamura Kunimitsu. "Kintarō no haha." *Tengu to yamauba*. Ed. Komatsu Kazuhiko. Vol. 5 of *Kaii no minzokugaku*. Tokyo: Kawade Shobō, 2000. 384–407.
———. "Onna no jigoku to sukui." Ed. Okano Haruko. Vol. 3 of *Onna to otoko no jikū: Nihon joseishi saikō*. Tokyo: Fujiwara Shoten, 1996. 31–80.
Kawatake Mokuami. *Kawatake Mokuami-shū*. Ed. Kawatake Shigetoshi. Vol. 30 of *Nihon gikyoku zenshū*. Tokyo: Shun'yōdō, 1928.

———. "Modoribashi." Ed. Kawatake Shigetoshi. Vol. 47 of *Meiji Taishō bungaku zenshū*. Tokyo: Shun'yōdō, 1930. 147–51.

———. "Tsuchigumo." Trans. Donald Richie. Ohio, 1949.

Kawatake Shigetoshi, ed. *Engeki hyakka daijiten*. 6 vols. Tokyo: Heibon-sha, 1960–62.

Keene, Donald. *Seeds in the Heart: Japanese Literature from Earliest Times to the Late Sixteenth Century*. New York: Henry Holt & Co., 1993.

———. *World Within Walls: Japanese Literature of the Pre-Modern Era, 1600–1867*. New York: Grove Press, 1976.

Keikai. *Nihon ryōiki*. Ed. Endō Yoshimoto and Kasuga Kazuo. Vol. 70 of *NKBT*. Tokyo: Iwanami Shoten, 1967.

Keown, Damien, ed. *A Dictionary of Buddhism*. Oxford: Oxford UP, 2003.

Kijima Hajime. *Shuten Dōji: Manshuin zō "Shuten Dōji emaki" yori*. Tokyo: Riburopōto, 1993.

Kikuchi Yūjirō. "Saichō to Shuten Dōji no monogatari." *Dengyō-daishi kenkyū*. Tokyo: Waseda Daigaku Shuppanbu, 1973. 347–71.

Kimbrough, R. Keller. *Preachers, Poets, Women, and the Way: Izumi Shikibu and the Buddhist Literature of Medieval Japan*. Ann Arbor: Center for Japanese Studies The U of Michigan, 2008.

———. "Tourists in Paradise: Writing the Pure Land in Medieval Japanese Fiction." *Japanese Journal of Religious Studies* 33. 2 (2006): 269–296.

Kimura Chizuko and Yagi Ichio, eds. *Daikokumai emaki: Kamakura Eishōji shozō*. Tokyo: Benseisha Shuppan, 2006.

Kinoshita Junji. "Minwa ni tsuite." *Minwa no sekai: jōmin no enerugī*. Ed. Iijima Yoshiharu. Vol. 10 of *Nihon bungaku kenkyū shiryō shinshū*. Tokyo: Yūseidō, 1990. 82–95.

Kitagawa Hiroshi and Tsuchida, Bruce T., trans. *The Tale of the Heike*. Tokyo: U of Tokyo Press, 1975.

Kitagawa Tadahiko. "Tanabe no bettō kuchinawa tachi." *Geinō kenkyū* 126 (1994): 1–6.

Kitajima Harunobu. Kaisetsu. *Naita akaoni*. Hamada Hirosuke. Tokyo: Popurasha, 1978. 190–201.

Kitakami shiritsu oni no yakata, ed. *Oni no yakata: jōsetsu tenji zuroku*. Iwate: Kitakami shiritsu oni no yakata, 1995.

Knecht, Peter. "Ise sankei mandara and the Image of the Pure Land." *Japanese Journal of Religious Studies* 33. 2 (2006): 223–248.

———. *Shi to sei to tsuki to hōjō*. Tokyo: Hyōronsha, 1975.

Knecht, Peter, Hasegawa Masao, Minobe Shigekatsu, and Tsujimoto Hiroshige. "Denshi 'Oni' to 'mushi'—'Kyōu shoya zō Denshibyō kanjin shō' ryakkai –." Vol. 6 of *Shōdō bungaku kenkyū*. Ed. Fukuda Akira and Nakamae Masashi. Tokyo: Miyai Shoten, 2008. 40–95.

———. "'Oni' to 'mushi'—'kokoro no oni' ron ni mukete –." *Academia* [jinbun shakai-kagaku hen]. Nanzan U 78 (January 2004): 245–286.

Kobayashi Nobuhiko. *Ichishōnen no mita "seisen."* Tokyo: Chikuma Shobō, 1995.

Kobayashi Yasuharu and Masuko Kazuko, eds. *Uji shūi monogatari*. Vol. 50 of *SNKBZ*. Tokyo: Shōgakukan, 1996.

Kodama Kazuo. *Horā eiga no hīrō-tachi*. Tokyo: Shinchōsha, 1986.

———. *Monsutā eiga no tanjō*. Tokyo: Seikyūsha, 1996.

Kōen. *Fusō ryakki*. Ed. Keizai Zasshisha. Vol. 6 of *Kokushi taikei*. Tokyo: Keizai Zasshisha, 1897.

Koike Masatane, ed. *Edo no ehon: shoki kusazōshi shūsei*. 4 vols. Tokyo: Kokusho Kankōkai, 1987–89.

Kojima Noriyuki, Naoki Kōjirō, Nishimiya Kazutami, Kuranaka Susumu, and Mōri Masamori, eds. *Nihonshoki*. Vol. 2 of *SNKBZ*. Tokyo: Shōgakukan, 1994.

Kojima Noriyuki, Kinoshita Masatoshi, and Tōno Haruyuki, eds. *Man'yōshū*. Vols. 6–9 of *SNKBZ*. Tokyo: Shōgakukan, 1994–1996.

Kokonoe Sakon. *Edo kinsei buyō-shi*. Banrikaku Shobō, 1919. Rpt. Vol. 32 of *Kinsei bungei kenkyū-sho: dai ni ki geinō-hen*. Ed. Kinsei bungei kenkyū-sho kankō-kai. Tokyo: Kuresu Shuppan, 1998.

Komatsu Kazuhiko. *Abe no Seimei "yami" no denshō*. Tokyo: Ōtō Shobō, 2000.

———. *Fuku no kami to binbōgami*. Tokyo: Chikuma Shobō, 1998.

———. *Hyōrei shinkō ron*. Tokyo: Kōdansha, 1994.

———. *Ijinron*. Tokyo: Seidosha, 1985.

———. "Ijin ron—'ijin' kara 'tasha' e." *Tasha, kankei, komyunikēshon*. Ed. Inoue Shun et al. Vol. 3 of *Iwanami kōza gendai shakaigaku*. Tokyo: Iwanami Shoten, 1995. 175–200.

———. Kaisetsu. *Tengu to yamauba*. Ed. Komatsu Kazuhiko. Vol. 5 of *Kaii no minzokugaku*. Tokyo: Kawade Shobō, 2000. 417–34.

———. *Kamikakushi to nihonjin*. Tokyo: Kadokawa Shoten, 2002.

———. "Ma to yōkai." *Kami to hotoke*. Ed. Miyata Noboru et al. Vol. 4 of *Nihon minzoku bunka taikei*. Tokyo: Shōgakukan, 1983. 339–414.

———, ed. *Nihon yōkai taizen*. Tokyo: Shōgakukan, 2003.

———, ed. *Oni*. Vol. 4 of *Kaii no minzokugaku*. Tokyo: Kawade Shobō, 2000.

———. "Onna no 'chikara', aruiwa chitsujo to hanchitsujo ni tsūtē surumono." *Kokuritsu gekijō* (January 2000): 35–36.

———. *Shinpen oni no tamatebako*. Tokyo: Fukutake Shoten, 1991.

———. *Shuten Dōji no kubi*. Tokyo: Seika Shobō, 1997.

———. "Supernatural Apparitions and Domestic Life in Japan." *The Japan Foundation Newsletter* 27. 1 (1999): 1–5, 20.

———. "Yōkai." *Kami kannen to minzoku*. Ed. Gorai Shigeru, Sakurai Tokutarō, Ōshima Tatehiko, and Miyata Noboru. Vol. 3 of *Kōza nihon no minzoku shūkyō*. Tokyo: Kōbundō, 1979. 330–55.

———, ed. *Yōkai*. Vol. 2 of *Kaii no minzokugaku*. Tokyo: Kawade Shobō, 2000.

———. *Yōkaigaku shinkō*. Tokyo: Shōgakukan, 2000.

———. "Yomigaeru Kusazōshi no bakemonotachi." *Edo bakemono sōshi*. Adam Kabat. Tokyo: Shōgakukan, 1999. 230–37.

Komatsu Kazuhiko and Naitō Masatoshi. *Oni ga tsukutta kuni nihon*. Tokyo: Kōbunsha, 1990.

Komatsu Shigemi and Akiyama Ken, eds. *Gaki sōshi, jigoku sōshi, yamai no sōshi, kusōshi emaki*. Vol. 7 of *Nihon emaki taisei*. Tokyo: Chūō Kōronsha, 1977.

Komatsu Shigemi, Kanazawa Hiroshi, and Kanzaki Mitsuharu, eds. *Nōe hōshi ekotoba, Fukutomi sōshi, Hyakki yagyō emaki*. Vol. 25 of *Nihon emaki taisei*. Tokyo: Chūō Kōronsha, 1979.

Komatsu Shigemi and Murashige Yasushi, eds. *Haseo sōshi, Eshi sōshi*. Vol. 11 of *Nihon emaki taisei*. Tokyo: Chūō Kōronsha, 1977.

Komatsu Shigemi, Nakano Genzō, Matsubara Shigeru, eds., *Kitano Tenjin engi*. Vol. 21 of *Nihon emaki taisei*. Tokyo: Chūō Kōronsha, 1978.

Komatsu Shigemi, Ueno Kenji, Sakakibara Satoru, and Shimatani Hiroyuki, eds. *Tsuchigumo sōshi, Tengu sōshi, Ōeyama ekotoba*. Vol. 19 of *Zoku nihon emaki taisei*. Chūō Kōronsha, 1984.

Komatsu Shigemi and Yoshida Mitsukuni, eds. *Nenjū gyōji emaki*. Vol. 8 of *Nihon emaki taisei*. Tokyo: Chūō Kōronsha, 1977.

Komatsu Shigemi, Yoshida Yūji, Shimatani Hiroyuki, Uchida Masanori, and Oshita Tamiko, eds. *Kuwanomidera engi, Dōjōji engi*. Vol. 13 of *Zoku nihon emaki taisei*. Tokyo: Chūō Kōronsha, 1982.
"Komochi yamauba." *Kabuki on stage*. Ed. Torigoe Bunzō. Tokyo: Hakusuisha, 1989. 41–82.
Kondō Yoshihiro. *Nihon no oni: nihon bunka tankyū no shikaku*. Tokyo: Ōfūsha, 1975.
Konishi Jin'ichi. *History of Japanese Literature*. Trans. Aileen Gatten. Ed. Earl Miner. Vols. 2 and 3 of *The Early Middle Ages*. New Jersey: Princeton UP, 1986 and 1991.
Kōnoshi, Takamitsu. "Oni: oni no uwasabanashi o megutte." *Kokubungaku kaishaku to kyōzai no kenkyū* 17. 11 (September 1972): 95–101.
Kosugi Kazuo. *Chūgoku bijutsushi*. Tokyo: Nan'undō, 1986.
———. *Nara bijutsu no keifu*. Tokyo: Heibonsha, 1993.
Koyama Hiroshi, ed. *Kyōgenshū*. Vol. 43 of *NKBT*. Tokyo: Iwanami Shoten, 1961.
Kumasegawa Kyōko. "Oni no imi to sono hensen." *Kikan jinruigaku* 20. 4 (1989): 182–219.
Kurano Kenji and Takeda Yūkichi, eds. *Kojiki, Norito*. Vol. 1 of *NKBT*. Tokyo: Iwanami Shoten, 1958.
Kuroda Akira. *Chūsei setsuwa no bungakushiteki kankyō*. Osaka: Izumi Shoin, 1987.
Kuroda Hideo. *Otogi zōshi*. Tokyo: Perikansha, 1990.
———. *Zōho sugata to shigusa no chūsei-shi*. Tokyo: Heibonsha, 2002.
Kuroita Katsumi, ed. *Azuma kagami* 3. Vol. 35 of *Kokushi taikei*. Ed. Kokushi taikei henshūkai. Tokyo: Yoshikawa Kōbunkan, 1979.
Kurosawa Akira, dir. *Dreams*. Perf. Terao Akira and Martin Scorsese. Warner Bros. 1990. Film.
Kusano, Eisaburō. *Weird Tales of Old Japan*. Tokyo: Tokyo News Service, 1953.
LaCapra, Dominick. "From 'Bakhtin, Marxism, and the Carnivalesque'." *Critical Essays on Mikhail Bakhtin*. Ed. Caryl Emerson. New York: G.K. Hall & Co., 1999. 239–45.
LaFleur, William R. *Buddhism: a Cultural Perspective*. New Jersey: Prentice Hall Inc., 1988.
Lederberg, Joshua, Robert E. Shope, and Stanley C. Oaks, Jr., eds. *Emerging Infections*. Washington D. C.: National Academy Press, 1992.
Le Guin, Ursula K. *The Farthest Shore*. New York: Atheneum, 1972.
———. *Tehanu: the Last Book of Earthsea*. New York: Atheneum, 1990.
———. *The Tombs of Atuan*. New York: Simon Pulse, 1971.
———. *A Wizard of Earthsea*. New York: Atheneum Books for Young Readers, 1968.
Lent, John A. "Japanese Comics." *Handbook of Japanese Popular Culture*. Ed. Richard Gid Powers and Hidetoshi Kato. New York: Greenwood Press, 1989. 221–42.
Li, HuoXong. "'Kiki' seiritsu ni okeru 'oni' to iu hyōgen oyobi sono hensen ni tsuite." *Minzokugaku kenkyū* 51. 4 (1987): 417–431.
Lillehoj, Elizabeth. "Transfiguration: Man-Made Objects as Demons in Japanese Scrolls."*Asian Folklore Studies* 54. 1 (1995): 7–34.
Ma, Y. W. and Joseph S. M. Lau, eds. *Traditional Chinese Stories*. New York: Columbia UP, 1978.
Mabuchi Kazuo, Kunisaki Fumimaro, and Inagaki Taiichi, eds. *Konjaku monogatarishū*. Vols. 35–38 of *SNKBZ*. Tokyo: Shōgakukan, 1999–2002.
Markus, Andrew L. "The Carnival of Edo: Misemono Spectacles from Contemporary Accounts." *HJAS* 45. 2 (1985): 499–541.
Masuda, Katsumi. "Minwa no seikaku." *Minwa no sekai: jōmin no enerugī*. Ed. Iijima Yoshiharu. Vol. 10 of *Nihon bungaku kenkyū shiryō shinshū*. Tokyo: Yūseidō, 1990. 96–101.

Matsui Tomo. *Mukashibanashi no shi to tanjō*. Tokyo: Yamato Shobō, 1988.
Matsui Toshiaki. "Henshin no mae no onnagokoro." *Kokuritsu genkijō* (January 2000): 32–33.
Matsumoto Ryūshin. *Muromachi jidai monogatari taisei hoi*. Vol. 1. Tokyo: Kadokawa Shoten, 1987.
———. "Otogi zōshi no honbun ni tsuite." *Shidō bunko ronshū* 2 (March 1963): 171–242.
Matsuo Ashie. "Heike monogatari tsurugi no maki kaisetsu." *Heike monogatari 4*. Ed. Ichiko Teiji. Vol. 45 of *Nihon no koten*. Tokyo: Shōgakukan, 1987. 406–07.
Matsutani Miyoko. *Gendai minwa kō V—anoyo e itta hanashi, shi no shirase, umare kawari*. Tokyo: Tachikaze Shobō, 1986.
———. *Minwa no sekai*. Tokyo: Kōdansha, 1974.
———. *The Witch's Magic Cloth*. Trans. Alvin Tresselt and illus. Yasuo Segawa. New York: Parents' Magazine Press, 1969.
Maxwell, T.S. *Eastern Approaches: Essays on Asian Art and Archaeology*. New York: Oxford UP, 1992.
Mayama Seika. *Saikaku goi kōshō*. Vol. 1. Tokyo: Chūō Kōron sha, 1948.
Mayer, Fanny Hagin. *Ancient Tales in Modern Japan: an Anthology of Japanese Folk Tales*. Bloomington: Indiana UP, 1984.
———, ed. and trans. *The Yanagita Kunio Guide to Japanese Folk Tales*. Bloomington: Indiana UP, 1986.
McAlpine, Helen and William. *Japanese Tales and Legends*. Oxford: Oxford UP, 1979.
McArthur, Meher. *Gods and Goblins: Japanese Folk Paintings from Otsu*. Pasadena: Pacific Asian Museum, 1999.
McCarthy, Helen. *Hayao Miyazaki: Master of Japanese Animation*. Berkeley: Stone Bridge Press, 1999.
McCullough, Helen Craig, ed. *Classical Japanese Prose: An Anthology*. Stanford: Stanford UP, 1990.
———, trans. *Eiga monogatari: A Tale of Flowering Fortunes*. 2 vols. Stanford: Stanford UP, 1980.
———, trans. *Ōkagami: The Great Mirror*. New Jersey: Princeton UP, 1980.
———, trans. *The Taiheiki: A Chronicle of Medieval Japan*. New York: Columbia UP, 1959.
———, trans. *The Tale of the Heike*. Stanford: Stanford UP, 1988.
———, trans. *Tales of Ise: Lyrical Episodes from Tenth-Century Japan*. Stanford: Stanford UP, 1968.
McGillicuddy, Karen. "Yumemakura Baku's Onmyōji: A Translation with Introduction." Senior Thesis. Mount Holyoke College, 2004.
Mihashi Kazuo. "Oni no matsuei." *Oni no matsuei*. Vol. 2 of *Mihashi Kazuo fushigi shōsetsu shūsei*. Tokyo: Shuppan Geijutsusha, 2005. 151–71.
Mills, D. E. *A Collection of Tales from Uji: A Study and Translation of Uji Monogatari*. Cambridge: U of Cambridge, 1970.
Minamoto Akikane. *Kojidan, Zoku kojidan*. Ed. Kawabata Yoshiaki and Araki Hiroshi. Vol. 41 of *SNKBT*. Tokyo: Iwanami Shoten, 2005.
Minamoto no Shitagō. *Wamyō ruijushō*. Ed. Masamune Atsuo. Tokyo: Kazama Shobō, 1977.
Minobe Shigekatsu and Minobe Tomoko. *Shuten Dōji e o yomu: Matsurowanu mono no jikū*. Tokyo: Miyai Shoten, 2009.
Minzokugaku kenkyūjo. *Minzokugaku jiten*. Tokyo: Tokyo-do Shuppan, 1951.
Mitamura Engyo. *Mitamura Engyo zenshū*. Ed. Mori Jūzō, Noma Kōkin, and Asakura Haruhiko. 28 vols. Tokyo: Chūō Kōronsha, 1975–83.

Mitani Eiichi. *Monogatari-shi no kenkyū*. Tokyo: Yūseidō Shuppan, 1967.
Miyake Hitoshi. *Shugendō: Essays on the Structure of Japanese Folk Religion*. Ann Arbor: Center for Japanese Studies The U of Michigan, 2001.
Miyamoto Kesao. "Fuku no kami no shinkō." *Shichifukujin shinkō jiten*. Ed. Miyata Noboru. Tokyo: Ebisu Kōshō Shuppan, 1998. 60–75.
Miyamoto Masaaki. "Ōeyama densetsu seiritsu kō."*Kinki minzoku* 48 (1969): 1–10.
Miyata Noboru. "Kankō ni atatte." *Shichifukujin shinkō jiten*. Ed. Miyata. Tokyo: Ebisu Kōshō Shuppan, 1998. 1–2.
———. *Yōkai no minzokugaku*. Tokyo: Iwanami Shoten, 1985.
Miyazaki Hayao. "Chihiro's Mysterious Town." *The Art of Miyazaki's Spirited Away*. Ed. Alvin Yu. San Francisco: Viz Communications, Inc., 2002. 15–16.
———, dir. *Princess Mononoke*. MiraMax. 1997. Film.
———, dir. *Spirited Away*. Walt Disney Home Video. 2003. Film
———, dir. *Tonari no totoro*. Buena Vista Home Entertainment. 1988. Film.
Miyazaki Kazue, ed. *Kunisaki hantō no mukashibanashi*. Tokyo: Miyai Shoten, 1969.
Miyazaki Michio. *Arai Hakuseki no kenkyū*. Tokyo: Yoshikawa Kōbunkan, 1984.
Mizuhara Hajime, ed. *Shintei genpei jōsuiki*. Vol. 1. Tokyo: Jinbutsu ōraisha, 1988.
Mizuki Shigeru. *Mizuki Shigeru no yōkai wārudo*. 1998. Web. May 2005.
———. *Yōkai gadan*. Tokyo: Iwanami Shoten, 1992.
———. *Yūrei gadan*. Tokyo: Iwanami Shoten, 1994.
———. *Zoku yōkai gadan*. Tokyo: Iwanami Shoten, 1993.
———. *Zusetsu nihon yōkai taizen*. Tokyo: Kodansha, 1994.
Mizuo Hiroshi. *Jaki no saga*. Kyoto: Tankō Shinsha, 1967.
Mizuta Noriko. "Yamauba no yume." *Yamaubatachi no monogatari: josei no genkei to katarinaoshi*. Ed. Mizuta Noriko and Kitada Sachie. Tokyo: Gakugei Shorin, 2002. 7–37.
Mochizuki Shinkō and Tsukamoto Zenryū. *Mochizuki bukkyō daijiten*. 10 vols. Tokyo: Sekai seiten kankō kyōkai, 1973–74.
Moes, Robert. *Rosetsu*. Denver: Denver Museum of Art, 1973.
Mori Masao. "Konjaku Monogatari shū: Supernatural Creatures and Order." *Japanese Journal of Religious Studies* 9 (1982): 147–170.
Moriya Takeshi. *Chūsei geinō no genzō*. Kyoto: Tankōsha, 1985.
Morley, James William, ed. *Deterrent Diplomacy*. New York: Columbia UP, 1976.
Morson, Gary Saul and Caryl Emerson. *Mikhail Bakhtin: Creation of a Prosaics*. Stanford: Stanford UP, 1990.
Motoori Norinaga. *Motoori Norinaga zenshū*. Ed. Ōno Susumu and Ōkubo Yasumasa. Vol. 9. Tokyo: Chikuma Shobō, 1968.
Mulhern, Chieko Irie. "Analysis of Cinderella Motifs, Italian and Japanese." *Asian Folklore Studies* 44. 1 (1985): 1–37.
———. "Otogi-zōshi. Short Stories of the Muromachi Period." *MN* 29. 2 (1974): 180–198.
Murasaki Shikibu. *Genji monogatari*. Ed. Abe Akio et al. 6 vols. Vols. 20–25 of *SNKBZ*. Tokyo: Shōgakukan, 1994–98.
———. *The Tale of Genji*. Trans. Edward G. Seidensticker. Tokyo: Tuttle, 1973.
———. *The Tale of Genji*. Trans. Royall Tyler. 2 vols. New York: Viking, 2001.
Murayama Shūichi. "Abe no Seimei to nihon onmyōdō taisei e no michi." *Abe no Seimei kō*. Ed. Seimei jinja. Tokyo: Kōdansha, 2002. 62–79.
———. "Kyūtei onmyōdō no seiritsu." *Engi tenryaku jidai no kenkyū*. Ed. Kodaigaku Kyōkai. Tokyo: Yoshikawa Kōbunkan, 1969. 359–86.
———. *Nihon onmyōdō sōsetsu*. Tokyo: Haniwa Shobō, 1981.

Muroki Yatarō. *Katarimono no kenkyū*. Tokyo: Kazama Shobō, 1970.

———. *Kinpira jōruri shōhon shū*. 3 vols. Tokyo: Kadokawa Shoten, 1966–1969.

Nagai Gō. *Debiruman*. 5 vols. Tokyo: Kōdansha, 1997. Comic books.

———. *Debiruman wa dare nano ka*. Tokyo: Kōdansha, 2004.

———. *Nagai Gō SAGA: Sakuhin hyōronshū*. Tokyo: Fuyōsha, 2003.

———. *Oni*. Vol. 1 of *Nagai Gō kaiki tanpenshū*. Tokyo: Chūō Koronsha, 1995. Comic books.

———. *Shuten Dōji* [A child handed from heaven]. vols. 1–3. Tokyo: Kodansha, 2001; vols. 4–5. Tokyo: Fusōsha, 1998; vol. 6. Tokyo: Fusōsha, 1997. Comic books.

Naganuma Kenkai. "Daikokuten saikō." *Daikoku shinkō*. Ed. Ōshima Tatehiko. Tokyo: Yūzankaku, 1990. 53–102.

———. *Fukujin kenkyū Ebisu to Daikoku*. Tokyo: Heigo Shuppansha, 1921.

Nagasawa Kikuya. *Keitai shin kanwa jiten*. Tokyo: Sanseidō, 1969.

Nagasawa Rosetsu. *Exhibition Nagasawa Rosetsu: The 20th Anniversary of his Death*. Tokyo: Nihon Keizai Shinbunsha, 2000.

Nakada Kaoru. *Tokugawa jidai no bungaku ni mietaru shihō*. Tokyo: Sōbunsha, 1956.

Nakada Norio, ed. *Nihon ryōiki*. By Keikai. Vol. 10 of *SNKBZ*. Tokyo: Shōgakukan, 1995.

Nakagami Kenji. *The Cape and Other Stories from the Japanese Ghetto*. Trans. Eve Zimmerman. Berkeley: Stone Bridge Press, 1999.

———. *Nakagami Kenji hatsugen shūsei*. 6 vols. Ed. Karatani Kōjin. Tokyo: Daisan bunmeisha, 1995–-99.

———. *Nakagami Kenji zenshū*. 15 vols. Ed. Karatani Kōjin. Tokyo: Shūeisha, 1995–96.

———. "A Tale of a Demon." *Snakelust*. Trans. Andrew Rankin. Tokyo: Kondansha International, 1998. 99–120.

Nakai, Kate Wildman. "The Naturalization of Confucianism in Tokugawa Japan: The Problem of Sinocentricism." *HJAS* 40 (1980): 157–99.

Nakamura Hiroaki. *Ueda Akinari no kenkyū*. Tokyo: Perikansha, 1999.

Nakamura, Kyoko Motomochi. *Miraculous Stories from the Japanese Buddhist Tradition*. By Keikai. Cambridge: Harvard UP, 1973. Rpt. Surrey: Curzon Press, 1997.

Nakamura Yukihiko, ed. *Ueda Akinari shū*. Vol. 56 of *NKBT*. Tokyo: Iwanami Shoten, 1959.

Nakamura Yukihiko, Takada Mamoru, and Nakamura Hiroyasu, eds. *Hanabusa zōshi, Nishiyama monogatari, Ugetsu monogatari, Harusame monogatari*. Vol. 78 of *SNKBZ*. Tokyo: Shōgakukan, 1995.

Nakane Chie. *Japanese Society*. Berkeley: U of California Press, 1970.

Nakar, Eldad. "Nosing Around: Visual Representation of the Other in Japanese Society." *Anthropological Forum* 13. 1 (May 2003): 49–66.

Nakazawa Shin'ichi. *Poketto no naka no yasei: pokemon to kodomo*. Tokyo: Shinchōsha, 2004.

———. "Yōkaiga to hakubutsugaku." *Yōkai*. Vol. 2 of *Kaii no minzokugaku*. Ed. Komatsu Kazuhiko. Tokyo: Kawade Shobō, 2000. 79–86.

Namekawa Michio. *Momotarō-zō no hen'yō*. Tokyo: Tokyo Shoseki, 1981.

Napier, Susan. *Anime from Akira to Princess Mononoke: experiencing contemporary Japanese animation*. New York: Palgrave, 2001.

———. *The Fantastic in Modern Japanese Literature: the Subversion of Modernity*. New York: Routledge, 1996.

———. "Matter Out of Place: Carnival, Containment, and Cultural Recovery in Miyazaki's *Spirited Away*." *Journal of Japanese Studies* 32. 2 (2006): 287–310.

Narayan, R. K. *Gods, Demons, and Others*. New York: The Viking Press, 1964.

Narazaki Muneshige et al., eds. *Ukiyo-e Masterpieces in European Collections*. Vols. 7 and 9. Tokyo: Kodansha, 1990 and 1989.
Narazaki Muneshige and Kikuchi Sadao. *Masterworks of Ukiyoe: Utamaro*. Trans. John Bester. Tokyo: Kodansha International, 1968.
Nicholson, Nigel. "Victory without Defeat? Carnival Laughter and Its Appropriation in Pindar's Victory Odes." *Carnivalizing Difference: Bakhtin and the Other*. Ed. Peter I. Barta et al. New York: Routledge, 2001. 79–98.
Nihon mukashibanashi jiten. Ed. Inada Kōji et al. Tokyo: Kōbundō, 1977.
Nihon no oni kōryū hakubutsukan, ed. *Ima Yomigaeru oni*. Kyoto: Nihon no oni kōryū hakubutsukan, 1993.
"Ninjin no okori." *Rikuzen mukashibanashi-shū*. Ed. Sasaki Tokuo. Vol. 29 of *Zenkoku mukashibanashi shiryō shūsei*. Tokyo: Iwasaki bijutsusha, 1978. 74–76.
Nobuhiro Shinji. *Rakugo wa ikanishite keisei sareta ka*. Tokyo: Heibonsha, 1986.
Nogami Toyoichirō. *Nō no yūgen to hana*. Tokyo: Iwanami Shoten, 1943.
Noguchi Takehiko. *Edo hyakki yakō*. Tokyo: Perikansha, 1985.
Nomura Hachiryō. *Muromachi jidai shōsetsu-ron*. Vol. 2 of Otogi zōshi kenkyū sōsho. Ed. Fujii Takashi. Ganshōdō Shoten, 1928. Rpt. Tokyo: Kuresu Shuppan, 2003.
Nosaka Akiyuki. *Otogi zōshi Shuten Dōji*. Tokyo: Shūeisha, 1982.
Nose Asaji. *Nōgaku genryū kō*. Tokyo: Iwanami Shoten, 1938.
Ōba Minako and Mizuta Noriko. *Yamamba no iru fūkei*. Tokyo: Tahata Shoten, 1995.
Ogawa Juichi. "Ōeyama densetsu kō." *Shūkyō to geijutsu* 9. 10 (1928): 33–43.
———. "Ōeyama ekotoba no kenkyū." *Rekishi to kokubungaku* 12. 1 (1935): 29–41; 12. 4 (1935): 15–24; 15. 3 (1936): 1–13.
Ōizumi Mitsunari. *Anno Hideaki sukizo Evangerion*. Tokyo: Ōta Shuppan, 1997.
Okano Reiko. *Onmyōji*. 13 vols. Tokyo: Hakusensha, 1999–2005.
Ōkawa, Shūmei. *Bei-ei tōa shinryaku-shi*. Tokyo: Dai-ichi Shobō, 1942.
Ōkubo Jun'ichi. "Kintaro to Yamauba." Vol. 9 of *Ukiyo-e Masterpieces in European Collections*. Ed. Narazaki Muneshige et al. Tokyo: Kodansha, 1989. 257–58.
Olson, Scott R. "Hollywood Goes Global." *World & I* 16 (February 2001): 263–275.
Ōmori Shōzō. "Kotodama-ron." *Sekai to chishiki*. Ed. Ōmori. Vol. 2 of *Kōza tetsugaku*. Tokyo: Tokyo Daigaku Shuppankai, 1973. 163–213.
Onmyoji. Dir. Takita Yōjiro. Perf. Nomura Mansaku. Pioneer. 2001. Film.
Onmyoji II. Dir. Takita Yōjiro. Perf. Nomura Mansaku. Geneon Pioneer. 2003. Film.
Onna daigaku takarabako. In *Onna daigaku-shū*. Ed. Ishikawa Matsutarō. Tokyo: Heibonsha, 1977. 27–59.
Ōno Susumu, Satake Akihiro and Maeda Kingorō. *Iwanami kogo jiten*. Tokyo: Iwanami Shoten, 1974.
Orikuchi Shinobu. "Haru kuru oni." Vol. 17 of *Orikuchi Shinobu zenshū*. Ed. Orikuchi Shinobu zenshū kankōkai. Tokyo: Chūō Kōronsha, 1996. 123–41.
———. "Kokubungaku no hassei." Vol. 1 of *Orikuchi Shinobu zenshū*. Ed. Orikuchi Shinobu zenshū kankōkai. Tokyo: Chūō Kōronsha, 1995. 11–66.
———. "Okina no hassei." Vol. 2 of *Orikuchi Shinobu zenshū*. Ed. Orikuchi Shinobu zenshū kankōkai. Tokyo: Chūō Kōronsha, 1995. 348–388.
———. "Oni no hanashi." Vol. 3 of *Orikuchi Shinobu zenshū*. Ed. Orikuchi Shinobu zenshū kankōkai. Tokyo: Chūō Kōronsha, 1995. 9–26.
———. "Oni to sanjin to." Vol. 17 of *Orikuchi Shinobu zenshū*. Ed. Orikuchi Shinobu zenshū kankōkai. Tokyo: Chūō Kōronsha, 1996. 117–22.
———. "Shinodazuma no hanashi." Vol. 2 of *Orikuchi Shinobu zenshū*. Ed. Orikuchi Shinobu zenshū kankōkai. Tokyo: Chūō Kōronsha, 1995. 253–92.

Oshima, Mark. "Komochi yamamba." *Kokuritsu genkijō* (January 20002): 64–65.
Ōshima Tatehiko. "Shichifukujin no denshō." *Shichifukujin shinkō jiten*. Ed. Miyata Noboru. Tokyo: Ebisu Kōshō Shuppan, 1998. 308–317.
———, ed. *Otogizōshi-shū*. Vol. 36 of *NKBZ*. Tokyo: Shōgakukan, 1974.
———. "Yamauba to Kintarō." *Tenmei bungaku*. Ed. Hamada Giichirō. Tokyo: Tokyodo Shuppan, 1979. 34–53.
Ōsumi Kazuo. *Nihon no bunka o yominaosu: bukkyō, nenjū gyōji, bungaku no chūsei*. Tokyo: Yoshikawa Kōbunkan, 1998.
Ōwa Iwao. *Oni to tennō*. Tokyo: Hakusuisha, 1992.
Oyler, Elizabeth. *Swords, Oaths, and Prophetic Visions: Authoring Warrior Rule in Medieval Japan*. Honolulu: U of Hawai'i Press, 2006.
Perez, Louis G. *Daily Life in Early Modern Japan*. Conn.: Greenwood Press, 2002.
Philippi, Donald D., trans. *Kojiki*. Princeton: Princeton UP, 1969.
Piggott, Juliet. *Japanese Mythology*. New York: Peter Bedrick Books, 1982.
Plutschow, Herbert. *Matsuri: the Festivals of Japan*. Surrey: Japan Library, 1996.
Prince, Stephen. *The Warrior's Camera: The Cinema of Akira Kurosawa*. New Jersey: Princeton UP, 1999.
Proulx, Mason. *Everything You Always Wanted to Know About Lum*. 1998. Web. March 2000.
Putzar, Edward D. "The Tale of Monkey Genji: Sarugenji-zōshi." *MN* 18 (1963): 286–312.
Quinn, Shelley Fenno. *Developing Zeami: The Noh Actor's Attunement in Practice*. Honolulu: U of Hawai'i Press, 2005.
———. "How to Write a Noh Play: Zeami's Sandō." *MN* 48. 1 (1993): 53–88.
———. "Oral and Vocal Traditions of Japan." *Teaching Oral Traditions*. Ed. John Miles Foley. New York: The Modern Association of America, 1998. 258–65.
Rabinovitch, Judith N. Trans. *Shōmonki: the Story of Masakado's Rebellion*. Tokyo: MN, Sophia University, 1986.
Rambelli, Fabio. *Buddhist Materiality: A Cultural History of Objects in Japanese Buddhism*. Stanford: Stanford UP, 2007.
Reader, Ian and George J. Tanabe, Jr. *Practically Religious: Worldly Benefits and the Common Religion of Japan*. Honolulu: U of Hawai'i Press, 1998.
Redesdale, Algernon. *Tales from Old Japan*. London: Macmillan & C., Ltd., 1928.
Reider, Noriko T. "Animating Objects: *Tsukumogami ki* and the Medieval Illustration of Shingon Truth." *Japanese Journal of Religious Studies* 36. 2 (2009): 232–257.
———. "*Ōeyama Shuten Dōji*: A Voice of Other and Carnivalesque." *Japanese Studies* 28. 3 (2008): 383–94.
———. "*Onmyōji*: Sex, Pathos, and Grotesquery in Yumemakura Baku's *Oni*." *Asian Folklore Studies* 66. 1 (2007): 107–124.
———. "Shuten dōji: Drunken Demon." *Asian Folklore Studies* 64. 2 (2005): 207–231.
———. "Shutendōji: *Oni* with a Righteous Tongue," *Estudos de Literatura Oral* 7–8 (2001–2002): 305–320.
———. "*Spirited Away*: Film of the Fantastic and Evolving Japanese Folk Symbols." *Film Criticism* 29. 3 (Spring 2005): 4–27.
———. *Tales of the Supernatural in Early Modern Japan: Kaidan, Akinari, Ugetsu monogatari*. New York: The Edwin Mellen Press, 2002.
———. "Transformation of *Oni*: From the Frightening and Diabolic to the Sexy and Cute." *Asian Folklore Studies* 62. 1 (2003): 133–157.
———. "Yamauba: Representation of the Japanese Mountain Witch in the Muromachi and Edo Periods." *International Journal of Asiatic Studies* 2. 2 (July 2005): 239–264.

Reichert, Jim. "Deviance and Social Darwinism in Edogawa Ranpo's Erotic-Grotesque Thriller *Kotō no oni*." *Journal of Japanese Studies* 27. 1 (Winter 2001): 113–41.
Richie, Donald. *Japanese Literature Reviewed*. New York: ICG Muse, Inc., 2003.
Robinson, Richard H. and Willard L. Johnson. *The Buddhist Religion*. 4th Edition. Belmont, Calif: Wadsworth Pub. Co., 1997.
Rosenstone, Robert A. *Mirror in the Shrine: American Encounters with Meiji Japan*. Massachusetts: Harvard UP, 1988.
Rubin, Jay. "The Art of the Flower of Mumbo Jumbo." *HJAS* 53. 2 (1993): 513–541.Ruch, Barbara. "Medieval Jongleurs and the Making of a National Literature." *Japan in the Muromachi Age*. Ed. John W. Hall and Toyoda Takeshi. Berkeley: U of California Press, 1977. 279–309.
———. *Mō hitotsu no chūseizō: bikuni, otogi-zōshi, raisei*. Kyoto: Shibunkaku, 1991.
———. *Zaigai nara-ehon*. Tokyo: Kadokawa Shoten, 1981.
Sadler, A. L. "The Heike Monogatari." *Transactions of the Asiatic Society of Japan* 46.2 (1918): 1-278; 49.1 (1921): 1-354.
Sadler, A. W. "The Spirit-Captives of Japan's North Country: Nineteenth Century Narratives of the *Kamikakushi*." *Asian Folklore Studies* 46 (1987): 217–226.
Saigyō. *Senjūshō*. Ed. Nishio Kōichi. Tokyo: Iwanami Shoten, 1970.
Saitō Mikihiro, ed. "Shuten Dōji kuruwa no hinagata." Vol. 2 of *Edo no ehon: shoki kusazōshi shūsei*. Ed. Koike Masatane. Tokyo: Kokusho Kankōkai, 1987. 58–71.
Saitō Ryōichi et al., eds. *Roman arubamu: Sen to Chihiro no kamikakushi*. Tokyo: Tokuma Shoten, 2001.
Sakakibara Satoru. *Edo no e o tanoshimu: shikaku no torikku*. Tokyo: Iwanami Shoten, 2003.
———. "*Ōeyama ekotoba* shōsai." *Tsuchigumo sōshi, Tengu sōshi, Ōeyama ekotoba*. Ed. Komatsu Shigemi, Ueno Kenji, Sakakibara, and Shimatani Hiroyuki. Vol. 19 of *Zoku nihon emaki taisei*. Tokyo: Chūō Kōronsha, 1984. 144–60.
———. "Suntory bijutsukan-bon 'Shuten Dōji emaki' o megutte." *Kokka* 107(1983): 7–26; 1077 (1983): 33–56.
Sakakura Atsuyoshi et al., eds. *Taketori monogatari, Ise monogatari, Yamato monogatari*. Vol. 9 of *NKBT*. Tokyo: Iwanami Shoten, 1957.
Sakamoto Tarō, Ienaga Saburō, Inoue Mitsusada and Ōno Susumu, eds., *Nihonshoki* I and II. Vols. 67 and 68 of *NKBT*. Tokyo: Iwanami Shoten, 1967 and 1965.
Sakurai Tokutarō, Hagiwara Tatsuo and Miyata Noboru, eds. "Kitano tenjin engi." *Jisha engi*. Vol. 20 of *NST*. Tokyo: Iwanami Shoten, 1975. 141–68.
Sanari Kentarō. *Yōkyoku taikan*. 7 vols. Tokyo: Meiji Shoin, 1963–64.
San'yūtei Enchō. "Shinkei Kasanegafuchi." *Rakugo, kaidanshū*. Ed. Nobuhiro Shinji. Vol. 6 of *SNKBT*. Tokyo: Iwanami Shoten, 2006. 1–395.
Sasama Yoshihiko. *Roman no kaidan: umi to yama no rajo*. Tokyo: Yūzankaku, 1994.
Satake Akihiro. *Shuten Dōji ibun*. Tokyo: Heibonsha, 1977.
———. "Yasaburō densetsu." *Kokugo kokubun* 29. 9 (1960): 16–27.
Satō Kenzō and Haruta Akira, eds. *Yashiro-bon Heike monogatari*. Tokyo: Ōfūsha, 1973.
Satō Tadao. "Akira Kurosawa Talks about Throne of Blood." In *Perspectives on Akira Kurosawa*, James Goodwin, ed. 51-53. New York: G.K. Hall & Co., 1994.
Sawa Shisei. *Oni no daijiten: yōkai, ōken, sei no kaidoku*. 3 vols. Tokyo: Sairyūsha, 1998.
———. *Oni no nihonshi*. Tokyo: Sairyūsha, 1990.
Schilling, Mark. *The Encyclopedia of Japanese Pop Culture*. New York: Weatherhill, 1997.
Schodt, Frederik L. *Dreamland Japan: Writings on Modern Manga*. Berkeley: Stone Bridge Press, 1996.

Segawa Jokō. *Shitennō Ōeyama-iri.* In *Kinsei-hen.* Ed. Takano Tatsuyuki. Vol. 10 of *Nihon kayō shūsei.* Tokyo: Shunjū-sha, 1929. 326–34.
Seimei jinja, ed. *Abe no Seimei-kō.* Tokyo: Kōdansha, 2002.
Seki Keigo, ed. *Folktales of Japan.* Trans. Robert J. Adams. Chicago: University of Chicago Press, 1963.
———, ed. *Nihon no mukashibanashi.* 3 vols. Tokyo: Iwanami Shoten, 1956–57. Rpt. Iwanami Shoten, 1981–82.
———. "Types of Japanese Folktales." *Asian Folklore Studies* 25. 2 (1966): 1–220.
Sekiyama Kazuo. *Sekkyō no rekishiteki kenkyū.* Kyoto: Hōzōkan, 1973.
Senjūshō Kenkyūkai, ed. *Senjūshō zenchūshaku.* Tokyo: Kasama Shoin, 2003.
Shibusawa Tatsuhiko. "Mittsu no dokuro." Ed. Yumemakura Baku. *Shichinin no Abe no Seimei.* Tokyo: Bungei Shunjū, 2001. 173–95.
———. "Tsukumogami." *Shikō no monshōgaku.* Tokyo: Kawade Shobō Shinsha, 1977. 95–101.
Shimada Shūjirō, ed. *Tenjin engi emaki, Hachiman engi, Amewakahiko sōshi, Nezumi nosōshi, Bakemono sōshi* and *Utatane sōshi.* Bekkan 2 of *Shinshū nihon emakimono zenshū.* Ed. Tanaka Ichimatsu. Tokyo: Kadokawa Shoten, 1981.
Shimazaki, Chifumi. *Troubled Souls from Japanese Noh Plays of the Fourth Group.* New York: Cornell U East Asia Program, 1998.
Shimazaki Tōson. *Hakai.* Tokyo: Shinchōsha, 1987.
Shimizu, Christine. "Kintaro to Yamauba." Vol. 7 of *Ukiyo-e Masterpieces in European Collections.* Ed. Narazaki, Muneshige et al. Tokyo: Kodansha, 1990. 231.
Shimizu Isao. "Kindai manga no seiritsu to sono imisurumono." *Kindai manga o tsukuriageta Kiyochika, Rakuten to 10-nin no fūshi gaka ten.* Tokyo: Ukiyoe Ōta Kinen Bijutsukan, 1984.
———. *Taiheiyō sensō ki no manga.* Tokyo: Bijutsu dōjinsha, 1970.
Shimo Yoshiko. *Ryūseimei—anata no jinsei jōrei shimasu.* Tokyo: Jitsugyō no nihonsha, 2002.
———. *Shimo Yoshiko no Ryūseimei fukuunjutsu: daikaiun supesharu gō.* Tokyo: Jitsugyō no nihonsha, 2007.
Shirane, Haruo. *The Bridge of Dreams: a Poetics of Tale of Genji.* Stanford: Stanford UP, 1987.
Siebers, Tobin. "Introduction: What Does Postmodernism Want? Utopia." *Heterotopia: Postmodern Utopia and the Body Politic.* Ed. Tobin Siebers. Ann Arbor: The U of Michigan Press, 1994. 1–39.
Simmer-Brown, Judith. *Dakini's Warm Breath: the Feminine Principle in Tibetan Buddhism.* Boston: Random House, 2001.
Skord, Virginia Susan. *Tales of Tears and Laughter: Short Fiction of Medieval Japan.* Honolulu: U of Hawai'i Press, 1991.
Steven, Chigusa. "Hachikazuki." *MN* 32. 3 (1977): 303–331.
Stinnett, Robert B. *Day of Deceit: The Truth about FDR and Pear Harbor.* New York: The Free Press, 2000.
Stronach, Bruce. "Japanese Television." *Handbook of Japanese Popular Culture.* Ed. Richard Gid Powers and Hidetoshi Kato. New York: Greenwood Press, 1989. 127–65.
Sugawara no Takasue no musume. *Yowa no nezame.* Vol. 26 of *SNKBZ.* Ed. Suzuki Kazuo. Tokyo: Shōgakukan, 1996.
Sugiura Yukio. *Manga.* 11. 6 (1943): 6.
Suntory Museum, ed. *Suntory bijutsukan hyaku-sen.* Tokyo: Suntory museum, 1981.
Suwa Haruo. *Abe no Seimei densetsu.* Tokyo: Chikuma Shobō, 2000.

Suwa Haruo and Kawamura Minato. *Otozureru kamigami*. Tokyo: Yūzankaku, 1997.
Suzuki, Beatrice Lane, ed and trans. *Nōgaku: Japanese Nō Plays*. London: John Murray, 1932.
Suzuki Zenji. *Nihon no yūseigaku*. Tokyo: Sankyō Shuppan, 1983.
Tachibana Kenji and Katō Shizuko, eds. *Ōkagami*. Vol. 34 of *SNKBZ*. Tokyo: Shōgakukan, 1996.
Taira Yasuyori et al. *Hōbutsu shū, Kankyo no tomo, Hirasan kojin reitaku*. Vol. 40 of *SNKBT*. Ed. Hiroshi Koizumi. Tokyo: Iwanami Shoten, 1993.
Takada Mamoru, ed. *Edo kaidanshū*. 3 vols. Tokyo: Iwanami Shoten, 1989.
Takagi Ichinosuke, Ozawa Masao, Atsumi Kaoru, and Kindaichi Haruhiko, eds. *Heike Monogatari*. Vols. 32 and 33 of *NKBT*. Tokyo: Iwanami Shoten, 1959–60.
Takagi Tadashi. "Kekkon, rikon." *Edo e no shinshiten*. Ed. Takahashi Shūji and Tanaka Yūko. Tokyo: Shin shokan, 2006. 97–115.
———. "Marriage and Divorce in the Edo Period." *Japan Echo* 30. 5 (October 2003).
Takahashi Masaaki. *Shuten Dōji no tanjō: mō hitotsu no nihon bunka*. Tokyo: Chūō Kōronsha, 1992.
Takahashi Rumiko. *Inuyasha*. 56 vols. Tokyo: Shōgakukan, 1997–2009.
———. *Inu Yasha*. 48 vols. Adapt. Gerald Jones and trans. Mari Morimoto. California: VIZ, LLC, 2003–2010.
———. *Urusei Yatsura*. Tokyo: Shōgakukan, 1998–1999.
Takasaki Masahide. *Kintarō tanjō tan*. Vol. 7 of *Takasaki Masahide chosakushū*. Tokyo: Ōfūsha, 1971.
Takeda Seichō and Anzai Atsuko, ed. *Tochigi no densetsu*. Vol. 44 of *Nihon no densetsu*. Tokyo: Kadokawa Shoten, 1980.
Takeuchi, Melinda. "Kuniyoshi's Minamoto Raiko and the Earth Spider: Demon and Protest in Late Tokugawa Japan." *Ars Orientalis* 17 (1987): 5–38.
Tanaka Takako. *Abe no Seimei no issen'nen: Seimei genshō o yomu*. Tokyo: Kōdansha, 2003.
———. *Ayakashi kō: fushigi no chūsei e*. Tokyo: Heibonsha, 2004.
———. *Gehō to aihō no chūsei*. Tokyo: Sunagoya Shobō, 1993.
———. *Hyakki yakō no mieru toshi*. Tokyo: Shin'yōsha, 1994.
———. "Uji no hōzō." *Denshō bungaku kenkyū* 36 (1989): 68–81.
———. *Zusetsu hyakki yagyō emaki o yomu*. Tokyo: Kawade Shobō Shinsha, 1999.
Tanba Tsuneo. *Ukiyo-e: Edo kara Hakone made*. Tokyo: Asahi Shinbunsha, 1963.
Tanigawa Ken'ichi. *Ma no keifu*. Tokyo: Kinokuniya Shoten, 1971.
———. "Seidō no kami no sokuseki." Vol. 5 of *Tanigawa Ken'ichi chosaku-shū*. Tokyo: San'ichi Shobō, 1985. 5–288.
Terashima Ryōan. *Wakan sansai zue*. Vol. 6. Ed. Shimada Isao, Takeshima Atsuo, and Higuchi Motomi. Tokyo: Heibon sha, 1987.
Thomas. Roger K. "Sound and Sense: Chōka Theory and Nativist Philology in Early Modern Japan and Beyond." *Early Modern Japan: An Interdisciplinary Journal* 16 (2008): 4-32.
———. *The Way of Shikishima*. Lanham: UP of America, 2007.
Thompson, Rosemarie Garland. "Introduction: From Wonder to Error—A Genealogy of Freak Discourse in Modernity." *Freakery: Cultural Spectacles of the Extraordinary Body*. Ed. Rosemarie Garland Thompson. New York: New York UP, 1996. 1–22.
Thurston, Robert W. *Witch, Wicce, Mother Goose: The Rise and Fall of the Witch Hunts in Europe and North America*. New York: Pearson Education, 2001.
Tōbu bijutsukan et al. eds. *Ukiyoe no kodomotachi*. Tokyo: Tōbu bijutsukan, 1994.
Todorov, Tzvetan. *The Fantastic: A Structural Approach to a Literary Genre*. Ithaca: Cornell UP, 1973.
Toelken, Barre. *The Dynamics of Folklore*. Utah: Utah State UP, 1996.

Tokuda Kazuo, ed. *Otogizōshi jiten*. Tokyo: Tokyo-dō, 2002.
———. *Otogizōshi kenkyū*. Tokyo: Miyai Shoten, 1988.
Torii Fumiko. *Dentō to geinō: kojōruri sekai no tenkai*. Tokyo: Musashino Shoin, 1993.
———. *Kintarō no tanjō*. Tokyo: Bensei Shuppan, 2002.
———. "Kojōruri ni okeru yōkai henge taiji mono." *Jissen joshidaigaku kiyō* 7 (March 1962): 23–38.
"Torii tachi gomi tōki yamu." *Mainichi shinbun* 24 Jan. 2003, evening ed.: 10.
Toriyama Sekien. "Gazu hyakki yagyō." *Toriyama Sekien gazu*. Ed. Inada Atsunobu. *Hyakki yagyō*. Tokyo: Kokusho Kankōkai, 1992. 19–96.
Tosa Mitsunobu. *Hyakki yagyō-emaki*. In *Nōe Hōshi ekotoba, Fukutomi sōshi, Hyakki yagyō emaki*. Ed. Komatsu Shigemi, Kanazawa Hiroshi, and Kanzaki Mitsuharu. Tokyo: Chūō Kōronsha, 1993.
Tsuchihashi Yutaka. *Nihongo ni saguru kodai shinkō: fetishizumu kara shintō made*. Tokyo: Chūō Kōronsha, 1990.
Tsuda Sōkichi. *Nihon koten no kenkyū*. Vol. 1 of *Tsuda Sōkichi zenshū*. Tokyo: Iwanami Shoten, 1963.
Tsuruya Nanboku, "Hakone ashigarayama no ba." *Modoribashi sena ni go-hiiki*. Kokuritsu gekijō kabuki kōen jōen daihon. Dir. Toshikura Kōichi. Tokyo: Kokuritsu gekijō, 1975. 59–75.
———. *Tōkaidō Yotsuya kaidan*. Ed. Gunji Masakatsu. Tokyo: Shinchōsha, 1981.
Tyler, Royall. *Granny Mountains: A Cycle of Nō Plays*. Ithaca: Cornell UP, 1978.
———. *Japanese Tales*. New York: Pantheon Books, 1987.
Ueda Akinari. *Tales of Moonlight and Rain*. Trans. Anthony H. Chambers. New York: Columbia UP, 2007.
———. *Tales of the Spring Rain*. Trans. Barry Jackman. Tokyo: U. of Tokyo P., 1975.
Ueda Nobumichi. Kaisetsu. *Nihon mukashibanashi*. Iwaya Sazanami. Ed. Ueda. Tokyo: Heibonsha [Tōyō bunko], 2001. 467–86.
Uegaki Setsuya, ed. *Fudoki*. Vol. 5 of *SNKBZ*. Tokyo: Shōgakukan, 1997.
Uekusa Nobukazu, ed. *"Sen to Chihiro no kamikakushi" o yomu 40 no me*. Tokyo: Kinema Jumpōsha, 2001.
Ury Marian, tr. *Tales of Times Now Past*. Ann Arbor: Center For Japanese Studies the U of Michigan, 1979.
Usuda Jingorō. *Usuda Jingorō chosakushū*. Vol. 5. Tokyo: Ōfūsha, 1995.
Uzuki Hiroshi. *Ugetsu monogatari hyōshaku*. Nihon koten hyōshaku, zenchūshaku sōsho. Tokyo: Kadokawa Shoten, 1969.
Viswanathan, Meera. "In Pursuit of the Yamamba: The Question of Female Resistance." *The Woman's Hand: Gender and Theory in Japanese Women's Writing*. Ed. Paul Gordon Schalow and Janet A. Walker. Stanford: Stanford UP, 1995. 239–61.
Vukov, Elaine. "Kamishibai, Japanese Storytelling: The Return of An Imaginative Art." *Education About Asia* 2. 1 (Spring 1997): 39–41.
Wakamori Tarō. *Kami to hotoke no aida*. Tokyo: Kōbundō, 1975.
Wakao Itsuo. *Oni densetsu no kenkyū: kinkōshi no shiten kara*. Tokyo: Yamato Shobō, 1981.
Watanabe Eri. "Seiai to tōsō—Nakagami kenji Kumano shū 'Chūtō no sakura' 'Oni no hanashi'." *Nihon kindai bungaku*. 72 (2005): 132–147.
Watanabe Shōgo, ed. *Nihon densetsu taikei*. Vol. 7. Tokyo: Mizūmi Shobō, 1982.
Watanabe Tsunaya and Nishio Kōichi, eds. *Uji shūi monogatari*. Vol. 27 of *NKBT*. Tokyo: Iwanami Shoten, 1960.
Watson, Burton, trans. *The Complete Works of Chuang Tzu*. New York: Columbia UP, 1968.
———, trans. *The Tales of the Heike*. New York: Columbia UP, 2006.

Watson, Michael, ed. *List of noh plays in alphabetical order of the Japanese titles*. 2009. Web.
———, ed. *Otogizōshi: Texts, Translations and Studies with additional information about Muromachi tales*. 2006. Web.
Weatherby, Meredith. "The Maple Viewing." *Three Japanese Plays from the Traditional Theatre*. Ed. Ernst, Earle. London: Oxford UP, 1959. 17–33.
Wilson, William R. *Hōgen monogatari: Tale of the Disorder in Hōgen*. Tokyo: Sophia U, 1971.
Wolfgram, Juliann. "Oni: the Japanese Demon." *Japanese Ghosts & Demons: Art of the Supernatural*. Ed. Stephen Addiss. New York: George Braziller, Inc., 1985. 91–101.
Yamada Yoshio, Yamada Tadao, Yamada Hideo, and Yamada Toshio, eds. *Konjaku monogatarishū*. Vol. 25 of *NKBT*. Tokyo: Iwanami Shoten, 1961.
Yamagata Bantō. "Yume no shiro." Ed. Mizuta Norihisa and Arisaka Takamichi. *Tominaga Nakamoto, Yamagata Bantō*. Vol. 43 of *NST*. Tokyo: Iwanami Shoten, 1973. 141–642.
Yamaguchi Takeshi. "Ugetsu monogatari hen'ei." *Kokugo kokubun* 1 (October 1931): 40–60.
Yamaguchi Yoshinori and Kōnoshi Takamitsu, eds. *Kojiki*. Vol. 1 of *SNKBZ*. Tokyo: Shōgakukan, 1997.
Yamamoto Yoshiko. *Namahage: A Festival in the Northeast of Japan*. Philadelphia: Institute for the Study of Human Issues, 1978.
Yamanaka Yutaka. *Eiga monogatari*. 3 vols. Vols. 31–33 of *SNKBZ*. Tokyo: Shōgakukan, 1995–98.
Yamaoka Genrin. "Kokin hyakumonogatari hyōban." *Zoku hyakumonogatari kaidan shūsei*. Ed. Tachikawa Kiyoshi. Vol. 27 of *Sōsho Edo bunko*. Tokyo: Tosho Kankōkai, 1993. 5–77.
Yamashita Kōmei. "Heike monogatari." *Nihon koten bungaku daijiten*. Vol. 15. Tokyo: Iwanami Shoten, 1984. 390–98.
Yan Xiaomei. "Saiyūki to Akinari no bungyō." *Edo bungaku* (October 1992): 110–117.
Yanagita Kunio. *Nihon mukashibanashi meii*. 2nd ed. Tokyo: Nihon hōsōkyōkai Shuppan, 1971.
———. *Shinpen Yanagita Kunio-shū*. 12 vols. Tokyo: Chikuma Shobō, 1978–79.
———. "Yama no jinsei." In vol. 1 of *Shinpen Yanagita Kunio-shū*. Tokyo: Chikuma Shobō, 1978.
———. "Yōkai dangi." Vol. 4 of *Teihon Yanagita Kunio-shū*. Tokyo: Chikuma Shobō, 1968. 285–438.
Yanase Kiyoshi, Yashiro Kazuo, Matsubayashi Yasuaki, Shida Itaru, and Inui Yoshihisa, eds. *Shōmonki, Mutsuwa ki, Hōgen monogatari, Heiji monogatari*. Vol. 41 of *SNKBZ*. Tokyo: Shōgakukan, 2002.
Yang, Xiaojie. *Oni no iru kōkei: Haseo sōshi ni miru chūsei*. Tokyo: Kadokawa Shoten, 2002.
Yōkai emaki. Mainichi shinbunsha, ed. Tokyo: Mainichi Shinbunsha, 1978.
Yokomichi Mario and Omote Akira, eds. *Yōkyoku shū*. Vol. 41 of *NKBT*. Tokyo: Iwanami Shoten, 1963.
Yokoyama Shigeru ed. *Kojōruri shōhon shū*. 5 vols. Tokyo: Kadokawa Shoten, 1964–66.
Yokoyama Shigeru and Matsumoto Ryūshin, eds. *Muromachi jidai monogatari taisei*. 15 vols. Tokyo: Kadokawa Shoten, 1973–85.
Yokoyama Yasuko. *Edo Tokyo no kaidan bunka no seiritsu to hensen—19 seiki o chūshin ni*. Tokyo: Kazama Shobō, 1997.
Yoshida Atsuhiko. *Mukashibanashi no kōkogaku*. Tokyo: Chūō Kōronsha, 1992.
———. *Yōkai to bijo no shinwagaku*. Tokyo: Meicho Kankōkai, 1989.

Yu, Alvin, ed. *The Art of Miyazaki's Spirited Away*. San Francisco: Viz Communication Inc., 2002.
Yumemakura Baku. *Onmyōji*. Tokyo: Bungei Shunjū, 1991.
———, ed. *Onmyōji dokuhon*. Tokyo: Bungei Shunjū, 2003.
———. *Onmyōji: hiten no maki*. Tokyo: Bungei Shunjū, 1998.
———. *Onmyōji: hōō no maki*. Tokyo: Bungei Shunjū, 2002.
———. *Onmyōji: namanari-hime*. Tokyo: Bungei Shunjū, 2003.
———. *Onmyōji: ryūteki no maki*. Tokyo: Bungei Shunjū, 2005.
———, ed. *Shichinin no Abe no Seimei*. Tokyo: Bungei Shunjū, 2001.
———. *Onmyōji: Takiyasha-hime*. 2 Vols. Tokyo: Bungei Shunjū, 2005.
———. *Onmyōji: tsukumogami no maki*. Tokyo: Bungei Shunjū, 2000.
Zimmerman, Eve. "In the Trap of Words: Nakagami Kenji and the Making of Degenerate Fictions." *Ōe and Beyond*. Ed. Stephen Snyder and Philip Garbriel. Honolulu: U of Hawai'i Press, 1999. 130–52.
Zolbrod, Leon M. *Ugetsu monogatari: Tales of Moonlight and Rain*. Vancouver: U of British Columbia Press, 1974.
Zuikei Shūhō. *Dainihon kokiroku: Gaun nikkenroku*. Ed. Tokyo daigaku shiryō hensanjo. Tokyo: Iwanami Shoten, 1961.

Index

A

abandoned women: lingering affection of, 58–60; oni, transformation into, 53–54, 55, 58–60, 137–38

Abe Masamichi, 164

Abe no Seimei (921?–1005): abandoned woman's husband protected by, 58–59; dog's supernatural powers noted by, 164, 164n21; Katō connection to, 117; oni, dialogs on, 138; as *onmyódo* practitioner, 13; as pop culture icon, 113, 139–40, 141, 142; in postwar fiction, 131, 132, 133, 134–35; Shuten Dōji abductions and cannibalism discovered by, 30–31, 186, 186n8; as Tsuchimikado clan founder, 116

Agi Bridge in Ōmi, oni at, 16, 125–26

Akimoto Kichirō, 21, 23

Akira/Devilman (fictional character), 147–48, 149, 169

Alice in Wonderland, 159

Amano Fumio, 46

Amaterasu (deity): deities, violently fought by, 19, 19n36; evil gods defined by, 5, 5n7

Ancient Matters, xx, 4

Anesaki Masaharu, 2, 10

anime: oni in, 144; overview of, 156–57, 157n12

apocalypse, Japanese *versus* Judeo-Christian view of, 145

apocalyptic fiction, 145–46

Arai Hakuseki (1657–1725), 90–91

Aramata Hiroshi, 112–19

aratama (malign spiritual entities), 9–10

Armageddon, 147–48, 169

Asanari (Fujiwara no Asanari, 917–974) as fictional oni, 122, 123, 124, 130

atomic bomb, 154

Aunt Picot (fictional character), 161, 161n16

B

Baba Akiko, 184

Baba Yaga (Russian witch), 61

babies born with teeth, beliefs and practices concerning, 21

bakemono: literary depiction of, 96; term, 95, 95n4

Bakhtin, Mikhail, 31, 32, 37, 38, 39

bandits, oni as, 48–49

Burakumin, discrimination against, 122

Bargen, Doris, 83

Bataan Death March, 110

beans, scattering (New Year's Eve custom), 25

Benkei (1155–1189), 72

Biblical literature, stories based on, 147–48

Blade Runner (1982), 146

Bō (fictional baby), 159

Book of Revelation, apocalyptic narrative in, 145, 145n3

Buddha, attributes of, 185, 185n6

Buddhism: death, beliefs and practices concerning, 141, 175; fallen world, saving in, 145; non-dualism in, 67, 172; oni in, xviii, 2, 3, 10–13, 177; rebirth in, 74

Buddhist deities and Shinto priests, 13

Buddhist hell: cannibalism in, 38–39; prison guards of, 7, 7n12, 11; sinners saved from, 201; supernatural creatures residing in, 10

Buddhist priests: oni disguised as, 93–94; villains, perceived as, 39

C

cannibalism: evil gods' practice of, 6; female oni practice of, xxiii, 55, 137, 156, 159; oni practice of, xix, xxii, 10, 14–16, 23, 27, 37, 40, 94, 115, 121, 135, 184. *See also* Shuten Dōji (Drunken Demon): cannibalism practiced by; *yamauba* (mountain ogress): as cannibal

carnivalesque (concept): folk culture swallowed into, 50; marginalization and otherness in, 42–43, 45, 46–47, 48, 178, 179; mother's milk and lifeblood in, 93; oni as literary figures in, 52; oni-warrior battle and, 51; Shuten Dōji story parallels to, 31–32, 37–42, 45

Caucasian man, Shuten Dōji as, 49
censorship, 70, 70n20, 85, 107
central authority: earth spiders defying, 166, 168; moral dilemmas from perspective of, 52; narrative prose concerning, 47–48; oni in opposition to, 30–31, 184
Chihiro (film character), 159, 161, 168
Chikamatsu Monzaemon (1653–1724): Shuten Dōji, de-demonization of, 92, 96–97; works of, 76–84, 85, 95, 157
Child Handed from Heaven, 151–55
children's literature, oni in, 108–10, 111, 170–73
Chinese literature, oni substance through, 177
Chinese tradition, oni in, xix, 2, 3, 4–10, 170
Chronicle of Pre-Grand Pacification (Zentaiheiki), 75, 76, 78
class boundaries, carnivalesque violations of, 31
Collection of Tales from Uji (ca. 13th c.), 116, 164
commercialization of oni: in current culture, 120, 139–40, 182, 183–84; overview of, xxi; sex, violence and, 119, 143; in tourism, xxv–xxvi; in urban culture, xxiv, 90, 95–103
Craig, Timothy J., 157
creation myth, Japanese, oni in, 3–4
criminals as "other" category, 45
customs, labeling of people with different, 21
cyberspace, oni in, 145, 163

D
Daijō-itokuten (Heavenly Great Merits): Sugawara Michizane transformation into, 12–13; as thunder god, 23–24
Daikokuten (Great Black Deity), 26–28
Dainkoku shiyajarai (female oni), 153, 155
Dakini, 27
Dante Alighieri, 147, 148
datsueba, 68–69, 75
daughter of Ikeda Kunitaka: abduction of, 185–86, 199; rescue and return of, 202–3
death: in Japanese tradition, 140–41; oni, becoming after, 4–5, 5n4, 19, 142, 174, 175, 176
Debiruman (Devilman), 146–51, 169, 182
deceit against oni, Shuten Dōji as target of, xxi, 43, 50
de-demonized oni, 90, 92–95, 171–72
deities: battles against, 19, 19n36; categories of, 3; disasters caused by, 45, 46n25; emperors as, 104; oni becoming, 115; warriors compared to, 51–52

Delacroix, Eugène, 147
demonic people, 98–103
demonic (Western term), 1
demon plays, 61, 61n3, 67–68
demons: human side of, 67–68; human transformation into, 150
dengaku (dance form), 40–42
dengaku troupe, oni as, 42
Dengyō Daishi, Priest (d. 822), 38, 39, 194
detective stories, oni in, 100–103
deviant, explorations of, 100
deviant individuals, eugenics as response to, 101
devil, Judeo-Christian, oni compared to, 146, 148, 169
Devilman, 146–51, 169, 182
Devilman (fictional character), 147–48, 149, 169
difference, attitudes toward those displaying, 21, 23
disasters, demon role in causing or preventing, 45, 46n25
discrimination, oni as objects of, 121
diseased, disenfranchisement of, 49
disenfranchised persons, oni as representatives of, xix, 52, 181
distant strangers as "other" category, 45
Divine Comedy (Dante), 147, 148
divorce, 83–84
dogs, supernatural powers of, 163–65
Dōjōji, 127–28, 127n16
doomed souls, affinity for, 140
Dower, John, 110
dragon, red, as thunder god symbol, 75
Dreams (film), 154–55

E
earth spiders: conquest of, 98; in films, 167–69; in manga, 165–67; as oni variant, 55, 165–67
East Japan Railway Company, oni images used by, xxv–xxvi, 183
Edogawa Ranpo (1894–1965), 100–101
Edo period: Shuten Dōji stories during, 69; supernatural, beliefs concerning, xxiv, 90–92, 95–96, 98, 104; women's status during, 82–83; *yamauba*, depiction of, 70
emperors: human status of, 112, 134, 134n31; oni, battles against, 18–20, 118; supernatural status of, 104
En no gyōja (ca. 7th-8th century), 20–21, 192
Enryaku-ji, founding of, 39, 39n15

erotic-grotesque-nonsense culture, oni in, 100–103
ethnic boom, 122
ethnic groups or races, non-Japanese: attitudes toward people of, 21, 23; as oni, 6, 181
eugenics, 101
evil people and oni compared, 99, 100
ex-convicts as "other" category, 45

F
famine, oni responsible for, 43
Faust, 147
female oni: decree to subjugate, 58, 58n3; fierce nature of, 9; origins of, xx, 4, 139; overview of, xxiii–xxiv; in postwar fiction, 121, 124, 125, 126, 129–30, 131, 136–38, 155–58; private role of, 59, 180; revenge of, 53–60; sociopolitical spaces of, 53. *See also* Uji no hashihime (woman at a bridge); *yamauba* (mountain ogress); Yomotsu-shikome (ugly woman of the other world)
female outcasts, *yamauba* as, 66
female sexuality as oni ploy, 18, 40, 126
Figal, Gerald, 104, 106–7
films, oni in, 139, 144, 182
fire-breathing head (of *yamauba*), 79, 79n31
food: deities of, 27–28; *yamauba* association with, 63, 64, 65
foreign enemies as oni: overview of, 104–5; in World War II, xxiv, 107–13, 179
foreigners: Japanese attitude toward, 3; as "other" category, 45
foreigners as oni: in ancient times, 6; in postwar fiction, 134
foreign influences, selective adaptation to, 2
fortune, oni as agents of, 24–29, 172, 177, 180
fortunetellers and prognosticators, 141
Foucault, Michel, 118
Four Heavenly Guardians, 10, 31
friendship as oni story theme, 172
Fudō Akira/Devilman (fictional character), 147–48, 149, 169
Fujiwara clan, 123, 123n5
Fujiwara Michinaga (966–1027), 20, 46, 164, 164n21
Fujiwara no Asanari (917–974), as fictional oni, 122, 123, 124, 130
Fujiwara no Kaneie (929–990) in postwar fiction, 132, 133
Fujiwara no Koretada (924–972), 123
Fujiwara no Tameyoshi (fictional character), 136, 137, 141

Fujiwara no Tokihira, 12
Fujiwara no Yoshifusa (804–872), 19
Fujiwara Regency: as Heian imperial court center, 31, 31n3; oni viewpoints concerning, 124; *onmyōdō* practice under, 14; peak of, 20, 46; suppressed people under, 46; warrior class rise under, 50

G
games, oni in, 144
Gazu hyakki yagyō (painting), 97–98
gender boundaries, 31, 66. *See also* women: role and status of
gendered oni, sociopolitical space of, 53, 57–58
gender switching as oni trait, 40, 55–56, 57, 138
Genji monogatari, female oni in, 60
Genshichi (fictional tobacco seller), 77–78, 80–81, 83
ghosts, 162–63
giants, oni depicted as, 9, 200
Ginza city, fictional recreation of, 118–19
gods: evil, Chinese influence on concept of, 5–6, 5n7. *See also* deities
Goki (posterior demon), 20–21, 102
gokusotsu (Buddhist hell prison guards), 7, 7n12
Golden Splendor Sutra, 45, 46n25
goryō: Chinese influence on concept of, 5; origin and Buddhist influence on, 12–13
graphic novels (manga), 144, 163–67, 169
Greater East Asia Co-Prosperity Sphere, 111
Great Mother figure, 65, 154
Grimm Brothers fairy tales, witches in, 61, 65, 65n12
grudge: motherhood as source of, 153; oni-caused disasters stemming from, 45–46; realm of, 152
guests in community as "other" category, 45

H
Hakuenden (Story of White Monkey), 49, 49n29
Haku (film character), 168, 169
Hamada Hirosuke (1893–1973), 170–73, 175, 176
Hanayo no hime, 66, 68, 74, 102, 161
handicapped persons as "other" category, 45
Hankai (fictional character), 122, 123, 129–30
Hansel and Gretel witch, *yamauba* compared to, 61

harvest, dancing and music for good, 40
Haseo sōshi (Story of Ki no Haseo), 28–29
hats, oni association with, 25
Hazama (actor), birth of, 73, 73n27
heaven, oni in, 174
Heian imperial court, 30–31, 31n3
Heike monogatari (Tale of the Heike), 51–52. See also Swords Chapter of Tale of the Heike
hell: oni as prison guards of, 7, 7n12, 11; sinners saved from, 201; sinners terrified by oni in, 10, 24
heterotopia (defined), 118–19
hierarchical system in supernatural realm, 106
Hirai Yasumasa, 116, 117–18
Hirata Atsutane (1776–1843), 91
Hirohito, Emperor: in fiction, 116, 134, 134n31; human status, admission to, 112
Hōjō Takatoki (1303–1333), 41–42
honesty as oni trait: in folk tales, 28–29; in postwar fiction, 130; in Shuten Dōji stories, 43
horns, oni with and without, 7, 174–75
Hōshō (Fujiwara no Hōshō or Yasumasa, 957–1036): background of, 187, 187n15; entertained by *dengaku*, 40, 41; Mt. Oe, old woman at met by, 34; oni, statements concerning, 96–97; oni attempts at snaring, 40; Shuten Dóji defeated by, 31, 35
household objects: as oni, 10, 57; supernatural possession of, 57
humanization of oni: demon plays, 67–68; female oni, 67, 80; in postwar fiction, 142–43, 147, 149; Shuten Dōji, 92
human-oni sexual encounters, 122–23, 134–35
human organs, oni consumption of, 115
humans: demon resemblance to, 67–68; demons, transformation into, 150; oni as product of, 138, 177; oni compared to, xxi, 139; oni rebellion against, 146; *yamauba* resemblance to, 67–68

I
Ibaraki Dōji, 30, 200–201
Ibukiyama (Mt. Ibuki) version of Shuten Dōji story, 32–33
Ichijō, Emperor (r. 980–1011): death of, 47; regent of, 46; Shuten Dōji activities during reign of, 20, 38, 56; stories set during reign of, 30
identification with oni, xx–xxi, 45
Iemon (fictional samurai), 99, 102

Ieyoshi, Shogun, 98
Ikeda Kunitaka, daughter of, 185–86, 199, 202–3
Ikeda Yuriko, xxi–xxii
ikiryō, 123
Ikuhōmon'in, Princess (1076–1096), death of, 41, 41n20
imperial authority, weakening of, 52
Indian cannibalistic beings, Buddhist oni originating as, 10
Indian deities, possible oni origin through, xix
industrialization, dehumanizing effect of, 171
infidelity, stories warning against, 59
Inoue, Yasushi (1907–1992), 170, 173–76
Inoue Enryō (1858–1919), 106
InuYasha (dog-demon), 163–67, 169
invisibility: as oni attribute, 13, 25–26; wealth connected with, 25–26
Ise monogatari (Tales of Ise, 945 CE), 14–15
Ishibashi Gaha, 3, 107
Ishikuma Dōji (demon), 41, 41n18
Issun-bōshi (Little One-Inch), 26
Iwaya Sazanami (1870–1933), 109
Izagani (male creator of Japan), 4
Izanami (female creator of Japan), 4
Izawa Banryō (1668–1730), 73–74

J
Jackson, Rosemary, xix, 48
Japanese as oni, 110–11, 179
Japanese Empire, supernatural paradigm, collapse of, 112
Japanese Fairy Tales (1894–1896), 109
Japanese homogeneity, myth of, 122
Japanese imperialism, allegory for, 109–10, 111
jealous women, oni transformation of, 54–55n1
Jigoku sōshi, 7, 38, 39
Jimmu (Jinmu), Emperor, 166, 167, 185, 185n1
Jippensha Ikku, 96
Jūniten, 11

K
Kabat, Adam, 95, 96
Kabuki plays, 99–100
Kadokawa Gen'yoshi, 117
Kagome (fictional character), 163, 165
Kaibara Ekken (1630–1714), 48–49, 82
Kaidan-mono (ghost plays), 99–100
Kamaji (spider-like film character), 167–68, 169

Kamakura shogunate, 42
kami: definition of, 92; of fortune, 28; oni relationship to, 3, 12–13, 138, 139, 173, 179; *yōkai* transformation into, 24
Kamo no Yasunori (917–977), 117
Kanawa (Noh play): female oni in, 58–59, 60, 139; Onmyōji compared to, 133, 135–36
Kannon Bodhisattva, 33, 122, 186; as Great Mother, 65, 65n11
Kansei Reforms (1787–93), 85, 85n45
Kashiwabara Yasaburō, 33
Kashiwaba Sachiko, 161, 161n16
Katō Yasunori (fictional oni), 113, 114–15, 116, 117
Kawabata Yasunari, 124–25
Kawai Hayao, 65, 65n11
Kawatake Mokuami (1816–1893), 114, 114n11
Kazan, Emperor (968–1008), abdication of, 132, 133
Keikō, Emperor, 18–19
kibyōshi (yellow covers), *bakemono* depiction in, 96
Kinpira: appearance of, 72; as oni's child, 72; physical strength of, 71, 72, 74; as warrior, 70
Kinpira jōruri (literary genre), 70, 74, 78
Kintarō (super-child), 62, 69, 83, 84, 85–88, 86, 87, 89, 159, 160. *See also* Kintoki
Kintoki (Sakata no Kintoki, Raikō's lieutenant): birth and origin of, 71, 72, 73–74, 75–76, 78, 79, 80, 81, 160, 187, 187n14; oni encounters by, 58, 58n3; physical strength of, 72; shrine, visit to, 188; Shuten Dōji defeat, participation in, 62, 71; son of, 70; stories of, xxiii–xxiv, 73, 73n26
Kiri no mukō no fushigina machi (Mysterious Town beyond the Mist), 161, 161n16
Kitagawa Utamaro, 121
Kitajima Harunobu, 170–71
Kitakami City of Iwate Prefecture, 184
Kojiki (Ancient Matters), xx, 4, 19, 65, 166, 173
Kōbō Daishi (priest), 39, 164, 165, 187, 194
Kōda Rohan, 115
Kōeki zokusetsu ben (Refutation of Vulgar Legends for the Benefit of the Public), 73–74
Komatsu Kazuhiko: Aramata Hiroshi dealings with, 117; *kami*-oni paradigm proposed by, 24; on *kami*-oni relationship, 13; on *oni* (term), xix, 2, 13; other or "strangers,"

notion of, xx–xxi, 45; on *shikigami,* 14; Shuten Dōji story interpreted by, 47; supernatural of the dark side, works on, 113, 113n8; *yamauba* studied by, 181; *yōkai* defined by, 163
Komochi Yamauba (Mountain Ogress with a Child), 76–84, 85, 157
Kondō Yoshihiro, 2
Kongōbu-ji, founding of, 39, 39n14
Konjaku monogatarishū (Tales of Times Now Past), 121, 130–31, 133–34
Konkōmyō saishōō kyō (Golden Splendor Sutra), 45, 46n25
Koretada (Fujiwara no Koretada, 924–972), 123
Kotō no Oni (Oni of a Solitary Island), 100–3
Kozuna (half-oni), 149, 149n7
Kūkai. *See* Kōbō Daishi
Kumasegawa Kyōko: on oni-warrior classification together, 51
Kunitaka, daughter of, 185–86, 199, 202–3
kunitsukami (deities of the land), downfall of, 67
Kurosawa, Akira, 154–55
Kyoto, *dengaku* fever in, 41, 41n20

L
lightning: oni associated with, 12, 13, 23–24, 51, 177, 184; *yamauba* related to, 76
Little One-Inch (folk hero), 26
local deities, Buddhist sect beliefs and practices concerning, 46, 46n26
Lum (fictional ogress), 155, 156–58, 182
"Lust of the White Serpent," 127–28, 131

M
Mahāvairocana, 27
maidens of Capital of Heian, kidnapping and consumption of, xix
Maitreya Buddha, 145
mallet, wish-granting: oni association of, 25, 28; wealth associated with, 26–27, 28
Manago (fictional serpent), 126, 128
manga, 144, 163–67, 169
Manga (cartoon magazine), 107–8
Maple Leaf Viewing, 18
mappō (Buddhist doctrine), 145
marebito, xix, 3, 25, 29
marginalized other: in carnivalesque, 42–43; female oni as, 57–58, 62, 137, 138, 181; moral dilemmas from perspective of, 52; oni as, xx–xxi, 18, 103, 133, 134, 146, 149,

178–79; Shuten Dōji (Drunken Demon) as, 31; *yamauba* as, 89. *See also* other, oni as
marital relationships, discord of, 138–39
Matsudaira Sadanobu, 85, 85n45
Matsui Toshiaki, 76
Medvedev, Pavel, 88
Meiji, Emperor, 105, 106
Meiji Restoration/period: ideal Japanese boy during, 109; supernatural beliefs under, 91, 106; Western influences during, 104
men and women, relations between, 138–39
Mephistopheles, 147
metal workers, oni as, 49
Miki (fictional character), 146, 147, 148
Minamoto no Hiromasa (918–?): oni, dialogs on, 138; in postwar fiction, 131, 134, 137
minority groups, discrimination against, 122
Miraculous Stories from the Japanese Buddhist Tradition (ca. 823), 15
Mishima Yukio, 124–25
Miyata Noboru, 181
Miyazaki Hayao, films by, 158–62
Miyoshi no Kiyotsura (847–918), 29
Mizuta Noriko, 66, 76, 83
modernization, dehumanizing effect of, 171
"Modoribashi" (dance piece), 114, 114n11
Momijigari (Maple Leaf Viewing), 18
"Momotarō" (Peach Boy) (folktale), 108–10, 111, 112
mono: concept, Chinese influence on, 5; oni compared to, 5, 5n5; oni relationship to, 6, 6n10
mononoke (evil spirits), 6–7, 11–12
monster-conquering stories, 30, 30n1
Montoku, Emperor, 19, 20n39
morals, decline in, 99
Moroboshi Ataru (fictional boy), 156
motherhood as oni story theme, 62, 153–54
Motoori Norinaga, 3
mountaineering ascetics, 47–48n28
Mountain Ogress with a Child, 76–84, 85, 157
Mouse's Palace, 158
Mt. Asakura, 25, 25n44
Mt. Ashigara, 71, 76
Mt. Hiei, 46
Mt. Ibuki, 33
Mt. Katsuragi, holy man of, 19–20, 102
Mt. Ōe: in modern times, 183; old woman at, 34, 37, 38; oni as bandits on, 48; oni fortress at, 33, 34
multiculturalism, 122

Muraoka no Masatoki (diviner), 186
Mysterious Town beyond the Mist, 161

N
Nagai Gō, works of, 146–55, 182
Nagasawa Rosetsu (1754–1799), 88, 160
Naita Akaoni (Red Oni Who Cried), 170–73, 176
Nakagami Kenji, 120, 121–31
Nakamura Hiroaki, 91
Namanarihime (2003), 137
namanari mask, 136
Nanking, atrocities of, 1937, 110, 179
Napier, Susan, 144, 145, 157
Naraku (fictional character), 163, 165, 166
Narutaki Jun'ichi (fictional character), 115, 118–19
natural disasters, oni responsible for, 24, 43, 45, 177, 178
natural history, supernatural beliefs influenced by, 97, 97n7
natural phenomena, oni arising from fear of, 51
New Year's Eve, lunar, customs observed on, 25
"Nezumi no goten" (Mouse's Palace), 158
Nihongi (Nihonshoki), 5, 19, 21, 65, 168
Nihon mukashibanashi (Japanese Fairy Tales, 1894–1896), 109
Nihon Ryōiki (Miraculous Stories from the Japanese Buddhist Tradition, ca. 823), 15
Nihon sandai jitsuroku (True Records of Three Generations in Japan, 901), 15–16
Noh plays, 61, 61n3, 67–68. *See also* titles of specific plays
non-dualism, 67, 172
nuclear technology dangers, films depicting, 154–55

O
Ōemachi, Kyoto, 183
Ōe Mountains, 49
Ōeyama ekotoba (Picture Scroll of Mt. Ōe, early 14th c.), 33, 41, 56
Ōeyama (Mt. Ōe) version of Shuten Dōji story, 32–34
oil as oni treasure, 112
Oiwa (fictional abandoned wife), 99
Ōizumi no haha, 141
Ōkagami, 124
Okano Reiko, 113, 113n8
Oken setsuwa (narrative prose concerning central authority), 47–48

one-eyed beings, 21, 23
oni: children and descendants of, 49, 49n30, 65, 65n10; concept, xviii–xix, 1, 5; etymology and definition of, 6, 6n10, 92, 117–18; fall of, xxiii, 51–52, 96–97, 178; influence, decline in, 182; nature and characteristics of, xix–xxi, 1, 14–29; origins of, xix, 2–14, 51; physical description of, 7–9
Onigumo (fictional character), 165–66, 167
oni museums, xxi, 183–84
"Oni no hanashi" (Story of Oni), 173–76
"Oni no hanashi" (Tale of a Demon), 120, 121–31
"Oni no michiyuki" (Oni's Journey [to the Palace]), 137–38
Oni of a Solitary Island, 100–103
Oni-sado (warrior), 52
Oni's Journey, 137–38
onmyōdō (way of yin and yang): oni in, 2, 13–14; smallpox, ceremonies to protect against, 49. *See also* yin and yang
Onmyōji boom, 141–42
Onmyōji II (film), 139
onmyōji, 14, 113, 116, 117, 119
Onmyōji (Yin-Yang Master), 113n8, 120, 131–43
onmyōryō (Bureau of Divination), 13–14, 14n27
Orikuchi Shinobu: Kadokawa Gen'yoshi as student of, 117; on oni etymology, 9; on oni origin, 3, 172–73; on *yamauba* as virgin, 69
Orpheus and Eurydice (Greek myth), 4
Osamu Tezuka (1928–1989), 144
Ōshima Tatehiko, 64
Ōsumi Kazuo, 11–12
other: categories of, 45; defined, xx. *See also* marginalized other
other, oni as: in detective fiction, 102; earth spider, 169; in film, 162; kind oni, 175; in modern times, xxv, 145; overview of, 18–23, 180; Shuten Dōji, 42–48; unity, sense promoted by, xxiv, 104–5; vilification of, 49–50
other world, 140–41 161, 161n17, 175
otogi zōshi (companion stories) genre: *carnivalesque* literature compared to, 32, 32n4; overview of, 32, 32n6; Shuten Dōji story as example of, 30, 35
Ōtsu-e (Ōtsu pictures), de-demonized oni in, 93–94
outcasts: discrimination against, 122, 122n2; fiction about, 124; oni as, 66, 121; in real life, 124–25

outer space, oni from, 144–45, 156
outsiders, oni as, xxiv
Ox-Cart Puller and Mountain Ogress, 63
ox horns, oni depicted with, 7

P
"Peach Boy," 108–10
performing arts surge seen as bad omen, 41–42, 41n20
Picture Scroll of Mt. Ōe (early 14th c.), 33
pleasure quarters: depicting, penalty for, 85, 85n45; in Shuten Dōji stories, 93
polygamy, jealousy and resentment caused by, 60
popular culture, oni in: early modern period, 98–100; media and films, xxiv–xxv; present day, xxi; World War II, 107
postwar fiction, oni in, 105, 112–19
praying oni, xxi, 93–94
pregnant woman (fictional character), oni encounter of, 62–63
Prince, Stephen, 155
promises of oni, 28–29
prosperity, oni as agents of, 24–29

Q
Queen of Hearts (*Alice in Wonderland* character), 159, 160

R
Rabelais and His World (Bakhtin), 37, 39
Raikō (Minamoto no Raikō or Yorimitsu, 948–1021): disappearances of persons in time of, 55–56; earth spider conquered by, 98; earth spider killed by, 168; entertained by *dengaku*, 40, 41; entertained by Shuten Dōji, 36; lieutenants of, 70, 71, 73, 75, 77, 78, 114, 160, 187–89, 190–92; Mt. Oe, old woman at met by, 34, 38; oni, relationship to, 50–51, 72; oni attempts at snaring, 40; rescues performed by, 93; Shuten Dōji defeated by, xxiii, 31, 35, 43, 179, 200; status of, 69; targeted by Shuten Dōji, 46; warriors under command of, 17, 58, 58n3; *yamauba*'s son adopted by, 71, 74, 75, 78
Rainuma, Professor (fictional character), 150
rasetsu (*rākṣasa*), 10
Rashōmon (Noh play), 56, 57
rebirth as *yamauba* story theme, 74
Red Oni Who Cried, 170–73, 187
Refutation of Vulgar Legends for the Benefit of the Public, 73–74

relationships, oni yearning for, 171, 175–76
religion influence, decline of, 182
religious beliefs, contemporary, 141–42
religious boundaries, violations of, 31
Revelation of St. John the Divine, 147–48
rice harvest, dancing and music for good, 40, 40n16
Rokujō Lady, revenge of, 60
Roosevelt, Franklin D., 107
ruling class, aristocratic, warrior ideal compared to, 52
Ryō/Satan (fictional character), 147, 148, 149

S

Saga, Emperor (r. 809–823), 54, 55, 56, 186–87
Saichō. *See* Dengyō Daishi
Saimei, Empress, funeral of, 25, 25n44
Sakata no Kintoki, Raikō's lieutenant. *See* Kintoki
samurai, rise of, 97, 98
San'yūtei Enchō (1839–1900), 106
Satake Akihiro, 33
Satan (term), 169
seasons, *yamauba*'s children associated with, 64–65
Segawa Jokō (1739–1794), 84
Seimei. *See* Abe no Seimei (921?–1005)
selfless oni, xxv, 170–76
self-sacrifice as oni story theme, 172
sensual pleasures, 99
Sen to Chihiro no kamikakushi. See Spirited Away
Serene (demon), 149
Setsubun (play), 25, 180
settlers, permanent, from outside community as "other" category, 45
Seven Fortune Deities *(shichifukujin)*, 26–27, 28
sex and violence in commercialization of oni, 119, 143
shape shifting powers of oni: contemporary, 182; demon subjugation in spite of, 97; overview of, xix, xxii. *See also* transformation power of oni
Shiba, Mrs. (fictional character), 152–54, 155
Shibukawa Seiemon, Shuten Dōji story version by, 33–34, 41, 41n18, 43, 43n22, 185–203
shikigami, oni as, 14
Shimo Yoshiko (b. 1952), 141
Shingon sect of Buddhism, 39, 39n14
Shinjuku no haha (contemporary figure), 141

Shinto priests, 13
Shinzei, Bishop as oni, 19–20n39
shitennō, 10, 11, 17, 31, 55, 62, 69, 70, 71, 73, 77, 78, 160; stories, 70
shunned natives as "other" category, 45
Shuten Dōji (Child Handed from Heaven), 151–55, 182
Shuten Dōji (Drunken Demon): birth of, 72; cannibalism practiced by, 15, 31, 34, 36, 37–40, 43, 115, 178, 190–91; commercialization of, 183; in early modern period, 69, 70; fall of, 20, 31, 35, 42, 43, 45, 52, 62, 71, 200; head, severed, 44, 47–48, 57, 58, 179, 200; honesty as trait of, 29; imperial ideal entwined with, 52; in modern fiction, 49–50n30; nature of, xix–xx, 180; origins of, 20, 30, 46, 48–51; as other, 42–48, 178–79; overview of, xxiii; as sympathetic figure, xxi, 92–93, 95; texts of, 32–35, 185–203; Uji no hashihime (woman at a bridge) compared to, 53, 55–58, 60
Shutendō Jirō (fictional character), 151–53, 169, 182
Sino-Japanese War (1894–1895), 109
smallpox, deity of, 49
smiths, lightning associated with, 23
Social Darwinism, 100, 100n9, 101–2
social isolation of oni, xxii–xxiii
Sōdō sect of Zen Buddhism, local deities recognized by, 46, 46n26
Sparrow's Inn, 158
Spirited Away (film), 158–62, 167–69
spirit possession as *yamauba* story theme, 83–84
Story of Ki no Haseo, 28–29
"Story of Oni", 173–76
Story of White Monkey, 49, 49n29
strange creatures *(bakemono)* as *dengaku,* 41, 41n19
strangers: categories of, 45; concept of, xx–xxi
Sugawara Michizane (849–903): artistic depiction of, 22; kami, promotion to, 179; oni, transformation into, 12–13, 178; Shuten Dōji compared to, 45–46n25, 51; as thunder god, 23–24
Sugiura Yukio (1911–2004), 107–8
superhuman abilities, 73–74
supernatural: belief in, xxiv, 73, 90–92, 104; commercialization of, 95, 120; contemporary attitudes toward, 121, 142; deities, categories of, 3; in fiction, 113; hoaxes,

95–96; post-World War II views of, 112; reconfiguration of, 105–7; tales of, 94–95
supernatural creatures: conquest of, 55; oni as, 45; as "other" category, 45
supernatural phenomena: interest, contemporary in, 143; logical explanation of, 75
suppressed people, oni as representation of, 46
Susa (human boy transformed into oni), 139
Su-shēn, attitudes toward, 21
Sutoku, Retired Emperor (1119–1164), 105–6
"Suzume no oyado" (Sparrow's Inn), 158
Swords Chapter of *Tale of the Heike*: female oni in, 53, 54–55; oni in, 16–18; Rashōmon (Noh play) based on, 56, 114, 114n11
symbolic jewel, 47–48
sympathetic figure, oni as: in current culture, 140; deceit against oni as factor in, xxi, 43; defeat followed by, 50; in films, 139; good/evil coexistence and, 43, 45; humans, resemblance to as factor in, 48; marginalization as factor in, xx–xxi, 31, 133, 142; possessions of weak, strong taking, 45–46; in postwar fiction, 135, 137, 138; sex and violence, 125. *See also* selfless oni

T

Taira no Koreshige (warrior), 18
Taira no Masakado (903–940), 113–14
Taira no Masakado (fictional collective entity), 115–16
Taizō (fictional character), 129
Takahashi Masaaki: oni as deity, concept of, 2; on Raikō (warrior), 50–51; on Shuten Dōji origins, 49
Takahashi Rumiko, 163–65
Takamimusuhi (deity), 5–6
Takegorō (fictional oni), 101, 102, 103
Takeuchi, Melinda, 95–96
"Tale of a Demon," 120, 121–31
Tale of Genji: "Lust of the White Serpent" compared to, 127–28; spirit possession in, 83; Ueda Akinari influenced by, 94
Tale of Nezame (ca. late 11th c.), 51
Tale of the Heike, 51–52. *See also* Swords Chapter of *Tale of the Heike*
Tale of the Imperial Capital (1983–1989), 105, 112–19
Tales of Ise (945 CE), 14–15
Tales of Spring Rain (1809), 129
Tales of Times Now Past, 121, 130–31, 133–34

Tawaraya Sōtatsu, 24
technology, oni's existence entwined with, 145
Teito monogatori (Tale of the Imperial Capital, 1983–1989), 105, 112–19
Tendai Buddhism: founding of, 39, 39n15; as nation's protectors, 46
Tetsuwan Atomu (Astro Boy), 144
Those Obnoxious Aliens, 155–58, 163, 182
three-fingered hands, oni depicted with, 7
thrift, cartoons promoting, 108
thunder: oni associated with, 12, 51, 177; *yamauba* related to, 76
thunder god: artistic depiction of, 24; oni association with, 24, 75–76; Raikō (warrior) associated with, 50–51, 72; shrines to, 2
thunderstorm, oni acts of cannibalism during, 23
tiger skins, oni depicted with, 7, 156
Tōkaidō Yotsuya kaidan (Yotsuya Ghost Stories, 1824), 99, 100, 103
Tokugawa shogunate: government, 31n3; oni beliefs under, 97; pleasure quarters in, 93, 93n2; status of, 70
Tokuko (fictional female oni), 136–37
tool specters, 10, 10n19
Torii Kiyonaga (1752–1815), 88
Toriyama Sekien (1712–1788), 88, 97–98
tourism industry, oni in, xxv–xxvi, *183*
town revitalization movement, 183
transformation power of oni: contemporary, 184; hunting and destroying, challenges due to, 34, 187; overview of, 16–18; in postwar fiction, 125–26; snaring attempts through, 40. *See also* shape shifting powers of oni
treasures of oni, 25–26
Tripartite Alliance Pact, 111–12
True Records of Three Generations in Japan, 15–16
trust as oni trait, 50. *See also* deceit against oni
tsuchigumo (earth spiders). *See* earth spiders
tsukumogami (tool specters), 10, 10n19
Tsuna (Watanabe no Tsuna, 953–1025): kidnapping, attempted of, 9; oni encounters by, 17, 55, 56, 58, 58n3, 114–15, 187, 187n13; shrine, visit to, 188
"Tsurugi no maki" in *Heike monogatari*. *See* Swords Chapter of *Tale of the Heike*
Tsuruya Nanboku IV (1755–1829), 99
Tsutomu, Ema, 162
Twelve, Mrs. (Jūnisama) and children, 64
Twelve Devas, 11

U

Ueda Akinari (1734–1809), 94–95
Ugetsu monogatari, 133
Uji no hashihime (woman at a bridge): Mrs. Shiba (fictional character) compared to, 153; overview of, xx; as private person, 57–58, 59, 60, 180; Rokujō Lady compared to, 60; Shuten Dōji compared to, 53, 55–58, 60; stories of, xxiii, 53–55
Uji no hōzō (treasure house), 47
Uji shūi monogatari (Collection of Tales from Uji, ca. 13th c.), 116, 164
urban consciousness, *yōkei* portrayals and, 97, 97n7
urban culture: oni in, xxiv, 90–103; supernatural, beliefs concerning, 105
Urusei Yatsura (Those Obnoxious Aliens), 155–58, 163, 182
Ushikata to yamauba (Ox-Cart Puller and Mountain Ogress), 63
Utamaro, *yamauba* portrayals of, 85, 88

V

Vaisravana, Heavenly realm, promotion to, 11
victim, oni as, xxiv, 139
virgin, *yamauba* as, 69
Virgin Mary, 65
virtual reality, oni in, 182

W

Wakamori Tarō, 3
warrior battles with oni, xxiii, 17–18
warrior class, rise of, xxiii, 42, 50, 51–52, 178, 179
Watanabe Eri, 124
wealth: oni as agents of, 24–29, 140, 172, 177, 180; *yamauba* as agent of, 65, 68, 68n17, 161
weaving and spinning, *yamauba* association with, 75
"Weeping Demon" (Kurosawa), 154–55
witches: *yamauba* (mountain ogress) compared to, 61, 65; Yubaba (witch), 159–62, 167, 168, 169
Wolfgram, Juliann, 94
women: emotions, reining in, 60; in private *versus* public sphere, 58, 180; role and status of, 82–83, 157–58

Y

Yaegiri (fictional courtesan): Lum (fictional ogress) compared to, 157; as *yamauba*, 77, 78–79, 81–82, 83–84, 85

Yamagata Bantō (1748–1821), 90–91
Yamamba (Noh play), 62, 66–68, 74, 78, 172, 181
Yamaoka Genrin (1631–1672): on oni, 91–92, 98–99; on *yamauba*, 75
Yamato Takeru, 18–19
Yamauba and Kintarō (painting), 160
yamauba-buyō (shosagoto) (dance sub-genre), 84
yamauba (mountain ogress): artistic depiction of, 97–98; as cannibal, 62–64, 69, 74; children and descendants of, 69–76; definition and overview of, xx, 61–62; in detective fiction, 102–3; dichotomous nature of, 68–69; dwelling place of, 71, 76; in early modern period, 69–76; film depiction of, 158–62; human side of, 66, 67–68; in medieval period, 68–69; as mother and nurturer, 62, 64–68, 69, 76–89, *86, 87, 89*; origins of, 63, 63n6, 65, 181; physical characteristics of, 68, 78–79, 84–89, *86, 87, 89,* 181–82; in popular culture, 181–82; stories of, xxiii–xxiv; term, 63, 63n6; thunder and lightning, relationship to, 76; weaving and spinning, association with, 75; Western counterparts of, 61; as wife, 79–80
Yanagi Sōetsu (1889–1961), 93
Yanagita Kunio, 117
yasha (yakṣa), 10–11, 163–65
yin and yang rationalism: in early modern period, 91–92; oni and, 177; supernatural phenomena explained through, 75
Yin-Yang Master, 113n8, 120, 131–43. *See also onmyōdō* (way of yin and yang)
yōkai (hobgoblins/monsters): beliefs concerning, 106; in fiction, 115; *kami*, transformation into, 24; in media, 144, 182; oni as examples of, 95–103; oni relationship to, 3; and oni variants, 162–69; term, 95, 95n4
Yomotsu-shikome (ugly woman of the other world), xx; in creation myth, 3–4; Uji no hashihime (woman at a bridge) as spiritual descendant of, 59
Yorimichi as Uji no hōzō (treasure house) guardian, 47
Yorimitsu. *See* Raikō
Yowa no nezame (Tale of Nezame, ca. late 11th c.), 51
Yubaba (witch), 159–62, 167, 168, 169
Yukari (fictional character), 116, 118, 119
Yumemakura Baku, 120, 131–43

Z

Zeami Motokiyo (1363–1443): Noh plays analyzed by, 67–68; works attributed to, 58–59, 172

Zeniba (film character), 161

Zenki (anterior demon): as En no gyōja agent, 20–21; Takegorō (fictional demon) compared to, 102

Zen-taiheiki (Chronicle of Pre-Grand Pacification), 75, 76, 78

Zhu Xi, 91

Zuikei Shūhō (1391–1473), 64